Harry Livingstone's
Forgotten Men

Canadians and the Chinese Labour Corps
in the First World War

Dan Black

James Lorimer & Company Ltd., Publishers
Toronto

For Ch'en T'ing Chang (No. 65855), Chou Ming Shan
(No. 39038), and Tung Shih Ch'eng (No. 92107)

James Lorimer & Company Ltd., Publishers acknowledges funding support from the Ontario Arts Council (OAC), an agency of the Government of Ontario. We acknowledge the support of the Canada Council for the Arts, which last year invested $153 million to bring the arts to Canadians throughout the country. This project has been made possible in part by the Government of Canada and with the support of Ontario Creates.

Cover design: Tyler Cleroux
Cover images: David Livingstone, Library and Archives Canada, City of Vancouver Archives, WJ Hawkings Collection

Library and Archives Canada Cataloguing in Publication

Title: Harry Livingstone's forgotten men : Canadians and the Chinese Labour Corps in the First World War / Dan Black.
Names: Black, Dan, 1957- author.
Description: Includes bibliographical references and index.
Identifiers: Canadiana (print) 20190160691 | Canadiana (ebook) 20190160799 | ISBN 9781459414327 (softcover) | ISBN 9781459414334 (EPUB)
Subjects: LCSH: Chinese Labour Corps. | LCSH: Foreign workers, Chinese—Canada—History—20th century. | LCSH: Foreign workers, Chinese—France—History—20th century. | LCSH: World War, 1914-1918— Participation, Chinese. | LCSH: World War, 1914-1918— Participation, Canadian.
Classification: LCC D520.C5 B63 2019 | DDC 940.3/51—dc23

James Lorimer & Company Ltd., Publishers
117 Peter Street, Suite 304
Toronto, ON, Canada
M5V 0M3
www.lorimer.ca

Printed and bound in Canada.

Contents

Foreword

"History's lessons are there to see. But one must always look."
— *Canadian Naval Commander Tony German*

The First World War means many things to Canadians and over the course of the anniversary years, 2014 to 2018, we learned about the major battles, the heroes and heroines, the divisiveness of conscription, the impact on individuals, families and communities and how Canada became a nation on the muddy slopes of Vimy Ridge.

For those interested in the history of the war, the past five years have been years of discovery with a seeming unending flow of books, documentaries, exhibitions and websites on almost every aspect. From attics and basements all across Canada, letters, diaries, photographs and wartime ephemera were retrieved and shared. And the service documents of every man and woman who served in the Canadian Expeditionary Force (CEF) have been digitized and are available online, allowing countless Canadians to document the wartime service of their ancestors.

Canada's war was not restricted to the Western Front. Canadian service personnel were called upon to serve in Bermuda, the Middle East, Russia in 1919 and elsewhere, and while many aspects of the war are well known, others are less so.

The war consumed manpower; all nations were severely affected by the enormous number of casualties in what was a war of attrition. In 1916, the situation became critical for the French and so Chinese labourers were recruited to work behind the lines and free men of military age to serve at the front. That same year, the British found themselves in a similar situation and, like the French, turned to China for much needed labour. About a hundred thousand men were enrolled in what became known as the Chinese Labour Corps (CLC) and, while recruitment presented significant and pressing challenges, the job of moving the men from northeastern China to the Western Front was also a daunting task.

The story of the CLC in the First World War is not unknown: several books have been published about the work of the Chinese in France and their contribution to Allied victory. What is hardly known at all, however, is the story of how the British transported corps members from China to France, and back again at the end of the war. It was decided that Canada offered the safest and most efficient route for moving such a large number of men from the Orient to Europe.

Canadian military personnel, missionaries, various government officials and the Canadian Pacific — its ships and its railways — collaborated in a secret and unprecedented scheme to transport the CLC across the Pacific Ocean and Canada from Vancouver to various East Coast ports for shipment to Europe. At the end of the war, the process was reversed and about fifty thousand returned home via Canada.

Logistics aside, this is a very human story of tens of thousands of young Chinese men who agreed to undertake a perilous journey that few understood to participate in a war that must have been equally mysterious to them. Behind the lines in France and Belgium, members of the CLC were employed to move supplies and war *matériel*; they worked on Allied railways and, after the fighting stopped, they assisted in clearing the battlefields before embarking on the long trip back to China. Being a member of the CLC was not without its dangers — a number of men died in

Canada en route to Europe, many more would die of accident, disease and enemy action before the end of the war.

With access to diaries, memoirs and official records, author Dan Black tells their story, from recruitment to war and home again, and describes how this story is also very much a Canadian one. We meet military personnel who were engaged with the CLC, especially Captain Harry Livingstone of the Canadian Army Medical Corps, whose diary of his experiences with the CLC provide a striking motif for the story. We are introduced to several Canadian missionaries who were recruited by the British not only for their language skills, but also for their understanding of the Chinese. Above all, we meet many Chinese who agreed to leave home for employment in a vicious war on the other side of the world. This and so much more is found in this long-awaited book, *Harry Livingstone's Forgotten Men*. It is a fascinating story, one that reveals details of a Canadian contribution to a wartime scheme few Canadians have heard anything about.

— Glenn Wright, military author and archivist
May 6, 2019

Preface

The idea for this book was inspired by a black and white photograph.

The "snap" was taken in 1917 while the camera was pointed at the side of a railway car on a sixteen-car train. In the frame are four men, all of them leaning through two raised passenger windows. The fellow on the left holds a wooden, bowed instrument, and appears to be playing for the photographer. There is a slight smile on his dark, almond-shaped face.

Although the photograph was taken at a small whistle stop in Western Canada, the passengers are not Canadian. They are Chinese, members of the Chinese Labour Corps (CLC) bound for Europe at the height of the Great War.

This book is about those men and more than 84,000 other Chinese labourers who arrived in Canada between early 1917 and 1918, the vast majority of whom journeyed across Canada on guarded trains kept secret from the Canadian public. It is also about the Canadian officers who accompanied them, who remained with the men in France and Belgium until well after the war.

Few Canadians have heard of the CLC, let alone the crucial role Canada undertook as part of a British scheme to secure the hard labour needed to unload ships, stack ammunition and repair roads and even tanks. Despite all the efforts made in this country to commemorate Canada's involvement in the war, hardly anyone has written or talked about what was the largest, most concentrated mass movement of Chinese from the Far East, across Canada to Western Europe.

Prior to the release of this book, I spoke to a group of Canadian veterans who were well versed on Canada's military history from their own experience. These men and women were avid readers, continually searching for new articles or book titles on Canada's wartime involvements. When I showed them the photograph of the men on the train and explained why the Chinese were travelling through Canada, their reaction was one I was familiar with.

All of them wanted to know why they had not heard or read anything on this before.

While some of the material for this book was hard to obtain, it has not been an overly difficult story to pursue. Files were declassified a long time ago, so there is no shortage of material at Canadian and British archives. The Chinese have also produced excellent scholarship that sheds light on the Canadian involvement, which they remain curious about. In the fall of 2018, I attended a CLC conference in China and was invited to speak about the Canadian connection. The conference centre was located on the same ground where the labourers were recruited and examined by Canadian doctors in 1917 and 1918.

Thankfully, there are a few Canadian academic articles and news features, as well as a documentary film entitled *Tricks on the Dead*, that have brought the subject to light in Canada. However, this book pushes beyond those good works to present a more detailed history about the CLC's link to Canada. To accomplish this, I have provided a more thorough account of Dr. Harry Livingstone, who served as a captain with the Canadian Army Medical Corps. The book also incorporates myriad subplots describing the roles of other Canadians, including missionaries and Canada's wartime censorship authorities, and the contributions of Canadian Pacific Railway officials.

The research led me to several locations across Canada, to China, and Europe. In Canada, the Canadian Agency of the Commonwealth War Graves Commission provided exceptional support and assistance in regards to locating and verifying the graves of labourers who died in Canada, which has resulted in the erection of new headstones. Including special collections, wartime files were examined at Library and Archives Canada, the British Columbia Provincial Archives in Victoria and the United Church of Canada Archives in Toronto. My travels also included a visit to the site of the old William Head Quarantine Station on Vancouver Island, now home to a federal minimum-security penitentiary.

In putting together this story, I have purposely avoided sanitizing the language used at the time. Therefore, the text includes terms that are now considered vulgar and derogatory. The word *Chink*, for example, was used often, before, during and after the time period. But while it was used frequently by people who were racists or thought of themselves as superior to the Chinese, the word was also used by those who simply considered it part of everyday vernacular. The point is, not everyone who used such terms hated the Chinese or looked down on them.

Also, anyone familiar with Chinese personal names and place names will know how much of a challenge it is to recognize old versus modern spellings. Of course, there are some easy and more familiar ones, such as Peking, which is an old Jesuit romanization, and the modern name of Beijing. Another one is "Canton" (the city) versus today's "Guangzhou," although care must be exercised because "Canton" the province is spelled "Guangdong." Three geographical place names loom large in this work, but if a modern map is consulted the names of "Shantung" province, "Weihaiwei" or "Tsingtao" will not be found, but "Shandong", "Weihai" and "Qingdao" will. While other historians have adopted modern spellings or Pinyin, I have respected what was used at the time. So readers will find "Peking," not "Beijing." Personal names have been treated this way as well with spellings as they appeared on the CLC Medal or nominal roll. However, since this may be confusing, I have added, to the best of my ability, modern spellings in brackets on first reference.

The reader should also note the small "extra" I have added at the end of the book, which briefly covers the various theories connected to the origin of the influenza pandemic of 1918–19. I have done this primarily to acknowledge that among the theories, one points to the CLC.

Overall, it is hoped this book will not only inform, but lead to other research within Canada on the CLC experience here. As William Faulkner, the celebrated writer, puts it in *Requiem for a Nun*: *"The past is never dead, it's not even past."*

Dan Black
Merrickville, Ontario
April 15, 2019

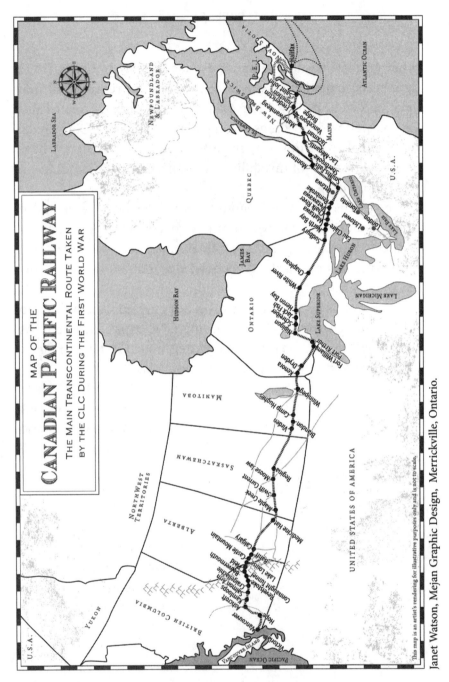

Janet Watson, Mejan Graphic Design, Merrickville, Ontario.

MAP OF THE

CANADIAN PACIFIC RAILWAY

THE MAIN TRANSCONTINENTAL ROUTE TAKEN
BY THE CLC DURING THE FIRST WORLD WAR

This illustration depicts the transcontinental railway route taken by members of the Chinese Labour Corps during and after the First World War. On their way to France in 1917-1918, the men entrained at Vancouver destined for eastern ports at Montreal, Saint John, New Brunswick and Halifax. The return trip in 1919-1920 covered the same ground, only in reverse.

The Urgent Need for Wartime Labour

"Dai fu lai la!" (Here comes the doctor!)

Birds' eggs . . .

Captain Harry Livingstone had dozens of them, tucked under glass in three wooden display cabinets at his home in Listowel, Ontario: each specimen carefully labelled and placed in its own cubicle, on a bed of cotton batting.[1] But while this fragile collection was safely stored, the small-town family doctor, grand-nephew to the world famous African explorer Dr. David Livingstone, was putting himself at tremendous risk.

It was August 10, 1917, and the recently commissioned officer of the Canadian Army Medical Corps was moments away from boarding a train at London, Ontario. The twenty-nine-year-old bachelor was on a top-secret, wartime mission aimed at delivering himself to a dusty recruitment depot in northeastern China, then back across Canada to the Western Front. More than once, the five-foot-ten, 145-pound physician was warned not to breathe a word about the assignment, at least not in public. Especially sensitive was the part about Canada's role in transporting tens of thousands of unarmed Chinese labourers across Canada in sealed, guarded railway cars.[2]

* * *

Starting in early 1917, special trains of the Canadian Pacific Railway raced day and night across the Dominion, working to keep pace with a highly complex British scheme that became the world's largest international mass movement of Chinese from the Far East to Western Europe. The trains rumbled past farms and through towns and cities, and the public had no idea what they were transporting or who was on board because the press was barred from reporting on the highly classified operation. Overall, nearly 81,000 members of the Chinese Labour Corps (CLC) were transported across Canada en route to Britain and France where they were assigned a variety of heavy work behind the lines.[3] Another 3,600 boarded the *Empress of Asia* and sailed from Canada's West Coast to the United Kingdom via the Panama Canal. Then, well after the Armistice was signed in November 1918, Canada again facilitated the movement of the CLC, only this time the operation was in reverse, sending more than 48,000 of the men home to China.

The land and sea logistics were enormous and involved multiple nations. But it was here — in Canada — where many of the Chinese formed their earliest impressions of Western civilization.[4]

Indeed, for those who had not travelled far from their villages, the enormity of Canada's varied geography and the time it took to cross the country was truly surprising.

The fact that most Canadians have never heard about the Chinese Labour Corps (CLC), let alone Canada's historic role in the larger British effort to utilize such labour on the Western Front, is understandable. Our military history rarely, if ever, touches on the subject. Yet it is a wartime story that goes well beyond the timely provision of a transportation network. Many individuals, including other doctors and Canadian missionaries, were called upon to officer CLC companies in France and Belgium. Several were employed at the large CLC hospital at Noyelles-sur-Mer

David Livingstone Collection

Captain Lou Sebert of the Canadian Army Medical Corps with the CLC at Weihaiwei, China, in 1917.

in northern France. But even before these highly educated men reached the Western Front, many assisted with recruitment in China and, like the Chinese workers, endured dangerous journeys, particularly across the stormy North Pacific to Canada and then across the U-boat-patrolled waters of the North Atlantic to Britain and France. But even the journey by rail across Canada was dangerous as well as tedious. Labourers died en route, some even before they entrained at Vancouver.

Those who crossed Canada made up more than 86 per cent of the nearly 95,000 Chinese recruited by the British between the fall of 1916 and early 1918. The French, who launched their own drive to recruit 50,000 Chinese in 1916, had, by 1917, approximately 37,000 Chinese navvies under their command, thousands employed in industry.[5] Meanwhile, tsarist Russia recruited between 160,000 and 200,000 Chinese to work at a number of places throughout Russia. Altogether, at least 300,000 Chinese men joined various labour schemes during the First World War. This book, however, is about Canada's largely unrecognized role in the British effort, which also coincided with the age of steam, not to mention the global mobilization of millions of armed combatants that began in the summer of 1914.

Throughout the war and later — during demobilization — massive steam ships and trains logged millions of kilometres while trying to adhere to schedules that relied on international co-operation and secrecy. The demands on ships and ports, locomotives and rolling stock, railway infrastructure and telegraph facilities were unprecedented. However, the movements themselves were largely dependent on people, from ships' masters, deckhands and dockworkers to the firemen on the trains, and those who issued the orders.

The recruitment of Chinese labour may not have changed the duration or outcome of the war, but it was an important measure. It came at a crucial time, owing to the desperate need for more men and equipment in war-torn Europe. And while the Chinese workers were non-combatants, they represented the largest and longest-serving non-European contingent in the war. What is also interesting is that the Chinese employed by the British were subject to military law and discipline, and not just in France and Belgium. One old photograph taken on Vancouver Island shows a labourer being caned in front of his peers. On the Western Front, at least ten Chinese labourers were executed during and after the war.[6]

Chinese labourers also earned medals for acts of courage, but most simply carried on with the hard and often dangerous work assigned to them. Some of the riskier and certainly more gruesome work came after the Armistice when the men cleared the battlefields and recovered the remains of soldiers for proper burial.

One of the CLC's final acts, which the Chinese Embassy in London expressed a strong desire for, involved carving names and inscriptions on headstones for fellow labourers who did not survive.[7] Sixty Chinese stonecutters, along with tens of thousands of other Chinese labourers and many of their Canadian officers, were the last to be repatriated in 1919 and 1920.

WJ Hawkings Collection, courtesy John De Lucy

With their kit, members of the CLC board the Empress of Russia *at Tsingtao, China, 1918.*

The reason the British and French went looking for labour is well told. Skilled, but mostly unskilled, men capable of hard work were recruited from every part of the globe, including South Africa, Egypt, the Seychelles and even as far as Fiji. However, the CLC was, without doubt, the largest workforce to go to France.

Such men were needed the moment war was declared, but no specific plan was developed until much later. For the British War Committee, pressure began to mount through 1915 and into the first half of 1916 with the alarming loss of frontline soldiers. The Ypres Salient, St. Julien, Festubert, Givenchy, St. Eloi and Mount Sorrel — all familiar places to Canadians — were among the battles that introduced stark efficiencies to mass killing, including the first use of chlorine gas.

The battles between early 1915 and mid-1916 produced horrendous casualty figures, yet the numbers were far less than those exacted on the Somme in 1916. During that battle, the British advanced less than ten kilometres and lost more than 432,000 men. The French suffered 204,000 casualties, while the Germans lost more than 500,000.[8] To the southeast, along the Meuse

River, the horrific Battle of Verdun, waged between February and December 1916, resulted in approximately 715,000 French and German casualties.[9] The war was deadlocked. Thousands of soldiers were simply buried where they fell in a landscape turned upside down by shelling that sowed the earth with millions of unexploded shells. By then, the Allies and their foes had more guns and the shells to feed them.

Meanwhile, elaborate trench systems and fortifications were added to the Western Front, which stretched from Switzerland to the North Sea. Courageous attempts by armed work parties to extend or repair these hard-won positions, including the roads and bridges leading to them, often proved futile and fatal. The war had become more mechanized, and greatly dependent upon the movement of men, munitions and other supplies, including food and horses.

Recruiting labourers from China and elsewhere allowed the British and French armies to release more of their able-bodied labourers behind the lines for frontline duty. Thousands could join the ranks of the fighting men, while the crucial supply lines — from the wharfs to the ammunition depots — were maintained by foreign as well as British and Canadian labour units. "The danger then was not so much of direct defeat in France through shortage of soldiers as an indirect defeat through failure to supply those who were there," wrote British historian Michael Summerskill in his 1982 book, *China on the Western Front*.[10] The British knew this before the first shots were fired in the Battle of the Somme, but it took them longer than it did the French to realize they, too, had to look further afield for manpower.

In June 1915, China, which was still a neutral country, proposed through its finance minister the idea of sending *armed* Chinese labourers to France. However, the British, for a host of reasons, balked at that, and by the fall of 1916 settled on the enrolment of unarmed labour. China did not declare war on Germany and Austria-Hungary until August 14, 1917. Meanwhile, in Britain, debate over the use of Chinese labour had been heard before, and none too quietly. The most recent and politically explosive instance occurred following the 1899–1902 Boer War after the British High Commissioner in colonial South Africa introduced measures in 1904 to legally import indentured labour.

During the next six years, nearly 64,000 Chinese workers were recruited and shipped to the British colony of Transvaal. The war had caused a severe labour shortage in the gold mines and it had become very difficult to hire native labourers, mostly on account of the wages and working conditions. The political storm in Britain centred on opposition charges that conditions faced by the Chinese in South Africa were "akin to slavery." It was one of the issues the Liberals hammered away at during the 1906 United Kingdom general election that saw the defeat of the Conservative and Unionist government. Soon afterwards, and largely due to the efforts of Winston Churchill, serving as under-secretary of state for the colonies, South Africa gained a new, self-governing constitution.[11]

Before and throughout the First World War, trade unionists opposed the idea of importing Chinese labour to the British Isles. Government discussions were top-secret, but when word got out through a leak to the press in late 1916 that it planned to recruit and ship to Europe thousands of Chinese workers, the unions and the workers they represented naturally felt seriously threatened. David Lloyd George, who was serving as minister of munitions and would become prime minister of the wartime coalition government on December 6, 1916, was, as historian Nicholas J. Griffin points out, "one of the moving forces behind the genesis of the Chinese Labour Corps." Griffin also notes: "Later, he lloyd George was . . . one of the politicians most effectively able to subdue the fears of British labour concerning the potential uses of the Chinese" labour in Britain.[12]

The first big decision to create a British-led Chinese labour force was made behind closed doors while the Battle of the Somme was underway. To fill the shortage of manpower on the

Western Front, the British needed not only a dependable source of Chinese labour and a practical approach to recruitment, but a timetable and a workable logistical plan to safely and efficiently transport tens of thousands of men around the globe. It did not take long for London's attention to turn to Canada, the young dominion "across the way" that in 1914 had demonstrated a strong commitment to Mother Britain by sending the first overseas Canadian contingent of some 30,600 soldiers.

For Canadian authorities in early 1917, ensuring the secret passage by rail and by ship of so many foreign nationals, travelling in successive "consignments" or drafts was another massive undertaking. By September 1918, when Ottawa submitted a claim to the War Office for $612,848.54 for the transportation and maintenance of the Chinese through Canada, the paperwork alone weighed forty-one kilograms.[13]

In addition to the high demands on the CPR, the pressure on available shipping grew. At least 50 per cent of the capacity of the Canadian Pacific Ocean Service (CPOS) fleet on the Pacific was requisitioned as a war measure in early March 1917. The Blue Funnel Line, British India Steam Navigation Company and Robert Dollar Steamship Company also contributed ships. By March 1918, dozens of sailings had transported labourers across the Pacific from China to Japan to Canada.[14] As the pressure grew to move the men as quickly as possible, safety regulations, such as ensuring an adequate number of lifeboats or lifebelts, were quietly waived by authorities in Ottawa.

The CLC journey across Canada was conceived as an "in-and-out" deal, carefully managed to ensure the labourers had no opportunity to get off the trains and disappear into Chinatowns or elsewhere. Preventing escapes was top of mind. However, the vast majority of Chinese labourers had no interest whatsoever in sneaking off the trains because they were obliged to earn money for their families at home, who stood to benefit from regular allotments promised by the British. Most of the men

This photo attests to the crowded conditions on board the steamships.

David Livingstone Collection

who enrolled were illiterate or semi-illiterate with very little formal education. This does not imply they were unskilled or not intelligent. However, the vast majority knew very little about the Western world. Canada was completely foreign to most of them and their exposure to the country and its people was limited by the tight security measures applied to their transcontinental movements. Still, when they stepped off the ships and onto the trains, they were entering a country that was very much part of the British Empire, populated almost entirely by people who had come from the British Isles and remained very loyal to the old country. For the most part, Canada was "white" and Christian. Then, and well before the war, significant efforts were made to keep it that way, as seen by the harm done to Indigenous people.

By late 1916, Canada was two years into a war that remained crucial, but seemingly without end. Canadians had returned home without limbs, with ghastly facial injuries, seared lungs and deep psychological wounds that were not well understood.

Many could no longer father children, maintain relationships or work. Thousands of families had lost husbands and sons, and thousands more were praying for the safe return of loved ones from the Somme, which by late October had accounted for more than twenty-four thousand Canadian casualties. For most households, there was little capacity to think of anything but the war and its terrible consequences.

The fighting overseas had stirred up tremendous hatred for people who had settled here from countries with which Canada was at war. However, Asians and other non-white minorities, who had lived here for decades and even supported the decision to go to war, continued to feel the brunt of racist attitudes. In the streets and in the press, these Canadian citizens encountered objections from people who saw it as their duty to openly treat them with disdain. Heard among the voices of prejudice were those expressing the fear that when the enlisted men returned home, there would be no jobs in a country they saw as being transformed by people who were "different." Anti-Asian hostilities were not unique to Canada. They were common throughout the Western world and expressed from all corners of society: politicians, educators, clergy, union leaders, immigration officials, landowners, community associations and church groups. British Columbia, which joined Confederation on July 20, 1871, was on the front doorstep of Asian immigration.

In the decade before the war, fear of South Asian immigration intensified, culminating with the 1914 standoff in Vancouver between immigration officials and the *Komagata Maru*. A lesser-known incident occurred in 1908 when the *Monteagle*, of the Canadian Pacific Ocean Service (CPOS), arrived at the same port.

By early 1917, the federal government, under Conservative Prime Minister Sir Robert Borden, had many pressing concerns, chief among them the ever-decreasing number of volunteers for the Western Front. In considering the CLC scheme, after being approached by Britain's Colonial Office in March, the Canadian government decided to waive the $500 head tax normally applied to Chinese entering the country. The volunteers of the CLC were arriving in droves, but they were not immigrants, and were therefore — in the eyes of government — not seen as individuals so much as a commodity passing through to war-torn France in aid of the British Empire. The Canadian Pacific Railway, meanwhile, had a lot of experience moving head-tax-exempt Chinese labourers across the country from Vancouver to Halifax. Chinese migrants destined for plantations in Cuba, the West Indies and the eastern United States had been moved regularly. The waiving of the head tax in early 1917, therefore, was not new, neither was it unusual for people who lived along the rail route to see Chinese on trains well before the CLC scheme began.

Still, the decision to waive the head tax for the CLC meant the labourers had to remain locked in guarded railway carriages. Lavatory windows in the CPR's Colonist cars were sealed shut to prevent escapes and guards patrolled the railway platforms whenever the trains stopped for coal and water. Doctors, including Livingstone, were assigned to the trains, but any labourer requiring hospitalization was escorted off the train and to the hospital by armed guard. Furthermore, when not in transit, the men were kept behind wire in guarded compounds.

The head tax had been introduced on July 20, 1885, as part of the *Chinese Immigration Act*, the first federal legislation to exclude immigration on the basis of ethnic origin.[15] At the same time, the federal government established the *Electoral Franchise Act*, which excluded "persons of Mongolian or Chinese race" from voting.[16] The enactment of this legislation occurred four months before CPR director Donald Smith drove the Last Spike at Craigellachie, British Columbia. The recognized irony here is that the difficult completion of the western stretch of the CPR would not have been possible without the thousands of Chinese navvies employed under harsh conditions to help clear the way. It is estimated at least six hundred died.

While the head tax was the most obvious symbol of Canada's desire to restrict Chinese immigration, other draconian measures were introduced just before the war to bar entry to any Chinese artisan or labourer regardless of the head tax. Then, during the last two years of the war, there were arguments going the other way, mostly from employers in Western Canada who wanted to ease the restrictions in order to make use of cheap Chinese labour at mines, mills and farms. However, as the war wound down, strong protests from organized labour sensed what was at stake and fought against this.[17]

When they arrived, the vast majority of CLC members knew little or nothing of these anti-Asian developments, although many had — even prior to their voyage — witnessed or experienced behaviour aimed at making them feel unwanted or inferior. While mostly shielded from the Canadian public, the Chinese were continually exposed to the Western officers in charge of their movements, the men guarding them and watchful Canadian immigration officials.

* * *

Stopping only briefly to take on coal and water, the CLC trains stuck to their schedules, starting in April 1917, only a month after London called Ottawa looking for help to transport its new source of manual labour. By then the CPR and its employees had already contributed greatly to the war effort. Fifty-two of its ships were pressed into service during the war, many of them requisitioned as troop transports that, altogether, moved roughly a million soldiers.[18] Enemy action claimed several and marine accidents sank two. Nearly 11,350 CPR employees enlisted for various types of service, and many of them lost their lives or were wounded overseas.[19] On the home front, some eighty constables from the CPR's Department of Investigation, many of them veterans of the South African War, helped guard the company's infrastructure, including tunnels, bridges and railway yards and stations.

Travelling from Vancouver's waterfront — and leaving only an hour apart — the CLC trains followed the transcontinental line across a seemingly endless landscape. The trains, some twenty cars long, followed the same route carved and blasted out of the landscape by that earlier Chinese workforce. They moved through tunnels into the clear, sudden brilliance of steep mountain valleys, across the Prairies and into the seemingly revolving vistas of the Canadian Shield. They came down the Ottawa Valley, past Chalk River and Smiths Falls, and on toward the St. Lawrence River and Montreal. In the summer of 1917, a special holding camp, enclosed with barbed wire and patrolled by guards, was erected at Petawawa, northwest Ottawa. Buried there in 1917 was a young Chinese labourer, Chou Ming Shan (Zhou Mingshan, No. 39038), who died on one of the trains.

The CLC specials that bypassed the docks at Montreal continued to Lac-Mégantic in Quebec's Eastern Townships. After a thirty-minute stop, they headed south, crossed into the United States and steamed over the hills and through the dense forest and swamps of remote northern Maine. From there, they continued over the Saint Croix–Vanceboro Bridge to Saint John, New Brunswick, and Halifax, Nova Scotia.

The United States was still not in the war when the international bridge at Vanceboro, Maine, was bombed on February 2, 1915. The railway through Maine was the shortest route between Quebec and New Brunswick and it was used regularly by the CPR to transport food and other wartime provisions to eastern Canadian ports. Around 1:30 in the morning, a suitcase of dynamite was placed on the Canadian side by an officer in the German army reserve. Werner Horn, who had been given the task while working at a plantation in Guatemala, lit the fuse with his cigar and then returned to his hotel in Vanceboro, shivering in the cold. The blast woke the town and shattered windows,

City of Vancouver Archives, CVA 139-17

Under the watchful eyes of Canadian immigration authorities, dozens of CLC members line up to entrain at Vancouver in 1917.

but did not destroy the bridge, which reopened within a couple of days.

Horn was arrested, suffering from frostbite.[20]

For the CLC trains, which began using that same bridge in early 1917, the journey did not always run on time or without incident. Despite careful planning, delays were caused by equipment failures, shipping shortages, the fear of sabotage, bureaucratic struggles and the weather. Among the accidents was a serious derailment in northern Ontario during the height of winter and a fatal crash between a CLC Special and a freight train near Sherbrooke, Quebec. However, the deadliest collision connected to the movements did not involve any labourers. It claimed the lives of several members of the Railway Service Guard who were returning to Vancouver after delivering CLC contingents to Halifax.

That tragedy, however, paled in comparison to the disaster that struck on December 6, 1917, when the Norwegian freighter *Imo* collided with the French munitions ship *Mont-Blanc* in the Narrows, a restrictive passage connecting upper Halifax Harbour to Bedford Basin. The accident caused a fire, and then a blast that levelled the city in what remains the largest man-made, non-nuclear wartime explosion in history.[21]

The explosion and tsunami killed more than two thousand people and injured at least nine thousand more and it happened at the height of wartime movements. One of the hardest hit areas was the district of Richmond in north Halifax, where whole families were wiped out when buildings and other infrastructure were obliterated. The Richmond Railway Yards and its station were destroyed, killing fifty-five railway workers. More than five hundred railway cars were destroyed or damaged.[22] The busy North Street Station, built by the Intercolonial Railway in the 1870s, was also heavily hit by the blast. Several Chinese labourers were among the sick at nearby Rockhead Military Hospital, a facility used to treat patients with various diseases. All seven labourers suffered lacerations after being hit by flying glass, which injured and claimed many lives throughout the city. Overall, the Chinese were lucky. None were killed and the injured were quickly treated and then assigned overseas transport.[23]

Halifax had no equal among Canadian cities contributing to the war effort, and its response to the disaster was quick and effective. The massive relief and recovery effort involved military personnel and ordinary citizens. It included rescue trains from other parts of the province, New Brunswick and the United States. However, there was no avoiding a temporary disruption in shipping and routine rail traffic in and out of the crucial port. Ships were re-routed to Saint John and trains were shuffled to other terminals, including six CLC specials re-directed from Montreal to New York City.

Overall, the CLC trains, which were sometimes coded in secret government correspondence as "silk trains," ran on schedule much like the actual silk-train traffic that crossed Canada in special boxcars under armed guard.

But whether the men were heading to France or returning to China, the vast majority spent time behind wire at the William Head Quarantine Station on Vancouver Island. The CLC encampment was only eighteen kilometres southwest of Victoria, situated on a rocky peninsula overlooking Juan de Fuca Strait. The time the labourers spent there constitutes a significant part of their story; one that, for most, marked their introduction to and their final days in the West. And while the quarantine station is long gone, the old cemetery is still there, within the perimeter of a federally-operated minimum-security prison. It alone provides chilling proof that not all the men survived the outbound and homeward-bound journeys.

Amazingly, only one ship with a large complement of Chinese labourers was sunk by enemy action. That disaster occurred along a route that took ships across the Indian Ocean, through the Suez Canal and then across the Mediterranean to France. The victim was the French transport *Athos,* torpedoed south of Malta on February 17, 1917, by U-65. Of 1,846 passengers and 328 crew members, 543 Chinese labourers — all recruited by the French — died, along with 211 others.[24] To the German U-boat commander, the transport, owned by the Messageries Maritimes company, was fair game because she was carrying troops as well as other passengers. At the time the Germans had recently resumed a campaign of unrestricted submarine warfare, targeting freighters, tankers, troopships and warships without warning.

The sailing orders for the transports carrying labourers recruited by the British did not begin with voyages to Canada. The first transport carrying CLC labourers, the *Teucer,* departed Weihaiwei (Weihai), China, on January 18, 1917, and took eighty-three days to reach Britain via the Indian Ocean. Although thousands of kilometres from the war's epicentre in Europe, the sea lanes across the Bay of Bengal and Indian Ocean had already proven disastrous for Allied shipping. Between the end of August and early November 1914, the German light cruiser *Emden,* dispatched as a lone raider from Germany's East Asiatic Squadron, had destroyed, disrupted and captured merchant ships before she was finally shot to pieces on November 9.

After completing her perilous crossing of the Indian Ocean, *Teucer* called at Durban on the south-east coast of Africa. From there she steamed around the Cape of Good Hope and reached the south coast of England on April 11. The British also sent initial CLC drafts via the Indian Ocean, the Suez Canal and Mediterranean for transfer to Marseille. But with the long voyages contributing to the rise of various illnesses and with Germany making good on her promise to target all Allied shipping, Admiralty had to find another way.

Many of the CLC ships that plied the route from China to Western Canada began their voyage in Hong Kong. From there they steamed north to the recruitment depot at Weihaiwei, where they dropped anchor and waited for labourers to be ferried out on crowded lighters. The first ship to call at Weihaiwei and transport labourers to Canada was the *Empress of Russia* of the CPOS. Her voyage was typical of other Canadian-bound ships. She began her journey March 15, 1917, called at Shanghai on the eighteenth, and arrived off Weihaiwei on the nineteenth, when more than 2,300 labourers were transferred to her steerage.[25]

From there, the *Russia* steamed southeast across the Yellow and East China seas. She called at Nagasaki, Japan, on March 21, where dozens of Japanese women with smudged faces and torn clothing relayed baskets of coal from flat-bottom barges up into the ship. Fully coaled, the *Russia* raised anchor and passed through the Japanese archipelago and then up the east coast, arriving at Yokohama on the twenty-third. Strangely incongruous to the secret scheme, regular paying passengers were welcomed on board and could see and even quietly photograph the labourers on the lower decks.

At Yokohama, the *Russia* took on more provisions while preparing for her 4,200-nautical-mile voyage across the North Pacific. The crossing typically lasted seventeen days, sometimes longer, depending on the weather. Travelling by the shortest distance, she followed a northeast bearing on a long arc that took her south of the Aleutians, then down along the west coast of Alaska and British Columbia. Probing through fog and against strong currents, she entered Juan de Fuca Strait that separates

Vancouver Island, British Columbia, and the State of Washington's Olympic Peninsula. On her left were the perilous Race Rocks, and just ahead the William Head Quarantine Station.

At that point a ship's schedule depended on the health of her passengers and crew. A single report of a contagious disease, such as smallpox or influenza, could place everyone — regardless of passenger class — in quarantine for days, even weeks. The *Russia*, unfortunately, arrived at William Head on April 3 with a labourer suffering from the highly contagious smallpox. Meanwhile, in Vancouver, health authorities had faced an outbreak of the same deadly disease introduced in late March.

Although inspections and quarantine interrupted and curtailed some travel, the vast majority of the nearly 85,000 Chinese labourers who arrived on Canada's West Coast boarded the trains at Vancouver. The only men who did not reach Europe this way after arriving in Canada were those who were too sick to carry on or those who embarked on the *Empress of Asia*, which, after passing through the Panama Canal, steamed north to New York for the Atlantic Crossing.

While the CPOS and Blue Funnel Line provided most of the ships, these vessels are remembered mostly for the time spent transporting tourist and business passengers to and from the Orient. The wartime service of the *Empress of Asia*, *Empress of Japan* and *Empress of Russia*, deployed in the Far East between 1914 and 1916 to help blockade German merchant ships, is also well known, particularly *Russia*'s and *Asia*'s in the long search for *Emden*. After the German ship was destroyed, *Russia* took on 230 of her survivors. Unfortunately, the historical wartime service of these ships as crowded CLC transports is seldom, if ever, mentioned.

* * *

Far more important to this story are the identities of the men who enrolled in the CLC. Most of the labourers are long

forgotten and few left anything behind to record their participation. Thankfully, recent scholarship and new exhibitions in
China and elsewhere have focused on who these men were,
their individual memories, experiences and ambitions, and the
psychology behind the choices they made. This has led to a better
understanding of why these men did what they did, and, more
importantly, what they and their families endured.

During the early years of the war many parts of China were
still drought-stricken. Millions were living in poverty and forced
to make hard choices, and there was — as there is today in China
— a large surplus of young men. "The struggle of the peasantry
to survive in the face of deteriorating agricultural conditions,
notably the scarcity of cultivable land, was certainly the prime
mover," noted Chinese scholar Zhang Yan. "Yet this could only
have translated itself into the spectacular outcome of 140,000
men being delivered to Europe by way of an effective medium."[26]

Within this wartime story it is also useful to understand that
while poverty was a motivating factor, it was not the main driving force. Scholars Thomas R. Gottschang and Diana Lary have
shown that China's long history of mass human migration is
based more on "the deep and unquestioned commitment of
millions of North Chinese workers to aid their families by any
possible means."[27] Those recruited under the British and French
wartime labour schemes were not all poverty-stricken peasants.
The recruiters were, after all, looking for men who were in reasonably good shape, which the poorest of the poor were often
not. Most of those who arrived at the recruitment depots easily
met the physical requirements, although a significant number of
unhealthy men were sent home.

Among the Chinese who were motivated to find work were
farmers, fishermen, students, cooks, shopkeepers, and artists,
as well as the unemployed or under-employed. "Most were
driven by a sense of filial piety and of obligation to their families,
manifest through the satisfaction of material needs," emphasized

Zhang Yan. The scholar describes one man, Wu Li-chung (Wei Lizhong, No. 57807) of Lin-tzu County who went abroad with the CLC partly because he needed money to redeem his eight-year-old brother, whom his family had previously sold.[28]

Through his extensive research in Shantung, Zhang discovered "most of the navvies were single, and had siblings who could take care of their parents . . . Many struggled with the thought of leaving China . . . yet going abroad offered the best guarantee of their material sustenance."[29] He also noted how men found quieter ways to slip away from home to the recruitment centres, especially if their parents had insisted they not leave. One young man, Yen Shih-cheng (Yan Shicheng), wanted to follow his brother overseas and began the journey after completing the chore of "collecting cow dung in the fields."[30]

Like Captain Harry Livingstone, who left Listowel and his childhood egg collection, and like the tens of thousands of other Canadians who served in the war, each CLC enrollee had an identification or registration number assigned by the military. And, also like Livingstone, they came forth with their own skills, personality, family history and physical qualities. Stereotypes of a race inferior to or physically smaller than whites often went unchallenged, but sometimes they were. One labourer, described by a Vancouver newspaper as a "placid Oriental," stood "seven feet six inches in his socks, and weighed over three hundred pounds."[31] There is also the extraordinary photograph of a tall, very muscular man balancing a barbell on his head.

Many of the labourers simply listed their pre-war occupation as "farmer" or "labourer," but Livingstone and others got to know men who were skilled tradesmen, musicians, painters, philosophers and storytellers. On the ships they drilled, worked and emptied buckets, but they also told jokes, laughed, cried, fought and gambled. On the trains, Livingstone, who kept a detailed diary, witnessed men marvelling at the landscape and wondering out loud how long it was going to take to "reach the end of Canada."

Character traits and emotion are seen in exceptionally rare letters to loved ones, often touching on subjects familiar to regular soldiers. Entering the picture was homesickness, the health of children and aging parents and, of course, the fears associated with safeguarding or providing for one's family while thousands of kilometres away. "We have arrived in English Canada from where we take a train and in about 16 days we will arrive in France," wrote Joe Hwei Chun to his father and mother-in-law. "I thank you for taking care of my wife as she is bound to fret about my absence."[32]

Canadians and other Allied military personnel travelling with the CLC formed both good and bad impressions. Livingstone was intent on learning from the Chinese while being mindful of the men's health. During his time at Weihaiwei, and on the long journey to France, he remained open to the language, and patient around cultural differences that were often ridiculed by other officers. When the doctor nearly missed his train in late 1917, a number of labourers became anxious and began to hang out the windows. When they spotted him running along the railway platform, they cried out: "Dai fu lai la!" or "Here comes the doctor!"[33]

Most of the Chinese who did not survive the war and its dangerous cleanup are overseas. Approximately two thousand are buried in some forty cemeteries throughout France and Belgium under the care of the Commonwealth War Graves Commission (CWGC) — their lives cut short by accidents, bombings and, mostly, by disease. The largest of those cemeteries, at Noyelles-sur-Mer, has 838 identified and four unidentified casualties.[34] Of those, more than 50 per cent died after the Armistice. Nearly forty others with no known grave are listed on the cemetery's memorial panel.

The Chinese also lie in cemeteries in the United Kingdom, from Shorncliffe to Liverpool to Plymouth. Here in Canada, their graves exist across the country, from William Head to Regina, to Winnipeg, Thunder Bay, Petawawa, Montreal, Quebec City and Halifax. At last count, more than fifty lie here, some of them without a headstone or defined location, a difficult situation that the Canadian Agency of the CWGC has made great headway with as part of its ongoing commemoration and in co-operation with research for this book. It is believed through this research that the body of one man, found by Livingstone on the troopship *Olympic* at Halifax, Liu Chih (Liu Zhi) of Tongshan, China, simply vanished after being taken ashore before the transport sailed to Liverpool. That was five days before the Halifax Explosion.

* * *

These men and their work in a "civilized" world undone by violence and far from home are at the core of this story. I have set out to chronicle their journey from Weihaiwei and Tsingtao (Qingdao) to Canada and on to the Western Front. For a story that is so unfamiliar, at least to Canadians, I have found it necessary to provide what I hope is proper context for a series of pre-war and wartime events that unfolded in China and in the West.

But what makes this book unique is its focus on the largely ignored or forgotten Canadian part of the CLC experience, offered with a fresh Canadian perspective. This, then, is mostly the story about Canadians who interacted with the Chinese, and the significant contributions they made — along with the Chinese — at a very crucial time.

Livingstone, fortunately, kept a detailed record of his time with the CLC. An adventure-seeker like his world-famous granduncle, he began his worldwide journey by heading to nearby London, Ontario, to enlist in the summer of 1916. The officer who put him through his physical and signed his enlistment papers was Captain Louis Sebert, a sprinter who had participated in the 1908 Olympics in London, England, before graduating from medicine at the University of Toronto.[35] Lou and Harry became close friends and travelled together to China with another officer, Lieutenant John McDonald. These three medical men had no idea what they were in for when they left No. 1 Canadian Army Medical Depot at London, Ontario, in August 1917.

But, then again, neither did many other Canadians, including men who were already in China or about to arrive, but were not — at least initially — connected to military service. These were missionaries, following deep spiritual beliefs as university-educated doctors, teachers and engineers. Among them were the Reverend Frederick Auld, W. Robert Reeds, Ernest Struthers and his brother Robert, Gordon Jones, James Menzies and Napier Smith. Each had studied the Chinese language and paid attention to the history and culture at their mission stations and in the surrounding villages. This was exactly the type of experience the British needed to break down the language and cultural barriers that came with such a massive foreign labour scheme.

It was awkward and very troubling at first, especially for the various church authorities and sponsors in Canada, but one by one Canadian missionaries signed up and received temporary appointments as British officers in the CLC. One of them, Thomas Arthurs, died in France. Another missionary, the Reverend Gillies Eadie, stayed behind in China and was singled out for his work at the British War Office's CLC Emigration Agency at Tsingtao. From early 1917 until well into 1920 when the last Chinese labourers came home, "Eadie ran the work of that office," stated York University Professor Margo S. Gewurtz in a 1982 presentation to the annual meeting of the Canadian Historical Association. Eadie handled "the paperwork; kept all the accounts and oversaw the distribution of some twenty million dollars a year."[36]

In France, the Reverend Gordon Jones of Brantford, Ontario, served close to the front lines as an officer with the CLC's 52nd Company. Throughout his journey from China to Canada to the Western Front, the professionally trained engineer wrote daily to his wife, Clara, and daughter, Eleanor. "Great excitement! We have just heard we are off," he wrote on June 17, 1917, while waiting to board a ship at Halifax. "At least we are moving up to the wharf in the city tonight and that almost certainly means we are leaving tomorrow or the next day . . . So perhaps this really will be the last from Halifax."[37]

Jones was right. Two weeks later, he was "Somewhere in France."

The Canadian story also involves CPR officials, immigration authorities, the press and military men, including a twenty-seven-year-old private from Toronto who was accidentally shot and killed during a CLC riot in France. The cast also includes undercover agents who scribbled down licence plate numbers while keeping an eye out for saboteurs on the West Coast. Looming large among Canadian officials is Canada's chief press censor, Colonel Ernest J. Chambers, who worked to keep the CLC scheme out of the press. On the West Coast he was aided by federal immigration inspector Malcolm Reid, who carried a lot of heavy baggage from his controversial days as federal immigration agent for Vancouver.

In Montreal there was Colonel Walter Maughan, the CPR's assistant general passenger agent who was responsible for issuing the top-secret train schedules and memos to select employees, high-ranking government officials and top military personnel. Among the shipmasters was Captain Arthur Wellesley Davison of the Canadian Pacific Ocean Service whose ship, the *Empress of Asia*, transported some fourteen thousand labourers in six Pacific voyages between 1917 and 1918.

* * *

Unfortunately, the years have erased much of what existed during the CLC's short lifespan. This book was written to shed light on the largely forgotten Canadian part of this fascinating story.

Part One: Canada to China

CHAPTER 1

Migrations

"I set no value on objects strange or ingenious, and have no use for your country's manufactures."

Pipes and drums . . .

The vibrations from the idling locomotive did not drown out the music from the small, but determined marching band. The pipes were still playing in Captain Harry Livingstone's head when he boarded the train at London, Ontario, bound for Vancouver.[1] It was a pleasant day with temperatures slightly below normal, but it was not raining, unlike the two previous days.[2] The five pipers and three drummers had rehearsed for the occasion, and now — with their ceremonial task complete — they were marching back to camp at Military District No. 1.

It was shortly after 1 p.m., Friday, August 10, 1917, and the train, with its massive steam-driven locomotive, loomed large — a defining point of departure for Canadians heading overseas from a country entrenched in war, but painfully divided on the hotly-debated issue of conscription, a controversy that, of course, burned well beyond the wreckage of the war.

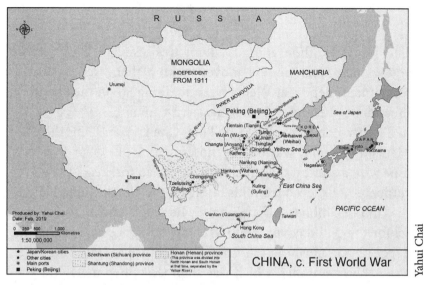

China at the time of the First World War.

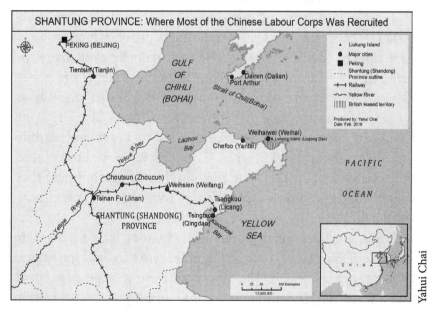

A map detailing Shantung province at the time of the First World War.

* * *

That summer, thousands of kilometres away in China, more young men were on the move, making their way to British recruitment depots at Weihaiwei and Tsingtao on the Shantung (Shandong) Peninsula in northeastern China.

Twenty-one-year-old Han Ting Chen (Han Dingzhen) of Tientsin (Tianjin) was one of those men. A muscular five-foot-nine with a scar on the left side of his broad forehead, the young carpenter journeyed from his home on the North China Plain to the Gulf of Chihli (Gulf of Bohai), where he boarded a small vessel for the two-day voyage to Weihaiwei.[3] Once accepted at the depot on the northeastern tip of the peninsula, Han Ting Chen was issued a number, which was stamped onto a metal bracelet. Although recruited by the British and destined for war-torn France, this man was not a soldier. He was a labourer, No. 47557 of the Chinese Labour Corps (CLC).

Tens of thousands of men just like him had travelled great distances to reach the CLC recruitment depot, which was not accessible by road or railway. The vast majority came from the provinces of Shantung and Chihli (Zhili, now Hebei province), although there were some who journeyed from as far away as Kansu (Gansu) province in northwestern China.[4] Like Han Ting Chen, the men made their way directly to Weihaiwei or into the towns along the Tsangkou-Tsinanfu Railway. From there, they boarded trains that took them east to Tsingtao, where they caught coastal steamers to Weihaiwei, roughly 240 kilometres to the north.

Either way, the journey was mostly by foot. These treks were rough and dangerous, but the Chinese were used to long migratory journeys. Pressures on resources from a large population and a severe lack of arable land led to abject poverty, starvation and death. For many, the choice was simple: Sit and try to eke out an existence at home, or travel to where work could be found.

And so every spring since the lifting of a travel ban in the 1800s thousands of peasants left Shantung and journeyed northeast to agricultural colonies in Manchuria.

Many Chinese, therefore, knew how to prepare for long journeys and separation from home and family. Most were used to walking in worn-out footwear or with nothing on their calloused feet. Generations had taught them to be resourceful and practical, carrying only what they needed. Some enterprising travellers pushed homemade carts or wheelbarrows equipped with large canvas screens that shielded their faces and bodies from the sun and abrasive dust. Into these practical wooden contraptions they placed what was necessary to sustain themselves, including items that could be sold or traded. Travelling alone or in groups, they ate and slept outdoors, each day continuing to pick their way through narrow valleys and along rivers dry as dust or suddenly swollen with torrential rain.

In late 1916 and early 1917, while contemplating their annual journey to the northern agricultural colonies, many men heard about the British scheme to hire Chinese labour for its war effort. The news came mostly by word-of-mouth but it was also found on posters tacked to the walls of post offices and railway stations. For the skilled and unskilled men of Shantung facing the usual hardships, including drought, flooding and political unrest, the British offer presented another option for work.

By March 1917, joining the CLC had become a lot easier for those living in Shantung province, within close proximity of the railway line. They did not have to travel as far as Weihaiwei; all they had to do was reach Tsingtao. By then the port on the Yellow Sea, which was under Japanese control, was no longer just a hub for sending men north. What had started out as a reception centre in an old German silk factory at nearby Tsangkou (Cangkou) had become a separate recruitment depot. For the logistically-minded British, this made sense because Tsingtao was not only served by the railway but had better port facilities. The men could

David Livingstone Collection

Four newly hired labourers eat at Weihaiwei in the fall of 1917. Shortly after this photo was taken the men underwent a physical examination at the recruitment depot in northeastern China.

go directly from the trains into the depot and then, if accepted, onto the ships.[5]

One of those men, twenty-four-year-old Chang Hung (Zhang Hong), was registered as No. 92560. The unmarried farmer from Tsingtao did not have far to walk, but, like many others who joined the CLC between late 1916 and March 1918, Chang Hung did not eventually return home. The young labourer made it only as far as the William Head Quarantine Station on Vancouver Island, where he contracted pneumonia in December and died on the evening of January 9, 1918.[6]

Coinciding with these travels to Weihaiwei and Tsingtao were the journeys of Chinese men who had opted to enrol in the French labour recruitment scheme, Service d'organisation des travailleurs coloniaux (Colonial Labour Service), which was up and running before the British recruitment effort began.

All of this interest in working overseas for the British or the French occurred less than six years after China experienced its 1911–12 revolution, which had brought thousands of years of imperial rule to an end. The Qing or Manchu dynasty was gone and in its place was a fledgling and tumultuous democratic republic.

* * *

Well before Livingstone boarded the train at London, Ontario, in the summer of 1917, images of crowds along wooden railway station platforms were embedded in the minds of thousands of Canadian soldiers already overseas. Many had left with the hope of returning after the war, but once overseas and in the trenches it was hard to be optimistic. Although the bands played on across Canada, enthusiasm for the war had waned, replaced by quieter farewells that put a brave face to the more authentic feelings of sadness and fear.

Captain Louis Sebert and Lieutenant John McDonald sat next to Livingstone in the coach; all three appearing rather confident in their uniforms. At age thirty, Sebert, born in Whitby, Ontario, was the oldest. McDonald, who had grown up on a farm at Lakeside, roughly thirty kilometres northeast of London, was the youngest at twenty-eight, but only by six months. The three physicians had attended medical school at the University of Toronto, and the two oldest had opened private practices before war was declared.

For the duration of their top-secret mission, Sebert took charge of the travel documents, tickets and cheques, while McDonald guarded the money and receipts. Livingstone was appointed "physician to the physicians," official historian and wartime scribe.

As the train pulled out of London to commence its journey across rural southwestern Ontario for a connection in Toronto, the "official historian" was careful to note in his small field diary the exact time of departure: 1:25 p.m.[7] Keeping track of such moments was important because over the next three months all three doctors were expected to travel to China, work there for an unspecified period of time and then escort large contingents of Chinese labourers through Canada while en route to the Western Front.

It all sounded rather challenging and perhaps a bit dangerous, but that was the assignment.

While Livingstone and McDonald were bachelors, they were leaving behind loving parents and good friends, not to mention promising professional careers. Sebert had that too, but was a married man. After graduating from university in 1912, he travelled to New York and completed postgraduate work at the famous Herman Knapp Memorial Hospital, where he became an ophthalmologist.[8] Eye doctors were in high demand during the war. On the Western Front, ocular assaults from flying dirt and other debris were common. There, as in China, men also suffered from various eye diseases, including highly infectious trachoma.

At Toronto's Union Station, the three doctors were greeted by Livingstone's father, John, who proudly led the way to nearby Walker House on the southwest corner of Front and York Streets.[9] The affable small-town druggist, who had travelled from Listowel to see his son off, treated the men to supper in the hotel's large dining room where they blended in with the crowd. Anyone who did pause long enough to notice the young officers probably assumed they were either on leave or en route to a troopship at Montreal or Halifax.

China was not on most people's list of probable wartime destinations.

While censorship kept a tight lid on troop movements and military operations, events were unfolding quickly in the countries these officers would eventually visit. Even as they dined, the British recruitment effort at Weihaiwei and Tsingtao

Captains Harry Livingstone (left) and Lou Sebert study maps at No. 1 Depot, London, Ontario, summer 1917.

David Livingstone Collection

was in full swing. There, moving eastward, Chinese labourers who had already passed through the recruitment centres were headed for work projects on the Western Front, in which some of their compatriots were already engaged.

Livingstone did not know much about China, but he was curious about its history, geography and people. Japan, which he would visit en route, also intrigued him and the other two doctors. The interior walls of one of the huts at the base in London were plastered with maps and the men had spent hours poring over them. They had picked out ports they were likely to visit as well as cities and ancient villages where life, they were told, still went on behind stone walls.

China's political situation, particularly its sudden and recent shift into a fragile republic, was another intriguing subject for the officers. While they were not aware of all the political developments unfolding in the Far East, all three had the capacity to wonder what life was like for the Chinese beyond the harsh stereotypical views shared by Westerners. Still, when it came right down to it, all three doctors believed they were being sent to work in a country that had been home to ancient civilizations and where millions of people still lived as they did thousands of years ago.

Beginning with the Xia and Shang dynasties and ending with the Manchu or Qing dynasty, the people of China had lived and died under imperial rule. However, these dynasties are also widely recognized for major advances along the road of human civilization. New political and social systems, philosophy, morality, complex writing systems, the discovery and use of iron and grain-based agriculture are just a few.

These and other great achievements were tied directly to the indigenous peoples' need to survive in a cereal-based agricultural environment that was, unfortunately, prone to drought and flooding as well as to invasion and rebellion. This was especially true during the Shang dynasty (circa 1600–1046 BC) — a time that is often thought to mark the beginning of Chinese civilization — and its successor, the Zhou (1046–256 BC), that arose in the Yellow River valley and developed a hierarchical political and social system that empowered aristocratic families. Over time, bitter rivalries among semi-autonomous states caused the system to fail, but it was during this period when the most influential thinkers, including Confucius, focused their minds on a desirable society in terms of individual morality and the role of governance.[10]

The last two dynasties — the Ming and the Qing — faced additional challenge and hardship caused by unprecedented population growth. For more than a thousand years the population of China had hovered around sixty million. During the Ming dynasty, which lasted only 276 years, it doubled, and by the end of the 268-year Qing dynasty it was between 400 and 500 million.[11]

Such numbers were hard to fathom for Livingstone, Sebert and McDonald. When they embarked on their journey, Canada's population was growing, but it was only around eight million.[12]

In addition to extraordinary population growth, the Qing also experienced severe famine, widespread rebellion, and violence. Major famines in 1849 and 1877–78 claimed nearly twenty-three million lives. The 1850–64 Taiping Rebellion left more than twenty million dead across seventeen provinces.[13] Many believe the toll was much higher. Hundreds of villages were destroyed and the once fertile landscape of the Yangtze River valley was covered with dead. The rebellion was finally suppressed when Qing forces — assisted by British Army regulars and American mercenaries — surrounded, then blasted through the walls of the Taiping capital of Nanking (Nanjing). The fourteen-year-long civil war, which coincided with massive migrations to North America to take advantage of the opportunities presented by the discovery of gold, weakened the Qing dynasty to the point where it was unable to establish effective control over the country. Stepping into this vacuum was a new decentralized armed force that had been organized from existing regional militias and used to help defeat the Taipings.

The ramifications of this carried over into the twentieth century.

Like most educated men of his day, Livingstone was somewhat aware of Europe's historical ties to the Far East, particularly when it came to trade and missionary work. In the late 1700s, Britain's King George III had sent an envoy to the Orient to establish an embassy and pursue trade opportunities. China was then the largest empire in the world with an estimated one-third share of global Gross Domestic Product.[14] Its ruler saw no need to import goods from Europe and made it clear foreign trade would continue to be confined to Canton (Guangzhou) on the south coast. The envoy, Lord George Macartney, was kindly refused and then asked to relay a message to the king. "As your Ambassador can see for himself, we possess all things. I set no value on objects strange or ingenious, and have no use of your country's manufactures . . . But as the tea, silk, and porcelain which the Celestial Empire produces are absolute necessities to European nations and to yourselves, we have permitted, as a signal mark of favour, that foreign hongs [business interests] should be established at Canton, so that your wants might be supplied and your country thus participate in our beneficence."[15]

Of course it was only a matter of time before China's hard protectionist stance on trade and foreign influence made it increasingly vulnerable to world powers, including Victorian England, which continued to perceive China as a backward country. "Chinese civilization during this period was for the most part commendable in so far as it measured up to European standards," wrote historian Mary Mason. "Westerners seemed to forget that Europe, until about the last quarter of the eighteenth century, had been just as backward, or possibly more so than China was in about 1850."[16]

The Opium Wars of 1839–42 and 1856–60 and other violence often stemmed from either foreign aggression or domestic humiliation prompted by foreign aggression, natural disasters or imperial weakness. The First Opium War was in response to a Chinese imperial commissioner sent to Canton to put an end to the illegal importation of the highly-addictive and harmful drug by foreign traders — most of them British — from India to China. Until it was prohibited in 1800, opium was imported legally through Canton. For the British, the Chinese opium market had been a way to correct a serious trade imbalance it had with China, mostly because of the importation of Chinese tea into Britain.

When Chinese efforts to stop the drug's importation failed, frustration grew, and in 1838 more than twenty thousand chests or 1,400 tons of opium were seized and destroyed. Warehouses were closed, and hundreds of black market merchants, including British traders, jailed. A letter to the queen of England in 1839 noted that her country knew full well how harmful opium was because it had passed laws prohibiting it.

Despite objections at home, British warships were dispatched and took control of Canton. Military forces then moved north, capturing and pillaging a number of cities, including Shanghai. It ended with China the big loser in the Treaty of Nanking of 1842, which ceded Hong Kong Island to Britain, established five open treaty ports and called on China to pay twenty million dollars in

compensation. A supplementary treaty in 1843 led to other benefits, including the assurance British subjects accused of crime in
a British concession would be tried by a British court or tribunal.
Several more concessions and privileges were granted to the British and French following the Second Opium War.

Augmenting the Qing dynasty's troubles during the mid-
nineteenth century was tsarist Russia, which was making good
on expansion plans. While moving eastward, Russia claimed vast
territories north of the Amur and east of the Ussuri rivers all
the way to Vladivostok on the Pacific. This, for a while, seemed
to work in the Qing's favour because it restricted movement of
traditional enemies from Inner Asia.

As the 1800s came to a close, little Weihaiwei did not escape
foreign interest or aggression. Home to China's Beiyang or
Northern Seas Fleet, the port was captured by the Japanese in
1895 during the last major battle of the First Sino-Japanese War.
The disastrous outcome proved how the Qing dynasty had failed
to protect China's sovereignty by not modernizing its military
forces. The victorious Japanese, meanwhile, continued to occupy
Weihaiwei for at least another three years.

The British lease at Weihaiwei, which covered approximately
750 square kilometres and included the town of Ma-tou, renamed
Port Edward by the British, was one of five signed between China
and foreign powers within a very short period. In November and
December 1897, Germany landed troops at Kiaochow Bay (Jiao-
zhou Bay) on the southern coast of the Shantung Peninsula near
Tsingtao. Russia, which by then had won the right to extend the
Trans-Siberian Railway through Manchuria, replied by sending
warships to Port Arthur on the Liaodong Peninsula situated on
the north side of the strait separating the Yellow Sea from the
Gulf of Chihli.

In January 1898, China yielded to the German aggression and
two months later signed long-term leases granting Kiaochow
to Germany and Port Arthur, which was a warm-water port, to

Russia. Meanwhile, France, not wanting to be left out, demanded Kwangchowwan (Guangzhouwan) on the southern coast of China, while Great Britain pressured for Weihaiwei as a counterpoint to the Russians at Port Arthur. Leases for these territories were signed in April, and in June another section of the Kowloon Peninsula adjacent to Hong Kong went to the British.[17]

Germany's decision to seize the Kiaochow Bay area was ostensibly in response to the murder of two German Roman Catholic missionaries. However, it had much more to do with the German Empire's desire to expand its trading and other political interests in China in order to compete with Britain, France and Russia. Perceiving China as a threat, Germany's Kaiser Wilhelm II used the phrase "Yellow Peril" to describe what he regarded as an inferior race. The ninety-nine-year lease Germany signed with China covered some 550 square kilometres and included the valuable port of Tsingtao.

The ugly crescendo that marked the end of the nineteenth century in China included a violent peasant revolt against the Qing dynasty. The Boxer Uprising of 1898–1900, which coincided with severe drought in Shantung province, spread mayhem across northern China and quickly developed into an attack on foreigners, which resulted in headlines around the world. Especially targeted during the massacres were missionaries and foreigners with railway interests.

By 1904, rival interests in China and Korea were creating conflict between Japan and tsarist Russia. In early February, the former launched a surprise naval attack on the Russians at Port Arthur, sparking the Russo-Japanese War. In addition to proving Japan's military superiority, the attack and subsequent war exposed serious weakness within Russia. By May, Japanese troops were on the ground and the port was under siege. Eight months later, with massive casualties on both sides, the Russians surrendered Port Arthur. The war ended in humiliation for Russia as well as revolution in the streets of St. Petersburg.

When China emerged from revolution in 1912 it elected popular anti-Qing rebel leader Sun Yat-sen as provisional president of the new republic. In early 1912, Yuán Shih-kai (Yuán Shikai), who had served as prime minister the previous year, was elected provisional president. In Peking, Yuán had the support of the powerful Beiyang Army. Sun Yat-sen, meanwhile, remained busy leading more diverse elements both in China and abroad. That August, the Kuomintang Party (KMT) was formed by Sun Yat-sen associate Sung Chiao-jen (Song Jiaoren), who campaigned to limit what he and others regarded as an abuse of power by the autocratic Yuán. In March 1913, a gunman assassinated the thirty-year-old Sung and, while many believed the orders came from Yuán, the president's involvement was never proven. However, the killing sparked widespread anger.

To finance his massive Beiyang Army, Yuán negotiated a multi-million dollar loan from international banks. The deal, which was considered unconstitutional, placed China under more paralyzing debt.

In August 1913, the KMT launched a second revolution, which it lost, and Yuán was confirmed as president with international recognition. However, just seven months before the outbreak of the European war, Yuán dissolved parliament. Democracy had clearly not worked, at least in his mind, and so he swapped civilian governors for more militarist leaders.

With war underway in Europe, China declared neutrality. However, it also had aims to recover the Shantung territory it lost to Germany in 1898.

But by November, Germany was no longer occupying Kiaochow Bay and Tsingtao. This is because shortly after German forces crossed into neutral Belgium in August 1914, China's neutrality was breached with long-term consequences. On September 2, ten days after Japan declared war on Germany, some twenty-three thousand Japanese troops, supported by more than 140 guns, landed in China, roughly 160 kilometres from

Tsingtao. The German-held port and surrounding territory was the main objective, but Japanese troops also moved westward beyond the leased territory to Weihsien and Tsinanfu.[18]

The invasion was accomplished without war-neutral China's involvement. Prior to the attack, the British had hoped Japan would restrict her military activity to the seas and focus on the destruction of German naval and armed merchant ships. But by mid-August — a week before it formally declared war on Germany — Japan was sticking to her plan to seize the German-controlled port, which they put forward as the best way to destroy German maritime activity.

So with the clock ticking, Britain contributed troops because it did not want the public at home to think their country was placing all the risk on Japan and because it wanted to maintain some influence over the Japanese occupation. Although China was still a few years away from declaring war on Germany, President Yuán asked if his country could contribute troops to the operation. However, nothing came of this.

Approximately 1,650 British and 500 Sikh troops, deployed from Tientsin and Hong Kong, participated in the attack. They arrived on September 22 after a second wave of Japanese forces landed. The British, in support of the Japanese, carefully avoided infringing on China's neutrality by landing their troops west of Tsingtao within the German-leased territory.[19] The invasion and bombardment — on and over Chinese soil and incorporating the deployment of naval carrier–based aircraft — was one of the earliest battles of the First World War, but remains largely unknown in the West.

Once a small fishing port, Tsingtao had developed quickly under German control into a bustling city with modern European-style features, including German architectural and engineering influences. Calling regularly at its deep-water port were a variety of commercial and naval vessels. Tsingtao was home to Germany's East Asia naval squadron, which in addition to patrolling the seas served as the port's first line of defence. Unfortunately for the German garrison, which had approximately four thousand men, the heavily-armed cruisers *Scharnhorst* and *Gneisenau*, commanded by Admiral Graf von Spee, had sailed off to avoid being caught in the bay at the outbreak of war. Months later, Spee and his two big cruisers, along with two light cruisers in his squadron, were destroyed during the Battle of the Falkland Islands on December 8, 1914.[20]

The siege of Tsingtao ended on November 7, 1914, with a German surrender and the Japanese — not the Chinese — firmly in control of Kiaochow Bay and Tsingtao. The fighting resulted in 1,518 Japanese casualties, including nearly 240 dead. The Germans suffered nearly two hundred dead and more than five hundred wounded. The much smaller British force, members of the South Wales Borderers, counted twelve killed and more than fifty wounded. Among the British casualties were soldiers shot accidentally by Japanese troops.[21]

Following the surrender, Japan continued to occupy what it had won. It also pushed the diplomatic boundaries of its wartime allegiance with Great Britain. In short, Japan knew or soon understood it could continue to exploit and entrench itself in China with very little interference from its European ally, which was pre-occupied with the war in the West and sensitive to keeping Japan onside.

In January 1915, Japan handed China a set of paralyzing demands that — when made public — caused domestic as well as international outrage. The United States, which also had a stake in trade with China, surmised that Japan's Twenty-One Demands would have major ramifications for China, but also for Britain and other world powers. If all of Japan's demands had been forced on China, the republic would have mostly relinquished control to Japan. China, for example, would have had to employ Japanese political, military and financial advisors and allow Japanese hospitals, schools and temples to buy

David Livingstone Collection

Both balance and brute strength are captured in this photo of a CLC labourer at Weihaiwei, 1917.

and own property in China. There were other demands, but the heaviest ones, which were not shared with Britain when the list was first presented, were dropped before a revised set was accepted by President Yuán on May 7, 1915. The amendments, however, did not go far enough and were understandably seen as a shocking betrayal by millions of Chinese. This resulted in riots, strikes and boycotts on what became known as National Humiliation Day.

The reaction was long and painful, but it gave way to the possibility that China could unify and even occupy a more significant place on the world stage once the war in Europe was over. This realization was important because throughout China's past its rulers had looked mostly inward, not outward. With a stronger world view, China could gain more international respect and hopefully use it to resolve past injustices, including Japan's control in Shantung province.

A large contingent of Chinese labourers pose in front of one of the accommodation sheds behind the wire at the Weihaiwei recruitment depot.

In the early summer of 1915, neutral China, mindful of what could be at stake after the war, offered the Allies 300,000 labourers with 100,000 rifles. The idea was eventually rejected by the British as being not practicable. So instead of combat labourers, China quietly suggested a willingness to provide non-combatant labourers for employment on the Western Front. Faced with ghastly casualty figures, the French quickly recognized an opportunity, while the British weighed the pros and cons before commencing recruitment in late 1916.

By then, President Yuán, disgraced and demoralized, had died of kidney failure. From this, the internal politics became more fractious and confused. Li Yuan-hung became president while Tuan Ch'i-jui (Duàn Qírui) served as prime minister. Tuan lasted until May 1917, when he tried to force the National Assembly to enter the First World War on the side of the Allies. Though the attempt failed and he was dismissed by the president, he very soon resumed control of the government and declared war on Germany in mid-August.

* * *

Dubbed "Way High" by British sailors, Weihaiwei, in spite of its shortcomings, was thought to be well situated for recruiting the type of men the British needed for France and Belgium. Labourers from Shantung, the British authorities were advised, were on average taller and hardier than those from Hong Kong and, therefore, more suitable for the European climate and the expectations of hard work on the Western Front.[22]

The leased territory featured one of the best natural, deep-water harbours on the Chinese coast and extended into Weihaiwei Bay and the island of Liu-kung Tao. A strip of land some sixteen kilometres deep and extending approximately 116 kilometres along the coast was also within the territory. The bay provided anchorage for large ships and a stone pier led to a narrow wooden wharf with a gate and two sentry huts. However, since the structure did not extend far enough to allow large ships to tie up, launches were employed to ferry passengers and cargo to ships at anchor. While this was a serious disadvantage when it came to moving large numbers of men and cargo, it was workable.

On the plus side, Weihaiwei had barracks, built and owned by the Witwatersrand Native Labour Association of Johannesburg. These large buildings, which occupied an exposed bluff not far from the water, had been built to accommodate labourers recruited for the South African gold mines. However, they were never used for that purpose.

Inland, past wind-swept dunes, and across the salty plains, time and nature had given rise to mostly treeless hills, some reaching 460 metres. Along the lower levels, amid the dusty scrub growth, generations of farmers and their families continued to hack and carve terraces for cultivation. British historian Michael

Summerskill notes that, prior to the war, separate and expensive afforestation programs, initiated by the British and Germans, were underway to plant an assortment of trees, including those favoured by the Shantung silkworm.[23]

In 1911, the territory had a population of roughly 150,000, including more than 200 Europeans. Most of the Chinese were used to living with the bare necessities of life. Traditions were strong, as were conservative values, even after the revolution. Among women, bound feet were not uncommon, while some men still wore the Manchu queue. The majority resided in crowded villages and faced daily struggles, including food and water shortages. Westerners were usually shocked by the sight of open sewers with children playing nearby.

Those adults who did not work small tracts of land handed down through generations ran small shops or made their living from the sea. Many others spent hours gathering mollusks and other edible treasures along the shore at low tide. While the homes they lived in were typically small, they usually housed more than one generation. Schools existed, but in 1911 fewer than five thousand children attended. The illiteracy rate among males at the time was nearly 85 per cent, and even higher among females.[24]

It was from such homes and villages where young men took notice of the British recruitment effort. Many, as did Livingstone, made a conscious decision to leave home and loved ones behind, each man driven by his own psychology and the reality he and his family faced. But while Livingstone was mostly propelled by patriotism, adventure and the wartime need for doctors, the Chinese were, again, generally motivated by an obligation to their family while struggling through very trying circumstances. "After the flood, which devastated a large part of Chihli and Shantung provinces in 1917, I was left penniless with not enough property to support the many mouths which belonged to my family," recalled one unidentified labourer after the war.[25]

In August 1917 alone — the same month Livingstone began his journey — 4,041 Chinese labourers left China or were preparing to sail as part of the CLC's monthly shipment from Tsingtao and Weihaiwei.[26] By 1918, more than eighty thousand men from Shantung had sailed overseas with the CLC, representing close to 80 per cent of the total number recruited by the British. Chinese scholarship has also pointed out, however, that the British and French schemes did not end or interrupt in any serious way the seasonal migrations to Manchuria. Nor was going to France considered to be a clear option for those looking for work to sustain their families. The migrations to Manchuria continued mostly unabated throughout the last two years of the war.[27]

CHAPTER 2

Starting Out

". . . unfit for full citizenship . . . obnoxious to a free community and dangerous to the state."

Fathers and sons . . .

With his life inextricably tied to a railway timetable, the moment had arrived for Captain Harry Livingstone of Listowel, Ontario, to say goodbye to his sixty-five-year-old father. After thanking Mr. Livingstone for picking up the tab at Walker House, the three officers and the older man walked back to Toronto's Union Station.[1]

It was mid-summer 1917: three years into the war and three months into what would prove to be the nastiest and most politically-charged period in Canadian history. The costly Easter victory at Vimy Ridge was a stunning achievement. However, on the home front it was followed by political decisions that nearly ripped the country apart in an extremely volatile election year that ended in December with a majority for Prime Minister Robert Borden and his new Union government. The conscription issue was front and centre all summer, driving an even deeper wedge between English and French Canada. By the end of August, the controversial *Military Service Act*, introduced to the House of Commons by Borden's Conservatives in early June, was law.

More divisiveness sprang from the *Military Voters Act*, which also became law by the end of August, and the *Wartime Elections Act*, passed in September. In addition to spawning more resentment and anger between French and English, these measures, individually and collectively, polarized huge sections of Canadian society. Farmers were turned against politicians, the working class and organized labour against the rich, women's organizations against women's organizations and Canadians of British stock against immigrants from countries Canada was waging war against.

While mindful of the worrisome conscription controversy, Livingstone was certainly not dwelling on it when he paused on the platform to shake his father's hand. Instead, it was a classic father-and-son moment with both men wishing each other well and hoping the war would be over soon. "Pa accompanied us to the train which left at 7 p.m. sharp," the grateful son scribbled into his field diary as the train pulled away, heading north through the city and leaving behind a swirling trail of smoke and steam.[2]

* * *

Left alone at the station, John Livingstone felt the sadness in his heart. While the tall, thin, white-haired father easily accepted the fact his son was only six months shy of his thirtieth birthday, it was still hard to say goodbye. The war, after all, issued no guarantees, and so all he and his dear wife Agnes could do was pray — often — and carry on.

With that, John followed his own advice and headed back along the platform, his long strides affirming an athletic past, one in which he had earned accolades throughout southwestern

The first page in Captain Harry Livingstone's Field Diary No. 1 describes the band that escorted the three officers to the London, Ontario, train station in August 1917.

Ontario as a top baseball player.

Life was good in Listowel, where the family was well known and respected. In keeping with the time period, both John and Agnes were habitually well dressed — regular churchgoers, proudly Presbyterian. John's drugstore occupied the ground floor of a four-storey brick building on the town's busiest corner. From behind the counter he dispensed pills and other popular remedies, but also stocked items found in most general stores, including paint and wallpaper, candy and children's toys.

During the fall and winter, two woodstoves — strategically located at the front and back — radiated heat throughout the building. Livingstone's Drug Store was a cozy, welcoming place; one of the most successful businesses in the southwestern

David Livingstone Collection

Captain Harry Livingstone takes a break in London, Ontario, before his departure to China, August 1917.

Ontario farming community. People often dropped by to sit or stand by the stove, chatting about the weather, the harvest, hockey or baseball.

Harry had also spent a lot of time behind the counter, learning from his Pa how to fill prescriptions and mix ointments. John was a patient, disciplined man who listened carefully to his customers and took the time to deliver orders to people who were bedridden or unable to make it into town. He worked a six-day week and his work ethic rubbed off on young Harry, who ran errands and slowly developed an interest in health care.[3]

But while the business was successful, the Livingstones were not wealthy. While Agnes had enjoyed a more privileged upbringing than John, she, too, lived a life of modesty and preferred a smile over a frown. The family's yellow-brick, two-storey home at the corner of Elizabeth and Argyle Streets was only a few blocks from the drugstore. It housed an unusually small family.

Besides Harry, John and Agnes had an older son, Roland, who was ten years Harry's senior. Despite the age difference, the boys got along well and remained close even after Roland headed off to medical school in Toronto. The big split came when Roland moved to Melville, Saskatchewan, where he established a family practice and acquired the folksy title "Doc Livingstone."

Harry's lifetime fascination with birds was John's doing. Their oological pursuits included springtime hikes into forests where they climbed trees in search of eggs to be collected, drained and catalogued. Although it was a hobby that was quickly falling out of favour, the father and son team assembled beautiful wooden display cabinets for their specimens. John and Harry also built and erected ornate purple martin houses that overlooked the town. On the Livingstone property, birds outnumbered people during the warmer months.[4]

Naturally, the Livingstones were quite proud of their blood connection to the world-famous medical missionary and African explorer. The great Dr. David Livingstone was the younger brother of John's father, John Sr. Born in Blantyre, Scotland, in 1811, John Sr., like most young people, went off to work at an early age. His childhood was divided between a few hours of school in the evening and fourteen-hour days, six days a week, as a "piecer" in a cotton mill in Blantyre, where he and David strung together broken cotton threads on the spinning machines.

In 1838, shortly before his adventure-driven sibling set sail for southern Africa, John Sr. emigrated from Scotland to Canada with his wife, Sarah, and their two young children, Neil and Mary. They settled in Lanark County west of Ottawa, where John — a kind of jack-of-all-trades — worked mostly as a tailor, but also as a tanner, and a partner in a lumber company. The couple had eight more children; John Jr. was the third youngest, born in 1852. Eight years later the family moved to Listowel, where John Sr. established a small farm in Elma Township and later opened a general store that was so successful he retired in 1873, the same year his brother died at age sixty in Chitambo, in south-central Africa, while searching for the sources of the Nile.

Included among the letters written by Dr. David Livingstone is one addressed to John Jr. in reply to a letter sent to him in 1864 by his then twelve-year-old nephew. The explorer, while still in Africa, compliments John Jr. on his excellent penmanship, and then explains there are several people standing around, watching him compose the letter. He noted how all the onlookers were amazed when he explained that people thousands of kilometres away will be able to receive the letter, open it and read the contents.[5]

John Sr. died at age eighty-eight in 1899. By then, John Jr. was forty-seven and his eleven-year-old son, Harry, was growing up fast, but still collecting birds' eggs and assisting at the drugstore. Slim, with light brown hair and grey eyes, the young student earned good marks in high school where he studied hard and benefited from a German language course. And like his father, Harry was quite athletic. But instead of baseball, he excelled at tennis and gymnastics.

In 1906, John and Agnes watched their eighteen-year-old son follow the path set by their oldest boy. Accepted by the University of Toronto's medical school, Harry boarded a train at Listowel and embarked for the big city. After waving goodbye to their son and returning to their empty nest, John and Agnes fully expected they would see him soon enough, and hear about his studies and time in the city.

As the small town faded from young Harry's view that day it was easy to appreciate what his parents had given him. His pleasant and supportive mother and his father's tireless work ethic had helped prepare him for a life of responsibility. Working in the drugstore had taught him to respect people's privacy and not to jump too quickly to judgment. There was, of course, still much to learn, but the lessons from his youth had been a good starting point.

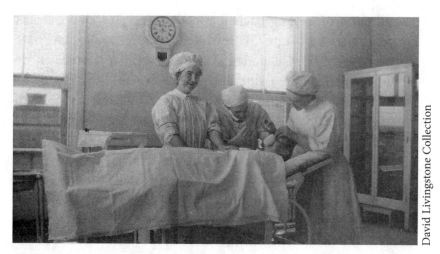

David Livingstone Collection

Dr. Harry Livingstone (centre) goes to work during his internship at Guelph General Hospital, 1910.

Toronto, of course, opened up a new and exciting world for Harry. He met interesting people and, when not in class, at the gym or cramming for exams in his rooming house overlooking Spadina Avenue, he cleared his head with long walks through the city, occasionally stopping in front of a bakery where his senses were teased by the sight and smell of fresh bread and doughnuts. Money was extremely tight, but each day brought him closer to his dream of becoming a doctor like his brother Roland. It was a goal quickly realized, because students could enter university right out of high school and four years later be full-fledged family physicians.[6]

After graduating in 1910 with a Bachelor of Medicine, Dr. Livingstone remained in Ontario and completed his internship at Guelph General Hospital. The following spring, the twenty-three year old had a decision to make: move from Guelph and open a private practice at nearby Elmira or return home to Listowel, where — word had it — an older doctor was set to retire. Still somewhat of a homebody, he opted for the latter and that summer established a practice above his father's drugstore.[7]

Although the young bachelor was a teetotaller, he loved his cigars, preferring White Owls, which he smoked while en route to the hospital to visit patients. If it was only a short visit, he would enter through a side door and leave the stogie with its smouldering end carefully balanced over the edge of a small wooden shelf. The cigar, which often caused a burn mark, was always waiting for him when he left the building.[8]

The respected role of small-town physician held Livingstone in place until August 1916 when the steady pull of wartime service and the cajolery of recruiters finally drew him to London, Ontario.[9] His medical training quickly opened the door to officer status in the Canadian Army Medical Corps (CAMC), and it was Captain Louis Sebert who certified his medical examination at Training Depot No. 1 on August 19, 1916.[10]

By then, the Battle of the Somme was underway.

* * *

While heading north towards Sudbury, Livingstone, McDonald and Sebert stared out at the diminishing twilight and chatted about a host of things, including the preparations they had made for their Far East adventure. All three, however, were conscious of the war's deadly toll and the political state of the country they were about to leave behind in the summer of 1917.

About the burgeoning controversy over conscription, Livingstone's field diary for 1917 makes no comment. This is not surprising, given the diary's intended purpose as a simple travelogue. However, like most well-educated men, the doctor read newspapers and more than likely felt the government was obliged to do something given the atrocious battlefield losses and the slowdown in volunteer enlistment. Conversely, as someone who had grown up in an agricultural community and provided health care for those who made their living off the land, Livingstone could understand why able-bodied sons were needed on the farm. The prime minister's attendance at the Imperial War Conference and his visits with wounded Canadian soldiers had convinced many that more men were needed overseas. However, by August the main controversy seemed more about patriotism and Canada's future than about finding more soldiers.

There is also nothing in the field diary to suggest how Livingstone felt about his actual assignment. He was clearly excited about the journey and the prospect of entering a strange and ancient world, but any thoughts on what he imagined the Chinese to be like were not recorded. Livingstone was, no doubt, aware of the widespread anti-Chinese immigration climate in Canada and how highly restrictive federal legislation had been introduced to control Chinese access. Likewise, he would know there was a head tax, and had presumably read about efforts by politicians, community leaders and labour representatives in support of Chinese exclusion. How all this might impact his mission is anyone's guess, but before leaving London it had certainly been impressed upon the three officers why the whole exercise involving Chinese labourers had to be kept quiet.

Although the head tax had been around since 1885, the new century had done little to change white attitudes; in fact, they became progressively worse. By 1900 there were approximately 17,400 Chinese settled in Canada. Two years later a royal commission delivered the message that Chinese and Japanese were "unfit for full citizenship . . . obnoxious to a free community and dangerous to the state."[11]

When the head tax was raised to $500 in 1904, it became even more prohibitive for Chinese men to move here in search of work, let alone bring along their wives or families. But while a lot fewer Asians arrived that year, the trend was short-lived as the decade played out: those who came, if they found work, earned much more here than they could in China.

In Canada, with few work options, the Chinese, segregated socially and economically, leaned on each other for support.

However, as their communities grew they became easy targets for racists, who regarded them as disease-infested ghettos that threatened white society. "They saw China as a weak nation of backward people who could never learn to live like white Canadians," writes Canadian historian Paul Yee. "Moreover, they said that Chinese people carried diseases and other bad habits that threatened Canada's well-being."[12]

In 1907, anger turned violent during an anti-immigration rally in Vancouver that spread through Chinatown and Japantown. There was also at that time strong antipathy towards East Indians. While the outbreak of war shifted much of the public's attention away from such matters, anti-Asian immigration attitudes remained strong. And so through 1917 and early 1918 these fears continued to influence government decisions in relation to the Chinese Labour Corps and its transportation across Canada. In the government's view, the less visible the labourers were, the better.

Before reaching White River, north of Lake Superior, Livingstone's train stopped several times for coal and water. They had skirted along Georgian Bay into Sudbury and then westward through places with unfamiliar names, including Pogamasing, Metagama, Woman River and Missanabie. "August 11, 1917: Spent most of the day in observation car admiring the scenery. At all stops we get out and exercise ourselves by walking up and down the platform."

In White River the doctor noticed something he thought would impress the folks back home. The object was billed as "the official thermometer," and it was not long before Livingstone and his travelling companions were duly informed that the standard temperature for winter in Fahrenheit in White River is sixty degrees below zero. Last winter, noted Livingstone, it "went as low as 71 below."[13]

The CLC transcontinental movements had been underway for months, and during the night of August 11–12 Livingstone's

Vancouver-bound passenger train and two east-bound Chinese Labour Corps specials met, heading in opposite directions, near Fort William, Ontario (Thunder Bay).

The CLC specials, fairly typical of their type, had departed Vancouver on August 8 and were an hour apart at Fort William. The first arrived at 9:30 p.m. Central Time and departed at 11 p.m. Eastern. Four hundred and fifty Chinese labourers occupied nine Colonist sleeping cars that were originally designed, as their name implies, to carry European immigrants from eastern ports to Western Canada. The armed guard, composed of one Canadian officer, three Canadian non-commissioned officers (NCOs) and thirty-two other-ranks, all of them Canadian, were accommodated in two Tourist sleeping cars, along with three British officers. The CPR manifests for these CLC trains — unlike the manifests for most others — do not list a physician from the CAMC or Royal Army Medical Corps.

In addition, the first special had four boxcars as baggage cars and a commissary baggage car, for a total of sixteen cars.[14]

For locomotive power, an E5-class locomotive, complete with its coal and water tender, had pulled the CLC specials across the western provinces. At Fort William, the E5 would have been switched with a G1- or G2-class engine. The E5 was a "ten-wheeler" locomotive of 4–6–0 wheel arrangement with four smaller wheels (two per side) at the front and six larger wheels (three per side) in tandem. The G1 and G2 were larger "twelve-wheelers" with a 4–6–2 arrangement. More powerful than an E5, these engines were better suited for the various grades on the lines through northern Ontario and Quebec.[15]

The second CLC special had ten Colonist cars and carried 489 Chinese. It featured a commissary car, and the same number of tourist and baggage cars for a total of seventeen. The train guard was composed of thirty-five other-ranks, three sergeants, a Canadian officer and two British officers.

Altogether, the two trains, which included an assortment of

railway staff, were transporting 939 Chinese who had travelled across the North Pacific on the Canadian Pacific Ocean Service ship *Empress of Japan.*

The timetable for this CLC "consignment" had been dispatched under great secrecy from the CPR's Passenger Department in Montreal by the punctilious Colonel Walter Maughan, the company's assistant general passenger agent. It shows the trains arriving at Camp Petawawa, northwest of Ottawa, at 8:45 and 9:45 a.m., August 13, 1917.[16]

Accommodations on the two trains were typical of the CLC trans-Canada movements, although the conditions on other specials were generally more crowded. Each Colonist sleeping car had thirty-six wooden-slat benches fastened to plank flooring with an aisle down the middle. The benches faced each other and the brass trim on the curved arm rests next to the aisle matched the coat hooks attached to the bulkhead and the light fixtures on the ceiling. In addition to transporting western settlers, these cars were the same type used to move Canadian troops to awaiting ships at eastern ports. With two people per bench, each car could seat seventy-two adults with larger or taller men preferring to sit next to the aisle.

Above the benches on either side of the car were nine single, upper berths. When dropped from the ceiling, each was suspended on two retractable metal chains. The lower berths were formed by folding down the facing seats and covering them with mattresses and other bedding supplied by the military. With two men sharing a lower berth and one man in each of the eighteen upper berths, there was enough sleeping space on each Colonist car for fifty-four men. These two eastbound trains, therefore, averaged fifty and forty-nine labourers per car. So while just about every sleeping space was occupied, the Colonist cars on these specials were not considered overcrowded during daylight.

In their current use, however, the guarded cars were not comfortable for long hauls. Motion sickness, claustrophobia and lack

David Livingstone Collection

While many of the CLC on board this train appear happy and content, the Colonist cars were very crowded with no time allowed for exercise during station stops.

of fresh air tested patience, as did the tight security measures. There was also the noise from the creaking undercarriage, the monotonous lateral sway of the car, and the various unwelcomed sounds produced by fifty men who ate regularly, but went without exercise. The labourers had been medically inspected before leaving China and again at the William Head Quarantine Station, but restrictions on movement within the cars increased the risk of catching a common cold or something worse, like the mumps, influenza or trachoma.

There were no showers on board and by day three the smell of sweat and other bodily odours and fluids were ripe while the trains sped east along the north shore of Lake Superior.

Fresh air was in short supply because, unlike the Colonist cars on regular troop trains, the windows on these cars were closed after the trains departed Vancouver, although there is no evidence to suggest they were, like the lavatory windows, nailed shut or not opened occasionally under the watchful eyes of the guards.

Adding to the passengers' general discomfort was another security feature regular trains did not have. Rare photographs show the inside of the windows blacked out or covered with thick paper, a measure that obviously blocked any view of the outside, even if the only views would have been of passing forests, lakes, the seemingly endless prairie or the ubiquitous swamps and rocks of northern Ontario. However, other photographs, taken while the trains were stopped at small watering and coaling stations, do not show the presence of such window screens. In some of these images, labourers are seen joyfully leaning out the open carriage windows.

For security-minded railway, military and immigration authorities, the use of window screens were deemed more necessary in larger, populated areas, especially during hour-long station stops. But while the screens hid the men from the public, the trains themselves no doubt attracted attention, especially when they rolled through towns during daylight and failed to pick up any regular passengers.

For the Chinese behind the closed windows and locked doors, sleep was sometimes the only escape from such limitations, but, unlike the Tourist cars, the Colonist carriages did not come with privacy partitions or curtains.

The two Tourist sleeping cars on the trains each had enough seating for fifty-six, which converted to sleeping space for twenty-eight. Fourteen more could be accommodated in the upper berths. However, only half of the guard detail slept at any one time because their duty was divided into twelve-hour shifts. Overall, the Tourist car was more comfortable, spacious and private than the Colonist car, and included sleeping space for each car's porter and the cooks from the commissary car. In addition to cushioned seats there were wooden partitions with curtains, CPR supplied mattresses, comforters, pillows and linen. The aisle was carpeted and each berth had a brass hook for hanging clothes or other belongings. For ablutions, there were two toilet rooms, and in addition to the steam heat provided by the loco-motive, each car was equipped with a heater for emergency use.[17]

The commissary car was a CPR invention, designed by W.A. Cooper, head of the company's Sleeping, Dining and Parlour Cars Department. Its wise development began when the railway company decided the cooking ranges in the Colonist and Tourist cars were too small to handle three meals a day for large volumes of passengers.

At the CPR's huge Angus Shops in east-end Montreal, Cooper supervised the practical conversion of twelve standard eighteen-metre-long baggage-express cars into practical kitchen cars, each capable of storing 5,410 litres of water. The serving capacity of a typical commissary car was a thousand meals, three times a day, an achievement that introduced marvellous efficiencies, not to mention an improved dining experience on the rails.

Orderlies filed in one end and out the other with ready-to-serve meals collected along the kitchen's full-length counter. "Essentially, each of the cars is a well-appointed hotel kitchen on wheels, and comprised of three main sections, kitchen proper, butcher shop, and pantry," extolled a company wartime news release.[18]

Such service was not, however, extended to the Chinese labour-ers. They were not waited on by the orderlies, nor did they line up and collect their meals individually. Instead, a half dozen or so from each Colonist car proceeded on schedule every morning to the commissary car to secure twenty-four hours' worth of rations for the men in their car. The food was prepared by the Chinese, cooked on ranges in the Colonist cars, then portioned out.[19]

In his succinctly worded memos, the CPR's Maughan reminded railway employees of the importance of maintaining the ranges in the Colonist cars. It is clear from his instructions that the CPR worked hard to prevent unrest on the trains due to various shortages or failing equipment. Having enough food and the means to cook it was vital. "On this account it is specially desired that the ranges be in good working order and a plentiful supply of fuel is carried for them," stated the assistant general passenger agent, who also cautioned staff about the importance of carrying enough water for the labourers for drinking and washing. "The water tanks in the Colonist cars only hold a small supply of water. It is asked that special attention be paid to this feature by seeing that they are replenished at all points where it is possible to put on water." Maughan also drew this distinction: "this class of passengers make very free use of water. It is also noted that they do not require ice, preferring water that is not chilled."

Referring to the need to sufficiently illuminate the cars for security, Maughan emphasized that the "lighting of the trains is very important. It is therefore asked that General Superintendents, Superintendents, and Assistants be advised to see that there is a sufficient supply of Gas and Oil in the cars at all times, also that the Military Officers on the Trains in Charge of the Coolies be given every possible assistance."[20]

Well before his train reached Fort William, Captain Harry Livingstone was impressed by the rugged Canadian Shield and how the railway skirted the north shore of Lake Superior. From Heron Bay on the lake's northern shore, the transcontinental, belching a pennant of black smoke, "wound through tunnels and gorges" before arriving at Jackfish, one of the CPR's main water- and coal-loading stations. Fur traders had made this a stopover before rugged Scandinavian settlers arrived and began fishing the lake, mostly for trout and northern pike. The town grew into a railway town during the 1880s after surveyors eyeballed and then measured the bay's potential for a coal dock. Soon freighters were steaming north across the inland sea into Jackfish to unload cargo, including kegs of dynamite, iron rails, fishplates and switches for the difficult Lake Superior section.

With solid rock, mosquito-infested muskeg and seemingly impenetrable forest standing in the way, the northern route along the lake had been one of the most dangerous and costly sections to construct. Blasting through rock and laying track and tamarack ties over many kilometres of swamp was forbidding. Near Jackfish, nearly five kilometres of track through rock cost a staggering $1.2 million. Further west, near Kenora, Ontario, then known as Rat Portage, workers toiled and swatted bugs while laying successive sets of track, which were swallowed by muskeg.

Some thirty years later, Livingstone stood in awe at Jackfish, staring up at the massive coal tower and the derricks used for unloading coal from steamers. Slowly introduced between 1885 and 1890, coal had replaced cordwood as the main fuel source for locomotives. By the turn of the century, a typical steam loco-motive could cover roughly forty-five kilometres with one ton of coal, depending, of course, on the route. With the introduction of the coal and water tender a train could run 160 to 240 kilo-metres without a refill. So in order to keep the trains moving day and night, coaling and watering stations were essential and their locations along the right-of-way gave rise to new communities, many of which did not fare well after the introduction of diesel engines decades later.[21]

Roughly a hundred kilometres west of Jackfish — while Livingstone's train was taking on water at Nipigon, Ontario — the three doctors disembarked to stretch their legs. They listened intently as locals described wealthy fly fishermen who had journeyed from as far away as Europe to fish the Nipigon rapids. Livingstone, who had frequently described himself as an "outdoors man," was impressed. "A trout weighing 14 pounds was caught here this summer," he noted, adding with envy that two fishermen "from the states" got off the train for a month-long expedition.

Back on the train, attention was drawn to a "young French girl" occupying a stateroom in transit with an elderly couple. It seems McDonald was particularly captivated by the woman's charms, but while he was trying to conceal his attraction the doctor's movements caught the discerning eyes of the elderly couple. "They keep her in continually and only let her out under guard," wrote an amused Livingstone, who assumed the young woman was the couple's daughter.

Concluding it was wiser to concentrate on other matters, McDonald raised what he confessed had been a rather nagging question since leaving Toronto. He wanted to know what he should do if one of the labourers under escort to France died while in transit across Canada. More specifically, he wanted to know what he should do "with the body" if the man died while the train was far from any city or town, on a journey that was, after all, supposed to be kept secret.

If McDonald's mind was put at ease it is not reflected in Livingstone's field diary. However, the Listowel doctor does describe a conversation with a fellow passenger and University of Toronto graduate who "gave us some pointers on how to look after the Chinese when our time comes." This, of course, was not in reference to the disposal of cadavers, but to the general supervision of the labourers once they came under their care.

Overall, the first few days of Livingstone's field diary recount an enjoyable, gastronomically pleasing start to their journey. "We are dining on the best of meals and are always the first in the dining car and always the last to leave," he noted. "A returned man is our waiter and we tip him generously every meal. We gave him thirty cents today — between the three of us. It is now elevenish and we are having ginger ale before retiring."[22]

CHAPTER 3

Overland, but Under Guard

"It was said that on one occasion the guards counted heads and found that the shipment lacked one coolie. Not at all dismayed, the ingenious guard who solved the dilemma merely strode over to a row of watching Chinese from the Vancouver Chinatown, seized one man by the scruff of the neck and flung him into the waiting railway car . . ."

Grinding it out . . .

While Livingstone sipped his beverage on the westbound train, the two Chinese Labour Corps specials rumbled eastward with the bright beam of their headlights illuminating a steel path through the dark, northern woods.

Earlier in the day, many of the Chinese had managed to escape long hours of boredom by doing what regular servicemen do: If they could write, they composed letters or kept diaries. Others sketched, told stories, daydreamed or played games. Gambling was prohibited, but it could not be policed all the time. Besides, the men were quite inventive when it came to finding ways to amuse themselves or just pass the time. One form of entertainment, played without cards, involved a group of men taking turns striking each other on the head or palm with increasing force until one man gave in to the pain. Boredom was boredom and such tests of endurance and masculinity were definitely not unique to the young men of the CLC. It is also more than likely that some of their games kept the guards entertained.

In some cars, singing and the welcoming sound of Chinese folk music rose above the monotonous clacking of the carriage wheels. More than a few labourers had brought along the four-stringed *sihu* or two-stringed *erhu*. Depending, of course, on the player's skill, the wooden, bowed instruments could lull a listener to sleep or send him into a world of irritability. In a crowded and secured railway car, such pleasure or displeasure could become rather pronounced.[1]

The *erhu* was usually played while resting the instrument on the musician's lap. Its light weight and lack of bulk made it easy to carry long distances and play in confined spaces. Losing the bow usually meant losing the entire instrument because the bow was attached, permanently placed between the two strings. For the men occupying the uncomfortable seats, the music helped free their minds. Few, if any, had a sense of where they were going or what the war in Europe would look like. But the sound of a well-played folk song took away much of the worry and made them think of home or paint their imaginations with stories of honour and adventure.

Later, while the Chinese slept or tried to sleep through the night between Fort William and a short 8 a.m. stop at Chalk River in Eastern Ontario, Canadian military guards were under strict orders to maintain their twenty-four-hour watch.

The work of the Railway Service Guard (RSG) began the moment they and the Chinese boarded the trains at Vancouver for eastern destinations. At any one time throughout the journey, there were always two uniformed guards posted in each Colonist car; one at either end. Armed with a Ross rifle equipped with a

David Livingstone Collection

A Chinese labourer proudly exhibits his bowed instrument while leaning through the window of a CPR Colonist car in Western Canada. Note how the glass in the window is covered with a screen.

bayonet, but no ammunition, the guards looked like they could handle anything.[2] Most of these men took the job very seriously and their vigilance extended to station stops during which they peered under the carriages while patrolling both sides of the train to ensure no Chinese got off.

No one wanted to be the man who allowed a labourer to escape.

This fear among the guards and among those who were much higher up in the chain of command was probably over-exaggerated. The Chinese very likely had no idea where they were or how they could live in such a strange land. So even if they did — for some reason — want to shirk their filial responsibility and slip away, the risk to health and safety was high.

Many of the men from Shantung had grown up in heavily populated villages next to other crowded villages. On the trains, when they could peer through the windows, what they saw was mostly unpopulated wilderness along the railway right-of-way. The prospect of disappearing into a dense, bug-infested forest or some other seemingly hostile landscape, especially during winter, was not appealing when compared to the relative warmth of the train and regular meals. Station stops in towns and cities were more appealing to would-be runaways, but in addition to the railway guards an escapee would have to get past the CPR's railway police who patrolled the platforms and yards.

During the previous decades, the CPR had begun to take very seriously the need for security and crime prevention. Railway constables were employed in 1886, soon after the company began operating its transcontinental service. Fourteen years later a Special Service Department was created with headquarters in Montreal and a branch office in Winnipeg. Joining that department were men previously employed as local "watchmen," constables, detectives and investigators. Most had little or no formal police training and were selected mostly for their competency and integrity. In the years leading up to the war, these were the same men who kept an eye on the head-tax-exempt Chinese migrants travelling to work sites in the Caribbean and United States.

In 1913, prompted by the endemic and costly theft of freight and other railway property by individuals and organized criminal gangs, the CPR stepped up its policing and established the Department of Investigations, a professional, centralized force ushering in a new era of railway security. While creating the department, CPR President Thomas Shaughnessy sent an important message by carefully selecting the man who would lead it. Rufus Chamberlin was in his early twenties when he joined the Dominion Police in Ottawa, established in 1869 to provide security services on Parliament Hill. By 1908, Chamberlin was serving as Vancouver's police chief, a job that increased his knowledge of the CPR and the large role it had in that city.[3]

With the country at war, Chamberlin's department increased its vigilance even more and was particularly on the lookout for possible terrorist or other subversive activities. Some two thousand special sentries were posted along the right-of-way, with particular attention paid to bridges and tunnels, and the movement of troops. Nefarious plots were indeed uncovered, including one to destroy the eight-kilometre-long Connaught Tunnel under the Selkirk Mountains in southeastern British Columbia near Revelstoke.[4]

The advent of the Railway Service Guard came without much public notice. Its status and brief existence during the war was never well known and it is hardly mentioned today. Even in February 1919, not long after the RSG ceased to exist, the chief inspector of the Department of Soldiers' Civil Re-Establishment wrote to the secretary of the militia council seeking clarification because former RSG men were applying for medical treatment.[5]

The Department of Militia and Defence replied on February 15, stating the men's "status was that of non-permanent Active Militia on service in Canada." In other words, they were not considered part of the Canadian Expeditionary Force.[6]

However, the militia department also noted, by virtue of Privy Council order 1569, under which all troops on pay in Canada were placed on the Canadian Expeditionary Force, personnel who come forward for treatment should be considered as belonging to the CEF. Therefore, any member of the RSG who incurred a disability due to service and required treatment "should be treated in a like manner to other members of the Canadian Expeditionary Force."[7]

It is not clear how many men joined the RSG in 1917 and early 1918, but there were several hundred with some lasting longer than others. Young men, including at least one seventeen year old, served in the unit, but preference was given to any over-age man, especially those from the conveniently located military districts and transportation hubs of Vancouver and Victoria. At the height of the CLC scheme, the age and health of these men became a factor, making it difficult for its commanding officer, Major Walter Haynes, to keep the unit up to strength. Unlike the men in his charge, Haynes, who saw service in South Africa, was a member of the CEF.[8]

Among the guards was Private Joseph Evans, a rancher from Kamloops, British Columbia, who at age fifty-seven fudged his date of birth and joined the RSG after a brief stint in the Rocky Mountain Rangers. At the other end of the age spectrum was Private George F. Roe who joined in Vancouver on January 15, 1917, twelve days after he turned seventeen.

Roe's enlistment papers show his occupation as "Student & Messenger," but his death certificate lists him as a law student. Born in Britain, he, along with his mother and sister, sailed from Liverpool to Quebec in late July 1911 on board the *Empress of Britain*. Roughly six years later, on December 3, 1917, while still assigned to the RSG, Roe was stricken with the measles and died at Vancouver General Hospital.[9]

The military service file for Evans points to three different years for his date of birth, namely 1862, 1870 and 1874. However, an examination of birth records in Britain indicates he was slightly older, born in 1860. He was also a married man when he moved to Canada with his wife in 1907.[10]

Evans's transfer to the Railway Service Guard occurred after an army medical board ruled he was unfit for overseas military service due to heart disease, initially detected as a "murmur" while training at Camp Vernon, British Columbia, in 1916. That same year he sprained an ankle while attempting to leap over a practice trench. By then he was living separately from his wife.

It is not certain if Evans and Roe were on the two trains that steamed past Livingstone's train that August, but the two guards were typical of the RSG who accompanied the movements. While the men maintained their watch, they were under orders not to communicate with the Chinese. Their job was to simply stand and keep their eyes open. But the more they watched, the more they realized that, with the exception of a few "bad apples," the Chinese did not pose a serious security risk. For the most part, the guards witnessed men who seemed to accept the fact they were on a long migratory journey with an honourable purpose, one that hopefully would return them home in good health and with some money.

Still, with hundreds of men per train, some guards were more nervous than others and their stiffness and mistrust was not lost on the Chinese. Undoubtedly, some of the guards saw the Chinese as inferior human beings and treated them like so much cargo. Donald C. McKechnie was not one of these men. In an interview after the war, that former Railway Service Guard said he believed most of the Chinese he travelled with were not interested in escaping and so the precautions seemed rather superfluous.[11]

It is not clear why McKechnie believed that. But it is possible he recognized the filial connection the Chinese had to their present circumstance and therefore could appreciate that for most it just made no sense to end their monthly wages by deserting. On the other hand, there were, no doubt, men among them who were running away from their families, had no family, or simply thought more about themselves.

A language barrier may have also contributed to keeping the men on the trains. At the time, there was no standard Chinese, only a common written language, and regional dialects. The Chinese community in Canada was composed of many people from Guangdong and Hong Kong, and these people spoke Cantonese. Few of them would have been able to understand the Shantung people from northeastern China.

This barrier may have made the CLC somewhat alien to the Chinese Canadian community and it certainly would have made it extremely difficult for a man from Shantung to easily and quietly blend in, let alone communicate. It is not clear how well this was understood by Canadian officials monitoring or chaperoning the CLC movements, but for the Chinese the idea of escape would have perhaps been more appealing if they had been recruited from southern China and, even better, if they had relatives in Canada. It is also important to remind ourselves of the physical differences between northern and southern Chinese — differences that would have also reduced the chances of blending in.

Perhaps more remarkable are the stories that circulated after the war regarding overzealous guards who accidently or intentionally grabbed men in order to fill quotas on CLC trains. Proving these stories is difficult given how much time has passed and the dearth of detail. But in his 1940 *Memoirs of an Ambulance Company Officer*, Harry Smith, who worked as an intern at Vancouver General Hospital in 1917, recalled how this happened after a steamer arrived at the city's busy port. "Vancouver, like many cities situated on the Pacific Coast had a rather large Chinese section and when a Canadian Pacific vessel loaded with coolies came into port, hundreds of Chinese would go down to the dock to watch their brethren disembark for the railway trains," he wrote, even though serious efforts were underway to keep the CLC movements quiet. "It was said that on one occasion the guards counted heads and found that the shipment lacked one coolie. Not at all dismayed, the ingenious guard who solved the dilemma merely strode over to a row of watching Chinese from the Vancouver Chinatown, seized one by the scruff of the neck and flung him into the waiting railway car, thus making the tally in the train agree with the tally that had been taken when the coolies had been loaded on the steamship in Asia, despite all the gibberings and struggles of the victimized Chinaman and the outrage clamour of his comrades whom he left behind."[12]

As one of the older guards, Evans probably wished he had something better to do with his time than stand and watch a carriage load of men he could not communicate with, at least verbally. It was monotonous work crossing the country time and again with little rest or fresh air. The confined spaces were hard on one's body, there was no privacy, and in winter it was hard to stay warm. For the Chinese, it was usually seven or eight days across the country and out the other side. But for Evans and the other guards, the end of each trip meant there was another whole week of deadheading back to Vancouver before getting a bit of rest and doing it all over again.

In addition to being tedious, the transcontinental journeys were not without risk to life and limb. On January 4, 1918, Evans was nearly killed in an accident west of Montreal near Dorval Station when his train was rear-ended while entering a siding next to the main through line. The accident claimed seven lives and occurred during an intense period of CLC movements.[13] On board were 250 RSG, all of them heading back to Vancouver and most of them, like Evans, tired and not in the best of health or the best of moods. One man had been discharged, but re-enlisted before the accident. Another had refused to write a will while a third wanted no notification made if he became a casualty during his service.[14]

At the moment of impact, Evans's five-foot-seven-inch, one-hundred-and-eighty-six-pound frame was catapulted out of his wooden seat. His back slammed into the wooden arm rest of the bench and he then flew through the air, doubled up like a rag doll, before crashing in a corner on the floor. Around him the air was a concentration of flying objects, including fellow guards, wood splinters and shards of glass.

Killed were RSG privates Percy Arthur, Richard Clark, Andrew Hunter, Thomas Kelly, Delore Lalonde, John Mackie and Matthew Shearan. Arthur was twenty-eight and married. He had been one of the first to join the RSG's 8th Platoon, after being told he was "unfit for overseas service." Clark was forty-one, a former teacher, school principal and editor of the *Nelson News* and *Hope Steamboat Nugget*.[15] Kelly had enlisted at Revelstoke in 1914 at age fifty-one. He got overseas, and served in France, but was sent home because of his age. Lalonde, whose crushed body was found beneath the train wreck, was from Rivière Rouge, Ontario. He had joined the RSG in April 1917.[16]

Injuries to the living ranged from severe facial cuts and scalp lacerations to bruised backs and broken legs. A long-time dining car waiter, P.J. Byrne of Vancouver, and porters I.P. Scarp and H.P. Pierce of Montreal were also among the injured, the latter two suffering from traumatic shock.

Dazed and in excruciating pain, Evans was carted off the wrecked train into the bitterly cold night, and placed on another train for transportation to Westmount Station. Doctors dealt with the injured while ambulances rushed the more serious to Montreal's Royal Victoria Hospital. With damaged vertebrae, Evans was still luckier than some. He remained in bed for several days before he was stretchered onto another train for the painful journey to Vancouver. Despite weeks of rehabilitation he was unable to walk more than a short distance without extreme pain in his lower back. "Patient walks with canes," observed his doctor. "Cannot stoop to lace shoes. If he attempts to bend over to touch the floor, loses control and falls forward."[17]

Evans was, therefore, not only unfit for overseas service, but unfit for service in Canada.

Nine months after the accident, on October 22, 1918, Evans died, not a result of his injuries but from the deadly influenza pandemic that claimed millions of lives worldwide, including some fifty-five thousand Canadians.[18]

CHAPTER 4

Crossing to Asia

"In the afternoon a terrific storm cut loose — one of the worst ever experienced by this boat. The bowsprit was smashed off and the wireless wrecked twice . . . We all thought our last hour had come. Captain Sebert said land was only a mile and a half away — straight down."

Railway men . . .

The waiter, otherwise known as the "returned man" the three doctors tipped in the dining car, was one of thousands of CPR employees who had answered the call to war. In August 1914, Thomas Shaughnessy, who was credited with turning the company into the most profitable railroad in the world, viewed the outbreak of hostilities as a tragic interruption. Like many Canadians he was doubtful the war would last longer than late winter or early spring of 1915, and believed when it ended there would be a return to the pre-war depression economy.

Even though the country was in the grip of an economic depression since 1913, the CPR president remained confident. Indeed, historians have noted how his attitude shone through in an announcement promising full pay to all permanent staff who enlisted in the armed forces for six months "or for any shorter time during which the men are engaged in the military service of the Empire."[1]

Initially, the war deepened the depression. Rail traffic and revenues plummeted during the early years of the global conflict. Between 1912 and 1915 freight carried by company trains declined from nearly thirty million to barely twenty-two million tons. The same two-year period saw a drop in gross earnings from about $140 million to less than $100 million. But as the war drummed on beyond Shaughnessy's hopeful prediction, its insatiable appetite for men and *matériel* restored economic prosperity, and not just for the railway. In 1915–16, rail traffic returned to almost thirty million tons and remained there throughout the last two years of the war. In 1915–16, earnings outstripped costs.[2]

In addition to encouraging its employees to enlist, the company saw its trains, telegraph services and ships put to the test. The latter were requisitioned to serve as fast transports or armed merchant cruisers. Nearly half of the liners used to transport the First Contingent from Canada to Britain were Allan or Canadian Pacific ships.[3]

At Hong Kong, one of the company's new Empress ships, the *Empress of Asia*, was requisitioned on the eve of war and outfitted at the Royal Naval Dockyard as an armed merchant cruiser.[4] Along with the *Empress of Russia* and the much older *Empress of Japan*, she helped with the blockading of German merchant ships around the Philippines. She and *Russia* had entered service in 1913, each weighing seventeen thousand tons with a top speed of twenty knots.[5] In the fall of 1914, crews from both ships could point to the fact they had been involved in the hunt for *Emden*.

By early 1916, *Asia*, *Russia* and *Japan* had resumed their trans-Pacific passenger service without any hint of being requisitioned to transport tens of thousands of Chinese labourers to France. However, within months these ships were transporting in steerage the first of thousands of CLC across the Pacific to

Canada. With pressure mounting for additional troopships to carry American troops overseas, *Asia* and *Russia* left the Pacific after being requisitioned again, joining the North Atlantic convoys in 1918.[6]

The CPR's wartime efforts were not limited to the transportation of troops and supplies and providing important telegraph communications. Its massive manufacturing shops were used for munitions production. In 1915, the company received an order for eighteen-pounder shells and brass casings, and work in the shops employed women as well as men. "Production continued twenty-four hours a day, seven days a week for over two years and a half," notes historian W. Kaye Lamb in his 1977 history of the CPR.[7]

* * *

Shortly after his train rolled into Winnipeg, Livingstone was greeted by his older brother Roland, who had journeyed by rail from his home in neighbouring Saskatchewan. The two doctor brothers were anxious to get caught up on each other's news while strolling around the limestone and red-brick grandiosity of the Canadian Pacific's Royal Alexandra Hotel. Roland surprised his younger sibling by telling him he was going to board his train and take it as far as Regina.

From Winnipeg, the train rolled past Camp Hughes Station, through Brandon, then Broadview. In his diary, Livingstone summarized the massive army training camp stretching across the dry, sandy plain west of Carberry, Manitoba. With recruitment slowed to a trickle, Camp Hughes sat idle, but during the previous years of the war, tens of thousands of recruited men bound for France had practised trench warfare and other forms of battle in the hot sun and blowing dust. With eight men to a bell tent, the recruits had had to get used to extremely tight sleeping arrangements. Movie houses and a large swimming pool, however, provided some relief from the heat, hard training and monotony. "No soldiers here now," observed Livingstone, who had only a passing glimpse of the camp. "All the shacks are standing and Government Property stamped on all."

A "perfect specimen of a rainbow" and a few hawks floating above fields and grain elevators, noted Harry after he and Roland emerged from a game of bridge. Amusing them was a young married couple from Winnipeg who were "quite spooney" throughout the day and night, occupying the berth above Sebert who, presumably with a pillow over his head, tried to get some sleep.[8]

Livingstone also noted "our intelligence service" reports the "mysterious French girl" first noticed while the train was crossing northern Ontario is "a daughter of 'Fighting Joe' Martin who had also boarded the train in Toronto." Described in the press of the day as the "stormy petrel," Martin had the distinction of "being the only man in the British Empire to hold a seat in four Houses," namely the Manitoba Legislative Assembly, the Canadian House of Commons, the British Columbia Legislature and the British House of Commons.[9] He had even been premier of British Columbia for a few excruciating months in 1900. Martin's bombastic style turned heads and generated headlines across the country, but as a lawyer Martin was known to defend clients with everything he had.

While the bird-lover in Livingstone could get the newspaper reference to a stormy black seabird with a hooked bill, the report from the men's "intelligence service" was short on facts. First, Fighting Joe Martin did not father a daughter, though he did have a stepdaughter named Irma Eaton who died at age nineteen on January 29, 1896.[10] Furthermore, Martin's wife, Eliza, who was born at Bell's Corners, now part of Ottawa, had died at age seventy in 1913. Prior to marrying Martin in 1881, Eliza had been married to the late George Eaton, a successful Ottawa-area lumber manufacturer who presumably fathered Irma.[11] Martin, who was still serving as a member of parliament in Britain, was on the train, but the identities of the "mysterious French girl" and the older woman sharing the stateroom with him remains a mystery.

Not long after drawing their assumption in regards to the young woman's identity, the three officers decided it was better not to pursue an introduction based on what they continued to perceive as strict parental watch. "None of us . . . has spoken to the daughter as yet," Livingstone noted.[12]

At Regina, Harry and Roland took a good long look at each other, shook hands and said goodbye. The train continued through Moose Jaw, Maple Creek and then across the Saskatchewan and Alberta border at Walsh. At Medicine Hat, Harry's Uncle Cy and Aunt Annie entrained and travelled with their nephew as far as Calgary. The diary does not mention what they talked about, but it can be assumed his aunt, who was his mother's sister, and his uncle were curious about Harry's big adventure, even though their nephew could not furnish many details.

Attention was also paid to a "smooth young lady from Ireland named Margaret McMillan" who rather boldly and oddly announced she "hated any man with his neck shaved." Livingstone must have assumed the woman was either joking or he and his well-groomed travelling companions somehow still "look alright with her." Moments later he learned the woman was suffering from a sore eye, which Sebert — the eye specialist in the group — quickly volunteered to treat.[13]

At Calgary, in preparation for a daylight journey through the mountains, the train swapped some regular cars for opened-topped observation cars. The stop gave passengers time to explore the city and admire the Rockies. The best view was from the top of the CPR hotel, where Livingstone dined on roast duck, a meal he found to be both expensive and tough to carve, demanding "a little physical training" with fork and knife. Serving them was an entourage of uniformed Chinese waiters who "all seemed to smile at us."[14]

By 5:30 the next morning, the train was following the historic line through the mountains. Riding along on the top of an

City of Vancouver Archives, SGN 917

The Empress of Japan *was a sleek-looking steamer resembling a sailing schooner. This was the ship Captains Harry Livingstone, Lou Sebert and Lieutenant John McDonald embarked on for China in 1917.*

open-air observation car near the back of the train, the easterners breathed in their surroundings as well as a little smoke curling back from the locomotive. "It is impossible to describe the grandeur of the Selkirks and Rockies, but two or three peaks made a special impression on us," wrote Livingstone. "The first group we saw was the Three Sisters, then Pilot Mountain whose snow-covered peak can be seen for miles." Castle Mountain, west of Banff, lived up to its name with its "turrets and battlements." In Banff, and in Field, British Columbia, west of Lake Louise, the men disembarked and "took several snaps" while envying the passengers who had left for the grand hotels.[15]

Continuing on their journey, the men were awed by alpine lakes, glaciers, great cascades of snowmelt and the barren, rock and timber-strewn paths left by landslides and avalanches. After skirting along the Columbia, the train entered the eight-kilometre-long Connaught Tunnel that the Germans had hoped to destroy with the help of an agent who had lived in Montreal and Calgary, but got his marching orders from a San Francisco contact. J.H. van Koolbergen was followed north, apprehended and then interrogated, spilling details about the plot and its architects, before any damage was done.[16]

The wild mountain beauty gave no hint of the old bureaucratic struggles behind the railway's construction through western Alberta and across British Columbia. But it was abundantly clear to Livingstone how daunting the challenge must have been, especially for the pick-and-shovel men, which included thousands of Chinese navvies employed along the western section.

Livingstone's train steamed into Vancouver on August 15, just as the breakfast dishes in the dining car were being collected.

After stepping off the carriage onto the platform at Granville Station, Sebert introduced his travelling companions to an old college pal who led them on a tour of the waterfront. Alongside was their ship, the six-thousand-ton *Empress of Japan*. Built as one of the CPR's first Pacific Empresses, the *Japan*, along with sister ships the *Empress of India* and the *Empress of China*, began transporting passengers and cargo across the Pacific in 1891. The *Empress of China* ended her service on July 27, 1911, when she struck a reef and was abandoned in Tokyo Bay. Three years later, following her two hundred and thirty-eighth crossing, the *Empress of India* was purchased by a wealthy maharajah and converted to a hospital ship for Indian troops. The war also interrupted *Japan*'s regular service, but by 1917, well past her prime, she was still plying the northern route across the wild Pacific and had many more years and nautical miles in front of her.

Japan's sleek graceful lines turned heads in every port of call. Powered by two independent triple-expansion engines driving twin screws, she and her sisters were for a time the largest and fastest passenger liners on the Pacific.[17] In addition to accommodating many first- and second-class passengers, she routinely accommodated up to seven hundred passengers, mainly immigrants from Asia and Japan, in steerage, a number exceeded in wartime.

Her role as an armed merchant cruiser had actually started before the war, in the summer of 1914, after she sailed from

Vancouver to Hong Kong where she had been requisitioned and fitted out. If Livingstone was impressed by her as a passenger ship, it is not reflected in his diary. Instead he seems to take the opposite view, describing her as "a rather small tug," a puzzling impression because most people did not view the *Japan* as small or tug-like, given her schooner-like hull and the large carved figurehead of a green and gold dragon beneath her bowsprit. It is hard to understand why Livingstone used those words. He was certainly unfamiliar with ships, or perhaps he was nervously expecting a larger vessel to handle whatever the ocean could throw at them.

Overnight accommodation for the three doctors was not on the ship, but in the luxurious Hotel Vancouver, which had opened the previous year. With seven hundred rooms, arched windows accenting the lower levels, terra cotta sculptures of wildlife and lavish furnishings, which included gold-plated hardware and marble sinks, the Italian Renaissance-style building was one of the grandest hotels in the British Empire. While the temptation to stay and marvel at the stunning architecture was strong for all guests, the three men from the east decided there was a lot more to see outside. So they loosened up, had lunch and boarded a streetcar to Stanley Park. They visited the park's zoo, laughed at the monkeys and strained their necks while admiring the towering grandeur of the Seven Sisters trees.[18]

The afternoon ended with a cool dip in English Bay.

Getting lost was out of the question, owing to the impressive flagpole in front of the court house next to their hotel.[19] The evening was spent at the Rex on West Hastings Street, where they caught Douglas Fairbanks and Eileen Percy in the Hollywood western comedy *Wild and Woolly*.[20] The silent motion picture is about the son of a railway magnate who tires of life in the East and is sent West where he saves the day for folks at Bitter Creek, Arizona. It is not clear why Livingstone, Sebert and McDonald chose the Fairbanks movie. There were movie houses closer to their hotel. Perhaps the film's story resonated with their journey or they just needed a good laugh.

Before bed, Livingstone picked up his fountain pen and wrote a five-page letter to his mother on blue hotel stationery. He told Agnes about the mountains and described Vancouver as "a dandy clean city" where he got his first taste of saltwater. This time he avoided describing the *Japan* as "a rather small tug," but his words were still laced with mild trepidation, stating she is "a small vessel built like a yacht . . . It looked pretty dirty, but I guess we will be alright." The doctor may not have realized it, but it is likely the ship looked dirty not because of being unkempt but because of the coal dust produced from bunkering. Livingstone finished his letter with: "This is our last night in Canada and we hate to leave it but the sooner we get away the quicker we will get back. The ocean is calm this month so I guess we won't be sick."[21]

If Livingstone and the other passengers who boarded the *Japan* on August 16 doubted her seaworthiness, they soon learned just how good a ship she was on this, her hundred and thirtieth crossing. En route to Victoria the weather remained calm as the ship and her "large cargo of missionaries" and crew of "nearly all Chinese" crossed the Strait of Georgia.[22]

In Victoria, the *Japan* and her passengers easily caught the attention of the local newspaper. However, wartime censorship prevented the paper from identifying her. "Probably never before has a liner gone out with so many missionaries aboard as did the vessel which left here yesterday," reported the August 17 edition of the *Victoria Daily Colonist*. "They hailed from all parts of Canada and the United States and are bound for China, Japan and India. The various liners arriving from the Far East during the past few months brought over numbers of missionaries who were going home on furlough and most of them are now returning to their posts."[23]

On August 17, after slipping through the fog and the powerful currents of Juan de Fuca Strait, the ship met the immensity of the Pacific, where Livingstone began to wonder if he had jinxed the voyage in his letter to his mother. "Woke up this morning and first thing we noticed was the heave of the ship," he scribbled with a nervous hand into his diary. "Everyone out for breakfast, but in the afternoon, oh boy, something seemed to tell us all was not well . . . Rest of the day spent wishing for home."[24]

"Sunday, August 19: Lou led off by coughing up breakfast . . . Two large whales appeared on the horizon and spouted several times. In the afternoon, a terrific storm cut loose . . . one of the worst ever experienced by this boat. The bowsprit was smashed off and the wireless wrecked twice and the waves were so high, the captain stopped the engines and let the boat ride out the storm. We all thought our last hour had come. Capt. Sebert said land was only a mile and a half away — straight down. We would have all parted with our cash to be in London again. Twice in the night we thought the boat had hit bottom."[25]

It is doubtful *Japan*'s captain "stopped the engines." It is more likely he slowed the ship down to heave-to.[26] The *Japan* was a very strong ship and such weather was common on the Pacific, although extremely unsettling for passengers who had never experienced a gale, including Sebert who succinctly summed up how he and his two companions felt: "Sick! Sicker! Sickest!"[27]

The *Japan* was still weathering the storm on the twenty-second when Livingstone noticed high above the swells the "first two volcanic peaks of the Aleutian Islands come in sight above the clouds." His interest in birds was also rewarded when he noticed "many black birds looking like ducks with yellow beaks" flying "quite close to the ship" with "large, brown, dark gulls following" above the rising and falling foam of the ocean. The gale subsided on the twenty-seventh, a full twelve days after *Japan* departed Vancouver, and so there was cause for celebration. "Had a dance on deck tonight. Gramophone music. Deck decorated with flags from all nations."[28]

Japanese fishing boats appeared the next day, and then a steamer came into view. "After two weeks without seeing any ships of any kind" the vessels were a welcome sight. The tops of mountains were noticed around 5 p.m., and on August 30 the weather-battered ship and its grateful passengers reached Yokohama harbour. "It was a dull grey morning and the mists had not cleared so we could not see much of the city . . . In the harbour were many peculiar looking vessels of the East with large, square dirty sails on small heavy looking boats and standing or sitting around these boats half naked Japanese fishermen or coolies. Puffing steam launches from the hotels were skimming through the water and big freight barges were lumbering along some towed by small tugs puffing out dense clouds of dirty black smoke."[29]

While the ship was at anchor in the harbour, Japanese doctors were ferried out on small, white launches. "They did not examine us at all, only looked at us," noted Livingstone.[30] The same was not so for other passengers and crew who were quickly lined up on deck. "It was a hurried examination they made, simply quickly walking along and grabbing each wrist with their thumb over the pulse. We thought it was more a case of show than any thing."[31] Being from the West, Livingstone found this strange because he had been taught to check the pulse using his forefinger.

Prior to disembarking at Yokohama, the three Canadian doctors made arrangements to spend the next two days in Japan while the ship sailed south to her next Japanese port of call at Kobe, on Osaka Bay. Once ashore, they "engaged a motor" car and spent a few hours exploring the seaport with a fellow traveller named Gubbay, referred to as their "Bombay friend." Tokyo was also on the day's itinerary and while travelling there by train Livingstone committed to memory passing scenes of life and landscape. Sliding past the coach window were neatly terraced fields, bright flashes of morning glories, ponds covered with white lotus flowers and houses topped with thatched or tiled roofs. Through open windows Livingstone noticed women cooking or doing the laundry while children ran around outside without clothes or shoes. Contrasting these rural scenes was the massive exterior of the Imperial Palace in Tokyo with its ancient stone walls, moat and brightly-dressed "guards posted all around." Nearby, youngsters chased singing cicadas with long bamboo poles dipped in bird-lime. The men also shopped for "curios," followed by a train of children who regarded them as curiosities.

The Shogun shrines and temples, which Sebert playfully referred to as "the Shotguns," were impressive, as were the holy trees and the *Ishidourou* (stone lanterns) marking the paths to tea houses tucked away in traditional Japanese gardens. It is unclear whether Livingstone grasped the full significance or symbolism of the lanterns and how that might apply to his journey, but he took time to sketch them. He thought they resembled tombstones,[32] but *Ishidourou*, introduced to Japan from China in the sixth century as part of the Buddhist tradition, were created to add balance, harmony and endurance to the life of the garden. Resting on stone pedestals, the lanterns have variously shaped portals and the light shining through them is symbolic of the teachings of the Buddha aimed at overcoming the darkness of ignorance.

Aside from a passing reference to a "pro-German" passenger who disembarked at Yokohama, there is nothing in Livingstone's diary for August 30 to suggest the doctor had arrived in a country at war. Japan, however, had been on the side of the Entente since August 23, 1914, and while her entry was tied to obligations under the Anglo-Japanese Alliance there was a very strategic, self-serving purpose behind the country's involvement. In addition to exploiting the opportunity to invade the German territory in China at Tsingtao in 1914 and present its Twenty-One Demands in 1915, Japan was pursuing opportunities to extend its reach into the Pacific.

In addition to being a major military power, Japan, when Livingstone arrived, was in the midst of an economic boom, a direct result of the war. In 1917, new and lasting industries were born with many brand names familiar to consumers today.

At Tokyo, the three Canadian doctors boarded an overnight train for Kyoto that took them south past Mount Fuji. In Kyoto they paid "rickshaw boys" to transport them to temples and Shinto shrines. They visited silk stores and ventured into a tea house where they were handed shoe covers and immediately led upstairs into a sparse room with matted floors and sliding wall panels. "Soon a man came in quickly who could talk English brokenly and asked us if we wanted tea. We told him we did so he disappeared with a bow and soon two Japanese girls that looked more like dolls came in, in their bright coloured kimonos and their greasy hair sticking up in a large roll over their head. They carried pillows and placed them at our feet . . . We found them laughing at our awkward movements in squatting down. They then brought in small round cups without handles of sweet tea with some small pink cakes and a dish of candies. They sat opposite us and smiled as we finished up the food. Then the man returned and asked us . . . questions about our mother's health and where we were going . . . and when we asked him how his Grandmother and Grandfather were he stopped the questioning. He wanted us to give him five yen each to see the geisha girls dance, but we had to hustle for our train . . ."

The men left in such a hurry that Livingstone forgot to remove the shoe covers he had been given and so he "went tramping off down the street" with several employees from the tea house in pursuit.

Kobe was reached on August 31, and by 11 p.m. the men were back on board the *Empress of Japan*. The evening had included a few hours at a club where ukulele-strumming Hawaiian musicians played the Japanese and French national anthems, forcing everyone to stand while their soup got cold. It was a hot, sweltering night, but relief was found on the hotel's rooftop garden from which Livingstone contemplated the twinkling lights of ships far out at sea. Much closer, in the harbour below, was a powerful Japanese dreadnaught.[33]

Before calling it a night, Livingstone tried to clear his mind of the story shared by a few American naval officers he had met at

David Livingstone Collection

It was mostly women who were responsible for carrying the coal onto the ships at Nagasaki, Japan. The fuel was shovelled from barges into baskets and then relayed up the side of the ship with the use of planks and ladders. It was dangerous and dirty work.

the club. After leaving the Philippines, the Americans had run into a typhoon that knocked their ship more than 322 kilometres off course. The waves, they claimed, "were twenty-seven metres high"; one man was swept overboard. "They say a typhoon is due today, but I hope not," Livingstone noted in his diary. The *Japan* sailed at midnight, bound for a coaling stop at Nagasaki before crossing the Yellow Sea to Shanghai.[34]

While Livingstone describes Nagasaki as one of the most beautiful places he has visited, it was the coaling of the ship on September 2 that stood out. In his diary he devoted two full pages and completed a small sketch showing how wooden planks, instead of ladders, were deployed by the labourers, many of whom were women. Skiffs, he wrote, were "laden with coal . . . gathered alongside on both sides of the ship. These were attached by ropes to the ship and a series of steps built up the side of the ship to the coal chute openings. The steps were suspended by ropes . . . on each step either a girl or a man would stand and pass small baskets of coal with amazing rapidity from the boat below up, from one to the other, to the top step where the person . . . would dump it into the hole then throw down the empty basket where young boys would gather them and distribute them to the shovellers. There were on average from 10 to 14 in each string of basket carriers and they passed about 40 baskets per minute, each basket holding two large shovelfuls of coal. The people would frequently relieve each other by changing positions. They can load 1,500 tons in six or eight hours . . . We saw youngsters of about six or seven almost naked with babies strapped on their backs all day waiting for their mothers who were working. We throw down coins to the little boys who searched for them in the coal."[35]

With the loading completed, Livingstone observed how the exhausted labourers no longer looked Japanese on account of the coal dust obliterating every inch of their faces, arms and hands. In addition to blackening their exposed skin, the dust entered their mouths, noses, eyes, ears and lungs. The doctor watched patiently as the workers headed to shore in their flat-bottomed skiffs, propelled by oars across the dark oily water.[36]

The doctors' fast, but concentrated tour of Japan marked their introduction to the Far East. From Yokohama to Tokyo to Nagasaki the men recognized how they stood out as minorities. At the same time they had observed many foreign influences. Nagasaki and Yokohama were, after all, important international transportation hubs and big passenger liners, warships and cargo vessels arrived regularly. There were other signs of Western commerce and culture as well, including the "flashy poster" Livingstone spotted along a busy street in Kyoto, advertising a Charlie Chaplin film.

With the sun setting and Nagasaki disappearing behind them, *Japan*'s passengers dined and then relaxed on deck as the ship journeyed past several islands and out into the East China Sea for its 725-kilometre crossing to Shanghai. Prayer services were routinely held on the Empress ships and so several passengers sang hymns, including William Whiting's popular ode to seafarers, "Eternal Father, Strong to Save," known for its last line, first verse, "For those in peril on the sea."

"The moon's rays are reflected in a long pathway across the water like last night and it is a night that makes one dream of the people at home and wonder what they are doing, no doubt wondering if we are safe," wrote Livingstone. "At the present moment the words of the appropriate hymn . . . echo along the deck and we all sing it in earnest as this Yellow Sea is very treacherous on account of the typhoons and this is the time for them . . ."[37]

Aside from a little ocean breeze, there was no bad weather.

It was a good crossing, with the doctor's observations limited to whale sightings and streaks of yellow fish spawn. On September 4, the ship dropped anchor at Woosung, where the Whangpoo River (Huangpu) joins the Yangtze. Livingstone watched as hungry women and children approached the ship in square-fronted sampans, begging *Japan*'s passengers to drop their orange peelings over the railings into their boats.

From the Yangtze, launches took passengers and their steamer trunks some twenty kilometres up the Whangpoo to the customs wharf on the famous Bund, the central riverfront business district of Shanghai. The three Canadians visited the British consul where a surprised and agitated civil servant admitted he had not been expecting them and therefore did not know what arrangements, if any, were to be made for the next leg of their journey.[38]

Shanghai had been a quiet fishing village until the British won the First Opium War in 1842 and named it one of five treaty ports. Foreign involvement turned it into a city divided into autonomous concessions administered by foreigners, including British, French and Americans, who were not subject to Chinese law. Foreign involvement in the city increased again following Japan's victory in the Sino-Japanese War of 1894–95. While many Chinese lived mostly within the walls of the old city, others chose to live in the settlements established by foreigners. As a result, cultures mixed and as the excitement of Shanghai grew it attracted even more interest from wealthy westerners. By the time Livingstone arrived in 1917, the population, which included many Eurasians, was roughly a million. A hundred years later it is twenty-six million.

Before checking into the Bund's Palace Hotel, the men spotted a few captured enemy ships and some American warships. In town, the old German clubs were closed and guarded by well-armed Sikh policemen. Under the hot sun, beads of sweat dropped from the brows of coolies as they drew their rickshaws in front of banks and other commercial establishments. The Canadians exchanged their money for large and heavy Mexican silver dollars, the common currency in southern and eastern China. The exchange rate was "very high" and so were the prices, noted Livingstone. There was a lot of "bad money" about.[39]

Shanghai was where the three men parted company with the ship, and where Livingstone and Sebert said goodbye to McDonald. Their friend had orders to embark on the *Bessie Dollar* of the Robert Dollar Steamship Line, and proceed — on a two-and-a-half-day journey — to the CLC recruitment depot at Tsingtao. "This was Mac's last night with us and we're sorry to have him leave us," wrote Livingstone. There was much to think about that evening, including Mac's sudden departure, and the journey Livingstone and Sebert had in front of them to Weihaiwei. Meanwhile, there were bats — great big ones — to keep an eye on as they flew around, picking off bugs, in his room at the Palace.[40]

On September 6, the same day Mac sailed, Livingstone and Sebert boarded the *Shuntien*, a shallow-draft Chinese riverboat bound for the northeastern tip of the Shantung Peninsula. The *Japan* was also scheduled to call at Weihaiwei, specifically to pick up CLC passengers, but not until September 16 as part of her regular return voyage from Hong Kong to Canada.[41] By taking the riverboat, Livingstone and Sebert cut seven days off their voyage to the recruitment depot. Built at Greenock, Scotland, in 1904 for the China Navigation Company, which was a major player in British trade with China, the steel-hulled *Shuntien* was a bouncy but durable flat-bottomed boat thirty-one metres shorter than the *Bessie Dollar* and fifty-eight metres shorter than *Japan*.[42]

From Woosung, the *Shuntien* proceeded down river to the mouth of Yangtze where she glided through brown, silty waters into ocean blue. Pigeons, Livingstone and Sebert were duly informed, while sitting down for their evening meal, were found daily on board and slaughtered for food.

Beyond sight of land, the *Shuntien* followed the coast north and was soon into rough weather, leaving the boat "in the trough all day." On September 8, Weihaiwei was in view. "Beautiful harbour with an island. In the distance we could see the shacks of the Coolie Encampment. Sampans came out . . . in a very rough sea . . . When the smaller boat came near the ladder of the *Shuntien* we jumped aboard but just as I was ready to jump the boat swung away and if I hadn't hung onto the chain I would have been into the sea. Finally landed at the wharf and this English soldier took us in rickshaws up to the camp . . . There are about five thousand Coolies here and they have physical drill and appear to be a healthy lot. They wear blue suits with white band around tunic which identifies them in case of escape and if they take band off their tunic falls apart."[43]

The doctors' quarters were close to the officers' mess and cost them two dollars and thirty cents Mexican a day. "The sleeping shack is thatched and has matting on floor and boys in attendance. The beds are covered with mosquito netting as malaria is bad here."

It had taken Livingstone, Sebert and McDonald more than a month to reach their destinations in eastern China, yet it was only the start of their transformative, trans-world experience. By then, tens of thousands of Chinese men were already in France or heading there on Canadian ships and trains. For those men the journey was less comfortable, and far less welcoming.

CHAPTER 5

The Missionaries

"Naturally I was anxious to do my bit in the struggle which was engrossing the whole world. There were more men in the Chinese Labour Corps than the Duke of Wellington commanded at the Battle of Waterloo."

Bibles and believers . . .

A few months before his death on August 26, 1953, the Reverend Canon Napier Smith picked up a pencil and began writing a brief memoir. The conscientious Anglican preacher lived long enough to complete the manuscript for his three children, but barely made it to his sixty-sixth birthday. "There has been nothing spectacular about my life," he explained in his opening paragraph, "just a steady continuation of hard plodding."[1]

Much of Smith's "hard plodding" began thirty-seven years earlier — at the height of the First World War — in September 1916, when, at age twenty-nine, he boarded a Vancouver-bound train in Toronto, accompanied by Ruth, his twenty-one-year-old bride. A week earlier, the couple had exchanged vows and ventured to Niagara Falls where they stayed at the Clifton Hotel. With its limestone walls and beautifully trimmed balconies and porches, the Clifton was the grandest hotel at the Falls, and was certainly far beyond anything Napier Smith had experienced in the way of service and comfort.[2]

When they settled into their seats in the railway coach at Union Station, the newlyweds were simply, but excitedly, carrying on with their honeymoon. Ahead of them, though, was the promise of great adventure — a trip halfway around the world to serve as missionaries in China for the Anglican Church of Canada, known then as the Church of England in the Dominion of Canada. It was an extraordinary opportunity to travel abroad, live among the Chinese, learn the language and culture and teach in a mission school while enjoying each other's company. It also presented the opportunity to practise the "social gospel" that had ignited passionate interest among college and university-educated men and women seeking to go abroad from Canada, the United States, Britain and Europe. The social gospel movement, which began after the American Civil War in 1865, aimed to fix the ills of society and it held a powerful religious, social and political influence as the world became more urbanized and industrialized in the late nineteenth and early twentieth centuries. The movement held that God demanded change through moral order and social justice.[3]

By the beginning of the First World War, international missionary work had evolved into a highly successful enterprise with huge budgets, corporate-like management, head offices and thousands of devoted participants. By the end of the war nearly 25 per cent of the North American missionaries assigned to China were Canadian and many were still in France serving as officers with the Chinese Labour Corps. "Canada's contribution to the world missionary enterprise, like its contribution to the First World War, was larger than its share: it has been said that in proportion to their size and resources, the churches of Canada sponsored more missionaries than any other nation in Christendom," notes historian Alvyn J. Austin.[4]

Born in Lunenburg, Nova Scotia, on August 13, 1887, Napier Smith was a small-town Maritimer through and through. There were plenty of Smiths around and Napier's parents, Charles and Georgina, shared the same last name before and after they were married. Charles, whose parents were devout Anglicans and loyal members of St. John's Anglican Church, was the master of a sailing vessel. He died of typhoid fever when Napier, the youngest of three children, was two months old. "My mother did not marry again until I was about twelve or thirteen. She must have been left enough to live on, but my recollection is that it was hard going. There were no luxuries in our home. Clothes were passed down. The only picture I have of us three children shows a huge darned patch on the knee of my stocking."

Despite the hardship, growing up in the picturesque port town was fairly pleasant for the closely knit family. The arrival of steamship technology had hurt the traditional wooden ship-building industry, but in Lunenburg the yards remained busy. And of course one of the most famous schooners of all, the first *Bluenose*, was built at the Smith and   yard and launched on March 26, 1921. Still, many families had to rely on each other and their neighbours. "Mother meant everything to us, and I cherish her memory as a happy, generous, lovable soul who made heroic personal sacrifices to keep her little family together."[5]

Family unity was visible on Sunday mornings when Georgina, a soprano soloist, and her children donned silk gowns, cradled cloth-bound hymnals in their hands and sang with fresh faces in the St. John's Church choir. Although "afflicted with a terrible shyness," young Napier gave it his best. The hymns, sermons, prayers and throaty tones from congregational responses had an effect on the boy, as did the smell of burning wax and the inspiring shafts of light falling on crowded pews. When storms rolled in and prevented the family from attending church, Napier found a way to work around the situation. Along with his sister, Laura, brother, Harold, and two cousins who lived in the other side of the duplex, he assembled a makeshift chapel in the living room. Wearing a bedsheet and standing precariously on a wooden chair, the shy, would-be minister proclaimed the gospel.[6]

Trouble came when his stepfather insisted the family join another church. Napier saw a man "possessed of childish peevishness" and resented the way he treated his mother, and how he pressed him to drop out of school at age fourteen to find work. Tired of the harping, Napier left high school after a year and took a job as a grocery delivery boy earning two dollars a week. He soon doubled his weekly salary at Rudolf's Men's Furnishings and General Dry Goods. As a clerk, he did not make deliveries, but loathed selling goods to women who challenged his shyness by asking "for the most embarrassing, intimate things" in the store. Whenever he was out on the street — running errands for his mother or walking to and from school — the young man usually went out of his way to avoid meeting girls. "Dances or mixed parties were anathema to me. Thus I never learned to dance."[7]

By age seventeen, Napier had put aside some money and moved to Halifax, where he enrolled at the Maritime Business College. Despite having just a year of high school, he did remarkably well and was encouraged to apply to the University of Toronto's Wycliffe College where he could pursue the ministry. Napier got to Toronto, but could not register for an Arts course until he completed high school. At Farquharson's Matriculation School, he crammed three years of high school into a year. After a few years at Wycliffe the shyness that had followed him from Nova Scotia began to disappear.

While on a date with a clergyman's daughter, he was "completely bowled over" when introduced to his date's roommate, Ruth Langlois. The honourable Napier kept his date with Carrie Marsh, a Saturday afternoon canoe trip on the Humber River, but he could not shake Ruth from his thoughts. The weeks passed slowly before they met again, but by April 1916, Napier and Ruth were engaged.

The Reverend Napier Smith served as an officer with the CLC. He and a group of Chinese interpreters reached France via Canada and the United States.

Courtesy Roger Smith

Five months later they were husband and wife travelling to the Orient.[8]

Nowhere in Napier's mind was there any knowledge of the Chinese Labour Corps, nor any notion that within a year and a half his missionary work in China would be interrupted by a long and risky voyage to war-torn France. He was — as many Canadians were — aware of the horrific slaughter unfolding on the Somme, but he and Ruth were called by another king, the "King of kings" to save souls in the Far East and were prepared to give themselves to that cause within the framework of the social gospel.

* * *

For many decades it has been difficult to look at those colonial attempts to convert native populations to Christianity with any inkling of approval. "'Christian pedantry,' when it is seen in the service of national interests automatically and at the same time equating paganism with savagery and Christianity with culture, invites condemnation," states historian Nicholas J. Griffin. But Griffin and others also acknowledge that the missionary movement did alleviate much poverty and misery.[9] Certainly by the time the

United Church of Canada Archives

The Reverend Gordon Jones graduated from civil engineering in 1906. He then went to China as a missionary. During the war he wrote often to his wife Clara (right).

CLC scheme was in full swing, missionaries regarded themselves as active proponents of a humanitarian cause. To many Chinese, hospitals and schools reinforced the idea that missionaries, backed by their convictions and financial support, were working to alleviate serious problems in the Chinese communities.

In the countryside, everyday contact between missionaries and the men and women they were trying to convert brought perspectives that were wider and deeper than what many British officials could gain. Missionaries had to learn the language and speak it every day. That is essentially why the British government eventually went looking for men like Napier to officer the CLC, although he came to it rather late in the war. But, in the early spring of 1918, the Maritimer said goodbye to Ruth and travelled by coastal steamer from Shanghai to Weihaiwei, and then to France with a secret contingent of Chinese language interpreters. "A strong call had gone out for Chinese-speaking Britishers to officer the corps," wrote Napier. "A fellow missionary, who had been in China six years and I volunteered. Even though he had longer experience and spoke the language much better than I, he was rejected and I was accepted. This I found hard to understand, but I was happy in the thought that I had been accepted for service."[10]

Of course, Ruth's work in China also came to a halt. For her, Napier's decision meant packing up and returning to her family in Toronto, where she would pray for her husband's safe return — whenever that might be.[11]

Months before, missionary Reverend Gordon Jones of Brantford, Ontario, passed through the same CLC recruitment depot on the northeastern shore of the Shantung Peninsula. Jones was also married, but, had a young daughter, Eleanor. He answered the British Army's call for Chinese-speaking British subjects while serving with the West China Mission of the Methodist Church of Canada. "In 1916 . . . I was due to proceed on furlough early the following year," he remembered. "Naturally I was anxious to do my bit in the struggle which was engrossing the whole world. There were more men in the Chinese Labour Corps than the Duke of Wellington commanded at the Battle of Waterloo. When I occasionally met old friends in France the question I almost always was asked was 'How did you get with the Chinks?' The answer was that I was in China when the Corps was being organized and joined up there. I reported at Wei Hai Wei [sic] on May 1st, 1917, and two weeks later was en route to France."[12]

Jones, who wrote regularly to his wife, Clara, was given charge of a CLC company. His ship, the *Empress of Russia*, crossed the Pacific with approximately two thousand labourers split into eight companies managed by eight officers.[13]

For Canadian Presbyterian missionary James M. Menzies there was a larger family to say goodbye to in March 1917, as well as very important archeological work. Familywise there was his wife, Annie, and their three children: Marion, who was not quite four, Frances, who was just under two, and three-month-old Arthur. With a heavy heart, Menzies watched his family and their beloved but strict Chinese nursemaid, Shen Dasao, board a steamer for Canada. Missing was his son David, affectionately known as little Laddie, who had died the previous year.[14]

As the ship carrying his family sailed from Shanghai, Menzies realized he had missed the "last good boat" to Tsingtao. For him, reporting late for duty at the recruitment depot in Shantung province was not an option, and so he convinced a Japanese fisherman to take him on board. Four days later the modest but determined missionary, accompanied by his faithful servant Hsiang, known affectionately as "Lucky Boy," reached Tsingtao and reported for duty — on time. "That fishing boat I remember had only raw fish and cold rice with some pickles," but the voyage north on the Yellow Sea presented the opportunity to "learn Japanese chess."[15]

At Tsingtao, "Lucky Boy" became Menzies's batman and the two, along with more than three thousand Chinese labourers organized into two battalions and eight companies, boarded the *Protesilaus*, a 9,500-ton steamer of the Blue Funnel Line. Menzies, then thirty-two, was a short, pensive fellow who was clearly not accustomed to military life and its massive forms of regimentation. He dreaded being around men who smoked, drank and swore or took the Lord's name in vain, but his solid religious upbringing and his education had given him patience, a strong sense of commitment and humility.

Born on February 23, 1885, in the rural southwestern Ontario town of Clinton, Menzies was attending high school at Leamington on the shores of Lake Erie when he wrote his entrance exams for the University of Toronto. His parents, David and Jane, were faithful, practical people who worked hard and brought prayer into the everyday lives of their children. James and his older brother, Robert, and younger sister, Margaret, were nurtured by this abiding faith, which remained with the family as it moved from Clinton to nearby Goderich, then to Staples, near Windsor, and finally to Leamington.[16]

On board the *Protesilaus*, Menzies was among ten officers, although most of the men had little or no military training. Among them were an insurance agent, two businessmen from Standard Oil and a printer who worked for the British American Tobacco Company. Menzies, the only missionary, was responsible for a company of 382 labourers. Needless to say, he was in high demand by virtue of being the only officer who spoke Chinese. The *Protesilaus* sailed from Tsingtao on March 17.[17] By the time she made Japan and began her journey across the North Pacific, Menzies had charge of two companies.[18]

Fellow Presbyterian missionary Thomas Arthurs was also shipping out that month from Shanghai. But instead of waving goodbye to his wife, Hilda, who was also a missionary, and his young daughters Helen and Doris, the thirty-four-year-old received "joyful news" permitting him to sail with his family to Canada. The Arthurs, who had been working continuously in China since 1912, departed Shanghai on March 31, 1917, on the *Empress of Japan*, and were very much looking forward to seeing family again. However, the voyage home and the disruption to their missionary work in North Honan (Henan) province would not have happened without the urgent call for Chinese-speaking missionaries to serve in the CLC.[19]

Skippered by W.D. Hopcraft, the sleek and reliable *Japan* sailed to Weihaiwei and then crossed to Yokohama, arriving on April 7. On April 19, at 6 p.m., the passenger ship — with no reports of contagious diseases — landed twenty-three children, all under the age of fourteen, and 112 adults in Vancouver. Arthurs also had the good fortune of being granted a few days leave before reporting to Halifax for the transatlantic crossing.[20]

The extra time Arthurs had with his family was providential, because he would not survive France.

* * *

Smith, Jones, Menzies and Arthurs were not the first, nor the last Canadian Protestant missionaries to venture overseas with the CLC. The first to offer his resignation in order to volunteer with the CLC — a few months ahead of Menzies — was medical missionary Dr. Percy Leslie of Montreal. The McGill University graduate joined the Presbyterian Mission in North Honan in 1897 and was almost killed three years later while helping other missionaries escape during the violent Boxer Rebellion.[21]

Leslie's wartime service was preceded by that of another medical missionary, Dr. Ferguson Fitton Carr-Harris, considered the best-trained doctor in North Honan.[22] But instead of joining the CLC he served with the Royal Army Medical Corps and was decorated with the Distinguished Service Order and Military Cross for conspicuous gallantry and devotion to duty. The citation for the former states: "Hearing that ten men of another battalion were lying wounded in front of the position, he volunteered on completion of the relief to go to their rescue. He was out for eight hours of the night, found nine of the men alive, took two of them back to headquarters, and organized the rescue of the remainder. He showed great coolness and self-sacrifice." The citation for his MC includes: "It was due to his fine example under most difficult conditions that a large number of wounded were evacuated from No Man's Land."[23]

On March 16, 1917 — the day before Menzies sailed — Canadian missionary Harry Forbes of Fletcher, Ontario, boarded the *Empress of Asia* at Weihaiwei.[24] The thirty year old had arrived in China in the autumn of 1914, served with the North Honan Mission, and married Maisie McNeely in 1916.[25] The couple raised two children, and during the Second World War their only son, Harry Malcolm Forbes, a member of the Canadian Merchant Navy, was reported lost at sea after his ship, SS *Vancouver Island*, was sunk on the North Atlantic following a torpedo attack.[26]

Overall, more than a hundred British and American missionaries serving in China joined the CLC for service in France or as labour corps recruiters and administrators in China. At the North Honan Mission alone, fourteen of the thirty-two missionaries volunteered for CLC service, and many of them, including Arthurs, Jones, Leslie, Menzies and Smith, were commissioned as officers.

Why did these well-educated men and others separate themselves from loved ones and religious calling in China to join a massive labour force in war-torn France? Before describing the personal reasons behind their decision to go, it is useful to start with a basic understanding of how the Canadian missionary service in China evolved during the late 1800s and early 1900s and the risks and challenges the missionaries faced by doing what they perceived as their "life's work." Within that exploration begins an appreciation for what was at stake not only for the individual missionaries who signed on the dotted line for overseas service, but for the work they left behind and how that disruption — coming at a crucial time — upset church authorities and sponsors in Canada.

* * *

Twenty-six years before war was declared in 1914, more than a thousand students marched by torchlight down Yonge Street in Toronto to old Union Station. The parade in late September 1888 was not a protest, but a celebration following a communion service at Knox Presbyterian Church. The prayerful had gathered to bid farewell — in the rain — to the first organized party of Canadian missionaries bound for China. The small group of travellers was united behind the charismatic and world-famous the Reverend Dr. James Hudson Taylor, the fifty-six-year-old British founder of the China Inland Mission (CIM). Altogether there were fifteen men and women, ranging in age from eighteen to early twenties. Thirteen were Canadian. Two were American.[27]

Taylor, who was a Protestant missionary, spent several years in China before his mind turned to the creation of the CIM in 1865. Born in the mining town of Barnsley in Yorkshire, England, Taylor sailed to China from Liverpool in 1853. The voyage to Shanghai took five months and not long after his arrival he began to feel isolated, lonely and rejected by the people he had come to proselytize. Taylor worked on despite being robbed, and nearly killed by a cannon ball during the Taiping Rebellion.[28]

As an educated man deeply interested in his work, Taylor looked the part, often dressed in a silk robe and cap with a false Manchu queue. His reputation grew, and he was credited with becoming the most famous missionary in the world after the death of Dr. Harry Livingstone's grand-uncle, Dr. David Livingstone.[29] The Yorkshireman's Chinese garb drew criticism from those who felt he had gone too far, but he countered the ridicule by explaining the clothes made him more approachable for the Chinese. By the time he visited Toronto in 1888, the CIM was the largest missionary group in China, with 294 missionaries working in fourteen provinces.[30]

Although many people stood on their toes to get a look at the physically small prophet with the giant reputation, much of the crowd's focus was on the young people boarding the Vancouver-bound train. What well-wishers and leading churchmen of the day so admired was the willingness — the courageous faithfulness — of this young generation to leave home and country behind to deliver salvation to the ends of the earth.

The attention paid that evening to the young, onward Christian soldiers was not unusual given the amount of everyday enthusiasm that existed in a society that was far more religious than today. A new energy had been switched on during the 1880s in British, Canadian and American colleges and universities and it was radiating around the world. Rising from this was the American-based Student Volunteer Movement for Foreign Missions (SVM), born at a student conference at Northfield, Massachusetts. Throughout the next thirty years the SVM was the primary recruiting agency for college students anxious to spread the gospel, and there was no mistaking the message in the motto: "The Evangelization of the World in This Generation." China, with its massive human population, was high on the list.

"During the 1880s . . . the complacent mid-Victorian church — what one may call the 'church sentimental' — was increasingly being taken over by the aggressive young people of the 'church militant' . . . Throughout the decade social reformers and evangelists had been challenging the churches of Canada to stop acting as comfortable waystations for the faithful on the road to heaven," notes Austin. "The time had come . . . to complete Christ's 'great commission' and 'Go ye into all the world and preach the gospel to every creature.'"[31]

While the Toronto group's departure marked an enterprising commitment to missionary work, it did not signal the first time Canadian missionaries travelled to the Far East, nor did it come anywhere close to the earliest Roman Catholic and Protestant missions to China. Some six hundred years had passed since the arrival of the Franciscan friars, whose work there lasted less than seventy-five years. However, other Roman Catholic missions followed and, with little opposition from the Chinese government, the church grew. By 1907, an estimated one million Chinese had been converted to Roman Catholicism. Two Franciscan Sisters of Mary were the first French-Canadian missionaries sent to China. They left Quebec in 1902 as replacements for French sisters killed in Shantung during the bloody Boxer Rebellion in 1900.[32]

British Protestant missionary Robert Morrison was in China by 1807, followed by thousands of other Protestant men with their wives and children. Missionary activities were restricted to Canton and Macau until the Treaties of Nanking and Tientsin were signed following the Opium Wars. During the second half of that century, while China was forced to open itself to all forms of Western activity, there was a major buildup of missions.

Missionaries and other Westerners were free to move and spread their various influences throughout the country. By 1900, there were approximately 2,500 Protestant missionaries in China, most of them British and American.

Prior to Ontario becoming one of four provinces of the Dominion of Canada through the *British North America Act*, which took effect on July 1, 1867, a lot of religious interest in China flowed mostly from congregations in what became southwestern Ontario. In the aftermath of what is known as the Great Disruption of the Scottish church, the Reverend William Chalmers Burns arrived in 1844 to solicit support for the secessionist Free Church. The twenty-nine-year-old preacher proved popular among Presbyterians before and after he left for China.

The first Canadian to go there was nineteen-year-old Adelaide Galliland from Farmersville (now Athens, Ontario) a short distance north of the St. Lawrence community of Brockville, which, in 1832 amid a cholera epidemic, became Upper Canada's first incorporated, self-governing town — two years before the town of Toronto.[33] Recently married to the Reverend Virgil Hart of the American Methodist Episcopal Church, Galliland, with her husband, began the journey in 1865, two years before Confederation. While she inspired her prominent husband, Adelaide worked quietly behind the scenes as they established numerous missionary stations along the Yangtze River.[34]

In the early 1870s, the Western Division of the Free Church sent the Reverend George Leslie Mackay to the island of Formosa (Taiwan).[35] As the stern, black-bearded Scotsman from southwestern Ontario conducted his rounds, he preached, led locals in hymns and even extracted teeth.

Seventeen years later, eight months before Taylor arrived in Shanghai with his enthusiastic Toronto group, the Presbyterian Church in Canada (Western Division) agreed to send Jonathan Goforth and his well-known artist wife Rosalind to North Honan, China, with the included objective of distributing famine relief funds in the province. The couple arrived at Shanghai, but Goforth's inability to speak the language made it necessary for him turn the funds over to others who could distribute the money. Goforth and his wife, who was more than two months pregnant, headed north to Chefoo (Zhifu, now Yantai) on the Shantung coast where the CIM had established a school for the children of foreign missionaries, businessmen and diplomats. There, the Goforths were joined by a handful of others, who became known as the Honan Seven. The group eventually moved inland where, in 1894, they acquired property north of the Yellow River at Changte (Zhangde, now Anyang).

"Goforth of China," as he was known, "was an unlikely leader," notes Austin, adding that he was described by a friend as a "'queer chap — a good fellow — pious — an earnest Christian, but simple-minded and quite peculiar.'"[36]

Missionaries who experienced sheltered lives in North America were shocked when they arrived in Shanghai. The city, with its brothels and gambling houses, was certainly an eye-opener for Taylor's CIM followers, who landed there in 1888. It was teeming with people, crammed into a couple of hundred square kilometres of space. Among the toiling young men working the streets along the riverfront were sweaty, bare-chested "coolies" toting bales of hay and other heavy objects imported from the West.[37] Occupying the relative comfort of their sedan chairs, carried on the shoulders of "coolies" past the stone facades of European-style buildings and lush gardens, the young Canadians also noticed English signs stating, "No Dogs or Chinamen Allowed."[38] From the thriving cosmopolitan city brimming with European and Japanese influence, Taylor's followers boarded steamers and then smaller craft that took them up the Yangtze to CIM language schools. The women went eighty kilometres to Yangchow (Yangzhou) on the Grand Canal while the men journeyed more than three hundred kilometres to Anking (Anqing), the capital of Anhwei (Anhui) province.[39]

It was a risky venture.

Anti-Christian sentiment among the Chinese had existed since the arrival of the Jesuits. The Taiping Rebellion, described as the bloodiest conflict in human history, was tied to a warped form of Christianity that evolved and spread across China. Fuelled by anti-Manchu or imperial sentiment, the Taipings crusaded as God Worshippers against imperial forces. Their leader, Hung Siu-ch'uan (Hong Xiuquan), believed he was the brother of Christ and named himself king of the Taipings. Initially, many missionaries embraced his ideas, but the support ended when he cited his brotherly connection with the Son of God. As millions died, most missionaries prayed for a quick end to his heresy. They got their wish when the Taipings were defeated and Hung committed suicide in 1864.

As the century drew to a close, the challenge for missionaries was not so much about finding ways to spread the word to the masses, but ensuring how well the message was delivered and received. Once delivered there was no controlling how any objections, misinterpretations or misrepresentations of the gospel could be used against foreigners. Language training for missionaries helped, but learning a new dialect did not come easy and did not always guarantee the Bible or the word of God would be understood, let alone accepted, by people who felt no need to be saved.[40]

Through all levels of Chinese society, anti-Christian sentiment grew during the latter half of the nineteenth century. Amid sporadic street violence, public notices appeared inciting hatred for Christians and other foreigners. One placard transformed the word T'ien-chu, the Catholic name for Lord of Heaven, into Pig of Heaven and featured an illustration of a crucified pig riddled with arrows.[41] American historian Harold Isaac puts it best when he describes the period between 1860 and 1900 as the "Age of Contempt." The foreign arrogance and sense of entitlement that flowed from British and French victories after the Opium Wars created a highly combustible situation.

Anger among famine-stricken peasants boiled over in 1899, directed at the Manchu imperial government and then at foreigners, especially missionaries. The Chinese felt stepped on and they were not going to take it anymore from white foreigners who saw themselves as superior and wanted everyone around them to become part of their God's master plan. The revolt began in Shantung, in the same dusty, drought-stricken villages that within seventeen years would gave rise to approximately 80 per cent of the nearly hundred thousand men who enrolled in the CLC.[42] Young, angry men appeared wearing red sashes and turbans inscribed with "Protect the pure. Exterminate the foreign."

This all led to the massive Boxer Rebellion, which swept through North China.[43] The Empress Dowager Cixi blamed missionaries and other foreigners and called for their immediate annihilation. Massacres of men and women and the destruction of foreign infrastructure, including schools, hospitals and railways followed. The violence culminated in the summer of 1900 with the siege of the foreign legations that had been established in Peking following the Second Opium War.[44] Dozens of foreigners, including Canadians, and their children were tortured, beheaded or hacked to death. The fact some had worked to bring health care and education to China did not matter to the Boxers, who wholly despised the religious agenda and Western influences.

When Dr. Percy Leslie headed overseas with the CLC in 1916 he was still feeling the wounds he suffered in July 1900. He and other missionaries and British subjects in North Honan had received a British consul telegram from Tientsin warning them to evacuate immediately. However, several days passed before the first group left. Another party, led by Goforth, ran into a mob that stared in ominous silence before their anger erupted. While attempting to lead his group through the crowd, Goforth had his white pith helmet slashed by a sword. He was injured, but his skull remained intact. Leslie, who was then a strong and healthy twenty-nine-year-old, suffered fifteen wounds while helping his fellow missionaries escape. One laceration was so severe it nearly severed his right hand. The group eventually crossed the Yellow River into South Honan.

Three other Canadians, all of them with the CIM, were not so lucky. William Peat of the Hamilton, Ontario, YMCA, and Margaret Smith of New Hamburg, Ontario, met violent ends in Shansi (Shanxi) province to the north. The third, Alex Saunders, escaped the Boxers' knives and broadswords by wandering for days in the harsh wilderness.[45]

Before attending McGill, where he graduated in 1896, Leslie worked at his father's Montreal-based steel and metal merchants company.[46] The young Presbyterian doctor had much to offer as a medical missionary. He got his wish on May 20, 1897, when he was appointed to the Honan mission. Leslie arrived in China five months later and on October 30, 1899, wed missionary Isabel Ogilvy, daughter of the well-known Ogilvy department-store family.[47] After their narrow escape during the Boxer uprising, the Leslies did not rule out returning to China. In 1901, Percy completed postgraduate work in Scotland and Isabel gave birth to a son, Marc. A second son, Charles, was born in October 1906. Returning to China, Leslie became superintending physician at the large mission hospital in Changte Ho, North Honan.[48]

The Boxer rampage ended in mid-August 1900 after military forces from eight foreign countries, including Britain, France, Germany, Russia and the United States, arrived and launched an offensive, killing Boxers and pretty well anyone who stood in the way. In defeat, the Manchu government was ordered to pay a paralyzing $450-million indemnity to the foreign powers.[49]

Of the three hundred foreigners killed during the Boxer Rebellion, at least 243 were missionaries or from missionary families, including dozens of children. The cold-hearted butchering of foreigners was horrific, but paled in comparison to the thousands of Chinese, Christians or converts, killed by the Boxers, and those who died at the hands of the vengeful foreign military forces.

When the blood first began seeping into the dusty streets, many foreigners were caught off guard even though there had been violent precursors and evacuation warnings, not to mention several years of unrest. The faithful were particularly vulnerable, and many, sadly, were ignorant of Chinese history. Their lessons and worldly views came mostly from the Bible, and those who spent their time in missionary compounds, behind brick walls and wooden gates, were sheltered from the rising tension. Others who ventured out or had more contact with Chinese could see or feel the slow-burning hatred. Some were blind to it and more than a few rested comfortably on privilege and arrogance, heaping scorn on the "heathens" with racial slurs and some physical confrontations. Reinforced in 1899 by a Chinese government edict that granted them special status — equal to that of a local magistrate — missionaries could, if they did not keep themselves in check, lose themselves and their work to pride. Leslie and other Canadian missionaries, living as they were among the Chinese in rural settings, were not sheltered and could see and feel the tension.

The cooling-off period and the safer times after the Boxer Rebellion ended around the time James Menzies arrived in 1910. By then, revolution was again in the air, this time aimed at ridding China of imperial rule in favour of democracy.

CHAPTER 6

Missionaries
Accomplished

"No one worthy of the British name would shrink from considering the question of duty at such a time."

Love, marriage, mission . . .

James Menzies's route to China in 1910 had been more circuitous than that of most Canadian China-bound travellers. Deeply in love and following his faith, the civil engineer, land surveyor and theologian left Toronto on May 21. After arriving at the port of Montreal, Menzies began his journey to Liverpool, arriving there June 13 on the White Star Dominion Line ship *Dominion*. He had decided to attend the World Missionary Conference in Edinburgh, Scotland, with his younger sister, Margaret, and then travel alone from London to Holland and through Russia to North China on the Trans-Siberian Railway. From London, the mostly overland journey to Peking spanned some nineteen thousand kilometres, but it was a faster route to the Orient; two weeks, compared to roughly forty days by ship.[1]

While Menzies's faith was leading him to the more central Chinese province of Honan, the cradle of Chinese civilization, his heart was pulling him further south to his fiancée, Annie Belle Sedgwick. That young missionary with the Anglican Church of Canada was enrolled at a language course in Kuling (Guling) at the foot of sacred Lushan Mountain. As the story goes, the town got its non-Chinese-sounding name from a missionary who established a retreat there for fellow missionaries. Kuling was a pun for "Cooling."

Three years older than James and entirely independent, Annie had also been raised on a farm in rural southwestern Ontario: one of seven children, six girls and a boy. Her parents, John and Marie, were devout Anglicans and owned a mixed farm at Cottam, southeast of Windsor, Ontario. At an early age, Annie Belle acquired her mother's skills as a seamstress. She also led a women's Sunday school class and volunteered as secretary of the Young People's Association. After John died in 1904, the Sedgwicks moved to Windsor, where Marie earned income from rental properties.

When James and Annie met in Toronto they were deeply involved in volunteer Christian work, but pursuing separate goals of becoming foreign missionaries. James's higher education began in 1903 at the University of Toronto's School of Practical Science where, as an honours student, he graduated with a Bachelor of Science in civil engineering in 1907. He then attended Knox College, graduating three years later with a Bachelor of Divinity. Annie and her sister, Maude, had enrolled at the Anglican Deaconess Training School, but the young deaconess also attended classes at Wycliffe College.[2]

The extent to which James was smitten with Annie became obvious in a letter to his mother before Annie and Maude left for China. "I love a lassie," he began. "She is loved by everyone from the little raga-muffins on the streets to the higher church dignitaries . . . So, I wrote a letter that took me three days. Well, I told her in a clumsy blunt brutal way that I admired her from the crown of her head to the soles of her shoes."[3]

Annie and Maude's arrival in China in April 1910 was preceded by a rather dramatic farewell for James at Toronto, for he
had resolved "to let my heart have its way." Clutching an engagement ring in his pocket, but separated from Annie at the busy
railway station, Menzies, who was not a tall man, had to find a
way to talk to her. He purchased a ticket to the next station, and
while on board asked Annie to marry him. She accepted, but
insisted she must first honour her five-year commitment to the
Anglican mission.[4]

Following the Edinburgh conference and a lengthy holiday
through the British Isles, Menzies bid farewell to his sister Margaret
and from London took a train northeast to Harwich on the North
Sea, where he caught a steamer to the Hook of Holland, northwest
of Rotterdam. He arrived on the continent at five in the morning
and after passing through customs boarded a train that took him
past "the lowland dykes, canals, and windmills," all of which were
of great interest to a civil engineer and land surveyor. At Moscow,
Menzies began the first leg of his Trans-Siberian Railway journey
to China. "We were swarmed by hundreds of Russian porters in
white aprons, long boots, and linen jackets . . . who shoved passengers through one door and their luggage through another," he
wrote on August 22, ". . . a man at the door took your passport and
there you were herded in the large building with the blinds down
and all the doors closed — without your baggage or your passport.
They went through your luggage and I saw them taking things in
spite of protest. They examined inside the collars and cuffs of coats
for signs of wear. They knew their business."[5]

After arriving at Peitaiho (Beidaihe) in North China in early
September, Menzies boarded a train toward Kuling. The last part
of his journey south commenced a week later and entailed a more
traditional form of transport: the ubiquitous sedan chair. Overall,
the young missionary, who confessed to being too nervous to eat
breakfast, employed seven coolies, including a baggage carrier.
"After travelling about two hours over the plain we came to the

foot of the hill and were just starting up when I met Annie and Maude who were coming down. We went back to the rest house, had some lunch and then started up, up, and up — those steps went for hours. Annie and I walked a good part of the way. We had cocoa and then went . . . to the top of the hill and sat down after tea . . . on the verandah. Master, make me worthy of Annie's great love . . ."[6]

Instead of the expected five years, which Annie had insisted on in Toronto, the engagement lasted less than a year. In the ancient Honan city of Kaifeng, on February 23, 1911, which happened to be James's twenty-sixth birthday, Annie appeared in a white silk dress and veil, which she had made. Next to her stood the proud groom in his brushed-up dark frock suit, clerical collar and polished black shoes. The couple exchanged vows, with James looking a tad shorter than Annie.[7] "You know we had expected to wait some years for Annie to honour her commitment but the Canadian missionary folks out here have decided it will be best for us to be married at once and then we can settle down to the language together," James wrote to his parents. It was a difficult decision for Annie because it meant giving up her dream of working among the Chinese with the Anglican mission. Instead, she would resign and join her husband at the Presbyterian mission in North Honan province, north of the Yellow River.

From the enthusiasm expressed in Menzies's Toronto letters it is easy to see how his dream of becoming an overseas missionary began. Taught from an early age to pay attention and to live a clean, purposeful life, Menzies was smart and ambitious, with evolving interests. He was nine when the family moved from Clinton to Silver Creek Farm at Staples in 1894. In 1897, at age twelve, he was editing the school newspaper, the *Friday News*. "We will be celebrating thanksgiving day [sic]. I suppose we will all enjoy our dinner of duck or chicken. But we do not want to go cackling around the school-room next morning because we will get the teacher cross and will be in danger of getting a threshing [sic]."[8]

Radio Canada International

James and Annie Belle Menzies on their wedding day in China.

Involvement with the Young Men's Christian Association and the Student Volunteer Movement (SVM) began soon after Menzies arrived in Toronto in September 1903. The SVM held a convention at Toronto's Massey Hall in 1904 that attracted some two thousand delegates, most of them college-age students.[9] The following year, at another SVM gathering, Menzies made up his mind to become a foreign missionary.

Summer field trips tested James's land surveying and engineering skills, although he also worked the farm, including organizing the payroll in his father's office and washing the buggy. In 1905, James recognized how his father's schedule had taken a toll on his health. While he suffered each year from hay fever, it appears David Menzies had never known life without a day's work. In addition to operating a farm, he ran a general store, sold lumber and quality organs and invested in property. "It has added ten years to his age," James wrote in his journal. "My I do wish we could get out of here and have them [sic] settle someplace where they would enjoy life and have a happy time . . ."[10]

Meanwhile, Menzies continued his soul-searching. "It is a lovely night — calm and still. Very dark," he wrote on August 22. "But the stars are out twinkling down on us light hundreds of years old. And so may we, even if it is not appreciated now, by letting our light shine help someone a hundred years hence."[11]

Six days later he added: "Oh to serve God better. I must get the rudiments of the Christian Life and I am determined to start over and over again until I get well versed in the beginning of it."[12]

On September 11, after visiting the Michigan State Fair, he noted: "The tight-rope walker was the best I have seen — he turned back flips on it and bounced every way imaginable . . . Oh, yes, I saw a human being that lived on rattlesnakes, enjoying being bit by them and living on the flesh. It was horrible to watch her . . . Well I must go to bed as it is late. And may I learn from this exhibition something that will benefit me throughout life. For I believe that there are things to be learned. God help me to be the man I wish to be . . . Help me to be useful instead of useless, cheerful instead of growly and in all a man living to the Glory of God."[13]

David Menzies was not enamoured with the path his son had chosen. He was proud of James's intellect and pleased he had selected civil engineering as his major at the University of Toronto School of Practical Science. David recognized how James took his studies seriously and earned top marks, but there was little he could do about how serious his son was about missionary work. The young man was certainly in the right place at the right time to make connections with powerful people who could provide a guiding light to such work.

Toronto's population in 1910 was roughly 380,000 and nearly all of it was Protestant, led by Methodists and Presbyterians. Throughout the city, the various denominations had tremendous influence, ran numerous colleges and seminaries, most of which are well known today. Many of the denominations had also established national offices there.[14]

Despite a disastrous fire in 1904, which destroyed more than a hundred downtown buildings, Toronto was thriving with other local and national businesses, although photographs show women and children salvaging coal from downtown streets to presumably sell or heat their homes with. It is hard to imagine today, but evangelism was flourishing in Toronto and other major cities with mainstream religion strongly associated with university arts programs. The Massey Hall convention was one example of the enthusiasm that existed on and off campus for Christian work.

In Toronto and across the country, newspapers regularly reported on church and student evangelical activities, including foreign mission work. This enthusiasm continued well into the war. As an example, in addition to reporting the large number of missionaries who joined Dr. Harry Livingstone's ship, the *Empress of Japan*, in Victoria in August 1917, the *Victoria Daily Colonist* described a reception held at St. Andrew's Presbyterian Church prior to the missionaries' departure. Most of the missionaries who left for China, South China or Korea were mentioned by name, along with family members.[15]

Although written in 1913, roughly three years after Menzies arrived in China, the opening paragraph of the executive committee report to the SVM North American convention in Kansas City is indicative of the kind of literature that emboldened the movement. "The Student Volunteer Movement for Foreign Missions, called into being nearly a generation ago under the influence of the mighty working of the Spirit of God, has already profoundly impressed the religious life of the colleges of the United States and Canada, widely influenced the missionary of the Churches, and furnished to the Mission Boards the greatest offering of lives ever made in one generation by two Christian nations."[16]

While the SVM's slogan "Evangelization of the World — in This Generation," had been introduced to a previous generation, it was still resonating among young people in 1914. Churches, colleges, universities and seminaries continued to be firmly behind the movement, including those in Toronto. By 1913, more than a hundred North American institutions were giving $300 or more per year to the SVM, and the University of Toronto was among the top contributors.[17]

In its review of the four previous years, the report stated a "larger number of new volunteers has been enrolled than during any corresponding period in the history of the colleges of North America . . . There are now on the foreign field approximately seven thousand five hundred volunteers who have gone out from North America, the British Isles, the Continent of Europe and the Christian lands of the Southern Hemisphere."[18] The "missionary uprising" has been "a mighty help in the direction of counteracting the perils of our modern college life. At a time when growing luxury, self-indulgence and the tendency to softness are manifesting themselves in our colleges, it is well that we have a Movement which makes such an appeal to the heroic, which summons men to such a stern and rugged self-discipline, and which assigns to them such stupendous tasks."[19]

No one knew in late 1913 that the world would be at war within a year. For young and healthy Christian men and women, educated at mainstream colleges or universities with strong Christian ties, going to "the front" was a term to describe the remote villages in distant lands where the seeds of Christian values could be sown.[20]

Menzies had registered at Knox College in 1907 and graduated in 1910 with a Bachelor of Divinity. At that point he was ready to fulfill his dream. On January 20, James wrote to his mother, Jane, explaining he would leave for China in May or June. "Dear Mother: I am enclosing a clipping from yesterday's Globe which explains itself. I have been medically examined and found perfectly fit, and been before the Foreign Missions Committee and appointed to Honan, China . . . A great joy fills my heart and yet a great sadness too. For it is hard, very hard to think of leaving the folks at home . . . We are linked so close together that separation even for a few short years seems a long, long time. And the stronger the love is at home the harder it is for one to think of going. But then when we think of the Great love of — 'For God so loved the world that He gave his only begotten Son' — and when we think of the vast millions who have never even heard of that love then we feel that we must go and do as He did who left His home that He might go to those who did not know of God's love . . . The real sacrifice is made by the parents — not the son who goes."[21]

David Menzies accepted James's decision, but stuck to the hope his son would pursue a career in civil engineering or land surveying. "We receive the news with pleasure and pain," he wrote on February 2, 1910. "We are glad to think you have been called by a higher power and chosen by your fellow men for the hard work, that of winning souls to Christ and I trust you and your mate Annie will succeed evangelising your share of the world in this generation. We are sorry when we think of being separated from you by so great a distance and in all probability never to see you again."[22]

David asked his son if he was going to complete the Dominion Land Surveyor licensing exam, stressing it would be a mistake not to. "Think the matter over seriously and if at all practical I would like to see you finish your DLS as that is the part of your education I took so much interest in and looked forward to seeing you at the head of some noted Engineering staff of national note."[23] With his father's financial help, James took the exam and passed.

Included in the 1913–14 SVM executive report is a twenty-four-page list of North American college students recruited and sent to denominational missions around the world from 1910 through 1913. More than 1,600 names are on the list. On page 32, under the heading Sailed Volunteers for 1910, are the names of James Menzies and Annie Sedgwick. Listed for the same year were two other professionals who would join the CLC as officers, namely the Methodist Gordon Jones, and medical missionary Frederick Auld of the Presbyterian Church.

Auld graduated from McGill in arts and medicine and joined the North Honan (Henan) Mission in November 1910. "By diligent study he acquired knowledge of the language that was both extensive and accurate, fitting him to meet all classes of Chinese," notes a brief biography. Accompanying him to China was his wife, May, a missionary who served with him for seventeen years, including postwar work in the dietetic department of a large hospital at Weihwei."[24]

Honan, the destination for Menzies and Auld in 1910, was rather isolated and had a history of opposing foreign influence. "Although North Henan people were curious about anything new, at the same time they showed a strong sense of animosity against anything too unfamiliar, which explains why it was one of the last provinces opened to Christianity," notes author Linfu Dong in his 2005 biography on Menzies.[25] With mountains in the west and floodplains in the east, the province is considered the birthplace of Chinese civilization. It occupies a piece of the North China Plain and winding through it, from the northwest, is the Yellow River, separating the smaller North Honan from South Honan.

Neighbouring Shantung province, where most of the CLC was recruited, lies to the northeast. Population-wise, Honan was anything but small. At the start of the First World War its population exceeded twenty-five million, mostly peasants living in thousands of hamlets and villages across some 167,000 square kilometres. For comparison, fifty-four Honans could fit into Canada's land mass, which at the time supported only seven million people.[26]

For foreigners wishing to work among the Chinese it was wise to pay attention to local traditions, customs and histories. However, most foreigners did not do this, being more interested in making money or advancing their various agendas, business or otherwise. But while the Christian churches were deeply focused on saving souls there had been a greater awakening, lit by the social gospel movement, that led to the establishment of hospitals, schools and social services. These developments were, of course, tied to the cause, but they still benefitted many Chinese.

Missionaries who paid attention or tried to learn from Chinese history and traditional customs while touring the countryside, treating patients or teaching school found the exercise beneficial to their own understanding. Their experiences, coupled with their ability to speak Chinese, became very advantageous while with the CLC in France.

In the backwaters of China, Westerners and their technologies were regularly shunned and not trusted. Many Chinese had never seen a sewing machine let alone machinery that could harvest millet, beans, wheat or kaoliang (sorghum). However, the tough resourcefulness of the Chinese, including their inherited farming skills, technologies and deep, time-honoured commitment to family, helped many through the cyclical flooding and droughts that caused widespread famine and death. Although there were vast differences between rural China and rural Canada, it helped that many missionaries embarking on rural evangelism were from rural Canada and had spent time on a farm.[27]

In the wake of the Boxer Rebellion and the massive indemnity imposed by foreign nations, the Chinese government was forced to open the door a little more to allow the penetration of Western goods and ideas. Many of these influences and items were found beneficial by the Chinese population and adopted in places like North Honan. Slowly, long-held impressions were replaced by a mentality that either embraced or quietly accepted that it was simply futile to resist foreign influence. Others saw an opportunity for China to step up onto the world stage. Meanwhile, foreign railway consortiums were busy laying hundreds of kilometres of new track and when the Imperial government abolished the Confucian educational system in 1905 the foreign churches and their supporters saw greater opportunity to establish more schools. Around the same time, the demand for Western products, including clothing, toiletries and cigarettes, began to displace many local and more traditional products.

The remote village of Wu'an (Wuan) became the Menzies' first posting as husband and wife. Although quite rural, the town was heavily populated and its reputation as a backwater was supported by how far it was from the closest railway station. Established in 1909 with funds from a wealthy Montreal businessman, the missionary outpost was still under construction when the newlyweds arrived in late February 1911. By the time they moved into the completed compound that fall, Annie was pregnant. China, meanwhile, was giving birth to the revolution that ended the long reign of the Qing dynasty, marking the beginning of its fragile experiment with democracy.

China was again a dangerous place for foreigners and by November the British and American consuls were advising their nationals to evacuate the interior. Nearly 150 Canadians left from the Methodist mission in West China, but in North Honan the main missionary stations remained open. There, amid much fear and chaos, on December 9, 1911, Annie gave birth to David Sedgwick Menzies, nicknamed Laddie.

A greater sense of optimism prevailed around missionary work in China when the country became a republic under the short-lived provisional presidency of Sun Yat-sen, followed by Yuán Shikai, head of the powerful Beiyang Army. Young Chinese men and women studied Christianity and subscribed to the ideals of Western-style education, intent on furthering their learning abroad. During the Boxer Rebellion there had been roughly two thousand Protestant missionaries and one thousand Roman Catholic missionaries in China. Ten years later — around the time the Menzies arrived — these numbers had risen to 5,144 and 1,469, respectively.[28] The change in attitude for missionaries was encouraging, especially for those who had escaped the violence of 1900.

Like many missionaries arriving in China for the first time, learning Chinese was the priority for James and Annie. James struggled, but caught on while managing a heavy workload that included running a primary school, a Sunday school and maintaining the station's books. His engineering skills also proved incredibly valuable when it came to construction projects, including the sinking of a deep well. While the work earned him great affection and respect from the people of Wu'an, his own experiences opened his heart and mind to the rural Chinese.

By the time the Menzies left Wu'an for the main station at Changte (Zhangde, now Anyang) in late 1913, they, along with their nanny, Shen Dasao, were also raising a daughter, Marion.

At Changte the Menzies worked closely with Murdoch MacKenzie, an eloquent Scotsman and Knox College graduate. As one of the senior missionaries in Honan, MacKenzie was very familiar with the area and its people. With a passion for rural evangelism, he took great pleasure in travelling the countryside and visiting villages. Menzies frequently participated in these sojourns, and the two men talked of many things, including the work of the church in China and back home. MacKenzie's wisdom and eloquence emerged a few years later, in early 1917, when the North Honan Presbytery, followed by the Foreign Missions Board (FMB) in Toronto, grappled with the divisive question of whether to grant consent to missionaries who wanted to go to Europe with the CLC.

Then, one day, months before the outbreak of the war in Europe, life handed Menzies a pleasant surprise. While riding horseback along the Huan River he noticed how farmers had unearthed ancient pottery shards. Menzies stopped and while taking a closer look at the shards he was approached by local boys who asked the curious missionary if he would like to look at some "dragon bones with characters on them." The boys led Menzies to a gully where part of the ground was covered with small, white bone fragments. Several years earlier, a Chinese scholar in Peking had made an important discovery while examining a medical ingredient called "dragon bones" used to treat everything from gallstones to paralysis. On the bones he found scratches resembling ancient characters. News of that discovery was not widely shared and the scholar is believed to have committed suicide during the Boxer Rebellion in 1900. Then, roughly ten years later, Chinese scholars began pointing to the Huan River as the original site of the "dragon bones." However, very few people visited the area before the children led Menzies to the bones in 1914.[29] What the trained land surveyor had stumbled upon were artifacts from the Shang dynasty (1700–1045 BC), later commonly called Oracle Bones because the Shang people believed they could be used to send questions or messages to their deity.

Although most Canadians have never heard of the Oracle Bones or the Waste of Yin, these ancient court records and archives are still well known to scholars worldwide. The discovery of this primitive bone script or oldest form of Chinese writing has been incredibly valuable to understanding Chinese civilization. It was, scholars agree, on par with or surpassing other major archeological discoveries around the world. The ever-modest Menzies was quick to deflect credit for his discovery onto the young Chinese farmers who unearthed the artifacts. However, he also realized he had found physical evidence for the location of the Kingdom of Shang and he grew into an avid collector, soon acquiring the nickname "Old Bones."

International scholars have since praised Menzies for being the "first foreign or Chinese archaeologist to visit the Waste of Yin with a purely scientific interest," explains Dong. "Shard by shard, he became the foremost non-Chinese expert on Bronze Age China and helped decipher the oracle bone script."[30]

While Menzies collected, catalogued, and published a vital book on the ancient bone script, he remained true to his calling as a missionary. By August 1914 the war in Europe was underway, but in North Honan the Menzies' missionary work and family life carried on as usual until early June 1916. That was when four-and-a-half-year-old Laddie died at the family's northern vacation home at Peitaiho.

Annie was pregnant and left to grieve the tremendous loss while taking care of Marion and Frances with Shen's assistance. Nearly paralyzed with grief, James wrote home with the sad news while escorting his son's remains to the cemetery in North Honan. "A sad hearted son sits in the corner of a Chinese baggage car writing this brief note to you. A little coffin lies before him — all that remains of Laddie. He died at 4.20 AM today, June 13, 1916, of Scarlet fever. I only reached Pei-tai-ho last night in time for the last and he did not even know me . . . At midnight he seemed better. His temperature began to drop and his breathing was more free [sic]. In fact until a very little of the end we were full of hope. And then he just slipped away out of our grasp . . . Away in Central China his little grave will anchor us here. Annie remains with the children while I take him to his last earthly home."[31]

Roughly five months later, on November 29, 1916, Annie gave birth to a boy[32] who would be named Arthur Redpath Menzies and grow up to become a future Canadian ambassador to China.

The war in Europe had by then stretched beyond two bloody years. The Battle of the Somme was over with not much gained on the ground for the Allies. The human cost was horrific. Faced with their massive casualties, the British could try to round up more men from the factories in England, but moving them to the front would create a problem at home by depleting the workforce needed to supply goods for the effort at the front.

In China, the names of all British subjects under the protection of the Crown were added to a register. From the beginning, British businessmen, government employees and others of military age living abroad were encouraged to join the fight. In Peking, British officials recognized "it would be helpful if headquarters of China Missions could be moved to inform their branches in China that, in view of special nature of service, members are at liberty to serve as officers or doctors if required."[33] The November 1916 cable between Peking and London noted that before the CLC scheme was initiated, staff from the English Baptist Mission in China had joined the military and were in Europe. The cable's focus was on Shantung, but in neighbouring Honan province Canadian Presbyterian medical missionary Dr. Carr-Harris had, by the spring of 1916, already applied and been accepted for military service. In response to his decision to join the Royal Army Medical Corps, the Foreign Missions Board of the Presbyterian Church of Canada had agreed to grant him leave of absence without pay.[34]

As news and rumours spread, more official information was sought by missionaries, particularly those in North and Central China. In November, the British consul in Tientsin, roughly 110 kilometres south of Peking, distributed enlistment applications for missionaries to complete. The top candidates would be British subjects who could speak Chinese and serve as officers in the CLC. In December the British legation in Peking ramped up its efforts by making a more formal appeal. The missionaries who wanted to go to France as well as those who elected to stay knew the departures would deplete staffing levels and interrupt significant Christian work. The disruption was immediately felt in North Honan, where current and well-drafted plans for exciting new work across the territory were soon crippled by not enough staff.

The Canadian Presbyterian Mission there "had a well-developed infrastructure for evangelical, medical, and educational work and represented the major Protestant presence in the northern half of the province," explains Professor Margo Gewurtz. "Together with the American Presbyterians in neighbouring Shantung province and British missionaries of the China Inland Mission, the Canadians participated in the China Continuation Committee (CCC), a joint venture for co-ordinating Protestant Evangelical efforts throughout North China."[35]

The timing was particularly bad because the continuation committee had just agreed to launch a significant evangelical campaign. Within that undertaking the North Honan Presbytery had initiated a province-wide, five-year Evangelical Movement in which the Chinese church was to take a leading role. At home in Canada the churches supporting and publicizing this work were looking forward to its launch in February 1917.[36]

However, young and healthy missionaries could not be faulted for wanting to put experience gained in China to work overseas in support of the war. But was service to God not more important than service to king? It was, as Gewurtz points out, a "crisis of conscience among the Canadians as well as a conflict with the home church" because even if the Honan Presbytery was prepared to work around the staffing shortage there was no guarantee the FMB in Toronto would go along with it. For the Presbytery, the matter came to a head in January 1917. By then Dr. Leslie had already left for overseas with the CLC, and, of course, Dr. Carr-Harris was also gone. Menzies, meanwhile, had submitted his application to the British legation in Peking, pointing out his academic qualifications and the experience gained while supervising Chinese workers at the mission.[37]

The Presbytery commended Leslie for his decision to go. More significantly, it soon took the position that the war demanded every effort against tyranny, even if it meant a serious disruption in mission work. As far as Presbytery was concerned, those leaving for France would have its support, but this position could easily be overruled by the FMB. The FMB was not blindsided by the issue because it had already heard — through contact with families in Canada — that some of its missionaries in North Honan had left for France or were intending to go.

When Menzies's close friend Murdoch MacKenzie wrote to mission board secretary Dr. Robert Peter MacKay on January 25, 1917, he zeroed in on the vital question faced by all. "Years ago they had listened to the voice of the highest King, and in obedience to His command had come to China. They studied Chinese for the express purpose of making Christ and His great salvation known to the Chinese people in North Honan. In many spheres they rendered whole hearted and cheerful service to their Divine Master. An opportunity, such as does not come often in an ordinary lifetime, has now led them to ask whether their lives, and all the knowledge they have gained of Chinese, may not be turned to account in the struggle now being waged. Britain is about to put forth its maximum effort. The weightiest issues for our Empire and the World depend on the result. No one worthy of the British name would shrink from considering the question of duty at such a time. It has been taken up seriously by all our brethren, and their response is only that which was to be expected of them."

MacKenzie also tried to assure MacKay that missionary work would continue whether in Asia or in Europe because the men who wanted to go were following where God was leading them.

In supporting its missionaries, Presbytery also cited the larger picture, noting the unparalleled crisis facing the British Empire, and noting how the labour battalions would free British soldiers for combat. Key to the CLC scheme was the opportunity the British had in North China to attract what was only a limited number of Chinese-speaking missionaries. As Gewurtz points out, the politically astute and seasoned MacKay, who had served as secretary since 1892, accepted the argument that missionaries had a distinct language advantage. However, he was a very rational man who was not swayed by any thinking around how great an opportunity it would be for missionaries to spread the gospel on the Western Front. There were simply far more souls to save in China than in France. Of course, another reason cited in support of sending missionaries to France was the possibility that if the Germans won the war, China missions — and missions elsewhere — would suffer under a new world order.

Formal approval from the FMB came on April 19, 1917, and above anything else it was the written and verbal skills of their missionaries in North Honan that won the day. By then, Menzies's application had already been approved and, like other missionaries, he had sailed for France via Canada.

The FMB's approval was a tough call, but the right call because missionaries did make a difference by bringing their experiences and language skills to a hastily prepared foreign scheme that featured sharp cultural differences between men from the East and the military-minded men from the West. The British were in charge, but it was the Chinese themselves who got the work done while often turning to those who understood them more than those who had never been to China and spent time with them in their villages or at the recruitment centres.

In time, the absence of missionary staff in China, which stretched well beyond the Armistice of 1918, further eroded the work in North Honan and elsewhere. Sponsors at home moved quickly to pull funding. In early 1917, an American-based sponsor withdrew financial support to the severely scaled-down hospital at Wu'an. A church in Montreal, meanwhile, was concerned about continuing the salaries of missionaries, including funding for Leslie. Overall, years of hard work, some of which was paid for in blood, was crippled by the disruption that flash-froze the North China five-year forward movement.

The newlyweds, Napier and Ruth Smith, arrived in China in late September 1916, shortly after the China Continuation Committee agreed to develop its evangelical campaign. The British legation's urgent call for missionaries to join the CLC came two and a half months later. By then the Smiths were in Peking, enrolled at the North China Union Language School. After boarding their train at Toronto, the couple had extended their honeymoon with a few extra days in Banff and Vancouver before boarding the *Empress of Asia*. The ship followed the usual route to Shanghai and met the usual weather on the North Pacific and Yellow Sea. Four days out of Vancouver the ocean was "smooth as a millpond," noted Ruth in a September 10 letter to her parents.[38] The crossing from Nagasaki to Shanghai was less comfortable. "We ran into a typhoon . . . I stayed in my berth nearly all day," Ruth noted on September 25 after arriving at Shanghai. "I was not sick as long as I remained lying down. Napier could not put his head in the door but had to spend the day in a deck chair with rain and spray blowing over him."[39]

From Shanghai the Smiths headed north to Peking, travelling most of the way on a railway under British management. At the ancient walled city of Nanking, Napier and Ruth boarded a ferry to cross the Yangtze. Another train took them to Kaifeng in Honan where they climbed into a covered mule cart for the bumpy ride to the missionary compound outside the city. "Each cart holds two people. You sit on the floor with your legs stretched out in front of you and hold your breath for the next jolt," noted Ruth. Early the next morning, October 2, they were back on the train to Peking, proud of the Chinese names bestowed upon them while they were touring Kaifeng. Napier's was Hsieh Tien Kuang, meaning Thanks, Most Heavenly Gift, while Ruth was honoured with Hsieh Lu Teh, meaning Thanks, Road to Virtue. "The women just stared and stared at my clothes," noted Ruth after leaving Kaifeng. "And on the train whenever we stop at a small station the people come right up to our window, look in and laugh at a great rate. I am becoming quite used to it now."[40]

By early 1918, Napier and Ruth had spent a year and a half studying Chinese in Peking, attending school at East Cliff in the refreshingly breezy northern port town of Peitaiho, and teaching at the Canadian church mission school at Kaifeng. Before arriving at Kaifeng, while returning from Peitaiho to Peking in August 1917, the Smiths saw what inclement weather could do to northern China. "Between Tientsin and Peking and also on the other side of Tientsin for miles and miles the train passed through great stretches of water — the floods. Only the railway embankment and rails remained above water. The houses, grain, every sign of habitation was covered. Only the tops of graves, which are built in pyramid shape, were visible," explained Ruth in a letter dated August 24, the couple's first wedding anniversary.[41]

Flooding also interrupted their journey from Peking to Kaifeng, which, on account of the deluge, involved trains, rickshaws and ferries. The railway was broken or covered in water, forcing passengers to walk through deep mud to where they could board the train or ferry. "All the trunks had to be carried by coolies and the poor men slipped so in the mud," noted Ruth on September 2. "We ourselves were sorry-looking specimens . . ."[42]

Life was far more difficult for the millions of peasants trying to survive through the cyclical flooding and drought, and the ongoing political and military strife. In Shantung, where most of the CLC members were recruited with the help of British Baptist and Anglican missionaries, these catastrophic events, along with myriad psychological and economic reasons, such as the need to earn a living and provide for one's family, continued to embolden young Chinese men to pursue working far from home.

Returning to Shanghai on Easter weekend 1918, Napier and Ruth shared a heart-wrenching goodbye and went their separate ways: Ruth homeward on the *Empress of Japan* via Vancouver, and Napier — a few days later — on a coastal steamer to Weihai-wei. "I shall never forget how my heart and tummy and throat were all mixed up as I watched the boat sail away and I was left behind, soon to make my own voyage to France."[43]

The list of Canadian missionaries who served in China and went overseas with the CLC stretches beyond Arthurs, Auld, Jones, Leslie, Menzies and Smith. From southwestern Ontario were Herbert Boyd of Newton, Homer Brown of East Nissouri, Harry Forbes of Fletcher, Ernest and Robert Struthers of Galt and Edward Wilford of Blyth. William Reeds was also from Ontario, born at Reaboro, northwest of Peterborough, while Arthur Lochead was from Valleyfield, Quebec. From Nova Scotia were James Hattie of Caledonia, Joseph Mowatt of Windsor and George Ross of Blue Mountain. Although Mowatt was born in

Nova Scotia, the 1881 census shows him residing in New Brunswick where his father, Andrew J. Mowatt, was a very successful minister who served in Stellarton, Windsor and Fredericton before he was sent to a church in Montreal, one that sponsored mission work in China.

While Jones and Menzies were professional engineers, six of the other missionaries, Auld, Leslie, Reeds, the two Struthers and Wilford, were medical doctors. All of their skills were urgently needed in war-torn France.

CHAPTER 7

Getting to Know
Weihaiwei

"I hardly recognized myself in the strange uniform which they gave me. My friends would not have known me either . . ."

Tennis and tiffin . . .

Doctors Harry Livingstone and Lou Sebert stared at the large timber beam lying on the ground in front of them and decided they could at least try to lift one end. Moments earlier they had witnessed the heavy post being carried up from the waterfront on the broad shoulders of four young local men.

But even with the leverage of a bamboo pole, the Canadians, who were in reasonably good shape, could not raise the beam to shoulder height.

It was September 9, 1917.

Livingstone and Sebert were spending their first day getting to know their immediate surroundings in the British-leased territory of Weihaiwei. Before setting out on foot from the depot that morning the doctors had wondered what curiosities awaited them along the crescent-shaped beaches and within the old walled town, which was only a short walk or rickshaw ride from the compound.

David Livingstone Collection

The waterfront at Weihaiwei as it appeared in 1917. Note the crescent-shaped beaches and rolling hills above the recruitment depot in the distance.

Shortly after breakfast, while the tide was out, the doctors left camp on foot, heading down towards the shore. Erected on the sand, but far enough from the water to escape high tide, was a modest home inhabited by a fisherman, his wife and their four children. The place was comprised of a few small, low buildings constructed out of "rough granite," each bearing a tiled roof. "Around them we see some small garden beds planted with cabbages and beans, and one small bed of peanuts with long straggly stalks of corn between and in the shadow of an old junk drawn up on shore, several black pigs sound asleep. Ducks are splashing in the shallow water along shore and some chickens are scattered around the garden. The fisherman's wife is washing dirty clothes in a small pool of water behind the house and as she kneels . . . she hammers the clothes with a small heavy stick, on a flat stone then rinses them out in the dirty greenish water . . ."[1]

Livingstone noticed how one of the buildings was covered in lime dust and was, therefore, likely used to make lime from stone collected on the nearby hills. "Not many feet away from the fish-

When not working, Captain Harry Livingstone spent much time touring Weihaiwei, which introduced him to a way of life he had not encountered before.

erman's house was the pier from which all the coolies sail away." Jutting "out into the water," the pier's "iron framework has been eroded by the saltwater so badly that in many places, the beams and girders have fallen away altogether."[2]

That same morning the two men picked their way on hands and knees over a steep, natural breakwater to get to the beach where local women waded into the water to collect oysters off rocks fringed with seaweed. The women used small iron picks with a wooden handle to break the shell and "a small tin affair attached to the forefinger of the right hand" to scoop the oyster into a small, tin dish. "They have their feet bound and we thought perhaps we would see how their feet were deformed as they would likely be barefoot, but were disappointed as they had slippers and stockings on," Livingstone observed from beneath the brim of his pith helmet.[3]

As the two doctors moved cautiously over the slippery rocks, they noticed the bleached exoskeletons of crustaceans and the limp remains of "sea creatures" caught in tidal pools or arrested by the sand. Further along, between the water and windswept bluffs, they crossed the flat, crescent-shaped beach used for CLC parade exercise. At Half Moon Bay they watched fishermen clean and prepare their catch next to bamboo shanties. Nearby were a few children trying to control a couple of rambunctious black goats. "We gave coins to some of the kids who knew how to salute," Livingstone noted in his diary, referring to the children, not the animals. Further along the waterfront stood "some swell bungalows owned by British and other foreigners from Shanghai who summer here."

Before testing their strength with the wooden beam, the officers had been the guests of Sir James Lockhart, the popular head administrator of the British territory of Weihaiwei. Commissioner Lockhart occupied the stately consular residence, which afforded a good view of the bay.[4] The Edinburgh University graduate and former colonial secretary of Hong Kong had presided over the territory since 1902, but had resided in China since 1878. Already fluent in Cantonese, Lockhart had developed a solid working knowledge of northern dialects and by the time Livingstone arrived he had co-authored a manual on Chinese quotations (1893) and a book on Chinese copper coins (1915).

Weihaiwei was a plum posting in a geographical area known for its fresh temperate ocean breezes, sandy beaches and vacationers whose seasonal visits took them away from the sweltering cities and foreign legations in Peking. Family picnics, bathing in the aquamarine surf, shopping for curios in and among the old shops and entertaining guests at formal dinner parties made life memorable, if not perfect, for tourists.

The native population within the territory was spread among hundreds of villages and small market towns. Frugality was essential on account of there being so little arable land, but the afforestation effort, which had occurred during Lockhart's administration, had paid off. The trees, mostly Acacia and firs, had been delivered to government nurseries, sold at nominal

David Livingstone Collection

The bound feet of a mother with her children in Weihaiwei, 1917. The practice was outlawed, but in the more conservative areas of China foot-binding had not disappeared. On the back of this photo Livingstone wrote: "notice shoes on lady."

David Livingstone Collection

Captain Lou Sebert rides a cart hauling water at Weihaiwei, fall 1917.

cost to villagers and then planted around the territory, including windswept Liu-kung Tao (Island), which until the afforestation began was practically treeless.[5]

Tiffin with the mustachioed Scot was followed by a tour of the gardens, where Livingstone and Sebert picked fruit and quietly observed a few local women scrubbing clothes in a stream.[6]

After passing through a local market the men arrived "downtown," where they shopped for souvenirs and visited the post office. On their way back to the depot they followed a dusty road bordered with small honey locust, scrub oak and pine. Magpies chattered and hopped about the trees that had been planted to encourage the Shantung silkworm. Variations of the silkworm larva are found from northern India to the eastern regions of Russia and, while their preferred food is the white mulberry leaf, in Shantung they munch on oak and juniper leaves. For thousands of years the caterpillars have been highly coveted because they produce a cocoon of strong, lustrous fibre that became the source of commercial silk, a multi-million-dollar market that thrived until silk was replaced by popular synthetics in the 1930s. In the 1920s, a ninety-kilogram bale of silk was worth $800 US.

Silk was perishable, and so to reach North American markets it had to be rushed from China across the Pacific in the secured holds of passenger ships, such as the *Empress of Asia*, and then by rail — in airtight, moisture-proof cars — across Canada on the CPR. Each car on a typical eight- to fifteen-car Silk Train hauled up to 470 bales, meaning that each train could transport more than six million dollars' worth of silk to the National Silk Exchange in New York City or to mills along the eastern seaboard. Like the CLC specials, the Silk Trains, with their special boxcars, were guarded and moved quickly across the continent, only stopping for coal and water.[7]

While the officers were returning to the fenced-in recruitment depot, their quiet stroll was interrupted by the harsh sound of several labourers banging on tin plates. The noise, according to Livingstone, was meant to chase the evil spirits away from people who had recently arrived at the depot. Guards saluted as the officers entered through the gate and passed in front of a large reception shed that "at a pinch could accommodate 800 men."[8]

Meanwhile, hundreds — even thousands — of men were accommodated in the large barracks that had been loaned free of charge by the Witwatersrand Native Labour Association of Johannesburg. The only stipulation was that the buildings had to be returned in good condition.[9]

As night fell, Livingstone undressed and crawled into bed beneath the mosquito netting. Hanging above him, too, was anticipation of the work he had been sent halfway around the world to do.

* * *

As mentioned in Chapter One, before the British decided to recruit non-combatant Chinese labourers and flag Weihaiwei as the location for its main depot, consideration had been given to the deployment of armed Chinese soldiers.

In the summer of 1915, the Chinese offered to send 300,000 military labourers and 100,000 rifles to Europe. The scheme, which would have seen the men serving under British officers, was proposed by the politically astute finance minister Liang Shih-i (Liang Shiyi). At the time, the Allied campaign to open a supply route to Russia through the Dardanelles and knock Turkey out of the war by bombarding Istanbul was underway, but not going well. The offensive was desperately short of reinforcements. In France, the Allies had suffered huge losses at Ypres, and by June 19 British attacks were called off after French efforts at Artois had failed amid mounting casualties. Among the questions facing the British was whether the Allied cause would benefit from an influx of armed Chinese labourers.[10]

The Chinese offer had also come shortly after the Chinese president accepted a watered-down version of Japan's Twenty-One Demands.

Liang believed if his proposal for armed labourers were accepted by the British it would provide China with a trained, modern, battle-tested army. More than that, the commitment would send the message that neutral China was willing to fight for the Allies. The aim was to gain a seat at the postwar peace conference, reduce negative foreign influence in China, restrain the crushing Boxer indemnity payments and, especially, regain the Chinese territory taken by Japan when it attacked and defeated the Germans in Shantung. Historian Michael Summerskill notes that the "dominant public preoccupations of men such as President Yuan and Liang had been the unity of China, which was threatened by Japan, and its [China's] financial status, dependent upon foreign loans given in return for promises of revenue not only from the (foreign-built) railways but from other internal sources of income."[11]

Sir John Jordan, the British minister in Peking, thought the proposal was beyond practical and so did Lieutenant-Colonel

David Robertson, the British military attaché in Peking, who described the scheme in a June 12, 1915, memo as "fantastic and improbable" in its given form. However, the subject of utilizing Chinese troops did not disappear and was revisited shortly before the British finally settled on the use of non-combatant labourers from China. By then, however, President Yuán had cancelled his imperial inauguration and died of kidney failure (June 6, 1916) amid much personal disgrace. Internal politics was once again in disarray with the tumultuous rise of warlords in the southwest and a debilitating north-south split.[12]

In a July 25, 1916, cable sent to the British Foreign Secretary, Sir Edward Grey, Jordan again expressed his misgivings about employing armed Chinese troops. His purpose was to share his thoughts on a July 23 memorandum written by Robertson. Jordan told Grey that Robertson's memo divided itself into two parts, one which was "practicable" and the other "hardly practicable" in the present circumstances.

On the practical side was the possible use of non-combatant Chinese labour.

"Both the French and the Russian Governments are utilizing Chinese labourers and artisans for non-combatant purposes in the European war and should it be found desirable to do so, there seems no reason why His Majesty's Government should not adopt the same course. But their employment for combative purposes stands in an entirely different category and would practically involve a revival of the proposal that China should discard her neutrality and join the cause of the Allies. There are no indications she would now be willing to do this or that if she were willing, she would be allowed by Japan to play such a part in European affairs."[13]

This last observation demonstrated the British priority of keeping Japan on side as a wartime ally and not wanting to interfere with its tremendous power and sphere of influence in Shantung province, including its control of Tsingtao and the vast area served by the Shantung railway.

Jordan viewed the internal condition of China as being "so disturbed as to preclude her taking more than a passive role in distant enterprises (such as the war)" and her new school of statesmen would not, in his opinion, "view with favour the prospect of seeing their countrymen assisting European Powers in a struggle on any terms which did not ensure them complete equality of standing and a voice in the subsequent post-war settlement."[14]

Robertson had begun his memo to Jordan with: "In view of possible prolongation of the war into 1917, it seems worth consideration whether it would not be to our advantage to utilize the resources of China more than we do at present for the direct prosecution of the war."

He cited the French scheme that was well underway. "The French Military Attaché here informs me the Chinese labourers are to be used for roadmaking, agriculture work, in factories, and general unskilled work for which able-bodied Frenchmen are required, the object being to release them for service with the Colours." He stated his French counterpart in Peking told him the scheme had been under discussion since the end of 1915, but owing to objections raised by trade unionists in France over the use of Chinese labour in France the idea, had been only recently pursued. "These difficulties were caused, he thought, more by workmen who were reluctant to make close acquaintance with life in the trenches than by fear of Chinese cheap labour," observed Robertson.

The Russian military attaché, meanwhile, had told him tsarist Russia was employing at that time "about 30,000 Chinese labourers" in two mining districts. He added that Germans in China were endeavouring to prevent the enlistment of labourers by "spreading rumours they are to be used in war." Robertson explained the French and Russians were looking at employing the Chinese only for work outside the war zone. "They thus avoid neutrality question. But should we attempt to carry out the

French scheme in England we should without a doubt meet with the same difficulties from our labour organizations as the French are meeting with theirs. For us, therefore, employment of Chinese in England seems out of the question."

British labour reaction to the importation of foreign workers during the war is a subject that demands a wider explanation than can be included here. For the most part, British factory and dock workers remained very patriotic and answered the call of duty throughout the war with tremendous sacrifice on the home front and abroad. Organized labour's resistance to foreign workers entering the country began slowly in 1916, but grew into a "recognizable wave of opposition" by early 1917. British labour had rightfully perceived a threat to their organizations and the livelihoods of those they represented. This opposition would have occurred earlier had trade unions been aware of any talk of importing Chinese labour.

Historian Nicholas J. Griffin believes the War Office's bid in the fall of 1916 to attract a large number of Chinese labourers had got off to a shaky start for a variety of reasons. He cited "unforeseen delays and adversities which dogged the production of the Chinese Labour Corps," the "important role women gradually began to play in keeping up levels of factory output in Britain," and the "inevitable and formal extension of conscription." However, Griffin concluded "the most important factor in late 1916 and early 1917 which militated against the large-scale introduction of Chinese into Britain and, by extrapolation, against the introduction of other types of alien labor was the unexpectedly strong, though brief, resistance of organized labor."[15]

In his memo, Robertson did explain how Chinese soldiers could be utilized, but in the end the British perceived there was only one avenue given the "insurmountable" diplomatic difficulties associated with utilizing Chinese soldiers. "As I have already said," explained Jordan to Grey, "I see no reason why Chinese should not be utilized for road making, transport work, and other subsidiary duties connected with the War for which they have in an eminent degree all the qualifications which Colonel Robertson so justly ascribes to them."[16]

* * *

While the British wrestled with what to do through 1915 and well into 1916, France, facing its own wartime manpower shortage, was recruiting Chinese labourers and sending them to France. It had negotiated terms under a revised scheme for the use of non-combatant Chinese labourers, and as that developed war-neutral China was careful to maintain the facade that the labourers without guns were hired by private contractors, not directly for government service in France. The Germans, of course, did not buy this. To them, one labourer sent to France from a foreign country like China meant at least one more Allied soldier being sent to the front. Despite protests to the Chinese government, the French scheme continued.

Retired French army Colonel Georges Truptil arrived in January 1916, nearly a year before Thomas Bourne, the British top agent for the CLC, arrived at Weihaiwei. The colonel showed up as an "agricultural engineer," pretending to be employed in a non-governmental capacity, but he was working for the French Ministry of War.

On May 14, a contract for recruiting Chinese labour was signed between Truptil and the conveniently established Huimin Company created and led by minister Liang and Wang Keming, the director of the Chinese Industrial Bank. The syndicate agreed to recruit 40,000, later increased to 50,000, labourers between the ages of twenty and thirty, and the first 2,500 were to be hired as soon as possible. The syndicate received a hundred francs for each hired man, a payment meant to cover the syndicate's costs up to the point of each labourer's embarkation.

The contract between the labourers and the syndicate featured more than twenty separate articles or clauses covering everything from length of employment to rations, rates of pay, clothing, medical care and levels of compensation paid to the man's family in the event of death. In broad terms, it stipulated a five-year term of employment that commenced when the labourer left China. Each unskilled labourer was paid a fixed wage of five francs per working day and was expected to work a ten-hour day. Labourers in receipt of board and those in receipt of board and lodging received three francs twenty-five centimes and three francs per day, respectively. Skilled labourers were paid according to their qualifications, determined after they arrived in France. There was also a signing bonus of thirty francs paid to the man's family at the time of embarkation, through a bank chosen by the syndicate.[17]

It also stipulated the labourer would not participate in military operations, but would be employed in public or private industrial or agricultural work in France, Algeria or Morocco. The freedoms guaranteed under French civil law to French citizens would apply to the Chinese labourers, including freedom of religion. In return, the labourer would abide by French law. The contract stated the employer would treat the labourer considerately and he would have the right to the same holidays as French employees at the same work sites. In addition, the contract allowed a day off for the Chinese National Day in October. Bad behaviour or persistent disregard of the rules could result in immediate repatriation.

The first five thousand Chinese labourers enrolled under the French scheme, Service d'organisation des travailleurs coloniaux, left China on July 10, 1916, in the Eastern and Australian Steamship Company's the *Empire*, a clipper-bowed ship of 4,496 gross tons. Occupying what was termed "coolie" steerage, the labourers were bound for Marseille, France. The French also recruited labourers from an area west of Nanking, and from Hong Kong, Shanghai, Tsingtao, the southwestern provinces of Yün-nan (Yunnan) and Szechuan (Sichuan) and southern China.

* * *

The British plan in late November 1916 was to recruit three thousand labourers by December 31.[18] This was to be followed by four thousand a month, starting in January 1917. However, by December 1916 only a hundred men had been enrolled at Weihaiwei. The British had initially considered raising Chinese labour through its colony at Hong Kong, but that was discarded for various political and practical reasons, including the availability of suitable men in Hong Kong and concerns over how well men from southern China could adjust to a colder European climate.

Bourne's appointment as the British War Office's top man at Weihaiwei was a worthy one. Like Canadian missionary James Menzies, Bourne, who left London on October 9, 1916, was an engineer and travelled to China on the Trans-Siberian Railway. Accompanied by a pair of assistants, he arrived on October 28, met with Jordan in Peking, and then completed his trek to Weihaiwei on October 31. Joining him was Robertson, who had favoured Weihaiwei over Hong Kong, and would long be remembered as the architect of the British scheme.

Paid an annual salary of £1,500 and given allowances for travel and incidentals, Bourne, not Robertson, had overall responsibility. Robertson had tremendous respect for Bourne and considered him well qualified. The man, after all, had spent twenty-eight years in China, a large portion of it as engineering chief of the Peking-Hankow (Beijing-Hankoo) Railway.

Unlike the French, the British did not enter into an agreement with a private Chinese syndicate or independent recruiting enterprise. Instead, each labourer signed a contract with what was called the British Emigration Bureau, an agency of the British government.

Seriously undermining the French and British efforts in October 1916 was the infamous Laoxikai Incident, in which French military forces brazenly seized land adjoining the French concession at Tientsin in northern China. French authorities in the concession had been negotiating concession expansion with the Chinese since 1902 and a deal was being worked out when the French rushed ahead, took over the district by force, detained Chinese police, and posted sentries around the new boundary. Public reaction to the sudden land grab was swift and predictable. Anti-French and anti-British news spewed from the press, fanned by German propagandists. Meanwhile, French goods were boycotted and Chinese working for French companies walked off the job. The French recruiting effort was forced to look elsewhere for labour sources within China.

The fallout reached the sputtering British recruitment drive in Shantung, where, in addition to negative Chinese reaction and interference from local officials, the campaign was still hampered by the location of its recruitment depot. The establishment of the second depot at Tsingtao helped to right the situation, as did plans for a second recruitment campaign, to be led by John Pratt, the British consul stationed at Tsinanfu, the capital of Shantung province.

By early 1917, Weihaiwei experienced a dramatic increase in activity.

* * *

British CLC officer Lieutenant B. Manico Gull penned a lengthy and often quoted article that affords a detailed look at the workings of the Weihaiwei depot. His story, published in 1918 in the Shanghai-based newspaper *The Far Eastern Review,* is quite complimentary and includes a description of the camp's layout and the process the men passed through on their way to being accepted or rejected. Beginning with recruits arriving at the pier by lighter, Gull describes recruits noticing the "large white godown (warehouse) with a thatched roof in the middle of a wired compound." Lounging inside and against the wire fence, and studying the new arrivals, were men who had reached the depot the day before "after a cold and hungry trek across country from Chefoo, but who feel already old in experience of comfort and good food." He observes how both "lots of men look pretty disreputable. Their wadded clothes, all very much the worse for wear, in some cases are in rags, odd makeshift bits of cloth untidily adjusted to stop rents and gaps."

The depot's reception shed, states Gull, featured three rows of double bunks running the length of the building: two along each side and one down the middle. Natural light and outside air entered through long, barred windows beneath the eaves. Gull describes the shed as "palatial" compared to the low, narrow confines of the homes the men left behind. There "is a chorus of approval and much merriment as the men stake out their claims on the bunks."

It is more likely the men were — on the whole — a lot less bubbly and simply relieved to have arrived at their destination.

In addition to the reception shed and administration offices there were eight accommodation sheds with the bunks arranged in similar fashion. Each shed accommodated a thousand men. Occupying a cubicle perched like a nest on one of the upper tiers was the shed's prefect, who held a commanding view of the entire room. One of the accommodation buildings was termed the "going away" shed, used on embarkation days, which are described as the most exciting days at the camp.

The depot had separate quarters for police and interpreters, a general hospital, isolation ward, bathing sheds, officers' mess and a large cookhouse with sixteen enormous stoves. Gull describes the general hospital as a "commodious brick building with trestle beds set in rows in a large airy room looking out over the entrance to the harbour." Remaining upbeat, he notes the hospital was never a quarter full. "It is perhaps from the hospital door that one gets the best impression of the depot as a whole," he observes, adding rather artfully that to "the left lies the sea, big with the unanswered questions and hidden possibilities into which, mistlike, each transport filled with coolies sails, diminishes, and disappears." Just to the right are "the hills of the great Shantung promontory sheltering Narcissus Bay" and the walled city. Immediately below, "dropping down in terraces to the white arc of sand beneath the road are godowns, offices, and compounds, all busily preparing for the next embarkation."

Captain Harry Livingstone's initial impressions are less detailed and not as complimentary. His journal was not written for public consumption and so there was no censor looking over his shoulder. "Whole camp is enclosed by high barbed wire fence," he wrote on September 9. "Guards walk around the shacks we occupy, night and day."

On September 10, less than a day and a half after their arrival, Livingstone and Sebert began examining their first Chinese, noting that "250 passed through our hands. Four at a time are brought in to each of us three doctors and by means of an interpreter we managed to get through them. Bracelets, with their number and station on it, were put around their wrist. Photographs and fingerprints were taken." The norm, Livingstone wrote, was for the medical staff to inoculate three thousand men a day. "The coolies are given rice and millet seed which is shovelled out of boxes into smaller boxes for disposal. They also have brown bread. Rained all day and very rough. Lots of mosquitoes in our rooms and also at night — as usual — killed some bed bugs."[19]

Canadian Methodist missionary Gordon Jones, who arrived at Weihaiwei four months ahead of Livingstone, formed his own impressions. "It is a beautiful spot here. Air fresh and crisp. Reminds me of home," he wrote to Clara on May 1, after checking in to a hotel with a nice view. "Situated on a pretty bay. Beautiful blue sky — beautiful blue water . . . quiet hotel, no noise." His only regret was that if he had been informed of how long he was going to be at the depot, he would have arranged for Clara to join him. "Why is it everything connected to the government is so stupidly run? They could have given us some idea of what we were going to do and as far as I can make out there is no reason in the world why I couldn't have waited until June 1st to report. There seems to be changes in dates of coming and going arranged daily."

Jones also outlined for Clara some of the routine work. "The drill we give them is very elementary and easily picked up. I also have to attend to having their hair cut, having them bathed, vaccinated, disinfected. We will have to pick a barber, a shoemaker, and eight policemen from my lot. Will have to find out the trades of the men, give them daily drill ... Meanwhile there is a staff at the depot who signs up the men, writes their contracts, photographs them, takes thumb prints, and gives them brass identity disks."

It is also interesting to note that many of the men had the same name, but were not necessarily related to each other. Others arrived with no name at all and had simply been known by their position within the family, such as "first son," "second son" or something else. This, of course, presented challenges when it came to registering the men.

Jones described for Clara what the men looked like when they emerged from the "sausage factory." "The coolies wore blue suits with some red trimmings, brown caps with red knobs and a brass badge on the cap," he explained, while leaving enough space on the page to sketch the CLC cap badge. "They then get brown canvas knapsacks with a change of clothing, a quilt, and a pair of blankets and a water bottle. The men seem to be a fairly husky lot, averaging better than our Szechuan lot, and their talk is different from ours, but I can get along."[20]

First-hand accounts from Chinese labourers are rare. The Kautz Family YMCA Archives at the University of Minnesota holds an undated article written by W.W. Peter under the title "Yellow Spectacles." Peter was a medical missionary based in Shanghai and the story is an account from a Chinese teacher Peter refers to only as Li. Scholars believe there is no guarantee Li was an actual person who served with the CLC, but suggest the story accurately reflects what labourers thought of the war, the dilemmas they faced prior to enrolment, and what they experienced at Weihaiwei.

"It is a fight between the Central Powers who are good or bad, and the Allies who are bad or good to determine whether right shall prevail against might," states Li. "My difficulty lies in my inability to say which is which. Since missionaries, business men, and especially diplomats from each of these contending nations have been active in China since before my father was born, all I can say is they are very much alike. Good and bad are found together, the good when foreigners work as individuals, the bad when they act as nations . . ."[21]

"One day I saw a notice put out by the British and French authorities calling for thousands of laborers. It was pasted on the walls of the city gate and had the stamp of the local official. Soon a great crowd gathered. We concluded the Germans were winning the war as they prophesied. Why else should it be necessary for England and France to appeal to Chinese to help them? Who was winning the war did not interest me. I saw in this notice an opportunity I had not dreamed would be mine. Then and there I resolved to become a coolie myself in order to visit these foreign countries."[22]

"My friends urged me strongly to give up this strange notion and stay at home where I belonged. They said that what was happening over in France among the foreigners was none of my affair. Let them fight. Only a fool would venture near them at such a time. They fought like very gods of destruction. Did they not have guns which could shoot a shell it took ten men to lift? Shells loaded with such powerful powder as to be able to destroy a whole village a day's journey away? Vapor which could be seen neither by day nor by night, without odor, but so deadly that one full breath killed instantly? Machines like birds able to fly overhead even by night and drop explosives? Boats which in the twinkling of an eye sank beneath the water and yet did not sink? Was it not all very terrible? What could I hope to find out which would make such risks worth while?"[23]

According to the article, Li enrolled in the British scheme, but only after a friend had done so and made it safely to France. "When I arrived there Weihaiwei I had to pass an examination. A foreign doctor felt of my body in different places. He held the flat of his hand over my chest, tapping the fingers with the fingers of his other hand. He examined the pulse of my left hand, but failed to examine the right one. He clamped an instrument into his ears and after shutting his eyes, applied the free end of the instrument to my chest here and there, front and back, while I had to count each time up to three. He opened my mouth to examine my tongue and teeth. He felt of my scalp. Even my eyelids he turned up. I confess I was glad when this gentleman moved on to the next fellow in the line for I had not the slightest idea what he might have in his head to try next. It was the strangest examination I ever saw. I was not asked to write a single character. However, I passed, and moved along inside the wire enclosure. There I found that I was but one of several tens of thousands.

"The day was a turning point in my life. For one thing, I was no longer my own master. I had nothing to say about the food I ate; the clothes I wore or how I wore them; the place where I slept or when I wished to sleep or get up; where I desired to go or the hour of my going or returning . . . My body seemed to be the important thing, for now none concerned himself over what might be going on in my head."

The story noted how the last link between old and new was severed when the clothes Li arrived in were taken and sent home. "I hardly recognized myself in the strange uniform which they gave me . . . I was a changed man outwardly and I was conscious of an inner change already beginning."

Labourer Chiang Ching-hai recalled how he felt when he enrolled. "One knew the teachings of the ancients by heart — one should not, save for a good reason, wander afar while one's parents are still with us," he wrote in his memoir, *Twelve Months as a Coolie.* "My going abroad is an act of impiousness. Chances, it seems, hardly ever come to the gentleman in penury. His desertion of ancestral lands, his traversing of oceans — would that be loyalty, or disloyalty?"[24]

The story of Han Ch'ün-fa is indicative of how some families wanted their sons to remain in China. After boarding a train for Tsingtao, he hid in a washroom to escape his family, which went looking for him. When an older brother caught up to Han at Tsingtao he was unable to convince him to return home. The older brother then took out a pair of scissors, cut off Han's queue, and took it home to his parents.[25] This was clearly a sign of how conservative Shantung was; that men still had queues. In many other parts of China, the queue, imposed by the Qing dynasty, was long gone.

Part Two: China to Canada

CHAPTER 8

Examinations and Inoculations

"The coolies were all stowed away in the hold. We said goodbye to some nice boys."

Trachoma sunrise and a "green-faced robber . . ."

When Dr. Harry Livingstone woke on the morning of September 11, 1917, the full weight of his assignment was on his mind. He was about to begin his first day at work and, in addition to being far from home in a strange land, he realized the recruitment depot was no small operation and more akin to a processing plant.

The trickle of recruits in late 1916 had turned into a torrent and the dusty camp had been bustling with activity for several months. In and around the depot, young Chinese men — accepted into the CLC for their strong bodies and tolerance for harsh weather — practised drill, while others stood or squatted on the dry earth or against sun-bleached buildings. All of them had been examined and inoculated for typhoid and the brass bracelet, riveted to their wrist, bore their registration number.

Livingstone had brought along a Kodak camera and he used it to great effect, capturing photographs of men exercising in the

David Livingstone Collection

Labourers exercise at the Weihaiwei recruitment depot, 1917.

yard, having their eyes checked, their hair cut or just hanging around outside the huts. Some of the images show groups of men, bare-chested or in new uniforms, complete with large, broad-brimmed hats, and soft shoes. Many, especially those from outside the traditionally conservative territory of Weihaiwei, looked forward to getting rid of the Manchu hairstyle and its long, plaited queue.

*   *   *

For the British there was no longer the serious problem of finding enough Chinese men to send to France. While recruitment efforts had been stepped up, it was mostly the Chinese who turned the scheme into a success because of the personal reasons they had for wanting to work, even if it meant travelling halfway around the world. British politicians and government officials in London, the British legation in Peking and hard-working men like Thomas Bourne, David Robertson and John Pratt developed many of the ideas and provided the wherewithal to get the men overseas, but these efforts would have failed without the men.

* * *

After an extensive tour of Shantung province in December 1916, including stops at Chefoo, Tsingtao and Weihaiwei, Pratt, who was working under the direction of British authorities at Peking, was focused on a new, concerted effort to recruit Chinese. He was relying on British subjects, mainly missionaries, to recruit labourers along the east-west railway corridor between Tsingtao on Kiaochow Bay and Tsinanfu (Jinan), a distance of roughly four hundred kilometres. The latter was the provincial capital where the railway connected to China's main north-south network from Peking through Tientsin to Nanking and Shanghai. Built by the Germans during their lease in Shantung, the Shan-tung railway — which some automatically called the "Japanese Railway" — had been controlled by the Japanese after its victory at Tsingtao in 1914. Pratt's assignment was to transport recruits to Tsingtao on the railway and then move them north by coastal steamer to Weihaiwei.

The Japanese, who preferred the British use of Chinese labour-ers over Chinese soldiers, were consulted and went along with the plan, which would not give China centralized armed forces after the war.[1] Naturally, there were concerns over whether neutral China would object to British recruiting beyond the boundary of their leased territory. Months earlier, British fears regarding interference from the Chinese government had been articulated in a cable dated September 30, 1916, while the leased territory at Weihaiwei was being considered as the best location for the recruitment depot.

Prior to dispatching Bourne to China and setting the "machin-ery going," the British Foreign Office considered whether it was "necessary or advisable to say anything to the Chinese Government first." The same cable also makes it clear the British were not shy of considering recruitment outside of their leased territory. "The procedure is that the local recruiting agents who would be Chinese should endeavour in Chinese territory to get coolies in large numbers to go to Weihaiwei where they would be regularly recruited as though they were the ordinary inhabitants of that district in order that the battalions may be externally British." The cable asked whether this was "practicable," then warned if the Chinese were told of the plan to recruit at Weihaiwei and if the Chinese government saw fit to obstruct, "the scheme would no doubt be bound to fail."[2]

So, without the sanction of the Chinese government, it seems the British had quietly moved ahead in the early fall of 1916 with their plan to recruit in the territory and even beyond. At the same time they were still worried about interference from local officials and others who had heard about the scheme or saw the recruitment posters in public buildings. Participation in a war that had given Japan an excuse to seize the German-held territory at Tsingtao and then issue China a set of paralyzing demands was not sitting well with influential people. Still, when local Chinese officials apprehended two British recruiters outside the Weihaiwei territory, the Chinese Foreign Ministry told the local officials not to interfere.

The idea to expand the recruitment drive was forwarded to London in mid-January and coincided with ongoing efforts to counter local opposition. The timing was rather crucial because many Shantung men would — in a few months — be commencing their annual migration to work colonies in Manchuria. The Chinese government knew of this new plan to recruit from a wider area, and on January 4 its foreign minister asked Beilby Alston, the British chargé d'affaires in Peking, whether China, which had yet to declare war on Germany or Austria, would gain representation at a postwar peace conference.[3]

Less than one-quarter the size of France, Shantung province at the time had roughly the same number of people.[4] It was, as

Pratt surmised, full of recruiting potential even if local officials objected. German agents and propagandists were, of course, also working against French and British recruitment by using the press, intimidating the Chinese government and exposing local officials, who were assisting the British effort, to bribery.[5] Many of the local agitators — foreign or otherwise — remained focused on the war as being "a European war," and said any man joining the CLC was putting himself and his family at great risk.

The anti-recruitment leaflets tried to frighten men into believing if they joined and died overseas their soul would wander forever because their death did not occur at home or in China.

A November 14, 1916, memo from the War Office to Sir John Jordan in Peking illustrates how concerned the British were about the interference and its origins. "Is the scheme being opposed by the Chinese Government and local officials, and, if so, would it be better to take them into our confidence as was done by the French? Or even to come to some private financial arrangement with them on the lines of what was openly done in the case of South Africa."[6]

An article dealing with recruitment efforts in southeastern China, attributed to an organization calling itself the Kung Ho Association of Amoy, is an example of the propaganda circulated by opponents: "Since the outbreak of the European war the rivers have been filled with corpses and the sea dyed red with blood . . . and young men are daily becoming less numerous." It went on to state that once the labourers were on board ship they would "be very ill and will be able neither to sit or lie down or eat [sic]; when they arrive in the Southern seas they will be beaten with whips and very likely die. Their families will not know whether they are alive or dead. All this is however of little importance compared to the probability that they will be sent to the front to do all kinds of coolie work . . . or be disguised and sent into the fighting to be killed by the enemy . . ."[7]

By late December 1916, the British had responded with posters and leaflets written in Chinese to counter the propaganda "concocted by the Germans" and distributed in Shantung that aimed to convince the Chinese that "certain death" awaited those who went overseas. "The ultimate result of distributing the leaflet may well be to increase in volume the stream of recruits at present trickling into Weihaiwei, but its immediate and ostensible purpose is merely to deny and counteract the lying German propaganda," stated Pratt.[8]

Titled "The Truth about Coolie Recruiting," the British posters and leaflets stated many of the "lying statements" were from "evilly disposed persons" who want to prevent "Chinese workmen from earning a living" while engaged behind the lines on railways, roads, factories, docks, mines, fields and forests. "They will on no account be used as soldiers, nor will they go anywhere where fighting is taking place." The same article stated the British "have not sent men to recruit coolies on Chinese territory, but are recruiting them on the leased territory of Wei Hai Wei and are offering most generous terms."

Clearly by then the British effort was recruiting men or attracting men from beyond the leased territory. The advantage of using Tsingtao as an independent depot had also become apparent, due to its railway connection and excellent port facilities. By March 1917, labourers were being sent directly from Tsingtao to Europe.

The "generous terms" and regulations outlined by the British in a notice issued around that time stated that on "no account will the labourers be made use of as soldiers, nor will they be appointed work in fighting areas, or in any dangerous places." Among the regulations listed on the notice were:

> 1) Coolies must be between the ages of 20 and 40 and must have a good physique and be free from sickness.
>
> 2) On arrival at the Emigration Bureau depot and after medical examination, if the examination be satisfactory,

a bonus of $10 Mex [Mexican] will be given, and on embarkation a further sum of $10 Mex. will be issued. This bonus is not included in pay or family allowances but is separate.

3) After the coolies have arrived in Europe pay at the rate of $12 Mex. per month will be paid and a further sum of $10 Mex. family allowance (paid in China).

4) After enlistment the coolies will be supplied by the Bureau with clothes, food, boots, and hats, lighting, lodging, and every other necessary [sic]. Not one minutest part of cash will be deducted from the coolies pay for these things.

5) Family allowance will commence one month after embarkation.

One of the men who embarked at Tsingtao was Pi Ts'ui Te (Bi Cuide) from the Shantung village of Zhuhutongyu (Shangyu). He was one of eleven from that village who joined the CLC and it is believed he sailed from Tsingtao in the fall of 1917 with the identity or registration number 97237. In an interview for this book, his granddaughter, Cheng Ling, explained her grandfather was married with five children and his wife was pregnant (with Cheng Ling's father) when he left for France. His wife was very much against his decision to leave, and warned him that if he insisted on going he should not bother to return home.

Sadly, Pi Ts'ui Te did not make it back. While with the CLC he was employed as cook, but on September 27, 1919, while members of the corps were still overseas mopping up the battlefields, he was killed after being sent out to detect and mark the locations of unexploded bombs. Pi Ts'ui Te is buried at the CWGC cemetery at Beaulencourt, France.

The man's wife never forgave herself for saying what she did, nor did the family. Of the eleven men from the village who joined CLC, Cheng Ling's grandfather was the only one who did not return. Asked why she thinks her grandfather joined the CLC, Cheng Ling offered: "The family, like many others from rural Shandong, was very poor and he wanted to earn extra money to feed the entire family."

She said there are no written records of the eleven men and everything she has learned about them has been passed down by word of mouth. Like many descendants, she is hoping to learn more about her grandfather, especially his date of birth and what he looked like, although she believes he may have been physically comparable to his brother and her father, "both heavy set and about 1.7 metres tall" (around five-foot-six).[9]

Lieutenant John McDonald, who had parted company with Livingstone and Sebert at Shanghai, worked at Tsingtao, but only until September 23, 1917, when he boarded the *Monteagle* with a CLC contingent bound for Vancouver.

The utilization of Chinese-speaking British missionaries living in towns along the Shantung railway proved to be the vital link between the labourers and their families. Also used as recruiting agents, these men were entrusted with the distribution of the CLC family allowances or allotments that made the scheme so attractive to the Chinese and so successful for the British. Although previously despised, missionaries were enjoying new-found respect and influence among the Chinese.

Scholar Zhang Yan states "No fewer than nine British Protestant missionary organizations were at work in Shantung during the Labour Corps recruitment drive."[10] It is clear that without the missionaries and the work they did from their locations along the railway, the recruitment drive would have continued to stumble.

Baptist missionaries Albert Castleton and George Fisk were among those who understood how their administrative duties in Shantung connected with the recruitment campaign and the financial arrangements necessary to support men's families while they were away.[11] The British-based Anglican Society for the Propagation of the Gospel also had much influence. Reverend Francis Griffith stated it was not at all difficult to recruit labourers for the British. "If I could say that I was going with them (the labourers) and to take care of them I could recruit up to indefinite numbers." He noted that thousands passed through his hands, starting in February 1917.[12]

With the British recruiting from a wider area and relying heavily on missionaries to help spread the word, the recruitment campaign moved ahead. More and more men considered the CLC as another viable option to generate an income.

By the time Livingstone and Sebert arrived at Weihaiwei in early September 1917, the British had already registered, examined, outfitted and transported thousands of men.

"Taken out of the reception shed in batches, they pass into a room in the centre of the Depot where, stark naked, they are tested in exactly the same manner as a British Tommy," noted Lieutenant B. Manico Gull. Wearing a brass bracelet, the successful candidates emerged "from the nude anxiety of the doctor's chamber to be clothed in Depot garments, his old clothes remaining in a heap on the floor." The next step was the paperwork to record the labourer's name, age, height, next-of-kin and date of enrolment. Also recorded was the name and address of the person who would receive his allotment while he was in France. From there each labourer was assigned to a fifteen-man section, tested on his ability to speak English and asked to state his previous occupation. Moving on, each man was handed a little identification booklet, which included a head-and-shoulder photo and his fingerprints.

Temporarily divided into groups composed of roughly 475 men each, these companies included some 440 ordinary labourers, an interpreter who also performed the duties of a clerk and a "head ganger" whose status within the CLC was similar to a company sergeant major. There were also half a dozen "class-one gangers," which was the equivalent to a sergeant, eight "class-two gangers" or corporals, and sixteen "class-three gangers" or lance corporals. The men who held these non-military positions of authority were usually elected by their peers for their leadership abilities or because they were more literate. Nothing, however, could guarantee these units would remain intact after arrival in France.

For the journey halfway around the world each labourer was issued a brown canvas raincoat, two sets of cotton summer clothes, a padded woollen winter coat, two pairs of shoes and a felt hat. He also received a canvas rucksack that included a blanket, brush, two combs, a small towel, soap, a plate, a cup, a water bottle and a pair of chopsticks. Finding a cheap but warm winter coat proved difficult because of the prohibitive price of serge, noted one memorandum. "The great disadvantage of wadded clothing, which is admirable for a dry cold climate like North China, is the difficulty in drying it once it had become wet. This disadvantage has been neutralized to a large extent by using a good quality of pressed cotton wool instead of raw cotton which gets into balls when wet, and by providing coolies with a raincoat ... The latter is made of brown canvas and though not absolutely waterproof is very nearly so."[13]

Historians have suggested the French contract was better than the English one. While the French hired the Chinese under a five-year term, the British stipulated three years. Both specified a ten-hour work day, but only the French offered overtime pay for assigned work. While the French paid a daily wage higher than the British, both schemes offered a signing bonus, free passage, accommodation, food, medical services and a uniform. Other differences centred on the levels of compensation paid for disablement or partial disablement, and death. Under the latter, a family whose son died while with the British scheme was compensated for 375 days after the death. Under the French scheme the assistance lasted between 54 and 108 days.

Another major difference between the two schemes was the legal jurisdiction they would live under in France. The French applied the use of civil law, while members of the British Chinese Labour Corps would be under British military law. Remarkably, this was not written into their contract or made clear to the labourers until they arrived in France. What makes this all the more interesting is that it was the French who insisted the British apply military law to those recruited under the War Office. The rationale appears to be that while the French were importing labour into their own country, the British were bringing the labourers to a foreign country, France. So, when it came to the law, the labourers would be treated as if they were soldiers in the British Army, subject to the various levels of court martial, including field general court martial with the possibility of execution by firing squad.

* * *

On September 11, 1917, Livingstone and Sebert were not so much concerned about the contractual arrangements as they were with the immediate health of the men lining up at the depot's hospital. There were twenty-one grounds on which a candidate could be rejected, including bad teeth, beriberi, bronchitis, epilepsy, hysteria, malaria, mumps, serious physical abnormalities or ailments, scarlet fever, smallpox, trachoma, tuberculosis and venereal disease. Reports of the rejection rate at Weihaiwei ranged from 30 to 60 per cent.[14] Some of the first recruits who journeyed to the depot during the bitter winter of 1916–17 presented with respiratory illness and frostbite.

Trachoma, one of the world's leading causes of preventable, irreversible blindness, was the most common medical condition diagnosed among the labourers, and one of the main reasons for rejection. Between March and December 1917, which includes the time Livingstone and Sebert were there, doctors discovered

678 cases of trachoma and 135 cases of conjunctivitis, equalling more than eighty-one eye cases per month. At least 35 per cent of the total in-patients over the same period suffered from the highly contagious disease caused by the bacterium *Chlamydia trachomatis*. Easily spread through human contact, shared towels and clothes, and transferred by flies that come into contact with the eyes or nose of an infected person, trachoma was extremely hard to control in camps and onboard ships. If left untreated it causes severe scarring of the inside of the eyelid and as the inner lining of the eyelid deforms, the eyelashes turn in and scratch the cornea, the transparent outer surface of the eye.

Livingstone, Sebert and other doctors looked for irritation of the eyes and eyelids, swollen eyelids, mucous or pus draining from the eyes, sensitivity to light and clouding of the cornea.

Diagnosing trachoma involved the delicate procedure of turning the eyelids of each patient inside out to look for scarring. For prophylactic treatment, doctors usually relied on daily instillations of zinc and boric acid drops. Individual examinations did not take long, but with hundreds of men for each doctor to examine in a morning or afternoon it was time-consuming. It also meant being on your feet — at eye level — most of the day.

The examinations were usually done outdoors under direct sunlight, and the doctor usually stood with his back to the sun, allowing the light to pass over his shoulder directly onto the eyes of his patient. To examine the right eye, the physician placed his right thumb on the lower lid and then grasped the skin of the upper lid between his left thumb and left second finger. The patient was then asked to look down or shut his eyes. A quick rolling motion backwards using the finger and thumb of the left hand everted the upper lid while a pull downwards at the same time with the thumb on the lower lid exposed the inner surface of that lid and also helped with the eversion of the upper lid. For the left eye the doctor's hands were reversed.[15]

The importance of a thorough eye exam became more apparent

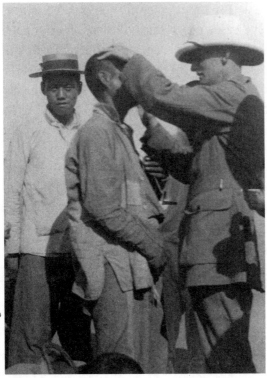

David Livingstone Collection

While conducting an eye exam at Weihaiwei, Captain Harry Livingstone looks for signs of trachoma.

as the CLC recruitments increased through 1917. Earlier that year, many trachoma cases were not caught and men suffering from the disease made it onto the ships, to Canada and France. Reports from medical officers travelling with the overseas contingents included long lists of Chinese men who were infected while crossing the Pacific or shortly after arriving in Canada, where they remained in quarantine on Vancouver Island.

In France, medical authorities, after discovering the disease among Egyptian and then Chinese labourers, issued the edict "that no cases with definite trachomatous granulations or any acute conjunctivitis should be allowed to embark from Egypt or China or to disembark in France."[16] A January 1920 article in the *British Journal of Ophthalmology* observed that examining doctors in China were constantly changed and so there was a varying standard of requirement for a "clean" eye, as well as a varying degree of experience in the detection of trachoma. The article also noted how life on a crowded transport ship "provides ideal conditions" for the rapid spread of the disease.[17]

One CLC company in France saw fifteen cases swell to eighty-one within eight weeks. This infection rate helped prompt medical authorities at the CLC hospital at Noyelles-sur-Mer to segregate men into companies using an X, Y, Z classification system. Each company had roughly five hundred men and those assigned to "X" had been declared infection-free and could be assigned to various companies. Those sent to "Y" companies may have had trachoma or only conjunctivitis, while those sent to a "Z" were definitely infected. There were fifteen and a half "Z" companies totalling 7,750 men, or roughly 8 per cent of the total number of men enrolled in the CLC.[18]

Livingstone and Sebert had read the reports and took them very seriously, but the pressure to catch all cases and prevent the disease from spreading beyond the depot remained high throughout their time at Weihaiwei.

After spending the morning of September 11 staring into the eyes of dozens of labourers, the two doctors took a break and while touring one of the old cities in the territory realized how easy it was for disease to spread. "You enter the city through a small arch and the streets were very dirty . . . a sewer ran right down main street." The next day the doctors examined 223 men and mixed among the usual trachoma cases Livingstone noted "some queer cases," including "morphine fiends" with large scars all over. There were men with abscesses, pin worms in their feces and those with a "peculiar pattern" on their chests apparently caused by "pinching the skin, which lasts seven days and cures indigestion."[19]

Such discoveries were not surprising to the doctors, who generally worked from early morning to late afternoon with most of their time taken up with vaccinations. "Inoculated all morning with Chinese assistants and did some dressings in dispensary. A couple of new boatloads of new coolies arrived today," he noted on September 13. Three days later, while he was conducting more examinations, the *Empress of Japan* arrived on schedule. "Nine-hundred-and-fifty coolies went away. First of all they came along in single file and were examined by the doctor. Then their small

David Livingstone Collection

Captain Lou Sebert and a Chinese interpreter enjoy bowls of rice in Weihaiwei, 1917.

parcels were examined for gambling devices and matches. Before this their old clothes were taken away, and after doctor looked them over they had another antiseptic bath and were dried off as they marched along. They were then given a new suit and underwear . . . a suit of dark blue with red cord buttons and . . . handed their kit . . . etc. Just before this they put on stockings, like our regular bandages tied on by a piece of blue tape . . . As they went out with their kits they were given straw hats with CLC on a band meaning Coolie Labour Corps [sic]. Then they form up outside and receive their different section numbers which is pinned on their tunic."[20]

Livingstone watched as the men eagerly accepted a five-dollar bill from the pay clerk before proceeding to the wharf. Then, as they marched towards their destinies, other Chinese lit firecrackers to

David Livingstone Collection

Columns of CLC recruits drill on the beach at Weihaiwei.

bring good luck to the voyage. Livingstone, Sebert and other doctors joined the men packed shoulder to shoulder on a lighter pulled by a tug to the awaiting *Empress.* "The coolies were all stowed away in the hold. We said goodbye to a number of nice boys we knew well as dressers (orderlies) and then headed back to shore."

One late afternoon, while out for a stroll, Livingstone encountered a Chinese man who had been rejected at the depot. "He remained on his knees and said he would not get up unless we allowed him to go to France." After handing the man a chit for food, the doctor continued on his way. Later, while passing by the same spot, Livingstone found the man "lying on ground with a rope around his neck." The desperate man eventually stood up and walked away.[21]

On October 5, it was time for Livingstone and Sebert to part. The *Teesta* arrived at noon and when she sailed that evening, Sebert, the man who had welcomed Livingstone into the CAMC in London, Ontario, was on board along with more than 2,050 labourers. "Went aboard and saw the labourers safely stowed away," Livingstone wrote. "Tang Loon Pèn and his friend left with the dressers and I was sorry to see them go. We had great fun together teaching one another the languages. Boat pulled out at 6:30 and we waved goodbye from the verandah . . . Lonely without Sebert."

The ship's manifest lists Sebert among "eight government officers." Skippered by T. Coleborn, the ship had departed Hong Kong on October 1, taking four days to reach Weihaiwei. She arrived in Vancouver on October 27, 1917, and the manifest indicates none of her passengers were quarantined. At three o'clock the next morning, Sebert boarded one of three trains bound for Montreal. Altogether the three CPR specials carried 1,837 Chinese labourers; 147 guards, including four Canadian officers and three sergeants; seven British officers and two doctors.

Arriving in Montreal on November 2, the contingent boarded the *Missanabie*, which arrived in Liverpool on November 19, roughly forty-five days after Sebert and the labourers began their journey from Weihaiwei. With enemy U-boats claiming ships and lives, there was no such thing as safe passage. The *Missanabie* was torpedoed just south of Ireland ten months later on September 9, 1918, by U-*87*. Forty-five souls were lost, ranging in age from fourteen-year-old cabin boy William Stuttle to sixty-four-year-old Charles Lodge, a bathroom steward. Built by Barclay, Curie & Co. Ltd., Glasgow and owned by Canadian Pacific Steamship (Canadian Pacific Ocean Service), she was sailing from Liverpool to New York when the torpedo found her eighty-four kilometres southeast of Daunt Rock, Ireland.[22]

For Livingstone, the rush of daily medical parades continued through October. He did, however, find time to stroll and learn more about the Chinese and their culture. After one long day at the hospital he attended a theatrical performance and was impressed by the "clever acrobatic work and tumbling," the beautiful costumes and the main character, a "green-faced robber."[23]

Three days after Sebert's departure, he headed down to the wharf where he caught the ferry to Liu-kung Tao. His purpose was to visit the island and say hello to Dr. Charles Crompton, who, like Livingstone, had been sent to Weihaiwei to examine the labourers. The Brantford, Ontario, doctor's wartime service had commenced in March 1915 when, at age twenty-three, he joined No. 4 General Hospital in Toronto. Three months later he was overseas, but by early September 1916, while he was engaged as a medical officer at Salonika, Crompton's health deteriorated and he was soon on his way to losing twenty pounds. The clinical diagnosis was dysentery and pulmonary tuberculosis.[24]

He was invalided to Malta, then Britain and finally to Canada in late November. On March 6, 1917, a medical board ruled he was "unfit for overseas service, but fit for home service." It seems "unfit for overseas service" did not apply to service in China with the CLC.

At the time of Livingstone's social call, Crompton had been at Weihaiwei for a month, but had suffered a recurrence of dysentery and was admitted to the Royal Navy hospital on the island. Livingstone welcomed the chance to get out on the water and breathe in the fresh air while making good on a personal promise to visit a colleague, not to mention a fellow Canadian. As it turned out, Crompton was "getting along fine from his attack . . ."[25]

There was not a lot of time for socializing, but on October 11, after conducting hundreds of examinations, Livingstone taught a few small children how to count to three in English. He then surprised himself by buying a dog with only three good legs. The impulsive buyer had no idea what he would do with the little creature, but it was hard to pass up the opportunity. The doctor was not an overly sentimental man and there is nothing in his diary to suggest he was overtly homesick, but he clearly missed his folks and Listowel. Letters did arrive from Canada, including one from dear Roland, but Livingstone seems to have been able to compartmentalize his life. For the time being, his work was here and someday, hopefully, it and the rest of his time would be spent back there in southwestern Ontario. Nevertheless, before turning out the light that night, what he wanted most were letters from home and "some war news."

The next day, Livingstone was shocked by the sanitary conditions he was shown at a local school. He also noticed more schoolgirls with bound feet, even though the painfully debilitating custom had been banned. The day ended with a riot in the compound when frustrations boiled over between two groups of labourers. Livingstone was called in to help separate the combatants who were "hammering each other with poles and shovels. I nearly received a shovel on my head."

Four days later it was the weather that got angry. High winds sent breakers onto the beaches while rain, mixed with sand and dust, blasted the camp. That was also the day Crompton was discharged from hospital. His help was needed, especially on the day three thousand men were lined up for inoculations. "Boy in inoculation room came out with many English words as we worked," noted Livingstone. "One was a prayer he had likely learned in a mission school." Impressed by this, the doctor, in anticipation of Crompton's return, taught the youngster to say, "Hello Charlie." All of this, of course, surprised Charlie Crompton when he entered the room.

Before leaving Weihaiwei for good, Livingstone took time to say goodbye to people he had worked with or met often during his long strolls outside the camp. His diary notes a purse full of "coppers" went to a vagrant he had frequently bumped into and that a little cash went to a couple of boys who worked in the depot's mess. The entry for October 29, his last full day at Weihaiwei, begins with: "Very wet and windy and big sea running. *Empress of Russia* arrived at 10 o'clock during the night and when I woke she was at anchor out in harbour."[26]

The small-town doctor was about to take his next big leap.

CHAPTER 9

Veil of Secrecy

". . . it is desired that the movement through Canada shall occur without any publicity whatever . . ."

Loose lips sink . . .

Rain dripped off men's faces onto their woolen coats while they stood in line in Weihaiwei on the northeastern coast of China's Shantung province. The storm had whipped the bay into a swelling grey mass streaked with foam and the cold spray from the huge breakers was "thrown up into the compound." It was October 29, 1917, and formed up along the crescent beach — facing the waves and the unknown — 2,290 labourers stood with the small cadre of British and Canadian officers assigned to accompany them to Europe via Canada.

A few hours earlier the labourers had awoken in their bunks knowing this was the day. The "different companies paraded in long lines, each man wrapped in his grey blanket and shivering in the cold air," wrote Livingstone, who would travel to France with a young, but very devoted batman named Chaug.[1]

Once again, hundreds of men entered the sheds and emerged

out the other side with a new set of clothes and the standard kit. As usual, gambling devices and matches were taken away, but also small vials of Chinese earth that some men had wanted to have placed in their coffin should they die and be buried in a foreign land.[2]

From start to finish, the factory-like processing of the men moved along with great efficiency. "They were completely changed in appearance and looked fine," noted Livingstone who stood at the end of the finish line. "Most of them had their brown raincoats on by this time and it was funny to see the men exchanging slippers in order to get a pair that would fit."[3]

The doctor watched as the men were organized into sections before each man had a small brass plate, identifying his section number, pinned to the front of his jacket.

The wharf was neither long nor strong enough for the ocean steamers, and so the men, many of whom had never been to sea before, faced a wet and rough transfer to the *Empress of Russia* on lighters pulled by tugs. One delay followed another and so it was decided to march the contingent back up the hill and out of the rain to the accommodation sheds while Livingstone and several other officers boarded the lighter *Alexandria*, which was being pounded against the wharf. Once away, the boat slowly worked against the waves toward the anchored *Russia* and when she finally came alongside she damaged her bow by slamming into the steamship.[4]

With the *Alexandria*'s party safely on board, the labourers followed; marched out of the accommodation sheds for the second time and then down to the wharf. Despite the rain, strings of firecrackers were lit by well-wishers lining the beach. Each fiery pop . . . pop . . . pop meant "to assure a good voyage, free from devils and submarines . . ."

The lighter, crammed with the first group of roughly a thousand men, was slammed by powerful waves while being towed by the tug *Hespeler*. Men were soaked and threw up their breakfast.

David Livingstone Collection

Captain Lou Sebert poses with young hospital orderlies at Weihaiwei.

It was the beginning of a nasty voyage.

Once on board the great ship, the Chinese were immediately "marched down and stowed in their bunks," wrote Livingstone. Anyone who tried to get up before the anchor was raised "got a crack from a stick."

Skippered by Captain Samuel Robinson, the *Russia* got underway shortly before 4 p.m. At that point the labourers were permitted to come up on deck. Most "crowded the rail . . . many with tears in their eyes as the old familiar hills and mountains of their native land faded from view and a big new world of wonders lay before them," noted the doctor, who was also leaving a place he had grown to like.

Compared to the *Japan*'s gross tonnage of 5,940 and length of 485 feet, the *Russia* was 16,810 and 592 feet, bow to stern.[5] By 1917 she was fitted to carry 296 first-class passengers, eighty-four second class, and 800 in steerage, the latter typically assigned to Asians on trans-Pacific crossings.[6] The war and the rush to get men overseas, however, guaranteed the number in steerage on many of the CLC transports greatly exceeded the number of passengers the ships were fitted to carry, which resulted in a shortage of lifeboats due to the waiving of safety regulations. So, with nearly 2,300 labourers crammed into her lower decks, the *Russia* was exceeding her normal steerage capacity almost threefold. As a second- or tourist-class passenger, Livingstone assumed his journey back across the Pacific that fall would be more comfortable than what he, Sebert and McDonald experienced on the much smaller *Empress of Japan* in 1916.

He was in for a surprise.

Like her sister ship, the *Empress of Asia*, the *Russia* was a coal-fired quadruple-screw vessel driven by immense turbines. She burned an average of 311.2 tons of coal per day to average 18.46 knots. On a typical round trip voyage between the Orient and Vancouver, the ship burned in excess of ten thousand tons.[7] Pennants of smoke from her three sloped stacks could be seen from several kilometres away. The *Russia* was a fast ship; her first trans-Pacific voyage in 1913, which took nine days, five hours, twenty-nine minutes from Yokohama to William Head (Race Rocks), beat the previous record set by the *Japan*.[8]

* * *

The first ship to transport CLC men to Canada had been, coincidentally, the same ship Livingstone boarded. Fortunately, detailed accounts of that earlier voyage, which began at Hong Kong on March 15, 1917, survive. After reaching Weihaiwei on the nineteenth, the *Russia* took on roughly the same number of labourers that accompanied Livingstone. From Weihaiwei she followed the usual route, heading southeast across the Yellow Sea and then dropping anchor at Nagasaki, where she took on 3,200 tons of coal — at the rate of 533 tons per hour.[9] She also boarded civilian passengers, who enjoyed comfortable, well-appointed berths, including first-class rooms with brass bedsteads and hot and cold running water.

The upper decks were strictly out of bounds for the Chinese, but occasionally one or two got a glimpse of how the other half travelled. "During the first night some of them, full of curiosity, made an uninvited tour of the ship, visiting staterooms, engine room, and even the bridge," recalled British soldier Frank Heath, who accompanied the CLC.[10]

Heath's memoir, written after the war, states he boarded the *Empress of Asia* at Hong Kong in early March 1917. However, the *Asia* was, at the time, in Vancouver and did not leave the Canadian port for the Far East until March 16. She did not arrive back at Vancouver until April 30. Heath and his escort party were clearly on board the *Russia*, and the passenger manifest for the *Russia*'s voyage from Hong Kong on March 15 confirms this, noting among other details that the ship arrived at Victoria on April 3.[11]

British Second Lieutenant Daryl Klein also noticed labourers in places where they should not have been. "They loitered in the galleys, befriended the cooks, and watched the rice bubbling and steaming in half a dozen enormous cauldrons. In the holds they climbed up into the topmost bunks and fondled the steel plates and rivets of the decks. Defying their own police, they ventured into forbidden places, the boat deck for instance, where the boatswain caught them and lashed at them with a davit rope."[12]

After welcoming additional tourists and businessmen at Yokohama, the *Russia* followed the northern route across the Pacific, and arrived with the first contingent of CLC labourers at the William Head Quarantine Station. From Weihaiwei to Canada's West Coast she had logged 9,083 kilometres.

* * *

Well before the *Russia* delivered the first CLC to William Head, Canadian authorities were busy preparing for the first top-secret consignments of "coolies" destined for the special trains at Vancouver. On March 12, three days before *Russia* sailed from Hong Kong for Weihaiwei, Canada's Superintendent of Immigration, William Duncan (W.D.) Scott, issued the highly classified instructions to the CPR's head office in Montreal and to Canada's chief wartime censor, Ernest J. Chambers.

The edict was clear: News of the CLC must be suppressed.

The government, under its controversial *War Measures Act,* certainly had the power to do that. Passed on August 22, 1914, but retroactive to August 4, the *Act* gave broad emergency powers to the federal cabinet. It paved the way to govern by order-in-council, bypassing the House of Commons and the Senate, when it perceived the existence of "war, invasion, or insurrection, real or apprehended (anticipated)." The *Act* and subsequent orders-in-council gave cabinet power to censor all forms of public communication and expression deemed potentially useful to the enemy, harmful to Canadian morale, critical of military policy or Canada's ability to contribute to the war. Anyone caught contravening the *Act* faced the possibility of a five-year prison term, a five-thousand-dollar fine or both, and unlike the practice under common law, it was up to the accused to prove his or her innocence.

A newspaper story that include sensitive information relating to the departure of the First Canadian Contingent in 1914 prompted the government to give authorities more power over the mainstream and non-mainstream press. The story had also triggered a concerned response from the British Colonial Secretary, who was very mindful of the U-boat threat. On June 10, 1915, the office of the chief press censor was established and by mid-July, nearly two years before the first CLC transports arrived on Canada's West Coast, Censor Chambers was in the driver's seat, where he remained throughout the war.

So who was Ernest John Chambers, how did he land such a powerful wartime job, maintain a surveillance network and hope to enforce news blackouts in a country with telegraph

Ernest J. Chambers served as Canada's Chief Wartime Censor.

Library and Archives Canada, c. 1824

wire services, over a hundred daily newspapers, dozens of weeklies and other foreign-language publications, next to a neutral country with hundreds more and a very large German population?

Born April 16, 1862, in the civil parish of Penkridge, Staffordshire, England, Chambers was the youngest son of Edward and Louisa Chambers. He attended English grammar school until 1870 when — at age eight — he with his family boarded a steamer and immigrated to Canada, settling in Canada's largest city, Montreal, which then boasted a population of roughly 107,000.[13] Like many adolescents of his day, young Chambers was drawn to the militia, and became captain of the Montreal High School Cadet Rifles. After joining the 6th Battalion "Fusiliers," which began as the 6th Battalion Volunteer Militia of Canada the same year he was born, Chambers rose to the rank of captain.[14]

The potential for adventurous travel as a newspaper man appealed to Chambers and in 1885 he headed west as a correspondent for the *Montreal Daily Star* to report on Major-General Frederick Middleton's campaign to crush the Métis and Indigenous uprising. His unflinching patriotism for the British Empire, coupled with his unflagging support for the military, appeared obvious when he put down his pen and volunteered for military service at Fish Creek, Batoche, and operations against Mistahi-maskwa (Big Bear). Years later, when asked about the medal and clasp he wore on his chest, Chambers stated it had been his "life's goal to take part on the field in defense of the Empire and of the Dominion."[15]

Before returning home and reconnecting with his beloved 6th Battalion, Chambers worked briefly as managing editor of the new *Calgary Daily Herald*, which in those days often got its news from talkative CPR passengers.[16] From 1893 to 1896, Chambers co-owned and edited the *Canadian Military Gazette*, and then began authoring a series of regimental histories and other books, including publications on the Montreal Highland Cadets, the Queen's Own Rifles of Canada, the Governor General's Body Guard and the Royal North-West Mounted Police. When the Corps of Guides — the intelligence arm of the militia — was formed in 1903, Chambers was appointed officer for the military district encompassing Montreal and southwest Quebec.

As the man's contacts grew, so did opportunity.

In March 1904, Chambers travelled to Ottawa and was sworn in as Gentleman Usher of the Black Rod, a prestigious protocol function in the Senate. A photograph shows a bespectacled, white-gloved Chambers with thinning grey hair and a thick, frosty-looking mustache, proudly standing in uniform with medals on the left side of his raised chest and the elegant ebony cane or black rod held in his right hand against his shoulder. His left hand, which is raised, supports a baton tucked under his left shoulder. It is a stiff, quintessential portrait of a man on a mission, reverently holding a symbol of authority in his role as personal attendant and messenger of the sovereign or his representatives.

Four years later, Chambers's responsibilities grew to include the editorship of the *Canadian Parliamentary Guide*, and in 1912 the fifty-year-old major, still attached to the Corps of

Guides, became secretary of the Canadian branch of the Empire Parliamentary Association. Soon his accomplishments and experience with the Guides led to more trust and opportunity, and from the early days of the war he began working as a censor, monitoring international wireless and cable transmissions while at Canadian military headquarters in Ottawa.

Promoted to lieutenant-colonel in 1915, appointed by the secretary of state that summer as chief press censor, his primary objective was to secure the co-operation of the press of Canada in suppressing news that would aid the enemy, be critical of military policy or interfere with recruitment and military discipline.

For censors, banning material that promoted despondency, distress or alarm on the home front was a high priority, because authorities did not want the enemy to use such material as a means of encouraging more resistance against the Allies. Furthermore, tied as the country was to the British Empire, Canada was duty-bound to keep an eye on any suspicious activity that could help the enemy abroad or disrupt the Allied cause.

As the war continued, Chambers gained more surveillance power, which included the interception of domestic mail and telegraphic messages. Much of the surveillance work was aimed at Canada's Chinese population, which the federal government viewed as a threat to national or public safety, and to the Allied war effort as a whole. Private individuals, Chinese consul officials and political organizations such as the Chinese Nationalist League, which was banned in 1918, were monitored or subject to monitoring.

For the Canadian government, the threat level increased dramatically the moment it signed on to the CLC scheme. Ottawa's concerns ranged from the spreading of seditious material and support for German interests in China to blowing up railway bridges and tunnels in Canada. All of it could impact CLC recruitment or even jeopardize the transportation network that crossed two oceans and a continent.

As a tireless military officer and respected journalist with more than thirty years' experience, Chambers was suited for the task. His work put him in touch with eminent people across the country, including federal and provincial politicians, senators, newspaper publishers, editors, police and immigration officials. He developed key contacts at the CPR and surrounded himself with hard-working, trustworthy people. Chambers proved demanding and forceful in following and pressing beyond the stream of draconian wartime measures that mirrored the country's dislike of pacifism and socialism, and its mistrust of foreigners. On a daily basis he exercised great tact and diplomacy and got along well with most mainstream editors and publishers, meeting with them and communicating regularly.[17]

On the whole, Chambers preferred to play nice, or give editors the benefit of the doubt or at most a slap on the wrist when it came to specific, inadvertent breaches. His warnings, if not heeded, could become threatening, but more often than not he characterized infractions as "a slip" or "simple, honest mistake" rather than a wilful effort to evade the law.

A thin man with steadfast eyes, Chambers was a workaholic who drew a modest salary against a job that filled his week Mondays to Saturdays and often on Sundays. His work and that of his small staff demanded patience, acumen and careful, confidential responses often written in secret code, the mastering of which in itself involved a steep learning curve for those sending and receiving the messages.

His surveillance network reached across the country and involved serious, but also laughable or embarrassing situations. Occasionally, Chambers received telegrams from blindsided senior government officials pointing to articles that should not have appeared. With equanimity he replied by expressing how grateful he was for the tip and promising to investigate. During his time as chief press censor, he banned more than 250 religious or political publications, most originating from the United States. Publications that appeared in a language other than English or French were also common targets, as were those that expressed leftist views.[18]

The suppression and censoring of CLC news was only one part of his job.

While he worked from a stuffy office on Elgin Street in downtown Ottawa close to Parliament Hill and the recently opened Grand Trunk Railway Central Station, his authority reached beyond the printed word. Chambers's decisions impacted public photo exhibits, filmmaking, plays and musical recordings. The pole distance (in kilometres) of telegraph lines under censorship in Canada at the time, reported Chambers, totalled 67,296. This included 23,734 belonging to Canadian Pacific Railway Telegraphs, 16,228 to the Great North Western Telegraph Company and 8,355 belonging to the Grand Trunk Pacific. Beyond that there were more than 2.5 million kilometres of telephone land lines.[19]

The telegraph machines and typewriters in his office produced a constant stream of instructions to newspaper editors and various transportation, communication and immigration officials. The office, of course, was also on the receiving end of a multitude of messages that provided everything from tips to apologetic responses from those who had been warned. In his numerous circulars to newspapers, Chambers or his staff went to great lengths to provide examples of the type of news that would cross the line.

Staffing levels, meanwhile, were maintained at minimum strength, which imposed a "heavy burden," frequently making it "very difficult to cope with the work . . ." Serving under him as press censors were Joseph Fortier, an experienced — and in Chambers's words — popular French Canadian journalist, and Ernest Boag, who had worked as press censor librarian for the Department of Militia and Defence. Boag, noted Chambers, possessed an intimate knowledge of Canadian military organization, personnel and practice, and had a close acquaintance with current military and civil literature that proved extremely useful.

When Boag was recalled to the Department of Militia and Defence on March 3, 1918, his responsibilities to Chambers were divided between Ben Deacon, who Chambers described as a "practical Canadian journalist with wide experience and recognized sound judgment" and Joseph Leslie, who had assisted Boag "most intelligently in the duties of office organization and direction" and had been responsible for the office's night routine. Fortier worked for Chambers until July 31, 1919, when office staff was reduced around the time of the military's demobilization, and not long before the *War Measures Act* was revoked in January 1920.[20]

Also serving Chambers in Ottawa was an office supervisor, a German translator who doubled as an assistant censor, a filing clerk, two stenographers, a clerk typist and a confidential messenger. There were also numerous translators employed when needed, including men fluent in some Chinese dialects. Outside the nation's capital, Chambers relied on press censors in Toronto, Winnipeg and Vancouver, men described as "day" or "night editors of the Canadian Press Limited, receiving honorariums for their service as censors."[21] Strangely, Chambers's final report listed no press censors working for him in Quebec or the Maritimes, but he most certainly had contacts there given the ever-growing unpopularity of the war in Quebec, and the massive volume of shipping into and out of eastern ports.

* * *

In his March 12, 1917, cable to Chambers, Scott, the superintendent of immigration, pointed to the imminent arrival of the *Empress of Russia* "with between 2,000 and 2,500 Chinese coolies . . ." He told Chambers the movement of men will "run anywhere from 6,000 to 20,000 per month," that the CPR will handle transportation through Canada, and that his department is "endeavouring to arrange with the United States Government the passage of these people through the State of Maine to the Port of St. John, [sic] N.B. When navigation opens on the St. Lawrence, it is probable that these coolies will be shipped to Quebec. An arrangement is being made to by the Militia Department to provide guards. This Department is interested in checking this Chinese labour into Canada at Vancouver and out of Canada at Atlantic Port."[22]

In addition to outlining the nature of the movements, Scott, who had also, since 1911, been working as Canada's chief controller of Chinese immigration,[23] made it clear to Chambers the scheme had to be carried out with absolute secrecy. "The transport through Canada of a very large number of Chinese coolies will doubtless cause considerable comment and as it is desired that the movement shall occur without any publicity whatever I would respectfully suggest that you Circularize newspapers to withhold any information. It is unlikely that the Imperial Government will say anything about this feature as from what I gather of the meagre correspondence it is left almost entirely to the Canadian Pacific Railway Company, the Militia Department, and this Department to handle the movement through Canada."[24]

Two days later, Chambers assured Scott he would "issue the necessary instructions to the press to observe silence . . ."[25] That same day, he cabled J.M. Gibbon, the CPR's main publicity agent, who occupied an office at Montreal's Windsor Station. By then, Gibbon, no doubt, was aware of the scheme and the need for secrecy. Chambers, however, still emphasized the point, noting he would be contacting "the press of the country and the correspondents of our . . . newspapers to co-operate to prevent the publication of any information relating to this movement. It appears to me to be highly desirable that a caution should be issued to the employees of the railways, particularly yours, as I understand the arrangements are practically in the hands of your Company. Probably your offices have already taken the matter up, but if they have not, I wonder if you would kindly draw the matter to their attention. It appears to me to be highly desirable that nothing should be said even about the arrangements made in advance for this particular traffic . . ."[26]

Chambers, who was promoted to full colonel that year, concluded his March 14 cable by suggesting he and Gibbon meet in Montreal "some evening" to "discuss the subject of maintaining secrecy regarding this movement with you or any of the officials of your Company." Gibbon wrote back, stating the necessary instructions had been forwarded to CPR operating officials along the line. He also told Chambers he had contacted H.W. Brodie, the CPR's general passenger agent in Vancouver; F.E. Trautman, CPR press representative in Winnipeg; Robert Stead, publicity agent for the Department of Natural Resources at Calgary; and J. McMillan, the CPR's manager of telegraphs in Montreal. "I think this covers the ground, so you need not be put to the trouble of having to come down to Montreal."

In his interdepartmental correspondence to Brodie in Vancouver on March 15, Gibbon attached a copy of Chambers's letter and noted: "Judging from what I see in the Vancouver papers, they are rather lax about news regarding incoming steamers and I think it would be a good thing to direct the Editors to be particularly careful in connection with this particular movement."

By then, Chambers had written to the general managers of the telegraph companies, seeking their co-operation. He also cabled the Dominion immigration inspector for British Columbia, Malcolm Reid, informing him he was about to issue a circular to the press. "I will be much obliged if you can find time to drop around to the newspaper offices and give them a personal caution with reference to this matter," he wrote on March 14. "And if you can do anything else to assist in drawing the necessary veil of secrecy about the anticipated movements of these coolies, in Vancouver, I will be much obliged."[27]

Reid was well known on the West Coast — both loved and despised. As immigration inspector he worked mostly behind the scenes with a variety of people, including Chambers. He was a key figure involved in news leak investigations and the Canadian government's persistent surveillance of the Chinese and South Asian communities and organized labour.

True to his word, on March 17, the chief press censor sent French and English versions of his confidential circular C.P.C. 48 to Canadian editors. As well as informing top newsmen about the CLC movements and the desire to transport the Chinese labourers through Canada without publicity, the instructions, which filled two pages under the heading "Not for Publication," drew attention to previous circulars detailing a host of other wartime sensitivities banned from print.

Incredibly, on the same day Circular 48 was issued, a two-paragraph news article appeared in the *Toronto Globe* newspaper under the headline "Toronto Doctor to Examine Chinese Coolies." It stated that "Doctor George P. Sylvester" had "been appointed by the "French Government as a medical examiner to conduct the examination of Chinese coolies who are to go to France as labourers. Last fall he and his wife went to China to visit their daughter who is the wife of a missionary. It is stated that large numbers of Chinese labourers are to be taken to Europe."

Although the article forced an immediate response from Chambers, it did not compromise Ottawa's secret plan for handling the CLC. On March 19, Chambers wrote to Sylvester to explain he had read the article. "No harm has been done by the publication of the item . . . but I wish to draw attention to the importance of your co-operating with us to prevent the publication of news indicating the route by which these coolies are to proceed from China to France." He noted how preparations had been made to transport the Chinese through Canada and that authorities had made every effort to keep it a secret.

The reply came the next day, but not from Sylvester. E.H. Ellis, Sylvester's son-in-law, opened the letter and was, by accident, suddenly made aware of the plan. He told Chambers he "does not understand or know how information in the *Toronto Globe* March 17th was given in to the News Paper [sic]. We might state Dr. Sylvester has been in China since November of 1916. In a letter to me which was written about six weeks ago he told us he had been appointed by the French Government to examine Chinese Coolies and that he was then at his work. I am sending forward to the Doctor your letter and circular and give below his address in China."[28]

The forwarding address for Sylvester was in Tsingtao, care of Jardine Matheson & Co. That company, which had begun with the opium trade, was then the most important and oldest trading company in Hong Kong and Shanghai. In addition to its other commercial interests in China, it bid on contracts to outfit the labourers. British Foreign Office correspondence, dated January 28, 1917, points to a Dr. Sylvester who was in Tsingtao, but apparently working under the British and not the French scheme. "Coolies recruited by Pratt will be sent by railway to Tsingtao where they will be medically examined by Dr. Sylvester at a charge of twenty cents per head (to be reduced to 10 cents per head after first five thousand)."[29]

Chambers followed up with Ellis on March 21, explaining he was "extremely obliged" for the reply and pleased the correspondence was being forwarded to the doctor. "You will understand this is quite an important matter, particularly as we expect to ship many of the Japanese [sic] through Maine and it is most desirable that too much publicity should not be given to this movement, for fear of arousing opposition among hostile elements in the United States. This is one of the chief reasons why we are anxious to keep the movement quiet."[30]

The mistaken reference to Japanese may simply have been the result of a long day or week at the office, or perhaps because to him all Orientals looked alike.

That same day, Chambers heard from Malcolm Reid in Vancouver who, immediately after receiving Chambers's March 14 cable, had "dropped round" to visit top brass at the *British*

Columbia Federationist, the *News-Advertiser*, the *Province*, *Van-couver Sun* and *Vancouver World*. "All these gentlemen have promised to co-operate with us in connection with this matter," he assured Chambers. He had asked his contact at the *News-Advertiser* to prepare a list of any known correspondents who might live in Victoria "so that word may be given them, as I am personally of the opinion that many stories which have been sup-pressed in Canada have been forwarded by mail to United States points by Victoria correspondents."

Reid also told Chambers he was arranging to interview the Japanese consul with reference to the Japanese newspaper, and would take the same action in connection with the Chinese news-papers, and ask the telegraph companies "to hold up any news items or despatches relating to these coolies."[31]

Impressed by Reid's initiative, Chambers replied on March 26: "As a result of your very intelligent action in connection with this matter, I have no doubt that nothing remains to be done further in connection with this matter in Vancouver."

Additional assurances in regards to press co-operation came from Gibbon, who informed Chambers on March 28 that Brodie, the CPR's general passenger agent at Vancouver, had written to explain that the "city editors of Vancouver and Victoria have all been interviewed, and have all promised to do as outlined."[32]

In the midst of those reassurances, a *Vancouver World* news-paper article stated that 70 per cent of the space aboard the Blue Funnel liners plying the Pacific between the Orient and Can-ada's West Coast and on the Orient-European route has been requisitioned by the British government. Datelined Victoria and published March 21, the article explained how the news became known following the arrival of the *Talthybius*. The article listed the Blue Funnel liners affected on the trans-Pacific route as the *Talthybius*, *Protesilaus* and *Ixion*, representing approximately twenty thousand net tons, with an aggregate carrying capacity of fifty thousand measurement tons.[33]

On the same day a story datelined New York stated the British government had requisitioned half the accommodation on CPR ships and 75 per cent of the accommodation on Blue Funnel ships on eastbound voyages from the Orient to Vancouver. "The action does not affect outward traffic and . . . is intended to insure adequate space for the transportation of Oriental merchandise to Canada. The demand for freight movement from the Far East has recently been so heavy that the reservation of this space has been regarded as a necessary step, particularly in view of the upward movement of freight rates."

The article listed the Canadian Pacific ships as the *Empress of Russia*, *Empress of Asia*, *Empress of Japan* and the *Monteagle*. "While the volume of freight moving westward from North America is adequately accommodated by the tonnage now in service, it was stated yesterday by shipping men interested in the Far Eastern trade, that the vessels available were not sufficient for the eastbound movement. The situation was easier for several months, but it is reported to be tightening up again . . ."[34]

The "transportation of Oriental merchandise to Canada" was an interesting choice of words, but neither article stated what the ships were actually being used for, an indication that censorship was working.

In addition to dropping in on newspaper editors, Chambers contacted government officials in Washington, D.C., in attempts to stamp out unwanted reportage south of the border. The heads of Canadian churches were also approached and cautioned when it was discovered missionaries in China had written home with news they had been recruited as officers for the CLC.

Beyond the government's security concerns, the waiving of the $500 head tax was another reason given for keeping news of the CLC movements out of the press. Introduced well before the war to prevent Chinese immigration, the tax had wide public support. Waiving it facilitated the CLC's quick entry into and movement across Canada, but the public might react badly if it discovered the tax had been waived, especially if the revelation came after one of the CLC transportees had escaped.

There were other aspects the government did not want the public to know about.

On March 20, 1917, in a secret telegram from the Colonial Office to the Governor General, it was clearly conveyed that in order to use each steamer to the fullest extent and expedite the arrival of the labourers in France, British Admiralty needed to cut corners. As alluded to in the Introduction, the Canadian government was asked to waive regulations in regard to boat accommodation for the labourers conveyed in Holt Company and Canadian Pacific Railway liners. In seeking the change, Admiralty gave assurances that life rafts at least would be provided for all on board in any cases where boat accommodation regulations could not be complied with. Two days later, assured that "some species of buoyant apparatus" would be provided for all on board, the Canadian government waived the regulations.[35]

Many of the CLC ships, however, remained dangerously overcrowded. This was partly because of the war effort, but also due to the long-standing view among whites that Chinese, unlike white passengers, could be packed tightly into steerage.

British Second Lieutenant Daryl Klein, who arrived at Tsingtao in late 1917, wrote about his journey to France in the company of some 4,200 labourers and thirteen officers. "The coolies are not passengers capable of finding each his cabin; the coolies are so much cargo, live stock [sic], which has to be packed away, so many head in a hold . . . Company officers, who are official packers, find that the best way of preserving order is to seize the kit-bag of the coolie as soon as he enters the hold, throw it in his bunk and bundle the owner after it. In this manner, and with the aid of Malacca canes and gloved hands, members of the O.K. Party created a record, stowing away no less than 1,700 coolies in an hour and thirty-five minutes."[36]

It is important to remember though that the ability of ships to accommodate such large numbers of men may be more attributable to successful refitting and adjusting, than to packing men like cargo. The announcement that there would be reduced cargo space on selected crossings from Asia indicates that a substantial amount of ship's space was reassigned to passengers. It is also worth noting that the *Empress of Asia* carried over 1,300 Canadian troops from Britain to Victoria via the Panama Canal in 1919.

In his memories of the transports, Frank Heath comments on the crowded conditions while he was completing the last leg of his journey from Canada to Liverpool. Most of his focus, however, is on how he assumed the Chinese would react in an emergency. "I have often thought . . . what would have happened if we had been torpedoed. I think we should have stood a poor chance of getting into a boat with all that gang. They would have rushed everything, because all the way across the Atlantic we could see they were absolutely scared stiff, but fortunately nothing happened."[37]

With the regulations officially waived, most of the labourers, especially those who had never been on board a ship, endured an uncomfortable voyage to Canada while mostly confined to individual spaces no larger than a broom closet.

While Chambers went to work and pointed to his "success" of muzzling the press in regards to the CLC movements, word did slip out from under the veil of secrecy. It began to escape soon after the *Russia* arrived with the first boatload.

CHAPTER 10

Death at Sea

"We had to stand to in the galley, armed with light bamboo poles — in case of trouble. It was not long before we got it."

Walls of water . . .

In the dining saloon on November 11, 1917, dishes smashed while tables and chairs slid across the room and banged against walls. The outside decks were awash and out of bounds, and far below in the holds, the labourers were sick. And that was not the worst of it during eight days of stormy weather on the North Pacific. On November 4, a despondent female missionary crawled through a porthole and threw herself into the raging sea; four days later a male passenger died of heart failure. Livingstone's diary for November 4 is noticeably brief — just eight and a half lines, noting the suicide and how he, while trying to keep down the bile in his throat, ventured through the *Empress of Russia*'s lower passages to check on the labourers, who looked at him with "longing eyes."[1]

The ship's master, the experienced Captain Samuel Robinson,

noted in his diary that a northeast wind had produced a swell that caused the ship to pitch heavily. While he left out the detail about how passenger Miss A.P. Davies, a Presbyterian missionary, gained fatal access to the sea, he noted she "committed suicide by jumping overboard." The male passenger who died on the eighth was identified only as Robert K. Douglas.

Two days before the really bad weather hit on the fourth, a labourer sent Livingstone a few words on a scrap of paper, which when translated by an interpreter read: "I have the honour to inform you that I am not only seasick but also homesick." That same day, while the *Russia* was anchored at Yokohama, the doctor performed minor surgery on a labourer's inflamed arm and monitored patients suffering from mumps in the isolation ward.

* * *

When it came to seasickness there was nothing anybody could do except heave into a bucket or over the side and pray for it to end. During gales people sometimes did not make it to a bucket and found themselves slipping in their own vomit or someone else's. The power generated by a storm was especially felt in the crowded holds and between decks where those not used to the sea were smashed into bulkheads or tossed down stairwells.

In addition to nasty weather, the CLC transports continually faced the possibility of being sunk by enemy action, not so much on the Pacific, but certainly on the Atlantic and elsewhere where U-boats and surface raiders roamed. A British naval and military intelligence report dated July 23, 1917, noted that since the "beginning of ruthless submarine warfare 4,671,000 tons of shipping" had been sunk up to the end of June.[2]

Adding to these various external threats were the psychological effects of being confined to a crowded ship week after week. Depression and severe anxiety, accompanied by suicidal thoughts, were not uncommon.

The Canada-bound ships from the Orient to William Head frequently encountered the colder, stronger weather as they approached the Aleutians. They took this Great North Circle route because it was in fact the shortest distance. Still, it could be a painfully long voyage.

Dozens of the Chinese labourers contracted by the British died at sea, as did a few regular paying passengers travelling on the CLC steamers. The CLC medal roll, which is essentially a nominal roll, includes the names of dozens who were listed as having "died at sea" or "died en route" between 1917 and 1920. It is very likely many more died on the transports because several individual entries appear to be missing from the medal roll. It is also likely some fatalities were never recorded as sea deaths on the medal roll because the individuals succumbed while the ship was at anchor or in a port of call.

But unlike those who perished on the French transport *Athos*, most of the men who died on the British transports succumbed to disease. There is, unfortunately, not much detail on these men, but among those listed on the medal roll as having died at sea or while en route from various causes in 1917 are the following: Hsieh Ch'Ang Hsu (Xie Changxu, No. 4486), March 23; Ch'en Hung K'uei (Chen Hongkui, No. 11348), April 18; Chu Yu Ch'uan (Zhu Yuquan, No. 10914), May 25; Li Chao Shun (Li Zhaoxun, No. 11029), August 2; Sun T'ai Shan (Sun Taishan, No. 42521), October 6; Wang Te Sheng (Wang Desheng, No. 97572), December 16; and Yang Kuang T'ai (Yang Guangtai, No. 72139), December 23.

All of these men had left China with the hope of earning a wage behind the lines in France or Belgium.

There were other labourers who signed CLC contracts, but died prior to even boarding a ship to Canada. A December 31, 1917, dispatch from Thomas Bourne, the British War Office representative at Weihaiwei, to the War Office in London stated fifty to sixty labourers and a British officer-candidate suffered serious blood poisoning after being inoculated against typhoid.

Six of the Chinese men died. The officer-candidate, Mr. R.D. Thomas, recovered after being sent to the Royal Navy hospital on Liu-kung Tao. An inquest was held and an autopsy on one of the labourers, Tu Lien-ho (Du Lianhe, No. 75474), who succumbed December 19, showed he suffered septicaemia after the inoculation. Bourne stated none of the other three thousand labourers inoculated at the same time suffered ill effects.[3]

Roughly two months later, Canadian medical officers at the same recruitment depot were working day and night to end what was described as a deadly typhus epidemic. Captains Charles Bastin, John Box, George Cronk, Philip Doyle, Donald Fraser, James McEwen, Leonard Panton and William Shepherd were all singled out by the War Office "for admirable services rendered during the epidemic . . ."[4]

The crisis began after two coastal steamers, the *Tungchow* and the *Kueichow*, arrived from Chingwangtao on January 30 and February 2, respectively. Altogether, the vessels carried 1,655 men. "There appears . . . no doubt that the Typhus was brought here from Tientsin and its recently flooded and starved districts by the two steamers," stated Bourne in his March 11 dispatch to the War Office in London.[5]

Altogether, nine labourers died and hundreds more fell sick.

Following the first two deaths in mid-February, which were attributed to pneumonia, doctors quickly isolated the cause. "About 16th of Feb. the Medical Officers of the Depot suspected some undiagnosed trouble and finally on 19th Feb. all the Doctors in Weihaiwei met and decided definitely that there was Typhus in the camp . . . The immigration of coolies was stopped at once, the camp was segregated from the Town, the whole of the coolies clothes were changed and sterilized, or where dirty, burnt; and the coolies themselves were again bathed and washed down with Kerosene . . ."[6]

At the peak of the epidemic, on the March 1, 251 patients were in hospital. By March 7, noted Bourne, admissions were declining.[7]

Panton, who was from Winnipeg, was put in charge of organizing and co-ordinating the effort after the depot's chief medical officer contracted the illness on March 2. Bourne noted how the thirty-five year old's previous medical military experience and organizational skills were "of the greatest possible value." The War Office's top CLC administrator in China also noted how the seven other Canadians provided valuable service, which included keeping an eye on the depot's closed exits and controlling the bathing and disinfection showers.[8]

The honours the doctors received from the War Office are noted in the *Lancet* (Canada) magazine of September 1918. The article identified the location of the depot and made it clear the epidemic had broken out among Chinese labourers.[9] This information probably did not concern Canadian censors because by the time the magazine came out the last eastbound CLC trains had already crossed Canada.

Panton had joined the Royal Army Medical Corps in Britain in June 1915. From July 10 to January 31, 1916, he was serving at Cape Helles, Gallipoli. On December 31, shrapnel from a high-explosive shell sliced into his abdomen and perforated his intestine. Before transferring him to a hospital in Egypt, doctors at a casualty clearing station removed two segments of his bowel and inserted a couple of drainage tubes. He eventually ended up back in Canada and by early December was serving with the CAMC. His personnel file notes he "Proceeded on special duty . . . with medical services in connection with the Chinese Labour Corps to Weihaiwei, China, December 8, 1917." His actual date of embarkation at Vancouver was December 20, 1917.[10]

Captain Bastin was also from Manitoba. The thirty-year-old doctor, whose hometown was Hamiota, had served at Canadian stationary and general hospitals in Salonika prior to "special duty" with the CLC. The six other doctors were from Ontario, four of them from the eastern end of the province. Box, who saw service in France and Salonika, was born in Calabogie, Cronk was from Parham, Doyle was born in Hawkesbury and Shepherd, who later saw service in Siberia where he became "dangerously ill" with pneumonia, was from Almonte. Fraser and McEwen had enlisted in Toronto and London, respectively.

Before joining the CAMC in 1917, Fraser enlisted in the RAMC while attending medical school at the University of Toronto in 1915. By December that year he was attached to a field ambulance in Egypt. In 1916, Fraser put his medical skills to good use on the Somme where he earned the Military Cross, awarded for acts of gallantry.

McEwen, whose service extended to Britain as well as China, had enlisted in July 1917 at the same London, Ontario, depot Livingstone had arrived at a year earlier. The officer who signed McEwen's medical sheet was none other than Captain Lou Sebert, who was then three weeks away from commencing his journey to China.[11]

Overall, members of the CLC received their first vaccinations prior to boarding ships at Weihaiwei and Tsingtao. Additional shots were administered at sea by the medical officers who accompanied the contingents. Detailed reports, written by a contingent's commanding officer, documented each leg of the journey with separate reports filed by the doctors, including members of the CAMC. The lack of medical supplies, even the most basic kit, deeply troubled doctors during inspections prior to sailing and while crossing the North Pacific.

Captain Arthur Connolly, born in Sherbrooke, Quebec, on April 4, 1873, was medical officer on board the *Monteagle* and his report, dated October 11, 1917, was highly critical of the quality and quantity of medical stores placed on board by contracted suppliers in Hong Kong. In keeping with the reporting protocols, Connolly's assessment was sent to the contingent's commanding officer, Second Lieutenant Matthew Ivy, and copied to Sir John Jordan at the British legation in Peking.

From Hong Kong the *Monteagle* travelled to Tsingtao, where

she boarded 1,681 labourers and sailed on September 23. Before calling at William Head in mid-October, each man was to receive two inoculations. "In order to do this work properly we required iodine," noted an exasperated Connolly. "Iodine was among the supplies, in concentrated strength, requiring to be diluted with rectified spirits before using, but there was no rectified spirits among the supplies. We had to make 3,362 post inoculation dressings and were furnished with four ounces of Collodion for this purpose, not nearly enough for half the dressings."

Married in Vancouver on February 12, 1907, Arthur and Mary Connolly were residing at Salmon Arm, British Columbia, raising an eight-and-a-half-year-old son, Daniel, when Arthur joined the CAMC at Victoria on May 11, 1917. Less than three months later, the doctor-surgeon was en route to Shanghai, where he received orders to embark for Tsingtao.

While crossing the Pacific on the *Monteagle*, several labourers began experiencing severe stomach cramps and diarrhea, accompanied with mucus and blood. Dysentery, an infectious disease seated in the large intestines, was spreading, affecting approximately twenty men. However, when Connolly and other staff searched the ship for "any preparation of Emetine," none was found.

"Among the supplies were 100 Colocynth and Hyoscyamus pills for 1681 Coolies! These pills, as you have seen, are old and cracked and in our hands they have proved worthless. You have seen the supply of adhesive plaster. Three rolls, 15 yards in all. This was so old that it had entirely lost its adhesive qualities, and yet we were given this with which to make at least 200 vaccination dressings to say nothing of the numerous other small dressings in which adhesive plaster is required."

There were other serious shortcomings.

"Conjunctivitis is so common among all coolies that regular eye parades are required and yet for this purpose the medical and surgical stores supplied us from Hong Kong contained only two eye glasses," wrote Connolly.

Other basic oversights led to more frustration.

"Labels were furnished for bottles, but there was no gum supplied to fasten them on with and the adhesive supplied refused to work . . . Among the supplies are two tourniquets. These are of a style discarded 50 years ago. Both are worm-eaten and falling to pieces."

For inoculating the labourers, doctors were supplied with two, two-cubic-centimetre syringes. "For one syringe there were 8 needles and this lasted through as we were able to get needles mended by the ship's engineers. The other syringe had two needles, both of which were used up long before the first inoculations were complete. There was also a metal hypodermic syringe with two needles, neither of which would fit . . . We could find neither tongue depressor, nor stethoscope, but for these wards of the British Government we were furnished with a plentiful supply of Cattle salts."

The Canadian doctor's criticism ended with: "We have endeavoured to give the coolies the square deal that the British Government had contracted with them to furnish, but at every turn our endeavours have been handicapped by the lack as well as by the useless quality of the supplies furnished at Hong Kong."[12]

Other CAMC officers drew similar conclusions.

Major George Lawson of York, Prince Edward Island, was senior medical officer on board the *Tyndareus*, which sailed from Tsingtao on November 26, 1917. Assisting him was the slightly younger Captain David Boddington, from the southwestern Ontario town of Sparta.

Before sailing, Lawson and Boddington conducted an inventory of the ship's medical stores. "It is regrettable that the result of our investigations showed that not only was the medical material placed at our disposal most inadequate in many respects, but many of the items quoted on the vouchers, as having been included could not be found. Material indispensable for the voyage was either included in insufficient amounts, or was not furnished at all. It is unnecessary to point out the omissions in

CLC men with their buckets and scrubbers on board a ship bound for Canada, 1917–18.

WJ Hawkings Collection, courtesy John De Lucy

detail, but one item may be referred to as deserving of the strongest of criticism, viz. the provision of two small forty minim glass syringes with which to carry out the inoculation against typhoid of over four thousand men. As the second dose of vaccine administered is two cubic centimetres it is quite apparent that the syringes provided were absolutely inadequate for the purpose for which they were intended."[13]

The two Canadians took matters into their own hands and purchased 8,000 units of diphtheria anti-toxin, 200 ounces of rubbing alcohol, two pairs of rubber gloves, glass syringes with needles and morphine.

The *Tyndareus* was tightly packed when she finally sailed. In addition to Lawson and Boddington and eight other officers, the contingent had ten interpreters, two medical assistants, seventeen sergeants, sixty-eight corporals, 271 lance corporals and 3,799 regular labourers. All of the men, with the exception of the British and Canadian officers, were Chinese. Total number of CLC officers and labourers on board: 4,177.

Three trains had been used to transport the men a relatively short distance from the depot at Tsangkow to the wharf at Tsingtao. Like other CLC transports, the ship was equipped with a hospital, which included twenty-four bunks, an isolation ward and orderly room. There was also a canteen, two prisons and enough bunk space for sixty-four cooks, bakers and various Chinese contractors. "The accommodation was good, warm and well ventilated, and the holds easily accessible and free from sweating," noted British Second Lieutenant Duncan Forbes, the contingent's commanding officer.[14]

The latrines, meanwhile, consisted of sixty seats, and for ablutions there were sixty-four wash basins. "The number was enough for this time of year, the weather being so cold the men did not wash more than was necessary. At the beginning of the trip a good deal of trouble was experienced through the outlet pipes getting chocked [sic] up. This was caused by the coolies washing their dishes in the basins and throwing rice and filth into them," explained Forbes in his report.

Discipline was good and for the most part the men policed themselves, answering to the "head gangers" or "gangers" of lesser rank. Several of these were on duty at one time, taking four-hour watches. This was augmented by guard duty assigned to white officers, each of whom, accompanied by an interpreter, supervised one of three watches in a twenty-four-hour period. Every four hours the officers reported to the ship's officer on the bridge. Meanwhile, daily routines for the labourers included cleaning the holds, scrubbing the deck and rinsing latrines.

While the ship coaled at Nagasaki, Lawson and Boddington went ashore and purchased the additional medical supplies, including towels for the ship's hospital and dispensary. The day after leaving that port, additional vaccinations against typhoid and paratyphoid (A and B) were commenced and completed in four days. "This, it is understood, is the first instance in which the primary inoculation was carried out at Tsangkow before embarking and the venture has proven most satisfactory in every way," explained Lawson in his senior medical officer's report, filed at William Head on December 14. "Abundance of time has thereby been obtained to complete the second inoculation without undue hurry or confusion, and to ensure the after effects of the operation have completely disappeared before the date of debarkation at William Head. In view, therefore, of the manifest advantages of this arrangement, both Captain Boddington and myself wish to place ourselves on record as strongly recommending the procedure be continued. In fact, should such an arrangement be feasible, it is suggested that both inoculations be carried out prior to embarkation so as to obviate the marked depression which frequently results from the combined effects of seasickness and the injection, which depression has been noted in many cases as fairly severe and lasting for several days. Those members of the party whose vaccination against smallpox had been judged unsatisfactory prior to embarkation were again vaccinated. It is considered that all the coolies are sufficiently protected."[15]

Out of approximately four thousand labourers, Lawson identified seventy-one hospital admissions during the crossing, and of those, average hospital time was less than two days. The most common ailments were acute indigestion and diarrhea, although cowpox and scabies also appeared. The former was transferred to humans when they milked cows infected with the virus. Abrasions or cuts on the hands allowed it to transfer from ulcers on the cows' teats. On the plus side, the virus produced immunity to smallpox. More recently, researchers had discovered that rodents were also natural reservoirs for the virus and responsible for most infections.[16] Scabies, meanwhile, was an infestation rather than an infection that left men scratching angry rashes as mites burrowed into the outer layers of the skin to lay eggs.

Lawson's report was written after *Tyndareus* reached William Head, and so he was on home turf when he found a typewriter and began banging out his conclusions for Forbes. Conscious of how easily it is for infectious diseases to spread across oceans and continents, Lawson strongly recommended ships be provided with a microscope, simple staining reagents and a small urine test case in addition to ordinary medical and surgical supplies. "In many cases which are encountered it is only by the aid of such appliances that a quick and accurate diagnosis can be made."

Forbes, meanwhile, had been trying to figure out what had happened to one of his labourers, who disappeared December 10 but was not reported missing until the December 11. The man, identified in his report as No. 92836, belonged to A Company and it appeared he had jumped or was pushed overboard, or had found a good hiding place. A search was underway until one of the labourers spoke up, claiming the man had been homesick and was trying to arrange a return voyage with the help of the ship's Cantonese crew. When crewmen denied any knowledge of the man, his plan or his whereabouts, they were warned of the serious consequences of being involved in such a scheme. "It being too dark and wet to have a general parade on the evening the ship anchored off William Head, which was 10:30 p.m., December 12, I had one the next day, but it failed to find any trace of the man. I do not think the man jumped overboard as he took all his kit with him with the exception of his quilt and kit bag."[17]

The "missing man" mystery was eventually solved, as reported a few months later by Second Lieutenant F.W. Ambrose, commanding officer of a contingent that also sailed on the *Tyndareus* from Tsingtao to Vancouver.

That time the ship had departed Tsingtao on February 27 at 7 a.m. with thirteen officers and 4,171 labourers. She arrived at William Head on March 16, but once more a man had gone missing.

In reporting the disappearance of twenty-seven-year-old Cheng Ping Kuang (Zheng Bingguang, No. 131705) Ambrose stated that man was reported missing March 15. A ganger on the ship reported he had seen and talked to him on the fourteenth and decided he was "queer in the head" so he sent him to his bunk. "All the party were paraded, and I personally checked the nominal roll without finding any trace of him," noted Ambrose. "It appears rather more than a coincidence that exactly the same time the last voyage of the *Tyndareus*, Mr. Forbes, the O.C., lost one of his men, also reported 'missing,' but who was later found hiding in the ship at Seattle."

That explained what had happened to Forbes's "No. 92836," but Ambrose's missing man stayed missing. On March 20, the ship's master said there was still no word of Cheng Ping Kuang.

In his report, Ambrose praised the work of Captain Charles Bouck, Canadian Army Medical Corps, senior medical officer, and of the ship's other medical officer, Dr. E.R. Wheeler, for their excellent work during the voyage. Shortly after the *Tyndareus* left Nagasaki one of the officers on board, G.W. Sinclair, developed scarlet fever. He, along with the officers who occupied the same cabin, G.W. Brown and G.H. Barringer, were immediately isolated. Hospital admissions among the Chinese included individual cases of pneumonia, a suspected case of syphilis, gonorrhoea and tuberculosis. Overall, the health of the labourers was excellent, noted Ambrose, who added that the average daily attendance in sickbay was forty, including minor dressings and seasickness. "The medical officers, Capt. Bouck and Dr. Wheeler, assisted in every way they possibly could and it is undoubtedly due to their thorough work that there were no further cases of scarlet fever."[18]

Bouck had grown up in the eastern Ontario village of Toyes Hill, near the town of Iroquois, where his father farmed. By 1906 the family had moved to Calgary, and in 1911 Charles graduated with honours in medicine from the University of Toronto. He returned to Alberta to practise and joined the CAMC at Calgary on December 3, 1917. Within weeks, the thirty-one year old was en route to China to accompany the CLC party to Canada. That detail, however, does not appear anywhere in his military personnel file. The file does not indicate his journey across Canada, but it states he sailed overseas on May 22, 1918, and served with the CAMC at Bramshott, Witley and Shorncliffe.

In July 1919, Bouck sailed from Southampton on the *Olympic* and arrived in Halifax a week later.[19] Before he died in 1944, Bouck had one of the largest surgical practices in Calgary, and was known worldwide in such esteemed places as the Mayo Clinic. Closer to home, he was warmly welcomed during his many house calls to farms and small towns in southern Alberta.[20]

Unfortunately, there are no reports from the labourers themselves, commenting on what they thought of the conditions on board the transports. The officers' reports commented regularly on the men, but did not give voice to the labourers. Undoubtedly, there would have been complaints, protests and even compliments as the ships crossed the North Pacific. It appears the men did what they were told and found ways to entertain themselves while not on clean-up duty, lined up for an inoculation or bowled over with seasickness.

British Lieutenant Hugh Lowder was in charge of a contingent of 1,899 labourers who embarked with seventeen officers at Tsingtao on the *Coconada* on March 2, 1918. Among the medical officers were Captains William Carr, Percival Faed and Gilbert Gunne, all members of the CAMC. At age thirty, Carr, who had grown up in the Fort Rouge district of Winnipeg, was the oldest and had previous militia experience with the Cavalry Field Ambulance. At one point he left for Britain and returned in 1912, presumably with his medical degree.[21] Faed, who was twenty-seven, born in Woodville in the Kawartha Lakes area west of Lindsay, Ontario, had graduated from medical school at the University of Toronto in 1913. On March 24, 1916, he married Helen Reid McIvor at Toronto and just over a year later, on August 29, 1917, he was dispatched to China and remained at

Tsingtao until he boarded the *Coconada*. During the course of his lifetime, Faed, who moved to the United States in late December 1928, became an expert in pathological chemistry. Gunne, born in Glenboro, Manitoba, was twenty-eight. He had joined the CAMC in Winnipeg on December 14, 1916. Compared to Faed's five-foot-seven, 110-pound frame, Gunne was huskier at five-foot-ten, 158 pounds.[22]

On the same ship was a labourer who had decided early on that the CLC was not for him. His identity is only recorded in Lowder's report as "No. 134185," but it seems the man found an ingenious way to get off the ship. While the *Coconada* was still alongside at Tsingtao he purchased a suit of clothes from a Japanese man standing below him on the wharf. The apparel was hauled up in a basket and just before the ship sailed for Moji, Japan, the labourer put on the suit and walked ashore unnoticed, like a regular passenger. [23]

Meanwhile, the selling of food by ships' crews was prohibited. Some contingent commanders turned a blind eye to the activity, but not Lowder. Chinese cakes, which the comprador's cooks planned to sell to the labourers, were confiscated and tossed overboard. Two days later a thousand eggs were sent over the side.

After Moji, as the *Coconada* resumed her voyage, the sea turned rough and so did the illicit selling. In separate incidents, three labourers assigned to policing duties were struck and injured by lumber-wielding crewmen when they tried to intervene. Lowder spoke to the captain of the ship, informing him he (Lowder) would not be responsible for any of the ship's crew caught selling below deck by policemen angered by the assaults. But crew members believed it was their right to make money off the labourers. "During the afternoon a company officer was approached by member of the crew with a statement that crew and firemen and cooks had invested all their savings in Hong Kong and Tsingtao on goods to sell to the coolies, that the officers in charge of the Chinese had winked at it on the last voyage, and

The front side of the CLC cap badge worn by members of the CLC.

Courtesy Sam Chiu

that unless they were allowed to sell openly from now on they would all be ruined as their stores would go bad."

Lowder held his ground, but could not do much to discipline the crew. He could, however, punish labourers. Some were fined what money they possessed, with the sum distributed among those who caught the buyer. Other offenders were sent straight to the stokehold, where they shovelled coal. The latter punishment was also ordered for men who refused to get out of their bunks or committed other offenses.[24]

The voyages clearly introduced or made men more familiar with military discipline, which included punishment designed to embarrass or make examples out of offenders. British Second Lieutenant William Rowlatt was in charge of a contingent that sailed from China on September 16, 1917. Roughly ten days later every man was issued a CLC badge and instructed to sew it onto his uniform. Two days later a trial was held for a labourer accused of both failing to comply with the order and striking his sergeant. "Evidence on both sides most conflicting, but I was satisfied he struck the sergeant and awarded him three days handcuffed to a stanchion on deck, two hours each day with a noticeboard hung around his neck stating the reason for his punishment and telling all the men to be warned," noted Rowlatt in his report.[25]

Daryl Klein described how a labourer who had stolen a handful of peanuts was court martialed and publicly disgraced during his trans-Pacific crossing. "For six hours he stood handcuffed to a winch. About his neck was hung a notice which detailed his crime, and warned his fellows against a similar breach of discipline."[26]

When Lowder's contingent crossed the International Date Line, which runs down the middle of the Pacific Ocean, March 15 became March 14, since travellers heading east across the line subtract a day. By then the sea was smoother, but morning parade was still impossible. Sadly, not much is known about labourer Wang Chia Pen (Wang Jiaben, No. 133230), who died of pneumonia at 4:15 p.m. His remains were committed to the deep at 5 p.m. at 49°18′N, 174° 31′W.[27]

* * *

The Canadian missionaries travelling with CLC contingents also wrote about their passage, mostly in letters to their wives or the secretaries of their foreign mission boards.

On April 30, 1917, thirty-nine-year-old Canadian missionary Arthur W. Lochead, born at Valleyfield, Quebec, accompanied the *Monteagle* from Weihaiwei. The McGill University and Presbyterian College graduate had sailed to China with his wife, Jessie.[28] Now a captain in the CLC, Lochead and six other officers were responsible for 1,633 Chinese en route to France via Canada. Writing to MacKay of the Foreign Missions Board in Toronto, Lochead noted on May 18 that the ship was due to arrive in Victoria on Saturday morning, May 19, so long as there was no delay at the quarantine station. "We have had no contagious disease or serious illness since leaving," he wrote, while continuing to pray for good health.

Lochead provided MacKay with a brief update on a few other Canadian missionaries in transit with the CLC. "We heard of Dr. Leslie's boat having arrived in England before we left Weihaiwei.

Dr. Frederick Auld and Mr. J.B. Hattie will likely be just a few days behind us on the *Empress of Russia*."[29]

Canadian Methodist missionary Gordon Jones, meanwhile, had boarded the *Empress of Russia* at 6:30 a.m. on May 14 and while making his rounds recognized some familiar faces from the YMCA and Canadian Methodist mission in West China. He also noted the presence of Auld and Hattie.

Jones's impression of the labourers, detailed in a letter to Clara, painted a much brighter picture of the men. "Our coolies are stowed away in the 3rd class, have lots to eat, have three Chinese bands, and are as happy as a bunch of kids. They might well be for the *Empress* is sailing along like a river steamer, only with much less vibration."[30]

Jones wrote how the first- and second-class passengers arrived in the dining saloon wearing suits or dinner jackets. Afterwards, there was music and dancing on the deck below. "At dinner I had to stop and convince myself that we were really moving as there was no roll, no pitch," Jones added. "I am in a four-berth cabin with J.B. Hattie and Dr. Auld of the Presbyterians. It is a second-class cabin being used as a first-class because of the rush . . . Of course with the coolies to look after we are all over the ship and can go anywhere."[31]

After coaling at Nagasaki, the ship bypassed Kobe and sailed directly to Yokohama. "One officer is on Orderly duty each day, but most of us take strolls around to see that everything is all right every now and then," Jones wrote on May 16. "We hear preceding Battalions have sailed from Halifax, but I am hoping we will sail from Montreal and will have long enough there to let me go around via Toronto from Sudbury. That would mean knowing our movements in advance which is rather unlikely so chances would seem to be slim."[32]

Jones's hope, of course, was to visit Clara, who he nicknamed "Kiddy," and his daughter, Eleanor. If censors had seen the letter, which did reference the labourers travelling with him, they more than likely would have crossed out his references to battalions sailing from Halifax or the CLC train's movement through Sudbury to Montreal. However, it appears the letter was not interfered with in any way.

On May 22, three days out of Yokohama, with the weather suddenly turning cold, Jones expressed how much he missed his wife and child. "Every mile we get nearer to Canada makes me love you and long to see you more," he wrote on Sunday, May 27, 1917. "Oh Kiddy, why can't I tell you just how much I love you and what a lovely warm homey feeling it gives me just to think about you. You can't possibly understand how much you mean to me girlie . . . I always feel helpless when I try to express these things to you. It is all in the simple words, 'I love you' and yet how can you know what those words mean because they mean more to me every day."[33]

The good news for Jones was his ship arrived at William Head on the same day he wrote that letter. On Monday morning, the labourers "filed out past a doctor and collected on the dock for medical inspection, then came back on. It didn't take long and none of our lot was quarantined." From there the *Russia* sailed to Victoria, and soon commenced her 133-kilometre, four-and-a-half-hour journey to Vancouver.

* * *

Although Livingstone was not a man of the sea, his description of the ferocious weather that pounded the *Russia* on her crossing through early November 1917 (detailed at the beginning of this chapter) was supported by the ship's master, who mentioned it several times in his diary. For the ship's captain to do that, it must have been rough.

By the morning of the twelfth, the gale had passed and land was in sight. There "above the clouds to the northward, the snow-clad peaks of the Rockies [sic] could be seen and every coolie was pointing to them and crying out that they would soon be on land again," noted Livingstone in his journal. "They knew it was Canada and dressers told them it was my home and you could hear the coolies say when I passed by 'Doctor's home — good.'"[34]

The rugged slopes Livingstone saw that morning, while tossing bits of cake to the seagulls, were, of course, the Coast Mountains, which extend some 1,600 kilometres north from the Fraser lowlands near Vancouver into the Yukon.

Beyond that was the rest of Canada.

CHAPTER 11

Quarantined at William Head

". . . we may have illness at any time."

Ports and pathogens . . .

On the afternoon of November 12, 1917, with Livingstone and his contingent aboard, the *Empress of Russia* entered the western approach to Juan de Fuca Strait between Cape Flattery and Tatoosh Island on the American side and Carmanah Point on Vancouver Island. She had done this many times, through all kinds of weather, and it was this same ship, in the same capable hands of Captain Samuel Robinson, that had delivered the first members of the Chinese Labour Corps to Canada on April 3.

For the time being it was relatively calm in the strait and the big passenger liner cut through the water with ease. Between eighteen and twenty-seven kilometres wide, the strait extends roughly 160 kilometres east from the Pacific to Haro Strait north of Puget Sound.[1] Known for its strong currents, gale-force winds, extensive fog, and tidal rips, the strait demands a great deal of respect from mariners. During storms there is more to worry about, but on this day the *Russia*, with 2,596 people on board, including the labourers and paying passengers, was making good time after her rough, fifteen-day journey from Weihaiwei.

Some sixteen kilometres from her Canadian destination the ship slowed her massive coal-fired Parsons turbines. At exactly 4:32 p.m., the *Russia* dropped anchor in Parry Bay, which, along with the dramatic headland, had been named by British surveyor Captain Henry Kellett in honour of the famous Arctic navigator and explorer, Rear Admiral Sir William Parry.

Seven minutes of sunlight remained, followed by thirty-four minutes of twilight, enough time for Livingstone to inhale the crisp, salty air, and catch a glimpse of the rugged coastline and the silhouette of the big wharf at the William Head Quarantine Station.[2] The station occupied a peninsula that curled east into Quarantine Cove between the towns of Rocky Point to the west and Metchosin to the east. "We docked . . . and many more coolies could be seen on shore in the camp and in the evening some of these came down and talked from the dock up to our men on the boat," noted Livingstone.

*   *   *

Opened in 1893, the facilities at William Head grew from the failure and closure of Canada's first West Coast quarantine station, located nearly five kilometres away on the east side of Parry Bay at Albert Head. When the Albert Head facility began operations in 1886, it represented new hopes for preventing the spread of contagious diseases on the West Coast, in the wake of a very troubling and embarrassing encounter with smallpox, one of the world's most virulent diseases. That encounter, which spawned a long series of difficult and tragic episodes, in no way marked the first time smallpox had been introduced to Vancouver Island. However, it did serve as a catalyst for establishing the short-lived Albert Head facility.

The triggering event itself unfolded on June 13, 1872, when a forty-year-old old steamship, the *Prince Alfred*, fought its way north through heavy seas from San Francisco until it dropped anchor in Juan de Fuca Strait, west of Victoria. On board was a five-year-old girl stricken with smallpox. The steamer's captain did what was required and raised the yellow quarantine flag on the vessel's foremast to signal there was infectious disease on board. He, along with his anxious passengers and crew, then waited for a response from shore, but nobody signalled the boat, let alone acknowledged the flag's presence.[3] This could be excused if it had been a fog-ridden day in the strait, but visibility was apparently good across the anchorage at Royal Roads off Esquimalt.

Frustrated by the lack of reply, the steamer's captain rowed ashore the next day and tracked down Victoria's health officer.

From that moment on there were many twists and turns in the saga, all of which worked to reveal how poorly prepared Victoria was for such an emergency. British Columbia had joined Confederation the previous year and the quarantining of ships and passengers arriving in Canada was a federal responsibility. However, there had been no appointment of a federal quarantine officer, never mind plans for a quarantine station, on the West Coast. It was up to Victoria's municipal council to decide what to do with the passengers on the *Prince Alfred*.[4]

Factored into the deliberations, of course, were the normal and longstanding assumptions on how people of different economic classes and races should be viewed, treated and accommodated.

Three sites were designated as quarantine detention camps, all of them fitting nicely into these expectations. Two days after the *Prince Alfred*'s arrival, a dozen detained first-class passengers, including their children, were shown to a cottage that was quickly brought up to the high standards expected by their class. Second-class and third-class passengers who had cabins on the *Alfred* were escorted to a separate camp where tents, mattresses, blankets, pillows and lanterns were provided. There was also a makeshift cookhouse. The little girl, Bertha Whitney, and her parents were led to an abandoned and dilapidated farm on Holland Point, just east of the entrance to Victoria Harbour.

The first-class passengers in the cottage were free to leave after nine days. Second- and third-class detainees were quarantined a few days longer. Bertha Whitney did not survive her time at what became known as the Pest House. She died of smallpox on June 23, ten days after the *Prince Alfred* arrived off Victoria. Her parents buried her there, near the water's edge.[5]

The girl's death, coupled with how the whole exercise was handled, prompted a public outcry. On June 25, the local newspaper lashed out at government, particularly Ottawa, for not taking seriously the needs of the province when it came to "Quarantine and the establishment and maintenance of Marine hospitals."[6] Approached for reimbursement, government officials in Ottawa finally took notice, but were not impressed with the invoices they received listing the costs associated with the creation and operation of the detention camps. Clearly, steps had to be taken to establish a better and more manageable quarantine facility on Canada's West Coast.

There were certainly other models to choose from.

Quarantine stations had been operating on the East Coast for years, screening passengers arriving from Europe for cholera, leprosy, meningitis, smallpox and tuberculosis. Despite these efforts, deadly pathogens occasionally got through with devastating results. Among the more well-known stations are New York's Ellis Island; the Lawlor Island Quarantine Station at the mouth of Halifax Harbour; Partridge Island Quarantine Station off New Brunswick, at the mouth of Saint John Harbour; and Grosse Île Quarantine Station in the St. Lawrence River, forty-six kilometres downstream from Quebec City.

From 1832 to 1937, more than four million immigrants were screened at Grosse Île, but during its first year in operation and again in 1834 cholera reached the mainland anyway, where it killed thousands.

In 1847, during the Great Irish Famine, thousands of Irish immigrants, many of them suffering from typhus, boarded ships destined for the port of Quebec City. Also known as "ship fever," that disease, often transmitted by lice and fleas and character-ized by a purple rash, fever and delirium, thrived in the damp, overcrowded and vermin-infested conditions during Atlantic crossings that lasted several weeks. Men, women and children felled by the disease were hastily buried at sea. Thousands more perished while the ships were in sight of land or shortly after they landed. The grim toll at Grosse Île included sailors, quarantine staff, health care workers and priests.

At the height of the epidemic the disease spread to Quebec City, Saint John, Montreal and Bytown (Ottawa). Further west it devastated communities along the St. Lawrence River and Lake Ontario, including Kingston and Toronto. In 1847, typhus claimed roughly twenty thousand lives.[7]

The West Coast was no stranger to smallpox prior to the *Prince Alfred*'s arrival and the sad demise of young Bertha Whit-ney. An epidemic in 1862 had been particularly devastating for Indigenous peoples.

The highly infectious disease, which has been traced to the Egyptian Empire around the third century BCE, had been killing and disfiguring millions in Europe and Asia for centuries. While exploring and charting North America's northwestern Pacific coast in the early 1790s, Captain George Vancouver reported evidence of smallpox among native populations living near Port Discovery (Discovery Bay) on the southeast side of Juan de Fuca Strait. A subsequent report from one of Vancouver's officers in 1792 described natives near Whidbey Island, at the mouth of Puget Sound, as being "pitted with smallpox."[8]

To form a basic understanding of the Indigenous popula-tion on Vancouver Island at the time of the massive smallpox epidemic of 1862–63, it is necessary to look at the people who inhabited the land when white settlement began. In the early

1840s, James Douglas of the Hudson Bay Company (HBC) was assigned the task of establishing a trading post on the southern end of the island. The Victoria area, then called Camosack, was deemed appropriate, because the landscape appeared to lend itself to the plough and the raising of livestock. The HBC's Fort Victoria was built in 1843 and many Lekwungen formed a village on the northwest side of what would become Victoria's inner harbour. Scholars point out this was around the time the Lekwungen came to be identified through their anglicised name: the "Songhees" or "Songish."[9]

The distribution of smallpox in 1862 was wider than the previous epidemics in the 1770s and 1830s. With gold-seekers coming north to seek their fortunes, Victoria was a bustling town with a white population of between 2,500 and 5,000 people in 1862. In addition to the local Indigenous population there were at least two thousand coastal people — from as far away as Alaska — who had come to Victoria to trade. When Indigenous people were infected with smallpox they were forced out of Victoria. It was not long before the disease spread up the coast and into the mainland. The Songhees were largely spared because many were administered the vaccine, which was available in Victoria. What also saved the Songhees was their decision to retreat to Discovery and San Juan islands.[10]

The epidemic killed tens of thousands of Indigenous people on coastal British Columbia, and its origin was traced to a white gold prospector who arrived in Victoria from the United States.[11]

The fact smallpox had been introduced by a white man from California did not alter public perception, which placed blame on other races. The Chinese, in particular, were singled out and the public's fear over living among or close to people with infectious diseases influenced government decisions. Before Albert Head was selected as the site for the West Coast's first quarantine station, the federal government had hoped to purchase land and locate a quarantine hospital at Esquimalt, immediately west of Victoria. The money for this was allocated in 1882 and in August the following year Ottawa appointed Dr. William Jackson as its first West Coast quarantine officer. However, the proposed location raised the ire of local citizens, including municipal, provincial and federal politicians, who felt it was too close to Victoria. The province, though recognizing the need for a facility, argued that Albert Head was better situated.

One of the more vocal opponents of the Esquimalt site was Noah Shakespeare who, as leader of the Workingmen's Protective Association (WPA), was fighting to eliminate Chinese job competition. The WPA had expanded to the mainland and by 1879 it was calling for the taxation of Chinese residents and the end of immigration. In January 1882, Shakespeare was elected mayor of Victoria and a few months later his upward trajectory continued when he was elected as a Conservative to the House of Commons. His success at winning one of two federal seats in Victoria was tied to the support he gave to the rising fear and anger expressed by working-class whites over the influx of Chinese navvies arriving to work for the CPR. Shakespeare's quick rise to federal politics occurred not long before the hiring of Dr. Jackson. In 1884, Shakespeare tabled a motion for a law to prohibit Chinese immigration. He claimed this was necessary because of unfair wage competition from Chinese labourers. Shakespeare's motion was amended and became law in 1885 as the *Chinese Immigration Act*, and introduced the head tax that had risen from $50 to $500 well before the CLC arrived.[12]

The protests against the Esquimalt proposal forced the government's hand and by early July 1884 the federal government designated Albert Head for the new quarantine station.

"With regard to the quarantine hospital it is satisfactory to know that Albert Head has at last been adopted," stated an editorial in the July 11, 1884, *Colonist* newspaper. "The apparently obstinate determination of the Dominion government a short time ago, against all reason and in the teeth of the strongest representations on the part of our city members and others, to locate the hospital at Esquimalt, promised to be a very serious matter indeed to the people of this place. A pest house at the Esquimalt terminus of the Island railway, in the very heart of what is in a short time destined to be an important town, was really something that could not be justified."[13]

Within seven years, additional measures were taken to deal with a disease the public found particularly abhorrent. In 1891, police and health inspectors rounded up five Chinese men in Victoria's Chinatown. All of them had the tell-tale signs of leprosy, a disease treated today as only mildly contagious.

That same year D'Arcy Island, on the western side of Haro Strait, east of Vancouver Island's Saanich Peninsula, was expropriated and became the city's leper colony. Over a thirty-three-year period, men suffering from the disease spent their final years at this lazaretto in small row-house units built by the city or in shacks constructed by the men themselves. The vast majority were Chinese.

On D'Arcy Island, contact with the outside world was mostly limited to quarterly visits to the lazaretto from supply vessels bearing clothing, food and wooden caskets for the dead.[14] Responsibility for the colony shifted from the city to the province and finally to the federal Department of Agriculture. An attempt to move the men from the island into the then-vacated Albert Head facility failed in 1906 after a Victoria petition landed on the premier's desk. The D'Arcy Island lazaretto finally closed in 1924 when a new lazaretto was established a short distance from William Head on Bentinck Island. At the time, the move affected half a dozen Chinese lepers.

The demise of the Albert Head Quarantine Station in April 1893 was caused by a series of bad decisions, misdeeds and deficiencies that proved problematic during another smallpox outbreak on the island and mainland, bringing widespread anger and mistrust between the provincial capital of Victoria and Vancouver. Lasting three years, the so-called "Smallpox

War" was characterized by panic, impatient ship masters, public finger-pointing, damning editorials, litigation and lasting frustration over bureaucratic indifference from Ottawa.

When municipal politicians in Vancouver were warned by their counterparts in Seattle that trade between those two cities would cease if passengers and cargo continued to arrive in Vancouver from disease-ridden Victoria, they declared a strict quarantine against Victoria. More than once, angry crowds tried to prevent ships from docking in Vancouver.

Historian Peter Johnson, who has written an excellent book on William Head, noted that four years after Albert Head began operations there was still no wharf, no resident medical director and no coastal vessel to convey doctors to the arriving ships. In addition to no heating, an inadequate freshwater supply and no disinfecting showers for the passengers, the station was understaffed and lacked the equipment to fumigate infected ships and disinfect passenger baggage. "The one thing Albert Head had going for it after four years was the hospital's yellow paint, which indicated its purpose was for quarantine," noted Johnson. "Remote and almost hidden in a wilderness miles from Victoria, there was no signage, no notice that the place had anything to do with the large-scale containment of contagious diseases. These structural and operational deficiencies reached out from the Albert Head Quarantine Station like the tentacles of some giant Pacific octopus, and it turned what was a masquerade of effort into a theatre of misadventure."[15]

Opened in 1893, the William Head station was a fresh start on an old idea. One of its earliest proponents was Dr. W. MacNaughton-Jones, who had succeeded Dr. William Jackson at Albert Head in 1890. As William Head's first medical superintendent, MacNaughton-Jones did not begin as a quarantine expert, but he was experienced in public health and worked diligently to avoid a repeat of the Albert Head disaster. Born in Cork, Ireland, he immigrated to the colony of British Columbia in 1862, at age thirty. Four years later he was British Columbia's coroner. The highly respected surgeon and family man moved to Vancouver Island where his career introduced him to a variety of working-class and professional people. In Nanaimo, on the island's east coast, he worked as a physician at a top colliery. In the Cariboo Gold Rush town of Barkerville he was the hospital's chief medical attendant, and in New Westminster he became superintendent of the new Provincial Asylum for the Insane. He was sixty-one years old when he landed the job at William Head.

The federal minister of public works had offered eighty-four-year-old Robert Weir $3,000 for sixty acres at the southwestern end of the William Head Peninsula. The aging "Laird" of William Head, as he was known, is believed to be the first European to settle on the peninsula. The widowed father of half a dozen children was, of course, originally from Scotland. He had arrived in Victoria in 1853 and was tenured as a land steward at Craigflower farm until he decided there were better opportunities to the west. In 1854, Weir purchased large parcels of land, including William Head peninsula. As a sheep and cattle farmer, the enterprising Scot made a name for himself in the nearby community of Metchosin, where he held positions on the school and church board and in 1873 served as district justice of the peace.[16]

When Robert's son, John, rejected the $3,000 offer as too low, the government expropriated a larger parcel of land from the Weirs. On March 23, 1893, the peninsula became the site for Canada's new West Coast quarantine station. By early May, contracts were signed and construction began.[17]

From the air, the peninsula resembles a dog's hind leg, jutting into Parry Bay with the foot pointing northeast toward Albert Head. In places, the rocky bluffs drop twenty metres into the sea. It is a beautiful, but often inhospitable place. There are inlets with gravel beaches and magnificent rock formations extending into the sea. The narrow peninsula is fringed with arbutus trees shaped by the wind. During storms, massive breakers curl and crash in thundering consequence against the coast, sending geysers metres into the air. On calmer days, sea lions bask on rocky ledges while varieties of sea birds wheel and dive above swells streaked with foam and ribbons of kelp. Across the strait are the snow-capped mountains of Washington State's Olympic Peninsula. To the southwest, along the dog's hind leg, is Pedder Bay with its long forked tongue separating William Head from Rocky Point. In the strait, just beyond the cliffs, are Bentinck Island and the treacherous Race Rocks.

In a report sent to Ottawa in August 1893, MacNaughton-Jones wrote: "The new buildings at William Head were completed about three weeks ago; they still however require furnishing, and like all large wooden buildings, have some considerable requirements; when these are completed and the furniture in, the quarantine station at William Head will be very complete and perfect."

This meant, of course, that the station would be ready to hold or quarantine passengers who were contagious or suspected of having come into contact with a contagious person. The latter included men, women and children who were perfectly fine, while the former included those at death's door. Not everyone, however, was entitled to the same level of accommodation while waiting to be cleared for entry or re-entry into Canada. The passengers disembarking from first-class cabins expected to be treated and accommodated according to the class hierarchy that still existed in Britain and elsewhere. This expectation extended beyond hotels and ships to hospitals, and even quarantine stations, where, in the case of the latter, it was not always the reality.

From the veranda of his residence at William Head, MacNaughton-Jones was afforded a good view across the strait. But while breathing in the pine-scented air, he could also survey his immediate surroundings and appreciate everything the modern station had to offer. In addition to a large hospital, there were the separate accommodations for first-, second- and third-class passengers.

The Princess Louise *and the much larger* Empress of India *sit alongside the pier at William Head, c. 1901.*

These were also identified as "Cabin" for first- and second-class, and "Chinese and Japanese" for third-class or steerage.

The hospital included an administration building with accommodation for medical staff. There was a dispensary, an impressive dining room and a large kitchen. Wings running off the main building contained wards with nearby bathroom and washroom facilities. There was electricity, hot and cold running water and the space was well ventilated. Approximately four hundred metres west of the hospital was the dormitory for detaining first-class passengers who were apparently healthy, but who might have been exposed to contagious disease. It featured long verandahs, overhanging roofs, a large dining room, kitchen and pantry. The *Colonist* in Victoria described the bedrooms as "very like the first-class cabins on a ship."[18]

The dormitories for steerage or Asian passengers were located along the southern side of the peninsula. They were sparse and usually cramped. Efforts were made to separate the Japanese and

Chinese from each other, and certainly from those occupying first- and second-class accommodations.

William Head also had the requisite facilities and equipment to deal with contagions. There was a steel and concrete disinfection chamber tucked inside a building near the wharf where passenger baggage, clothing and other personal effects were carted in and steamed at high temperature. On the wharf was the fumigation hut, which contained equipment to spray sulphur dioxide into the ships. The station also had a laboratory with a nearby isolation hospital, laundry facilities, a steam plant, a generating station, a water reservoir, vegetable gardens and a cemetery.

Unlike Albert Head, the water supply, noted MacNaughton-Jones, was "abundant and very perfect," as was the disinfecting chamber. Conscious of how remote the station was, the medical superintendent recommended a telephone be installed, and the main road from Victoria be extended to the hospital grounds. "At present there is only an approach to the city by water, owing to the fact that a small stretch of about one and a half miles on land is impassable. It would cost very little." He also requested that furnishings for the station be added as soon as possible because "we may have illness at any time."[19]

The doctor's assessment of the water supply and the station's other amenities proved accurate, but only for a time. MacNaughton-Jones, who left in 1896, was succeeded by Dr. George H. Duncan, whose brief time as medical superintendent ended in 1897 with the appointment of Dr. Alfred T. Watt.

Watt's work at the station lasted sixteen years. He was both highly qualified and popular, but his time came to a tragic end in the summer of 1913. Watt had become the subject of a Royal Commission of Inquiry to investigate complaints from a small group of first-class saloon passengers who had been held at William Head. The lead complainant in the group was Dr. Judson Burpee Black, a well-known physician and politician from Nova

Scotia who had served as a member of parliament and was past-president of the Canadian Medical Association.[20]

The inquiry was called a few months after Watt had detained the *Monteagle*, which arrived at the end of March 1913 with two people suffering from smallpox. One of the cases was a white saloon passenger while the other was a Chinese steerage passenger. In total, the ship carried 379 passengers. Forty-six of them were travelling in first-class while the remaining 290 were Chinese in steerage.

While William Head had separate accommodations for all economic classes and different races, this was not enough to satisfy expectations among five of the well-to-do. It took about a week for the mood among them to shift from displeasure to anger. Led by Black, they formed a committee to protest what they regarded as conditions well below their expectations. They raised their concerns with Watt, who knew the station was a work in progress and definitely needed a few improvements, including more accommodation. The committee then wrote a letter and — without sharing its contents with Watt or gaining the signatures of other passengers — sent copies to the Victoria newspaper and to Watt's political boss, the minister of agriculture, in Ottawa. Feeling blindsided and betrayed, Watt wrote to the minister directly and sent a rebuttal to the newspaper.[21]

The acrimony continued as the inquiry unfolded, and among the chief witnesses was Watt's assistant and bacteriologist Dr. Joseph Douglas Hunter, who had previously written to the minister supporting the need for an inquiry. Hunter, who had resigned while the *Monteagle*'s passengers were under quarantine, was highly critical of how the station was being operated. "Dr. Hunter attacked Medical Superintendent Dr. Watt, stating that on his arrival he was given no specific instructions as to his duties," noted a newspaper story. "He alleges that the Government launch vessel was used for other purposes than those for which it was intended."[22]

Hunter also asserted "a flock of sheep had been allowed to invade the grave inclosure [sic] at William Head" and the animals had "broken into his garden and destroyed it." However, the local newspaper also reported that when Hunter was cross-examined he could not clearly recollect many of the dates of the various incidents.[23]

An experienced medical practitioner, Hunter, who was born at New Westminster, British Columbia, on August 27, 1881, had, in July 1909, joined the *Empress of Japan* as ship's doctor.[24] Well-connected politically, his father was a Conservative member of the provincial legislature while his maternal grandfather was former British Columbia premier John Robson. After the war, Hunter served as a Victoria alderman and later as a Conservative member of the Legislative Assembly.[25] In examining his differences with Watt it is not difficult to see him more as a strongly contentious politician than as compromising administrator.

Additional testimony, however, proved favourable to Watt. In particular, various witnesses offered assessments that differed from passenger complaints. Captain Rupert Archibald, described in the press as "Ship's Husband" for the CPR's trans-Pacific service, explained how the station could be improved, but stated the passenger complaints were exaggerated, and that "Dr. Watt always would do his utmost to help passengers in detention." The only trouble, according to the newspaper's coverage of Archibald's testimony, was "that Dr. Watt was not in a position to supply first-class passengers with the accommodations and the surroundings — more or less of the luxurious nature — to which they were accustomed."[26]

Also working in Watt's favour was a letter written to the minister of agriculture by R. S. Kinney stating he was not part of the group of five, nor did he share its criticisms. He cited a conversation he had with Black that suggested "the grounds of his complaint against Dr. Watt are more personal than anything" and that the "so-called protest is more political than anything else ..."[27]

When the evidence was weighed by Commissioner H.W.R. Moore of Victoria, Watt was exonerated. Sadly, the Commissioner's final report to the minister, dated September 22, 1913, came too late for Watt. His health had taken a dramatic, downhill slide and there were serious family health issues to attend to in Ontario, including the illness of his eldest son, who contracted pneumonia, and the death of his younger brother, claimed by cancer.

On July 27, 1913, before the commissioner issued his report, Watt died when he fell from a third-floor window at St. Joseph's Hospital in Victoria. He had been undergoing treatment for neurasthenia, a condition characterized by physical and mental exhaustion. Today, this condition is sometimes considered similar to or identical to chronic fatigue syndrome. "Towards the close of the week he appeared to be improving and on Saturday night he managed to obtain some two hours of natural sleep," noted one newspaper report. "Afterwards a sleeping draught was administered and shortly before 5 o'clock he appeared to be in a sound slumber. Seeing him thus . . . his nurse stepped across the corridor to get some fresh water. On her return she found an empty bed and the window curtains disarranged."[28]

A month later, Canada's director general of public health, Dr. Frederick Montizambert, arrived in Victoria to conduct his annual inspection of the station. Asked by the press about Watt's death, Montizambert said he knew the man "intimately, both as a friend and officer of the department, and I have every reason to grieve for his loss from both points of view. Under his hand the local station performed wonders in its limited way and I am sure that whoever succeeds him to the office cannot better the record for conscientious work which he set us. During the past few years I have had occasion to observe his work here and I must say that it gave me personally, and also as head of the department, the greatest pleasure to testify to his many excellent qualities. I always found him extremely sensitive, and that trait perhaps wrought him harm: he was the sort of man who would rather suffer in silence than speak it out to the world."[29]

Montizambert also proudly told the press that among the structures being built at William Head was a new building for first-class passengers.[30]

After tendering his resignation at William Head, Hunter, who lived in Victoria, pursued additional studies in England. He returned to Canada in September 1914.[31] On January 10, 1917, he was commissioned with the rank of captain in the CAMC. He served at the Esquimalt Military Hospital until the end of January 1919.[32] When he died in 1970 at age eighty-nine, he had been predeceased by his twenty-four-year-old son John who, while serving as an air gunner in the Royal Canadian Air Force, was killed over Germany on June 26, 1943.[33]

Overall, 1913 was a year of much fear and unrest on Vancouver Island. That summer, while the inquiry was underway, a thousand members of the militia were deployed to restore order in the midst of a large and often ugly coal miners' strike. The unrest began in mid-September the previous year when a miner was fired at Cumberland. When other miners walked off the job, the company locked them out and hired strike-breakers, including Chinese and others from Britain and the United States. The striking miners demanded union recognition as well as safer working conditions.[34] The position taken by the Cumberland colliery found support among other island collieries opposed to unionization. By spring 1913, some 3,500 miners were off work. When the bloody confrontation ended in the summer of 1914, the striking miners were no better off, but the mines were doing well after hiring new labour.

Watt's good work at the station had an impact, one that was felt well after the appointment of his successor, Dr. Henry Rundle Nelson, who was dropped into an unenviable situation two months after the inquiry. The work of these two men set the stage for the wartime challenges, which included the most fascinating period of all for William Head: the arrival of the Chinese Labour Corps.

CHAPTER 12

New Arrivals,
Old Assumptions

"I thank you for taking care of my wife as she is bound to fret about my absence."

Under canvas . . .

It is not clear how well Captain Harry Livingstone knew the history of William Head and the controversy it had experienced just prior to the war. As a nature lover he would have been more interested in the flora and fauna, which included a variety of winged species. Seabirds and raptors, including bald eagles and osprey, could be spotted above the peninsula and along the rugged coastline, as could an abundance of sea mammals. Wildlife also roamed in the nearby woods, including black-tail deer, black bears and cougars. But unlike Dr. Henry Rundle Nelson, Livingstone had less than twenty-four hours to observe the place before the *Russia* was off to Victoria with its steerage still crammed with labourers.

While the quick stopover was welcomed, it was definitely not the norm: most CLC contingents spent days, even months at the station, and often for reasons other than illness.

*   *   *

Doctor Nelson's annual reports from 1913 through 1916 describe the work of dealing with a variety of infectious and non-infectious passengers, including men, women and children who arrived during the early months of the war. People suffering from smallpox, measles and dysentery were identified and quarantined while those at risk were examined and detained until it was safe for them to leave.

Most of the passengers who disembarked at William Head were tired, but otherwise healthy.

Between the outbreak of war on August 4, 1914, and March 31 of the following year, 154 vessels arrived at the station. Not including crews, they brought 16,189 passengers, most of them in steerage. This was a decrease of more than six thousand from the previous year.

Of the vessels that called that fiscal year, sixty-five were routinely inspected between April 1 and early August. Another forty-three were examined between August 4 and December 8 when the German East Asiatic Squadron was destroyed off the Falkland Islands. The remaining forty-six ship inspections occurred between then and March 31, 1915. "It will be seen that before the declaration of war . . . we had an increase of three ships over the same period of the previous year. During the next period of activity of the German Pacific fleet, there was a decrease of 17 ships, and the next period, after the victory off the Falklands December 1914, and the sinking of the *Emden*, November 9, 1914 a decrease of only one ship."

Interestingly, Nelson's report for that year also noted: "No ship billed for this port was captured by the enemy."[1]

Improvements to the station's Chinese and Japanese quarters in 1915 included the addition of an "Oriental Kitchen" with steam cookers. Flush toilets were also installed for the Chinese, Japanese and second-class passengers.

Sudden emergencies included a spectacular brush fire that nearly destroyed everything. Erupting on land just beyond the station, it required "all hands available at work for two days and two nights." The extremely close call underscored the need for better fire protection. "The water supply to the Station is totally inadequate to meet an emergency such as this," stated Nelson in his report to Ottawa.[2] It is worth remembering here that during the 1913 Royal Commission, Dr. Alfred Watt was accused of allowing his sheep to wander onto government property. Watt had defended his actions by stating the grazing reduced the risk of fire.

When contingents of the Chinese Labour Corps began arriving with the *Empress of Russia* in April 1917, seven months before Livingstone's arrival on the same ship, Nelson faced a daunting task. The number of passengers nearly tripled from the previous year and there was simply not enough indoor accommodation and not nearly enough freshwater for the CLC men who were held until their passage to Vancouver could resume.

At most, the William Head station could accommodate eight hundred people. Each CLC ship, however, brought between 913 and 4,171 labourers at a time, as well as regular passengers.[3] The station had a deep-sea wharf with a couple of jetties and there were many useful buildings, but not nearly enough accommodation for everyone.

Fortunately, land, tents and wire fencing were available for the Chinese.

Nelson's first and worst fear, however, was clearly centred on contagious disease. He had dealt with and managed that risk before, but the wartime movement of the CLC took this work to a whole new level, causing him to wonder what he and his staff might face if even one case of smallpox arrived on the *Russia*.[4]

While staring out at the ship on April 3, 1917, the nervous doctor did not have to wait long for confirmation.

In his annual report ending March 31, 1918, written for Director

General Dr. Montizambert, Nelson listed a Chinese labourer suffering from smallpox who arrived on that first CLC ship. All the labourers, he noted, "were quarantined together with such passengers as I considered possible contacts." He then explained how the *Russia*'s departure from William Head was delayed because there was simply not enough shelter on land for the men. Some seven hundred had to remain on board the ship that night.[5]

While responding to the emergency, Nelson was, no doubt, aware of a fatal smallpox outbreak in Vancouver only a few days earlier, which had put everybody there on high alert.

Then, within a few days of the *Russia*'s arrival at William Head, a second case of smallpox emerged at the quarantine station. Also diagnosed was scarlet fever, contracted by several labourers and a young girl who had travelled over on the *Russia* in first class. "As I had to land 2,058 people on this occasion I found our buildings of course totally inadequate and our Staff could not possibly handle such a number."

Of those passengers, 1,996 were CLC.

In addition to the extra workload and frustration over accommodation, Nelson had difficulty obtaining decisions from Ottawa. He informed Montizambert "it was almost impossible to keep in touch with you . . . on all points cropping up and requiring immediate attention." The director general of public health, of course, had responsibilities that stretched across the country.

Nelson told Montizambert he had "accepted the Military aid immediately placed at my disposal . . . and the Coolies were got under canvas supplied and erected in an enclosed camp by the Military Guards . . ."

Meanwhile, foul weather made life miserable. "During the period of detention of these Coolies it rained almost continuously, and as no floors were supplied with the tents the Coolies helped themselves to anything that would keep them off the wet ground, this included doors of buildings and sheds and the entire walls and roof of the blacksmiths shop, and fences."[6]

Metchosin Museum Society, Metchosin, B.C.

Three members of CLC pose outside their bell tent at the William Head Quarantine Station.

When the second case of smallpox emerged, the tents were dismantled and then fumigated. Nelson ordered a new camp with clean tents on thirty acres adjoining the station, and the labourers went directly into these following their disinfecting baths. "It became necessary to hold this extra land as time went on as large numbers of Coolies have been detained for Military and Transport reasons and this camp was the logical detention point."

British soldier Frank Heath, who arrived on the *Russia* on April 3, recalled the case of smallpox and the onboard medical examinations and vaccinations while the ship was alongside at William Head. He also described some bad behaviour. "We were only about two or three days from Vancouver, when a case of smallpox was discovered. When we landed at Vancouver Island, there were several cases, so, of course, we had to go into quarantine. All the passengers were allowed to proceed after their medical examination; the majority had been vaccinated on the boat. The whole of the ship had to be fumigated, and then she was allowed to continue. We were left with a few Canadian troops to look after our coolies, who went under canvas. That was when they started to be rather troublesome, continually scrapping amongst themselves with stones, knives, or anything else that was handy. Tent slashing was another favourite pastime. I suppose they had to have some amusement; there was nothing else for them to do."[7]

Chinese labourer Joe Hwei Chun also arrived that spring and, contrary to the behaviour described by Heath, the young man was philosophical and in good spirits when he wrote home.

> *My Dear Father and Mother-in-law,*
>
> *Your son-in-law left on the 5th month, 3rd day. We went aboard ship and started on our journey and travelled till the 24th. We have arrived in English Canada from where we take a train and in about 16 days we will arrive in France . . .*
>
> *My journey has been one of peace and tranquility under the protection of the Heavenly Father and I have met with no dangers or hardships. Every day we have all we want. Our eatables, clothing and everything we want are excellent.*
>
> *I hope that Mother and Father-in-law have no anxiety about me. I hope that all members of the Church prosper and don't backslide because the Kingdom is near and we are controlled by destinies.*
>
> *I thank you for taking care of my wife as she is bound to fret about my absence and furthermore present my compliments to the two families, my sister-in-law and the eldest daughter-in-law, and I wish you all a tranquil farewell.*
>
> *Your Son-in-law,*
> *Joe Hwei Chun, in reverence.*[8]

Not much is known about Joe Hwei Chun and whether he survived the war. His letter makes it clear he and his family were religious, and so there is the possibility he had heard about the CLC through the missionaries recruiting in Shantung province.

Meanwhile, the Canadian missionaries who had been granted temporary appointments as officers in the CLC were also making their way to France. James Menzies's ship the *Protesilaus* arrived in Vancouver on May 9, 1917, after being cleared at William Head. Ten days later, missionary Arthur Lochead arrived on the West Coast on board the *Monteagle*, and, as noted earlier, Gordon Jones reached William Head at the end of the month. By then, Percy Leslie, one of the senior Canadian doctors from the Honan Mission, had completed his trip across Canada and was in northern France at the CLC hospital at Noyelles-sur-Mer.

Nova Scotia-born missionary George M. Ross, who was educated in Halifax at Dalhousie University and Pine Hill Theological College, also passed through William Head, but his journey to Britain took much longer. "There is a letter today from Mr. Ross who evidently had a tedious journey of 88 days before he landed in England," noted the Reverend MacKay of the Presbyterian Foreign Missions Board in a September 5, 1917, letter to Lochead, who by then had reached France with the 42nd Company of the CLC. "He, however, seems to have had an encouraging time amongst the men . . ."[9]

At this time, Napier Smith, the preacher from Lunenburg, Nova Scotia, and his wife, Ruth, were still in China. Several months passed before he finally said goodbye to Ruth as she boarded the *Empress of Japan* in Shanghai in March 1918. From there, Smith caught a steamer to Weihaiwei, but his journey to Canada followed a different route. Instead of embarking on a large CLC transport, Smith and fourteen others boarded a coastal steamer and travelled north across the Gulf of Chihli to Port Arthur. Before proceeding to Japan via Korea, they travelled to Mukden, Manchuria, where the climactic land battle had been fought during the Russo-Japanese War of 1905. "In time we found ourselves comfortably housed in a Japanese hotel in Shimonoseki" on the southwestern tip of Honshu, the main island of Japan. After sitting around for three or four days, the captain in charge of Smith's small party received a telephone message. "The British consul gave instructions for all, except me, to proceed to the southern end of Japan and take passage on the *Empress of Asia*," recalled the missionary.[10]

The *Asia* arrived in Vancouver on April 29, completing a normal trans-Pacific crossing without carrying a large contingent of CLC. On May 22, she departed Vancouver for William Head where 3,600 Chinese labourers were embarked for a voyage to France via the Panama Canal.

Smith was ordered to remain in Shimonoseki and await passage to Canada on the *Monteagle*. He was to conduct a party of English-speaking Chinese students to France, where they were to work as CLC interpreters. "This was indeed an answer to my prayer and another evidence of God's strange working," Smith noted in his memoir. "I had hoped so much that we might be sent to France by way of Canada in order that I might be able to see your mother again — and here I was, singled out from fifteen others to conduct this party by that route."[11]

While each of their ships came alongside at William Head, the missionaries caught a glimpse of the quarantine station. Writing to his wife, Clara, on June 2, 1917, Jones explained the *Russia* had reached "Williamshead" Sunday night and the ship was still tied up there Monday morning. "The Coolies all filed out past a doctor, collected on the dock and came back on. It didn't take long and none of our lot was quarantined."[12]

While scribbling his letter on Canadian Pacific Ocean Service letterhead, Jones was both homesick and suffering from tonsillitis. "But you must not judge from the writing that it has taken every ounce of my strength and that I am writing you a last letter with my remaining few ounces of strength."[13]

* * *

By November 1917, "owing to increasing difficulties of transportation," Dr. Nelson noted how military authorities considered an additional receiving and clearing camp for the labourers, but after examining four sites on the mainland and two on Vancouver Island — they decided to stick with William Head.[14]

On November 5, shortly before Livingstone arrived, Lieutenant-Colonel Charles Milne became camp commandant, a position demanding a close working relationship with Nelson. Although enlarged to accommodate more than five thousand men, the camp, Nelson noted, soon swelled to 7,500 men, all CLC. The largest influx occurred on the morning of January 8, 1918, when 8,900 labourers disembarked. By afternoon, some 1,500 had departed for trains in Vancouver.[15]

When it came to contagious diseases, mumps usually topped the list. "Practically all Coolies were infected more or less," noted Nelson. "During the year we have removed and treated 229 such cases." From the ships, the disease seemed to hop from tent to tent and calls were made to hire two medical officers and orderlies to work in the camp hospital. "On two occasions, in October 1917 and January 1918, serious outbreaks occurred . . . and as many as 230 cases were under our care at one time."

Other illnesses resulting in hospitalization included bowel disorders, bronchitis, mental illness, rheumatism, septic arms from inoculations and tuberculosis. Venereal disease and scabies were isolated in tents in the compound around the hospital.

In the same paragraph, found on page four of his eight-page annual report for 1917–18, Nelson notes nine labourers died after arriving at William Head during the fiscal year of his report. He does not list them by name nor does he list the cause of death, but research for this book indicates the following:[16]

Wei Chen Shan (Wei Zhenshan, No. 31996) died July 28, 1917. The cause of death is listed as "dysentery, exhaustion due to

Lieutenant-Colonel Charles Milne (right) with Dr. Howard Miller and a young boy named Ronald outside the officers' mess at William Head.

Metchosin Museum Society, Metchosin, B.C.

prolonged dysentery." He was a twenty-two-year-old unmarried man from Shantung.

Ch'en T'ing Chang (Chen Tingzhang, No. 65855) died October 23, 1917, of an "acute intestinal obstruction" shortly after being admitted to Victoria's St. Joseph Hospital. The death certificate for the thirty-six-year-old unmarried man was signed by Livingstone's former travelling companion, Lieutenant John McDonald (who, by the time Livingstone arrived at William Head, had just, on that same day, left for Vancouver).

Hsi Chi Jong Wang (whose number is not available) died October 28, 1917, of pneumonia after suffering through tuberculosis. He was a twenty-seven-year-old married man from Shantung and his death occurred fifteen days after he was hospitalized at William Head.

Ting YenYu (Ding Yanyu, No. 65376) died December 4, 1917, of "acute hysteria, terminal dementia." The twenty-one-year-old farm labourer from Tsingtao was a married man.

Kuo Te Sheng (Guo Desheng, No. 94941) succumbed to "arteriosclerosis, apoplexy" on December 19, 1917. He was thirty-seven and had recently arrived at the station.

Chang Hung (Zhang Hong, No. 92560) died January 9, 1918, of "lobar pneumonia." He was a twenty-four-year-old single

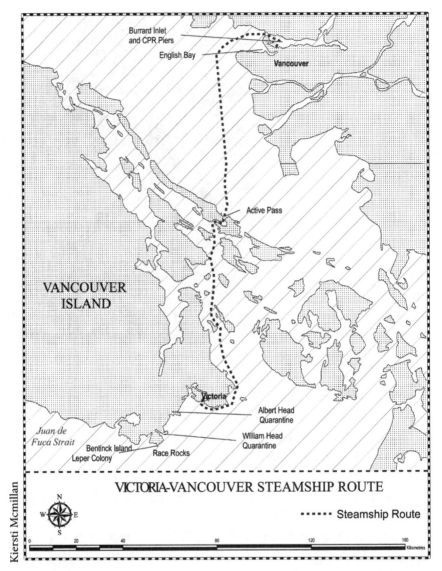

This illustration depicts the route the labourers took from William Head on
Vancouver Island (via Victoria) to the city of Vancouver, where they entrained
for the East Coast.

farmer from Tsingtao and had been at the quarantine station for about a month.

Chang Pao (Zhang Bao, No. 106053) succumbed March 15, 1918, of "tuberculosis, exhaustion and edema of the larynx." He was thirty-six.

Chang Yu Ts'ang (Zhang Yucang, No. 76539) died March 25, 1918, of "septicemia following inoculation, previous operation with drainage incisions, exhaustion." He was thirty-one.

Hou Yuan Ch'eng (Hou Yuancheng, No. 108671) also died March 25, 1918, of "acute tuberculosis." The twenty-four year old had been at William Head nine days.

Liang Feng Hai (Liang Fenghai, No. 131682) died March 26 of tuberculosis. He was twenty-nine.

On March 7, just before Nelson submitted his report to Ottawa, an unidentified soldier travelling with the CLC developed "a case of mild smallpox," a situation that resulted in the station being closed to outsiders. In April, four more labourers died. Fan Mao Chih (Fan Maozhi, No. 100495), age twenty-eight, on the first; Chang Cheng Li (Zhang Zhengli, No. 132781), also twenty-eight, on the third; Yen Chih Hsiu (Yan Zhixiu, No. 75135), age thirty-three, on the sixteenth; and Chang Kung Ch'ang (Zheng Gongchang, No. 130573) on the twenty-seventh. These men were not the last Chinese labourers to die in Canada.

Throughout 1917 there were ongoing problems with the camp's infrastructure. "The water supply has given me constant anxiety this year and I am glad to see the 10-inch pipes being distributed for the laying of the new supply from the City Main," noted Nelson. "As a measure of precaution, I laid a three-inch galvanized pipe from the deep sea wharf up the hill to the reservoir water tank, as at any time in the summer we may find it necessary to convey water by scow from Victoria to be pumped into this tank for distribution over the station and Coolie camp. So far I am glad to say we have been able to avoid this expense and all pipes laid for this purpose and in the camp will be available for use in the construction of

British Columbia Division of Vital Statistics

The death registration for Hou Yuan Ch'eng (Hou Yuancheng, No. 108671) who died at William Head on March 25, 1918.

the new laterals from the main supply. Last November our little lake from which we are now supplied, had sunk from 12 feet to 15 inches and we were only saved from conveying water from Victoria by the timely rains. The construction of the new main should be urged forward with all dispatch this summer."

Heavy use and misuse of the camp's latrines caused other problems. When the fresh water supply from the small lake near the camp proved inadequate, a pump was installed along the sea front and a water main extended to six latrines. This meant the latrines could be flushed every five minutes as opposed to every fifty minutes. It also prevented the wastage of some five hundred gallons an hour from the small reservoir.

Many of the Chinese were unfamiliar with flushing toilets. Most limited their intrigue to observing and using the technology, and then marvelling at the convenience. However, more than a few decided to test the latrines. "As months passed over and Coolies were being detained almost continually in large numbers we found that their curiosity or love of mischief caused them to throw large stones into the latrines for the fun of seeing the water flush the stones away," reported Nelson. "These caused endless trouble in stopping the drains and finally we had to close the water-flushed latrines and erect wooden platforms over sea-swept gullies."

Meanwhile, supplying enough food was another significant challenge. Initially there were only two steam rice cookers and the staff member in charge of the boilers, an engineer, worked twenty-hour days and even slept next to them to ensure enough rice was cooked. From the nearby Esquimalt navy yard, Nelson secured two additional steam cookers, but it seemed even that was not enough. "Great credit is due to Engineer Tracey for the willing way in which he has stuck to his post night and day, sometimes for two weeks on end," wrote Nelson.

Meanwhile, transferring passengers from ship to shore depended on the massive sea wharf, a substantial structure that rested on wooden, copper-covered piles driven well into the seabed. Instead of extending straight into the bay, the wharf ran somewhat parallel to the rocky shoreline. "It has had hard usage this past year and the tender piles have been renewed, also two of the approaches have been rebuilt, but the third still remains to be replaced and a lot of reconstruction on the main wharf is urgently required in the near future. The small wharf also needs considerable repairs."

Gales and fierce winter storms made it difficult and dangerous for large passenger liners to come alongside. Some ships overlapped the wharf by 160 metres, and so their masters requested the addition of a substantial dolphin. Consisting of a number of piles driven into the seabed, that wooden structure extended above the surface and provided another mooring point beyond the end of the wharf. This "proved its utility on March 4th (1918) when the *Empress of Asia* was probably saved from getting her stern ashore, as she hit the dolphin hard and rebounded into safety," explained Nelson.

Overall, between April 1, 1917, and the end of March 1918, the quarantine station saw the inspection of 127,602 passengers. Among them were 84,473 members of the CLC, 6,840 first- and second-class (cabin) passengers, 12,201 additional steerage passengers, 24,073 crew and fifteen stowaways. They arrived at William Head in 198 vessels. Forty of those ships carried contingents of CLC.[17] By comparison, the annual report ending March 31, 1917, listed 230 ships, but only 44,909 passengers. The fewer vessels in 1916–17 was, Nelson surmised, due to the withdrawal of ships from the Pacific to the Atlantic and also the result of the Japanese placing larger vessels on the trans-Pacific route, thus reducing the number of ships, but increasing the tonnage of their trade.

While it is likely apocryphal, the labourer described by medical missionary W.W. Peter in his article titled "Yellow Spectacles" is said to have arrived at William Head in April 1917. Known only by the name Li, this man described how "the great ship *Empress of Asia* forced its way through the water day and night" until land was finally sighted on the tenth night after leaving Yokohama. "There were no signs of fighting on shore. Only foreigners were in evidence, most of them in military uniforms, but so far as I could see and hear, all was peaceful." It was only then Li realized he had not landed in France, but in Canada.[18]

"Well, we left the boat and marched to a camp finer than the one we had in China. After a number of days we left on a train . . ."[19]

Doctor Harry Livingstone's friend Lieutenant John McDonald, along with Captain Arthur Connolly, also of the CAMC, arrived on the *Monteagle* on the night of October 12, 1917. After leaving Tsingtao on September 23 she had taken on coal at Moji, Japan, and called at Yokohama before facing the North Pacific. There were 1,681 labourers on board, eighteen more than she was supposed to carry. Lieutenant Matthew Ivy, the commanding officer of the CLC contingent, noted the extra men "found room on the hatches where they were quite dry and comfortable." During sick parades men presented with mumps and venereal disease. "The men had no opportunity of contracting the latter while in camp at Tsangkow and I am of the opinion that our stay at Moji was largely responsible for these. Coal is loaded chiefly by women in the midst of the men's quarters and in spite of extra guards being placed and a special watch being kept I fear it was impossible to prevent some of the women getting through to the men."

Everybody was tired as the ship neared Juan de Fuca Strait, but, as Ivy noted, the behavior of the men was excellent.

A day out from William Head, the *Monteagle*'s captain received a wireless message instructing him to land the contingent at the quarantine station. Ivy subsequently received a message from Canadian Pacific Railway authorities stating that, owing to transportation difficulties on Canada's East Coast, the contingent was to remain at William Head until further orders. "We disembarked at William Head at 6:45 AM on 13th October, each man being examined by the quarantine doctors. Eight men were suffering from mumps and a few others from various ailments which I trust will be cured during our stay here. The question of returning to China men suffering from venereal diseases is being considered."

Ivy's report describes the men as being quite content and happy to be off the ship. Drill, fatigues and eye parades kept them busy. "In addition, they are being trained to camp discipline, keeping their lines clean, erecting tents, hewing wood, using European implements, and, incidentally, learning a considerable amount of English with astonishing ease."

Labourers from Ivy's party also assisted with camp construction projects, frequently unloading cement, bricks and timber for the erection of buildings for military use. "This work was willingly done and the authorities in charge commented on the cheerful spirits of the men and the rapidity with which they worked. I was somewhat concerned, however, since the men's clothing and their shoes were fast going to pieces on the rocky ground and in the wet weather there was no means of drying them."

The men, noted Ivy, were not compensated financially for the work they performed, and while this did not seem to be an issue among them, it did not sit well with Ivy, to employ the men for a month without pay. He raised the issue with a Canadian military officer, but nothing happened while the contingent was at William Head.

Ivy's party was anticipating leaving the station on October 27. However, the day came and went without any movement because of a severe outbreak of mumps. Another party of CLC sailed to Vancouver instead. The next departure date was November 8, but this, too, was cancelled.

While the contingent was lucky to escape weeks of rain, the weather was cold. Ivy noted four labourers were returned to China on the *Empress of Asia* on October 25, and five more followed on the *Coconada* on November 3. The commanding officer's report also included a reference to the labourer who died October 23 at hospital in Victoria "while being operated on for acute intestinal obstruction." However, the man's name, which was Ch'en T'ing Chang (No. 65855), was not mentioned in the report.

When it finally came time for Ivy's contingent to depart William Head, the commanding officer had no choice but to leave twenty-three men behind for medical treatment, nine of whom had the mumps. In offering some constructive criticism, Ivy stated there was no efficient method in place to account for each man left behind. "Officers commanding battalions advise their depots of the registered number of the men they leave behind and of those they pick up and it would appear to be necessary that the military authorities in Victoria should render a statement periodically to the depot at Tsangkou and at Wei Hai Wei, showing the dates labourers are left behind at William Head, sent forward or returned to China, and the reason they are detained should be given."[20]

One of the largest contingents arrived December 13 on the *Tyndareus*. In her steerage were 4,167 Chinese labourers. "The day was the wettest I have ever seen here, over two and a half inches of rain being recorded, and a nasty wind was blowing," noted Nelson. "Owing to the high tide and height of the large vessel, owing to carrying practically no cage, it was impossible to use our two gangways, and all Coolies came ashore by one companion ladder, the time occupied being from 9:30 AM to 5:30 PM."

In commenting on the lack of a "cage," Nelson may have been referring to a cage that could be deployed to transport passengers and crew between ship and wharf when gangways or companion ladders could not be used. "As there was very little shelter ashore I made a point of having every man strip to the waist, we all got very wet, and cold, and several officers were in bed for some days afterwards with influenzal colds," noted Nelson. "Fearing a repetition of this occurrence I asked authority to cover two approaches to the wharf, and this has been done giving us over 500 feet of shelter which has been a great improvement during the rainy season. On March 16th the *Tyndareus* brought in 4,171 Coolies, but the tide being lower we were able to use our two gangways and the ship was cleared in two and a half hours . . ."

* * *

On November 12, 1917, Livingstone thought he might have the opportunity to reconnect with his friend John McDonald, who had been at William Head since mid-October. But on the same day Livingstone arrived at William Head on the *Empress of Russia*, McDonald had embarked for Vancouver on the *Princess Charlotte* along with 1,399 Chinese labourers. A second coastal vessel, the *Princess Alice* with 253 CLC on board, left later that day. The vessels reached Vancouver at 1:10 p.m. and 6 p.m., respectively, and by 4:30 p.m., McDonald, Ivy and 650 labourers were on one of the trains heading east.[21]

Life and Death at William Head

"Periodically the officers would invite prominent ladies from Victoria to come and see some of the crafts the Coolies made and quite a number would supply silks and embroidery threads and put in orders for cushion covers."

Arts, crafts and flogging . . .

The *Empress of Russia* spent the night of November 12 alongside the wharf at William Head while doctors examined her 2,596 passengers, including twenty-eight children all under the age of fourteen.[1] "Next morning the labourers were all marched out on the docks and examined by the doctors who stopped six with mumps," noted Livingstone. The rest, it seems, including several with sore throats, were good to go.[2]

The *Russia* was not cleared to sail for the provincial capital until just before 9 a.m. November 13, and so by the time she landed her first- and second-class passengers there at 9:55 a.m, the question for Livingstone was whether he would have time to tour the city.[3] Gone was any hope of seeing the sights with the two officers he had travelled to China with. While Lieutenant

John McDonald had already commenced his transcontinental train journey from Vancouver, thousands of kilometres to the east Captain Lou Sebert had almost completed his journey to Britain.

Sebert had arrived in Vancouver on board the *Teesta* on October 27. By early November, a CLC special had delivered the large party of labourers he was with to the port of Montreal, where the *Missanabie* was ready to sail. The former Olympic athlete turned eye specialist arrived at Liverpool on November 19, five days after his buddies passed through Victoria.[4]

The fact *Russia*'s time in Victoria was held to just an hour was either lost on Livingstone, not communicated to him directly or simply forgotten in the excitement of being in a Canadian city again. While the ship was coming alongside, the doctor believed he had time to disembark and take a quick "ride around town." His confidence was buoyed by the man he went ashore with, namely the officer in charge of the party, P. Edward Nettle. Livingstone had known Nettle prior to the trans-Pacific crossing and had even accompanied him on a route march with five hundred labourers at Weihaiwei.[5] Unfortunately, Nettle's decision to leave the ship and his party of labourers was one that, over the next twenty-four to forty-eight hours, had the potential to disrupt train schedules at Vancouver and even troopship departures at Halifax.

* * *

Meanwhile, at William Head, the hundreds of white bell tents remained as the only option for accommodation as the fast pace of the CLC movements continued through the rainy season and well into 1918.

From the military's standpoint, the circular cotton canvas bell tents, supported by a single pole up the middle, remained the perfect solution since first being pitched that spring, presumably with some difficulty on the rocky peninsula. After all, living

City of Vancouver Archives , MIL P194

A panoramic view of the CLC at William Head Quarantine Station, 1917–18.
In the background to the right are the ubiquitous bell tents the Chinese
occupied.

under canvas had — for centuries — been part of a soldier's life. In southern England, during the winter of 1914–15, the non-waterproof tents were assigned to members of the First Canadian Contingent, who slogged and griped it out in water and mud up to their shins on Salisbury Plain. Not surprisingly, those appalling conditions, and some of the bad moods they created, led to serious brawls in local pubs that spilled onto village streets.

Most of the Chinese assigned to the tents were used to spending time working outdoors through all kinds of weather. While some found it difficult, wet or harsh cold weather and crowded communal living did not bother most of them. The weather at William Head is generally pleasant all year, but it is not without storms or seemingly endless weeks of rain. A retrospective on the quarantine station written in 1961 and published in the *Victoria Sunday Times Magazine* noted that when it is pleasant at William Head there is "a lazy sea" and one can "look out over it for many miles to all the beautiful horizons. But when the winds blew and the waves crashed against the rocks or pounded up in a fine fury on the beaches, it was frightening in its immensity. It wiped out the hills, the distant land views until there was nothing else but the endless, towering breakers."[6]

The bell tents accommodated anywhere from six to twelve men, although British 2nd Lieutenant Daryl Klein remembered fifteen labourers per tent.[7] With their kit and few personal belongings, it was extremely tight, but not unlivable. Confinement mixed with foul weather, boredom and the risk of infectious disease did, however, produce a toxic atmosphere that pushed some men beyond the breaking point with sudden flare ups between the men and the guards.

Assigned to camp security and discipline were members of 5 Company, Royal Canadian Garrison Artillery (RCGA). The core of this unit was formed after British artillery and engineering companies were withdrawn from Victoria in 1906 and replaced by two smaller, but Permanent Force Canadian units. While most of the British regulars left that year, three officers and nearly fifty other ranks from the Royal Garrison of Artillery remained behind to form the nucleus of the company. At the same time, thirty-one members of the Royal Engineers helped form 3 (Fortress) Company, Royal Canadian Engineers. Even before the outbreak of war, both units were well trained and highly respected.

With thousands of men to supervise at William Head, 5 Company, RCGA, relied on CLC intermediaries to help explain camp rules, routine, and discipline. This was easier said than done, for many reasons. First, there were the obvious language and cultural barriers between the military and the Chinese; interpreters arrived with the CLC, but misinterpretations were common. The cultural divide was perhaps an even bigger hurdle, because no matter how well a message was delivered or received, its significance or level of importance could be judged differently by members of the CLC and by the military. These differences marked the CLC's entire wartime experience, from China, through Canada and on the Western Front.

Secondly, the labourers were not soldiers and, while the vague contract they signed with the British Emigration Bureau at Weihai-wei and Tsingtao established various terms, it did not specifically state the labourers would be subject to military discipline. Incredibly, it seems the men were informed of this only after they arrived in France. Regardless, life at the recruitment depots, on board ship and at William Head had exposed them to military hierarchy, discipline and punishment. From the start, the "non-combatant" labourers were treated somewhat like soldiers, and, while they were not given military titles, they were, as noted earlier, arranged into military-style units with their "head gangers" and "gangers."

The British military, with its command structure, rules and age-old traditions was, on the whole, a foreign concept for the Chinese, who preferred to depend on friends and personal resources, and on the various instincts acquired from childhood to adulthood. The sentries and other Canadian soldiers they witnessed at William Head were, collectively, a definite fixture, but their purpose was not always well understood by the Chinese, who simply wanted to get on with their journey. Although mingling, playing games, hijinks and joking with the guards was part of daily life, there were moments of mischief. From the guards' point of view, the Chinese were definitely an oddity; they were not soldiers, yet were expected to act much like trained soldiers. And while they appeared in a common uniform, the state of their dress was not consistent, although they all did wear slippers, not boots. The guards also witnessed men come off the ships with torn sleeves and holes or patched holes in their trousers.

It is also evident that with so many labourers arriving and being ordered into quarantine or cleared for the trains at Vancouver, it was a challenge for the guards to make sure the correct information got through to the men in a timely and useful fashion. Complicating this and the cultural and language barriers was the fact that the quarantine station, while incredibly important to the scheme, was but one step along the way to Britain and France.

Decisions made overseas in Britain and China, or by Canadian railway and military authorities in Ottawa or Halifax, in regards to the movements, had serious consequences for William Head and for men waiting there.

Backlogs due to shipping schedules on the East Coast or to the unavailability of trains on the West Coast caused a great deal of stress accompanied by frustration and lost tempers. Add to this the unpredictable nature of war and nature herself when ships could be lost to enemy action, the weather or mechanical malfunctions, which also occurred along the busy railroads.

Men who lashed out through boredom or got caught damaging property, stealing or fighting were dealt with harshly. As an example to others, those found guilty of serious crimes were stripped and fiercely caned in front of large gatherings at William Head. Australian-born Captain Edward Stuckey recalled how one big, strapping fellow fainted while another Chinese man was whipped.[8] One of the more dramatic photos from William Head, taken around the same time, shows hundreds of labourers lined up — three or four lines deep — forming a tight perimeter around a large field or parade ground. In the middle is a man whose trousers have been pulled down around his ankles. Two fellow labourers support him on either side while a man in a military uniform vigorously applies either a whip or a cane. Nearby, within the perimeter, four armed guards stand at ease while officers and a few other Chinese bear witness.

Also living under canvas were members of the Railway Service Guard. Most of the guards got along well with the labourers, but for some familiarity bred contempt, and confrontations arose. British Lieutenant Hugh Lowder, who led a CLC party from China to Canada in early 1918, noted how trouble began when a RSG man poked a labourer with his stick while the Chinese men were engaged "in some private drill." When the labourer protested, added Lowder, he was stuck harder by the guard, causing a wound.[9]

A member of the Chinese Labour Corps, who was found guilty of an offence, is caned in front of his peers at the William Head Quarantine Station on Vancouver Island, 1917-1918.

Military drill and various unpaid work details assigned to the Chinese were as much about keeping men busy and relieving tension as they were about improving camp infrastructure. And although the men were being sent overseas as non-combatants, they still marched regularly and dug trenches, dugouts and gun pits. These drills and fatigues, especially the marching, drew both attention and imitative responses from children whose parents worked at the station.

As more ships arrived, British officers leading the contingents formed opinions on how things were being run. British Lieutenant Horace Finlayson was in charge of a large party of labourers on board the *Protesilaus*, which dropped anchor off William Head at 2 a.m. January 8, 1918. With him, serving as medical officer, was Captain David A. MacFarlane of Clarendon, Quebec. In four days, MacFarlane, who had enlisted in Kingston, Ontario, as a private in 1915, would mark his thirty-third birthday. His appointment to captain in the CAMC had come in October 1917 after he received his commission in the Royal Army Medical Corps.[10]

The long process of unloading the *Protesilaus* began at 11:30 a.m., after the ship weighed anchor and came alongside the wharf. An hour later the first labourers were seen parading down the gangways. It took two full hours for the men to disembark. Once the all-clear was given following the medical inspections on the wharf, the men were formed into neat lines and then marched into camp, where a sergeant-major assigned tents. "We had taken with us from the ship 24 hours ration and this we distributed to the men that night," wrote Finlayson. "There was just some difficulty about food, but this was due to the strange surroundings and the darkness of the night."[11]

It had been a long and exhausting voyage for everyone, but especially for MacFarlane and his assistants, who treated large numbers of men, twice daily, during sick parades. Two labourers died, but neither their names nor their numbers appear in Finlayson's report. The first man succumbed December 23 of acute peritonitis — inflammation of the thin layer of tissue lining the inside of the abdomen. The second man succumbed a week before the ship arrived and his death was attributed to enteritis — inflammation of the small intestine. MacFarlane was, like the hundreds of men he had treated at sea, glad to be on land.[12]

Finlayson described the camp as being "in a shocking condition of mud, but after a few days it was transformed into something like a real camp . . . Companies were paraded twice daily for various fatigues, such as the carrying of wood, the breaking of rocks, and the procuring of gravel from the shore for the making of roads throughout the camp . . . It has proved an excellent preliminary training for all. To my staff it has provided an opportunity of seeing what camp life, camp routine, camp discipline really mean; it has shown the men what sort of work they will be called upon to perform in France."[13]

The lieutenant had kind words for the tall, slender and mustachioed camp commandant, Lieutenant-Colonel Charles Milne.

He "has been the very essence of kindness and has smoothed over many a difficulty by reason of his sympathy and rich experience. Nor has he omitted to look after our entertainment in the Officers' Mess. He has provided us with dances and lantern-slide lectures. In every possible way it has been a sojourn on which every one of us will look back with complete joy."

Milne was a curious figure to the Chinese. Appearing rarely, he was always in dress uniform; sitting ramrod straight in the saddle on his large steed or standing with his swagger stick under his arm. "Up and down their camp lines he would canter," noted Klein. "A kingly figure," he would also "gallop across the parade ground, raising a cloud of dust, regally regardless of them the Chinese."[14]

During inspections, Klein noted, Milne was "too royal to speak to them, but right royally he acknowledged their salutes. And *such* a salute he gave . . . There was something gracious about him; he held aloof; yet there was something intimate in the way he smiled when saluting. He did not come near enough to be recognized with love." Klein concluded the Chinese were endeared to him either through respect or fear because they assumed he would take care of them.[15]

Military service records make no mention of Milne's time at William Head, although a Vancouver newspaper story published on September 12, 1917, notes he was en route to Victoria, where "he expects to find orders as to his future activities." This is not surprising, given the secrecy around the CLC. However, a photograph, taken in 1918, shows Milne, a young child and a doctor standing outside the officers' mess at the quarantine station.

Born in the civil parish of Huntley, Aberdeenshire, Scotland, on September 25, 1866, Milne had served in the Gordon Highlanders before immigrating to Canada in February 1890. During the early 1900s he worked as a grocer in Dawson, Yukon, and at age forty-nine, on December 10, 1915, in Vancouver, he joined the 158th Battalion, Duke of Connaught's Own. He became the unit's commanding officer and worked hard to recruit men. On June 9,

1916, thousands of people lined streets to cheer the battalion as it marched with the colours to the CPR depot. The men were about to begin training at Camp Vernon in the British Columbia interior. Milne was fifty when he sailed overseas on November 1 on the troopship *Olympic* and he saw service in France before returning home on the *Megantic* in the summer of 1917.

While being interviewed by the Vancouver newspaper in September 1917, Milne spoke about the "oozy mud" and other slime his men marched or waded through in France, some smoking Player's cigarettes and just about everyone "singing with that forced and indefinable gaiety which is the spirit of the troops." At one point the reporter noticed how Milne "swallowed hard and his hands shook when he detailed some of the incidents."[16]

It was raining heavily when Lowder's ship, the *Coconada*, called at William Head on March 24, 1918, with a large party of tired and restless CLC. He, too, found the camp in a "filthy condition." When the 1,898 labourers disembarked they had nothing but leather slippers on their feet and, not wanting to ruin their only footwear, many decided to take them off and go barefoot.[17] Lowder ordered boots and woolen socks, but it appears from his report only the socks arrived and the delivery took several weeks. Like Lieutenant Matthew Ivy, who had already passed through William Head with a CLC contingent, Lowder saw how quickly the socks, along with the slippers, disintegrated on the wet, rocky surface.[18] "Coolies socks and shoes nearly worn out completely," he noted in his diary after a regular morning route march that took place more than a month after his party arrived.[19]

Lowder stated the filthy conditions were remedied and a drainage system added, which "took some time to complete, but kept the men occupied in their spare hours." Three Canadian doctors were among the handful of officers who arrived with Lowder's contingent. Right away, one of the British officers, suffering from tuberculosis, was taken to Victoria's Royal Jubilee Hospital while another unfortunate soul, a military man, who accompanied the party from China, was arrested and briefly jailed for intoxication. Later, the same man was reported absent without leave. He was found six days later in a Victoria hotel room, suffering from a hangover.[20]

On March 28, two of the Canadians, Captains Percival Faed and Gilbert Gunne, were granted leave from Lowder's unit. A month later, while the lieutenant's contingent was still at William Head, another Manitoban, Captain William M. Carr of Winnipeg, was granted leave. Carr had spent part of his time travelling back and forth between William Head and Victoria checking the health of the British officer suffering from tuberculosis.

The amount of work these doctors experienced was significant during their voyage and brief time at William Head. As with other movements, crowded conditions on board ship and at the quarantine station worked against the hope of maintaining men's health, even several months after the first contingents arrived. "Mumps were contracted the day after arrival, the greatest daily total being 160 men sick with this complaint at one time," noted Lowder. "The isolation arrangements were poor in the extreme, the men being placed in a brick building inside the camp lines, their food coming from the one kitchen in the lines." Lowder's report also noted the April 3, 1918, death of Chang Cheng Li, adding how the man's funeral took place at the William Head cemetery beneath a canopy of coniferous trees on the peninsula's south side, near the shoreline.

Three days later, a labourer suffering from leprosy was quarantined and later sent back to China on the *Tyndareus* along with seven others with contagious diseases. In early May an outbreak of conjunctivitis resulted in isolation for some 220 men. Lowder, who frequently consulted his Canadian doctors, believed the lack of soap and clean towels contributed to the outbreak.

Lowder was also somewhat of an innovator. Within a few weeks of arriving at William Head, he envisaged a labour scheme that would put the Chinese to work outside the camp for local farmers and land owners. Details of his proposal were sent on April 15 to Major General Robert Leckie, commanding officer at Military District No. 11 in Victoria. "I have the honour to request permission to make enquiries of land owners near William Head regarding the employment by them of some of the Chinese labourers I am conducting to France," he wrote to Leckie.

The lieutenant was convinced it would be good for all concerned, especially the Chinese, if a deal could be struck. The first step was to get Leckie's permission to approach local land owners. If that were granted he could find out from the land owners if they were interested in using Chinese labour from William Head. If so, he would ascertain how far the work site would be from the camp, the number of Chinese labourers required for employment, the nature of the work, and whether the men would be paid in money or in kind.

For Leckie's benefit, Lowder included in his proposal a copy of the British Emigration Bureau's contract signed by the Chinese at Weihaiwei and Tsingtao. "I have this day some 1,650 men fit and available for work. As will be seen by enclosed copy of contract, the Chinese are under obligation to work for 10 hours daily which, for them, is an easy day's work. The daily wastage of labour at present is, therefore, 16,500 hours. I landed here with these men on the 24th March last, and at the lowest computation at least 350,000 hours of valuable labour have been neglected."

The lieutenant told Leckie the men were "servants of the British Government" on a three-year contract. "They are from the north of China, are quiet, well-disciplined, and easily controlled, and as labourers cannot be surpassed. Their pay does not begin until the day they commence work in France, though their family allotments commence from the date of sailing from China."

Lowder made it clear the men would return to camp at the end of each working day for their evening meal and for sleeping. The number of men employed at a given work site would depend on the type of compensation, the rate of pay and the amount of

Metchosin Museum Society, Metchosin, B.C.

One of the tallest members of the CLC to arrive at William Head was this man who wore the stripes of a sergeant. The giant more than likely served as a "head ganger."

work involved. He assured Leckie he would provide adequate officer supervision for large work parties, but not smaller groups. "These men would excel at taking tree stumps out of the ground and destroying them, cutting cord wood, digging drains, etc. They could also very quickly be taught modern farm work, road-making and repairing, or anything connected with the land. They are nearly all farmers by profession, and they come from a province where husbandry is universal and unprofitable as a rule."

He noted the labourers are to be paid one franc per day in France by the British government and so if they were employed on Canadian government work in Canada they would, of course, have to be paid. This, however, was clearly not the case when members of the CLC assisted with construction projects at the federal quarantine station. But, as Lowder pointed out to Leckie, in the event of the CLC "working for private individuals on work that was productive or on work that would assist in the conduct of the war I would beg to say I could obtain at least 1,000 volunteers who would work for the pleasure of working and for having something to do whilst detained here."

Lowder believed regular work would assist in keeping the men fit and healthy. "Payment in kind, such as pork, of which the Chinese are very fond, could be made by farmers for such volunteer work."[21]

There does not appear to be any available record to reflect what the Chinese labourers themselves thought of Lowder's scheme. It is not clear how many of the men even knew about the proposal, let alone what they thought of the lieutenant and the impressions he had of them outside of their ability to perform manual labour.

In emphasizing the productive nature of the project, Lowder stated there is a "great shortage of white labour" due to the number of men who have enlisted and there is now "timbered land which farmers are unable to clear of stumps," thereby limiting the production or usefulness of their land. To allay any fear the project could disrupt CLC movements from William Head, Lowder assured Leckie any timber clearing or drain digging outside the camp could be commenced or stopped at a moment's notice. He concluded his proposal by stating "no productive effort should be left unemployed" when it came to utilizing wartime labour.

There were, of course, obvious drawbacks, not the least of which was the possibility labourers might walk away from work sites, never to be seen again, a notion that certainly would have driven immigration officials crazy. It was also going to be tough, dangerous work and so men could easily be injured or killed on these projects, thus unable to honour their contract and complete their journey to France. Interaction with the public outside the camp also increased the likelihood of confrontations between labourers, land owners or farmers.

Incredibly, Leckie approved Lowder's plan and communicated his decision to Milne. Soon, the enterprising Lowder fielded an offer from Cuyler Holland, manager of the British Columbia Land & Investment Agency Limited, which had an office in Victoria but was headquartered in London, England.

Holland proposed his agency start out with fifty labourers and raise the total to four hundred if the first batch of men hired to clear stumps worked out. In return, Holland proposed that when the land, measuring roughly 350 acres, was cleared he would place it at the "disposal of the authorities for returned soldiers, for five years rent free."

In his report, Lowder stated the work scheme died when Milne made it clear to him he did not want to see the Chinese working on any site other than a location he had approved, specifically a nearby farm that could take no more than twenty men. This may have been the Crosby farm at Metchosin, where CLC labourers were employed and accommodated in three or four bunkhouses on the property. "I do not know if there were specific individuals designated to live and work at Crosby, but Dad spoke as if he knew them quite well as a little boy," recalled Frances Weir, whose father grew up on the farm and was awed by one labourer who was "over seven feet tall. I do remember Dad telling me the Chinese were very friendly and hard-working and often played with him and his little sister."[22]

The well-meaning Lieutenant Lowder was also informed by Milne of the "political consequences" that could arise if any of the men escaped. Lowder may or may not have been reminded or told by Milne about the $500 head tax that had been waived for the CLC's passage through Canada. It is certainly not mentioned in his report.

Timing also had a role when it was learned Lowder's party was about to resume its journey to France. But instead of crossing to Vancouver and boarding trains to Halifax, his group boarded the *Empress of Asia* in late May, nearly two months after the contingent arrived at William Head. The *Asia*, with some 3,600 labourers on board, sailed south, passed through the Panama Canal, and then up the eastern seaboard to New York. She arrived at Liverpool in mid-June 1918.

While Lowder's proposal failed, there was plenty of work to do inside the camp. There were vegetable gardens to weed, clothes to wash and dry and lots of driftwood to collect off the beaches. Chinese work parties were also routinely dispatched within the camp to haul out trees felled or damaged by wind. The wood was cut, stacked, dried and eventually burned in campfires for cooking.

Rice was, of course, a staple for the Chinese, and there was a right way and a wrong way to prepare it. With so many mouths to feed, boilers were in short supply. In Victoria, Leckie thought he found the perfect solution when he suggested in a telephone conversation on October 17, 1917, that boilers from one of the ships could be dismantled and transferred to the quarantine station. He was politely informed by the CPR that the ship's boilers were an integral "part of the galley equipment" and could not be taken apart and used to cook rice. "I told him I would make some enquiries and would see if I could give him any suggestions as to how the difficulty they are experiencing at Quarantine Camp could be overcome," explained CPR Passenger Agent H.W. Brodie in a cable to the CPR's city passenger agent in Victoria.[23]

While the idea of using a ship's boilers evaporated rather quickly, Brodie did make some calls and did pass on a few suggestions, specifically about how the Chinese cooks at the Dominion Immigration Building in Vancouver used a "shallow dish with a high cover" to cook rice. Perhaps conscious of the importance of maintaining good relations with the military, Brodie asked the passenger agent in Victoria if he would telephone the general and let him know Brodie had at least made some enquiries.[24]

Violet Rhode, whose father, Frank, was a caretaker at the William Head station, was among the children whose parents found employment there. During the school year and through the summer she noticed a great deal, especially after the Chinese arrived. "The Station's landscape was covered with white bell tents with huge cauldrons set up for cooking," she recalled. "I can remember a Chinese man that stood out, or should I say, stood above the rest of his countrymen. He was well over six feet . . . and went off to war one day dressed in his pale, blue-grey uniform of baggy pants, front button jacket and little round hat."[25]

The large cooking pots were introduced after complaints over the quality of the rice prepared in the kitchens. A *Victoria Sunday Times Magazine* article noted the cauldrons were so heavy "it took a small crowd of them to drag them around."[26]

In his January 1918 report on William Head, Finlayson noted a different setup. "The cooking was done by our own men in four spacious kitchens provided," he explained. "There was some little difficulty at first but it was wonderful how they fell into the routine . . . The feeding arrangements were excellent and the only fault perhaps was an over-abundance of the ration. The whole battalion draws the day's ration every morning . . . consisting of bread, rice, vegetables, beef, salt, tea . . . There has been no lack of evidence the men have been given too much."[27]

The rocky landscape fringed with arbutus, fir and oak yielded many natural "treasures" that were saved and not burned beneath the cauldrons. Along the shore there were odd shapes of drift-wood, perfect for wood carvings. Also found were sea shells, polished stones and pieces of glass that had been worn down by the surf or regurgitated by the sea. The artists among the CLC turned these items into crafts that were displayed, sold or traded to first- and second-class passengers or to people who had business at the station.

As word of this talent spread, orders were placed. Visitors even supplied their favourite artist with stock material to be fashioned into original creations. "Periodically the officers would invite prominent ladies from Victoria to come and see some of the crafts the Coolies made and quite a number would supply silks and embroidery threads and put in orders for cushion covers or (etchings on) brass (artillery) shells," recalled F.R. Rockhill, the daughter of Doctor Henry Rundle Nelson, who donated a photo album belonging to her father to the British Columbia Provincial Archives. "This all helped to keep some of the Coolies occupied, which was quite a problem with so many there. This brass shell I have was done around 1918 by No. 132 of the Coolie Labour Corps; they just sharpened a nail to make the design."[28]

On the CLC Medal Roll, labourer No. 132 is identified as Wang Te Tseng (Wang Deceng).

Larger artistic creations took shape around the tents and at other locations throughout the camp, and all of them, noted Nellie de Bertrand Lugrin, told a story with a Chinese perspective. "They spent hours making what they termed "pictures." They would build a platform of rock and earth about eight by ten feet, level the top and construct the picture. It was meant to represent a story or play, and they made it by using pebbles, bits of coloured glass, flower blossoms or tiny shrubs. The children were delighted with their handiwork."[29]

George E. Cormack, who led a group of five hundred labourers from Tsingtao to northern France, recalled how the elaborate designs were set on a background of sand, with ground brick, coal, lime and ochre. "Those dragon designs would have made an excellent pattern for a carpet and the pictures of mythological characters seemed to transplant to Canadian soil the traditional art of China stretching back through the centuries."[30]

Lowder noted in his report how officers who had come to inspect the men were impressed with these ground murals and by the "drainage scheme carried out by the coolies, and the decorations around their tents."[31]

Like the tides, tension between station staff, the military and the Chinese labourers came and went. The most serious and well-documented episode occurred when a child belonging to one of the staff went missing. A newspaper account described her as a "beautiful little child" of five years with "golden curling hair, blue eyes, and of course, beloved by everyone." Panic ensued and there were some who jumped to conclusions with their suspicious minds set on the Chinese. The more rational responses considered other possibilities. With some forty buildings on site, there were many places — large and small — that could easily draw a child's curiosity, even though most children had been strictly warned where they could and could not go.

The search party, initially composed of station staff, quickly grew to involve every available man, woman and child. The girl's home was searched top to bottom as were other residences, inside and out, but there was no sign of her nor any response when her name was called. From their encampment, the Chinese watched the drama unfold, and soon more than two thousand Chinese joined the search. Within hours after her disappearance, the girl emerged from one of the buildings. Her golden hair was rumpled and she was rubbing her eyes; she had crawled into a laundry chute and taken a nap.[32] The Chinese spotted her first, and their willingness to assist in the search earned praise from the girl's parents, station staff and the military.[33]

From time to time, labourers also went missing. However, it was not easy for the men from Shantung to blend in, because of how tall they were compared to southern Chinese. One man who tried to hide out in Victoria's Chinatown was quickly spotted, apprehended, and then escorted back to William Head.[34]

*   *   *

Thousands of kilometres away in Ottawa, Canada's chief press censor, Lieutenant-Colonel Ernest Chambers, continued to keep a close eye on the CLC's movements and the press. It had not been easy, and by mid-1917 a few stories had appeared that required immediate attention. Meanwhile, those orchestrating the train movements were also working overtime to keep the CLC specials running on time. In mid-November that year, across the Georgia Strait in Vancouver, a normally mild-manned CPR passenger agent was checking his watch and seeing red over what he perceived as lack of co-operation from Captain Harry Livingstone's commanding officer, Lieutenant P. Edward Nettle.

Part Three: Canada to France

CHAPTER 14

Off the Water,
Onto the Rails

The man "took a very arbitrary stand . . . and appeared to be quite prepared to hold up the movement for five hours regardless of our protest and explanation . . . this would mean further delay in sailing of Atlantic transport . . ."

In the fog . . .

Captain Harry Livingstone and his commanding officer, P. Edward Nettle, were not on board the *Empress of Russia* when she left Victoria harbour on November 13, 1917. They had opted to tour the provincial capital, and when they returned to the wharf in the city's inner harbour all they could do was watch as their ship, with its large contingent of Chinese labourers, sailed away. "We certainly laughed when we saw *Russia* pulling out . . . and so we sent a wireless message to the ship, explaining our misfortune," noted Livingstone, who was a lot more concerned than his diary suggests.[1]

Making the best of a bad situation, the two officers headed for the city's grandest hotel, which at the time was less than ten years old. Overlooking the inner harbour and its steamship terminal, the Empress Hotel was among the CPR's crown jewels, built to exceptional standards on prime real estate and catering to the wealthy and famous. By 1917, this gilded chain included other hotels Livingstone had either stayed in or visited while en route to the Orient. In addition to the Hotel Vancouver, Calgary's Palliser, and Winnipeg's Royal Alexandra, there was the grand Chateau Lake Louise, Banff Springs and Quebec's Chateau Frontenac.

These establishments, along with the steamships and transcontinental trains, were all part of a business master plan tied to international shipping and personal travel. In addition to carrying people and cargo, the trains and ships were worked day and night against penalty to meet strict delivery deadlines for the Royal Mail. Promoted as the "All-Red Route," the transportation network guaranteed "safe" passage between Liverpool and the far reaches of the British Empire. A traveller could book passage on an Empress steamship in Liverpool, cross the Atlantic, check into a CPR hotel in eastern Canada, cross the continent by rail, settle into another CPR hotel on the West Coast, then cross the Pacific on another Empress ship bound for Hong Kong or board a Canadian ship bound for the South Pacific and Australia.

All this, including return passage, could be accomplished without ever having to leave the British Empire. Furthermore, by catering to the high expectations of the wealthy, the service was in line with the common assumption of the day that white people, particularly those with social standing, were ethnically and culturally superior and, therefore, entitled to better treatment than people of other races. So while travelling first class brought great comfort and excellent service, it was also sold on the idea of venturing forth and seeing the world within the company of one's economic class and race.

Livingstone certainly could not count himself among the wealthy, but throughout his journey he was drawn to local attractions, whether a thermometer in White River, Ontario, the Imperial Palace in Tokyo or a fancy hotel like the Empress. His lunch there with Nettle, however, was preceded by an unavoidable visit to the ticket office where both men secured passage to Vancouver on the next available vessel.[2]

Often called "pocket liners," the vessels of the "Princess" fleet offered a downsized version of the impeccable service and amenities found on the company's ocean liners. With names beginning with "Princess," many of these vessels were built to the specifications of American-born steamship Captain James Troup, a talented and energetic ship designer and businessman who, after his appointment as steamship operations manager, convinced the CPR to build first-class vessels and quality port facilities, including the terminal at Victoria.[3]

The *Princess Charlotte*, which had arrived in Vancouver on November 12 with Livingstone's friend John McDonald and nearly 1,400 Chinese labourers, was one of the finer vessels in the fleet.[4] Built in Glasgow, Scotland, and launched in late June 1908, she was a three-funnel vessel, converted to oil in 1911. She had a length of just over one hundred metres and a displacement of 3,926 tons.[5] However, when the *Charlotte* sailed that morning she had nearly two hundred more passengers than she was certified to carry in daytime service. But, this was wartime, and the men of the Chinese Labour Corps had to be moved.

After passing through the ornate entrance hall with its teak paneling and tiled flooring, McDonald had time during his four- to five-hour voyage through the Gulf Islands to the mainland to explore the vessel while keeping an eye on the Chinese passengers. The *Charlotte*'s first-class passenger accommodation featured two- and three-berth rooms complete with electric radiators, plush sofa beds and washstands. There was a large central hall with crimson seats, a ladies tea room, a barber shop, smoking rooms and a dining saloon for 133 people. Topping the accommodations were four bridal chambers, affirming *Charlotte*'s reputation as the "honeymoon boat" and "the bridal ship."[6] The Chinese experience was more limited. The men were jammed in tightly, but those on the open deck could breathe in the fresh, salty air, and, if it was not too foggy, marvel at the stunning island vistas.

Sea fog, of course, is no stranger to the south coast of Vancouver Island and the Georgia Strait. Much of it, along with marine stratus often lying over the colder waters off the island's west coast, is easily drawn toward the mainland through Juan de Fuca Strait. These inflows create days or weeks with very little visibility. The Gulf Islands and Active Pass are particularly treacherous under such conditions. In the days before and even after the introduction of radar, ships or coastal steamers have been compelled to slow down, maintain a steady heading, and sound the horn.

The journey from Victoria to Vancouver was part of the CPR's busy Triangle Route connecting the two Canadian ports to Seattle, Washington. From Victoria, Vancouver-bound steamers and ocean liners entered the Juan de Fuca Strait, travelled east to the Haro Strait, and then north past D'Arcy Island. Maintaining a north-eastward heading along Vancouver Island's Saanich Peninsula the vessels passed between James and Sidney Islands, across Moresby Passage and into Swanson Channel. After passing between North Pender and Prevost Islands, large ocean-going ships as well as coastal steamers entered the tight and unforgiving "S" curve of Active Pass before reaching Georgia Strait southeast of Galiano Island.

In the report from McDonald's commanding officer, Lieutenant Matthew Ivy, there is no indication the *Charlotte* and *Alice* were delayed by weather. However, fog was present or rolling in over Georgia Strait. It was thick before Livingstone and Nettle completed their voyage to Vancouver on the thirteenth, although the first three hours out of Victoria afforded some excellent views. To Livingstone, the Gulf Islands reminded him of the Seto Inland Sea separating the Japanese islands of Honshū, Shikoku and Kyūshū. Around 5:30 p.m. the coastal steamer Livingstone was on encountered heavy fog "and almost ran into a small freighter. They kept blowing the whistle all the time."[7]

When the fog is thick off Vancouver, coastal steamers and ocean-going vessels usually drop anchor in English Bay before attempting passage through First Narrows to the piers in Vancouver Harbour. The wharfs were located roughly in the same area where Canada Place stands today, jutting out from land that had been granted to the CPR as part of its massive transcontinental railway venture. The piers served the CPOS ships as well as other long-haul vessels carrying passengers, the mail and various commodities to and from the Orient. However, the wharfs also served the many coastal and river steamers that plied the routes to deliver people and cargo to ports on Vancouver Island, along the Fraser River, and the mountainous coast, from Puget Sound to the Lynn Canal, an inlet into southeastern Alaska.[8]

The loggerhead moment between Nettle and CPR Passenger Agent Brodie occurred shortly after Nettle and Livingstone arrived in Vancouver around 7 p.m. on the thirteenth. The episode reflects how personalities, the weather and equipment malfunctions interfered with carefully orchestrated plans — spearheaded by the CPR — to move the Chinese across Canada as quickly as possible.

Nettle was frustrated after missing the *Russia* at Victoria. Brodie, on the other hand, was fuming over the response he got when he asked Nettle to land his CLC contingent immediately and make preparations to board the trains.[9]

Much of Brodie's angst stemmed from his awareness of the tremendous pressure behind the urgent need to keep the CLC movements rolling at a time when more ships were arriving and disembarking labourers at William Head and Vancouver. Eleven days before the *Empress of Russia* arrived at William Head on November 12, Brodie's boss in Montreal, Walter Maughan, had told naval authorities in Ottawa there were 4,050 labourers from the *Monteagle* and *Coconada* waiting to move forward from William Head. The cable, sent November 1 to the navy's Lieutenant-Commander S.H. Morres, noted the *Russia* was carrying roughly 2,300 labourers. Sometime between then and November 5, there was a phone conversation between Morres and Maughan in which the latter was informed of the possibility of changes in the steamship arrangements on the East Coast, particularly the expected arrival of the troopship *Olympic*. Maughan was instructed to "hold up sending" the Chinese from the *Monteagle* and *Coconada* until the steamship was available at Halifax. Maughan promptly informed Brodie of the development.

Colonel C.S. MacInnes, adjutant general of the Department of Militia and Defence, meanwhile, was confident up to 9,500 labourers could be accommodated at William Head, and, if push came to shove, transports sailing from China could be delayed.

In a cable sent to Morres on November 5, Maughan asked what he should do when the *Russia* arrived at the quarantine station with 2,290 more labourers. "Will it be in order to send them forward immediately on their arrival? Presume this will be necessary as the Detention Quarters at Williams [sic] Head is at present full to capacity with Coolies."[10]

Morres replied by explaining the adjutant general's views on the capacity at William Head, noting there were at present about 6,500 labourers there and the draft from the *Russia* will "bring them near the limit." He explained if more labourers arrive before the labourers at William Head could be moved then the Chinese "will have to remain on shipboard."

The cable did not specifically answer Maughan's query on what to do with the *Russia*. However, the ship was ordered to proceed to Vancouver via Victoria as soon as possible. In the interim, Maughan told Morres, the buildup of labourers at William Head meant local coastal steamers would probably have to be taken completely out of regular service. And given the smaller size of these vessels, he estimated it would take four days to move thousands of men to the mainland.[11]

After leaving Victoria, the *Russia* was expected to arrive at Burrard Inlet at 4 p.m., November 13. On account of heavy fog, the ship had to drop anchor in English Bay and remain there overnight Tuesday. "The fog was very heavy on Wednesday morning and provision was made to send out a tender to take off the saloon passengers and the mail," noted Brodie in a cable to Maughan.[12]

Meanwhile, the steamer Nettle and Livingstone had caught in Victoria landed in Vancouver while the *Russia* was still on her chains in English Bay. Nettle elected not to visit Brodie's office until 11 a.m., Wednesday, November 14. In his cable to Maughan, Brodie explained he had told Nettle "it would be impossible for us the CPR to make definite plans for the movement of the Chinese from Vancouver until the *Russia* had docked."[13]

Brodie had also explained to Nettle that arrangements could be made to send boats out to the *Russia* to collect the labourers and transfer them to the dock. Nettle, however, was not in a good mood. He told the passenger agent he had missed his ship in Victoria on account of being misled by one of the ship's officers, who had told him the *Russia* would remain in Victoria for an hour and a half before sailing to Vancouver. "He acknowledges, however, that he was cautioned by the 2nd officer just as he was going ashore that it would not be safe for him to figure on the ship remaining for that length of time as she would probably sail earlier," Brodie told Maughan. "I have since been informed that he was told the steamer would sail at 11 AM and I understand she did sail at that hour."[14]

Insisting it was the fault of the ship, Nettle told Brodie he had three to five hours work to complete before he could get his contingent ashore. Shortly after Nettle left Brodie's office, the fog lifted and the *Russia* raised anchor, steamed through the First Narrows, and arrived at the pier by noon.[15]

This development, however, did not end the matter.

With the *Russia* alongside, Brodie contacted Nettle and told him the CPR was prepared to move the CLC men immediately, owing to the availability of the *Olympic* in Halifax. He asked Nettle to get his men ashore by 1 p.m. "He told me he would not

City of Vancouver Archives, , CVA 152-8.3

An excellent view of Pier A at Vancouver; the Empress *ships used both.*

be able to do this and repeated his previous statement that he had work to do that would take him three to five hours," Brodie explained to Maughan. "I told him the transport was already being detained at Halifax for the arrival of his Chinese and that my orders were to forward them immediately. He again replied the delay could be put down to his missing the steamer at Victoria which was the fault of the C.P.O.S., and again stated he would not allow the Chinese to be landed until he had completed the work which it was necessary for him to do."[16]

Now seeing red, Brodie forcibly called Nettle's attention to the seriousness of holding Atlantic transport. He explained he would have to wire Maughan to explain there was a delay due to Nettle's refusal to land his passengers. "This did not seem to impress him and he was in my office when I dictated the wire to you," an exasperated Brodie told Maughan. "After leaving my office, however, he was either able to complete his work in a shorter time . . . or possibly on second thought decided it would be better for him not to delay the movement . . ."[17]

Members of the CLC cross a small foot bridge on their way to the Dominion Immigration Building at Vancouver.

At 2 p.m., Brodie received word from Nettle he would be disembarking the Chinese at 2:30 p.m. The Chinese disembarked at 2:45 and by 6:30 all of the men were on board the trains.

Adding to Brodie's woes were other delays. Freight unrelated to the CLC was loaded on top of CLC stores, which slowed down the loading of the trains. A further delay was caused by "breakdowns which necessitated holding the fourth train until November 15."[18]

Still, it was Nettle who frustrated Brodie the most, noting the man "took a very arbitrary stand in regard to the prompt unloading of his coolies, and appeared to be quite prepared to hold up the movement for five hours regardless of our protest and explanation to him that this would mean further delay in sailing of Atlantic transport which would be awaiting his arrival in Halifax."[19]

In conclusion, Brodie suggested to his boss that a report should be made to Ottawa and that some further instructions be given officers in charge of these movements by the Admiralty at Hong Kong."[20]

Nettle, meanwhile, continued to defend his actions by pointing to the information he received at Victoria.

Lost, of course, in the whole kafuffle were the Chinese who, for the most part, remained stoic while staring into the lifting fog or coming down the gangways, and across to the Immigration Building. For them, long stretches of idleness often ended abruptly with orders to grab their kit and move from shore to ship or ship to shore, and suddenly onto trains that left day and night. Men who had become ill since leaving William Head and others who had been sick longer, but overlooked during regular sick parades, were sent to hospital in Vancouver. Those men were either treated and put onto later trains or sent home.

Four labourers died in hospital at Vancouver that summer and were interred at the city's Mountain View Cemetery. They were Ch'u I Kung (Ch Yigong, No. 14057), who died May 31, 1917; Han Shu Ch'ing (Han Shuqing, No. 30896), who died July 9, 1917; Ch'en Wang Feng (Chen Wangfeng, No. 33258), August 4, 1917; and Ts'ao I Hsiang (Cao Yixiang, No. 61935), August 25, 1917. The death certificates for all of these men were signed by Dr. A.S. Monro. Furthermore, the United Kingdom Book of Remembrance indicates the remains of all four were exhumed and repatriated to China. A fifth labourer, Li Ju Ying (Li Ruying, No. 106855), was also interred at the cemetery. He died on February 21, 1920, while returning to China. The CLC Medal Roll states he "Died at Sea," but the British Columbia death registers note the place of death as "CP Ry Depot" and the burial ground as Mountain View.

* * *

Meanwhile, in Ottawa, Canada's chief press censor and his staff continued to have their work cut out for them.

Seven months before Livingstone arrived on the *Empress of Russia*, the same ship had been in the news. The attention paid to her by the press on April 4 was not on account of her CLC passengers, but on account of a smallpox outbreak in Vancouver in late March. The contagion did not arrive in Vancouver with the *Russia,* but had originated from another steamer that came from Hong Kong. A number of longshoremen were infected and at least three deaths occurred in Vancouver before the contagion was halted. The *Russia* arrived at Vancouver on the fourth, but at the time of the outbreak she was still far away, not even at William Head. She did have smallpox on board, but it had been quarantined on the island.

Two stories appeared in the *Vancouver Province* on April 4. One pointed out how the disease had claimed the life of a nineteen year old named Harry Olson, "who passed away this morning in Vancouver at the isolation hospital. Altogether there are nine cases, including one at North Vancouver. The city medical health department, however, has the matter well in hand, every contact having been followed up and vaccination imposed on all persons suspected of the least liability to have taken the infection."[21]

The other story was longer and named the *Empress of Russia,* focusing on how the ship had been held a full day at William Head. The newspaper reported that the ship "reached port Vancouver about 2 o'clock this morning after touching at Victoria last night to land passengers and mail for that city. She came to her berth at Pier "A" and this morning the passengers disembarked and the cargo began to pour out of the holds of the big liner." The article noted there were 205 first-class and 134 second-class passengers as well as "a large number in the steerage."[22]

Chambers felt rather satisfied after reading the clippings sent to him by his West Coast contact, Malcolm Reid, the former federal immigration agent for Vancouver who was working as the federal immigration inspector for the province. Although the news of smallpox was terrible, neither story contained any information regarding the CLC or its movements. Chambers replied to Reid on April 12 telling him the information was useful as it indicates "the Vancouver newspapers are doing their "bit" and observing our instructions . . ."[23]

Canadian mainstream editors and publishers had read Chambers's circulars and took each one seriously. Most of these newsmen saw themselves as performing a valuable wartime service by not publishing information that could compromise the lives of military personnel or the safe delivery of wartime supplies. Chambers had also continued to benefit from the cooperation of the various telegraph companies.

But while the circulars were very clear, Chambers had to respond to a newspaper article in the *Toronto Globe*, April 6, 1917, two days after the *Empress of Russia* reached Vancouver with the first Chinese labourers. The headline read: "Coolies in Civil Work Supplant Men in Trenches." "News from the Presbyterian mission field in Honan, China, is especially interesting just now, owing to the fact that the British and French Governments have decided to employ a large number of the natives of that district as coolies in civil work in France to take the place of men who have been drafted to the front," the article stated. "For this purpose an offer has been made to the mission staff both of ordained and medical men to accompany them in the special capacity of interpreters and guides. Out of the staff of thirty-one at the station, fifteen have expressed their readiness to undertake this new and patriotic mission. Among them are Dr. W.R. Reeds, formerly of the Y.M.C.A at Toronto, and Dr. P. C. Leslie, and Rev. J.A. Mowatt, Montreal. While some of these Chinese labourers will go to Europe by an all-water route, it is likely that some . . . may pass through Canada."

The page-four article did not attribute the information to any source, but it is clear the news came from one of the missionaries in China who thought, innocently enough, to write home about the scheme and how missionaries were "answering the call" and "doing their bit."

On April 7, Chambers wrote a courteous letter to the newspaper's editor, stating he would "be much obliged if you will kindly draw the attention of your local staff to the importance of a close observance of the Order recently issued regarding the preservation of secrecy as to the movements of the Chinese coolies in Canada."

Chambers emphasized how "instructions received from the Home government" make it clear "why every effort should be made to preserve absolute secrecy . . . as to their transportation from China to France."

It is noteworthy that Chambers ended his letter with: "Exactly what the reasons are, I do not know, but the request for secrecy by the Home Government is very specific and they appear to consider the matter of great importance." At the time, Chambers understood why wartime movements demanded secrecy, but he may not have been entirely convinced, at least at first, why there had to be so much surveillance and secrecy in Canada surrounding the Chinese. His soft approach with the editor, however, had much to do with his desire to maintain a co-operative posture with the large, mainstream press.[24]

On the same day, Chambers sent a "Confidential and Secret" cable to high-level Canadian church superintendents and administrators. Included on the receiving end were the Reverend Samuel Dwight Chown, general superintendent of the Methodist Church of Canada; the Reverend Sydney Gould, general secretary of the Missionary Society of the Church of England in Canada; the Reverend W.J. McKay, editor of the Canadian Baptist; the Reverend Thomas Stewart of the Presbyterian Church of Canada; and the Reverend John Somerville, agent and treasurer of the Presbyterian Church of Canada.

Chambers told these officials what they already knew through their correspondence and from conversations with Canadian relatives of missionaries in China. The chief press censor was obviously aware of this, but his goal was to prevent further leaks. "The Imperial Government has asked us to attempt to preserve secrecy as to the movement of these men and it is giving me much concern to notice that certain very broad hints as to what is going on have appeared in certain papers as a result of leakages of information received from missionaries of various bodies, whose services have been secured in China . . . I will be deeply thankful if you will kindly pass word around to members of your staff, in Canada and among those of your clergy who are in touch with Chinese missionaries, impressing upon them the importance of co-operating with us to secure secrecy . . ."

On April 9, the Reverend Somerville replied, stating: "I am afraid we are a little late in trying to suppress information. However, we shall send out confidential letters to all our Missionaries who are home on furlough, not to give out any information in any way regarding these men, which may be received from Missionaries in China. I can well understand the embarrassment it may cause when information of this kind is scattered abroad through the Public Press. Many people think such information is a real scoop for the local paper, and they are glad to publish it with their own embellishment."

Somerville promised the church "shall do what is possible to aid you in the matter."[25]

". . . I thoroughly appreciate the kindly spirit in which you so kindly agreed to co-operate in connection with this very important matter," Chambers replied, April 10.

That same day, Chambers was informed by the editor of the *Vancouver Province* that newspapers south of the border were enquiring about Chinese labourers arriving at Vancouver. The editor's cable explained how the Seattle manager of Associated Press contacted him, wanting to confirm the story. "Extremely obliged," replied Chambers. "I wish you would say to the Seattle Associated Press manager that censorship requirements forbid you from making any statement further than that authorities deem it of importance that reports regarding the rumour be suppressed."

Chambers immediately contacted Fred Livesay, former president of the Western Canadian Press Association, who had become his Winnipeg-based press censorship aide for Western Canada. He also cabled C.O. Knowles of the Canadian Press in Toronto, explaining it is "most desirable to stop this story. Can you make a polite request on my behalf to suppress to the management Associated Press in the United States. Important." Chambers also cabled the telegraph companies, specifically G.D. Perry of the Great North Western Telegraph Company in Toronto and J. McMillan of CPR Telegraphs in Montreal. He wanted to know if any message regarding the *Russia*'s arrival had been sent over their respective telegraph wires. McMillan stated the telegraph office in Vancouver found nothing in recent files to indicate the message was sent over their wires. Perry's investigation also turned up nothing. Livesay, meanwhile, reported that Chambers's directive to "kill" any news from Seattle regarding the Chinese had been forwarded to western Canadian editors.

McMillan suggested Chambers check with the British Columbia Telephone service. "I am very much obliged for the information regarding the B.C. Telephone service," wrote Chambers on April 11. "I have been in communication with them on this very subject, but you realize as I do, that the only effective way to censor a telephone line is to cut it out, and I rather hesitate to do that . . ."

Chambers also followed up with Livesay, thanking him for his assistance. "I appreciate your action in this matter very much, and may say that I hope, within a few days to leave for Washington to make arrangements for a satisfactory system of co-operation between our Press Censorship and that just organized in the United States."

However, muzzling the Canadian press was a lot easier than preventing American mainstream newspapers and other publications from publishing news and photographs on the CLC. This remained a much larger and mostly futile challenge even after the United States declared war on Germany in April 1917.

On April 8, two days before the wires began humming over the threat of a news leak on the West Coast, the *Seattle Sunday Times* went to press with a story under the headline "New Arm of War Machine Organized By British Staff Important Factor in

Trench Fighting." Below this was a large photograph showing Chinese labourers crossing what appears to be a foot bridge. "Section of Pick And Shovel Brigade" states an additional heading over the story, which begins: "Maybe the Seattle citizen-soldiers who are sent to Europe with the proposed expeditionary force will not have to dig trenches after all.

"For according to M.H. Crawford, who has just returned from an extensive tour of the Orient, the Allies have already organized a force of 45,000 "trench specialists" to prepare the fighting fronts for the soldiers.

"This photograph shows 2,500 of these gunless war experts — Chinese coolies every one of them — arriving at Vancouver, B.C., on their way to the fighting front. From all appearances they are men of remarkable physique and should be able to stretch a line of trenches in a short time.

"According to Crawford's story, Great Britain has 'enlisted' more than 45,000 Chinese coolies for 'war labor' at a small British port in China. The men are all outfitted in a standard uniform and are furnished with rations the same as the actual fighting men.

"Instead of being armed with rifles, however, they are equipped with picks and spades and plans for laying out the most scientific trenches that the art of war has developed.

"The coolies landed at Vancouver, B.C., will be rushed to Eastern Canada and then to Continental Europe. Their ultimate destination is France. Military experts agree, said Crawford, that permitting these men to dig trenches, thereby saving the regular fighting troops, would be an economy of energy necessary to the success of the Allies' cause.

"'They have no drills to go through,' said Crawford. 'They must learn just one command and that's 'dig.' If they do that well they have earned their share of the glory.'"[26]

While Crawford's account deeply upset Canadian censors, it was fairly accurate. The labourers, of course, were not organized as a force of "trench specialists" and during the war a lot more than 45,000 arrived in France. The most annoying aspect for Canadian officials was reference to the "coolies landed at Vancouver" and plans to rush the men "to Eastern Canada and then to Continental Europe."

On April 11, the *San Francisco Examiner* published a photograph showing Chinese being taken on board the *Empress of Russia* at Weihaiwei. The caption stated the photograph was taken by an American named John R. Noggle and the Chinese labourers "were landed at Vancouver and immediately entrained for the Atlantic Coast . . ." It also identified "the battle front in France" as the destination.[27]

These two stories were sent to Chambers on April 20 by Livesay. By then the reports had presumably been shared via the news wire service south of the border. So, even before the first special trains left Vancouver with their Colonist cars full of labourers on April 18, the proverbial cat was out of the bag, at least south of the border. In Canada, it would take longer for the public to learn the secret.

Meanwhile, other stories appeared containing much erroneous information, but pointing out how Canada's West Coast was a transportation hub for the scheme. Chambers thanked Livesay for the news clippings, informing him on April 25 he had been trying to have some satisfactory communication with the censorship authorities in the United States and was in the process of addressing the United States consul general in Ottawa. "A curious thing about the leakage of this news through the United States is that secrecy regarding this movement of coolies is insisted upon largely for the purpose of obliging the United States government, who (for your secret information) has given permission for the transportation of these coolies through the state of Maine."

That same day, Chambers cabled Colonel J.G. Foster, consul general for the United States. From his office along Ottawa's

Wellington Street, Foster read Chambers's diplomatic request for co-operation. The chief press censor gave the example of how censorship had worked to hide a visit to Washington by British Foreign Secretary Arthur Balfour until the politician and his entourage safely reached Washington. Authorities had requested a news blackout and newspapers quietly heeded the instructions. "What every newspaper in the United States or the Authorities might have done would have been useless without co-operation from this side of the line," explained Chambers. ". . . for had our papers carried reports of the arrival of the party at Halifax and their progress through Nova Scotia and New Brunswick, the object aimed at by the Censorship Authorities of the United States would have been defeated."

Chambers explained why the CLC movements must be cloaked in secrecy, and then asked Foster to put him in touch with the proper Washington authorities.

Early in the morning, just three days later, Chambers received a cable from C.F. Crandall, editor of the *Montreal Star*, stating the *New York World* newspaper had published a story on Chinese labour travelling across Canada. An exasperated Chambers thanked Crandall for the tip.

It is easy to view Chambers and his staff as workers with their fingers stuck in the holes of a dike, trying desperately to contain leaks while running out of fingers. It was an unenviable task to stay ahead of the leaks, rumours and various underground surveillance channels that in addition to obtaining some useful information produced false leads and silly dead-ends. One of Chambers's newspaper contacts in Vancouver suggested some of the leaks on the West Coast of the United States might originate with crews of various Japanese steamers.[28]

On April 30, Chambers wrote to the consul general for Japan in Ottawa, who in turn cabled the Japanese Consulate in Seattle with instructions to investigate. A month later, on June 2, the Japanese consul in Ottawa told Chambers there was no evidence to suggest a

Japanese leak. It pointed to the *Seattle Times* story, which was based on information supplied by the American, Crawford.[29]

Despite these and other measures, Chambers's muzzle on Canadian newspapers was not airtight into the summer and fall of 1917. On May 4, the *Toronto Globe* reported four Canadian doctors were on a "Special Mission." According to the newspaper, captains W.G.M. Smith and H.A. Abraham, along with lieutenants F.H. Boone and D.G. Finlayson of the CAMC were "chosen by the Militia Department for special service of a confidential nature." It stated the "officers will leave for Vancouver tonight, proceeding to China on a special mission, and then to France on overseas service. The officers . . . are the first Canadian officers to be used in this service which is understood to be the care of the Chinese coolies on their way to France. Numbers of these have been already transported to France and used as labourers."[30]

Chambers wrote to the editor on May 7, explaining that while the story did not state the labourers and the doctors would be passing through Canada, the piece, he believed, was not helpful to his cause. Once again, it was "the desire of the Imperial Authorities and of the Chinese Government that silence should be observed regarding the movement of Coolies to the battle area."[31]

On June 21, Chambers replied to an article published by the *British Columbian*, based in New Westminster. Headlined "Illegal Use of Chinamen," the June 14 story was based on assertions made by a delegate named William Yates at the Trades and Labour Council meeting on June 13. It stated the "Canadian Northern Railway Company had 'borrowed' three hundred Chinamen from the Imperial Munitions Board, and shipped them out to work on the Goose Lake section of the railway. Mr. Yates said his information had come from a Chinese employment agent in Vancouver who was sore because he had not had the privilege of supplying this labour and taking his usual rake-off on the transaction."

It stated the "Chinamen in question were one of those parties which are constantly passing through Canada from China en route to France where it is understood they are being employed by the thousands in rehabilitating the devastating areas wrested from the Germans. They pass through Canada in bond, paying no head tax, and it is therefore illegal, Mr. Yates pointed out, to employ them in Canada."

Yates told the crowd he could not guarantee the accuracy of his information and still had to verify it through the Department of Labour in Ottawa. When the newspaper contacted the railway about the assertion, officials stated they had no knowledge of any Chinese employed on the Goose Lake section in Saskatchewan.

Chambers cabled his Ottawa bosses, including Scott and General Willoughby Gwatkin, informing them of the story. He also wrote to the editor of the British Columbian, reminding him of the instructions circulated in regards to censorship. He then asked the editor for Yates's contact information. Six days later Chambers wrote to Yates demanding the source of his information. He told Yates the assertions are "utterly without any foundation" but were of serious concern because they made public facts regarding the CLC movements. "I am sure I can depend upon you for complete information as to the origin of the untruthful stories which have been put in circulation in the manner indicated, for I consider it very likely these stories emanated from paid agents of the enemy."[32]

Yates replied on July 7 stating his information was based on rumour and, as the article pointed out, he had planned to contact the department of labour to check its accuracy. "Had we known the movement through Canada of these Chinese was to be kept secret, we would not have mentioned the matter in the meeting, but would have done so in private session of the executive, but as it is common knowledge here that they are passing through Canada no harm was thought of when the question was asked in the meeting, if the street rumours had any foundation."[33]

Scott weighed in on the matter with a confidential cable to Chambers. "I am surprised that any newspaper would publish information of this sort without asking your permission," he stated. "There is, of course, not a word of truth in the rumour as we have been checking the Chinese in at Vancouver and checking them out at Montreal or Saint John or Halifax."[34]

On July 12, Chambers wrote Yates again, re-emphasizing the importance of secrecy and how the incident illustrates the "great importance of exercising care in aiding the circulation of rumours . . . which in all likelihood are circulated by the paid or subsidized Agents of the enemy. There is more activity in this respect in Canada and the United States than the general public has any suspicion of . . ."

Chambers assured Yates every CLC labourer was accounted for on arrival, during their journey across Canada, and when they left. He stated "in not one single case has the checking revealed the disappearance of a Chinaman in transit."[35]

Yates was from New Westminster, employed as a motorman with the British Columbia Electric Railway. He was also an official with Division 134 of the transit workers' union and one of the more influential leaders of the New Westminster Trades and Labour Council. During this period organized labour in New Westminster was more conservative than the radical Vancouver Trades and Labour Council, which led the organizational drive to create the One Big Union and call a sympathy strike in support of Winnipeg strikers.

Yates's co-operative and nearly apologetic reply to Chambers reveals his position as a more moderate voice. He became a member of the Win the War campaign and a member of the Federated Labour Party, in contrast with the more radical elements that opposed the war and supported the Socialist Party of Canada. The end of the war period in Western Canada was a time of incredible labour unrest.

However, Yates seems to disappear from union activism in the early 1920s.

CHAPTER 15

The Wanted and Unwanted

"The (railway) cars were on the whole cold and the part of the coolies anatomy that seemed to suffer the most was their noses which they would stick well down in their sleeves."

Pain and suffering . . .

While the *Empress of Russia* was still on her chains beneath a blanket of fog in English Bay, Captain Harry Livingstone grabbed a bite to eat and then checked into a familiar place, the Hotel Vancouver. It was nice to be on the mainland, but the doctor's mood improved even more when an acquaintance he had arranged to meet at a vaudeville show arrived with a package of letters from home.[1]

When the *Russia* finally came alongside the pier in Vancouver Harbour at noon, November 14, Livingstone went on board, collected the rest of his belongings and then disembarked with a company-size group of labourers he had gotten to know well. It had been a long couple of days since leaving William Head and so far the Chinese, now marching to the Dominion Government Immigration Building, had seen more fog than land. The fog, however, was apropos because as far as they were concerned their journey was leading them deeper into the unknown.

Canadian Immigration officials huddle at the port of Vancouver. Shown, second from left, is the legendary hockey star and immigration official Fred "Cyclone" Taylor who had a connection to Captain Harry Livingstone's hometown.

It had been sixteen days since the men boarded the steamer at Weihaiwei. Most looked healthy and many were smiling as they walked single file down the *Russia*'s gangways into the fresh autumn air. Missing were several sick who had been detained at the quarantine station for minor ailments.

Meanwhile, the plainclothes immigration officers waiting for the labourers at the port of Vancouver had known what to expect. They had seen it before, since the first CLC ship's arrival that spring. Still, the scene before them continued to challenge basic North American assumptions about the Chinese. The men advancing towards the Immigration Building at the foot of Thurlow Street were not small, nor did they appear out of shape. Even in their white socks and dark slippers many of the Shantungers looked tall.

For the guards and other officials it was apparent, once again, that the standard issue trousers and wadded jackets for this CLC draft were worn by men who were quite robust. Many of them also wore puttees, which on some of the men looked improvised or as though they had been scrounged along the way. But while the leggings provided support and a little warmth they did nothing for the men's thinly wrapped feet.

Atop their shaved heads, the labourers in this draft wore the familiar dark round cap with its golden oval containing the letters "C.L.C." Sitting squarely on top, like a small beacon, was the bright red tuft or pompom. When worn correctly, the badge was positioned above the centre of the forehead. Headgear similar to the straw sailor hat, a flat-crowned affair with a wide brim and a band, had also been issued in China, but appeared more suited for warmer weather. However, no matter what topping the men wore en route, once they arrived in Europe it was usually replaced with a mix of local headgear, including the ubiquitous bowler.

Hanging from each man's back was his brown haversack packed with his effects, while bouncing off one hip was the canvas-covered water bottle attached to a strap over the opposite shoulder. Personal possessions too large or fragile for the haversack, including any wooden musical instruments, were tucked under an arm or held in place by a shoulder strap. A mass-produced, shiny tin cup dangled from the rear of the haversack, near the top. Many of the men must have been quite thirsty because the cup was in hand by the time they reached the front of the Immigration Building.

Symmetrical in layout with a central tower, the Immigration Building, roughly situated between Pier A and the railway yard, had the look of a fortress with emphasis on function. Despite its exterior, there was a hard beauty to it because the architect, Edward Blackmore, had gone with what is known as a Romanesque Revival/Edwardian Institutional design. Elements of the former included the rounded-arch windows on the main and top floors, the pediment over the entrance and handsome vertical pilasters on the facade.

Inside, the basement included separate kitchens for whites and for Chinese. It also contained rooms for storing, fumigating and sterilizing baggage. There was a laundry, a few stoves, coal storage

City of Vancouver Archives, CVA 139-14

While waiting to entrain at Vancouver, a young labourer displays a traditional Chinese plucked instrument.

and rooms for the building's machinery and electrical equipment. One floor up was the passenger reception hall, which included toilets, examining rooms, a medical officer's room, four waiting rooms, a couple of inspectors' rooms, a chief inspector's room, guard room and a large vault. Separate dormitories for white and Chinese travellers were one floor above that, where there were also segregated dining rooms, more toilets and a room known as the "deport" room. Still further up, the building, which was served by both an elevator and an iron stairway, contained more dormitories, toilets, dining rooms, a private detention room, male and female infirmaries, a matron's room, another vault and offices for more inspectors.

The highest floor, located in the centre tower, was smaller, but provided a bird's eye view of the waterfront, including sightlines to passengers arriving by ship and departing by train, or vice versa.[2]

As Livingstone walked with his company of labourers into the crowded reception hall, he spotted, among the white faces, a famous individual.[3] Standing with his broad shoulders and thick powerful legs beneath business attire, was the personage of an athlete whose chiselled face and solid neck seemed to sprout like a tree trunk from a high, tight collar. The man was four years older than Livingstone, and although born in Tara, Ontario, he grew up in nearby Listowel and had become known as "the Listowel Wonder."

Fred "Cyclone" Taylor was a hockey sensation — a household name in Canada, still playing for the Vancouver Millionaires, but also employed as an immigration officer. By then, Taylor had won several scoring titles and played on two Stanley Cup winning teams, the 1908–09 Ottawa Senators, previously known to fans and the media as "the Silver Seven," and the 1915 Millionaires, later renamed the Vancouver Maroons. When Livingstone spotted him in the fall of 1917, Taylor was on his way to scoring an astounding thirty-two goals in eighteen games. His white-collar employment had been assured in 1907 when he signed with Ottawa, insisting on a player's contract and a daytime government job.

His work with the Canadian Immigration Branch of the Department of the Interior kept him busy and occasionally in the public eye. On May 23, 1914, he had been working as an immigration official when the immigrant ship Komagata Maru arrived in Vancouver and was prevented from landing most of her 376 Hindu, Muslim and Sikh passengers.[4] Taylor eventually rose to become commissioner of immigration for British Columbia and the Yukon, but during the First World War he worked alongside top immigration officials, including the well-known and controversial Malcolm Reid, one of Ernest Chambers's most valued contacts.

There are many assessments of Reid's performance during the Komagata Maru crisis and they provide fascinating reading. There is not enough room here to explore them all or the complicated and tragic story of the Komagata Maru in any great detail. However, since Reid had a part in the Canadian effort to secretly transport the CLC across Canada less than three years later it is useful to have some idea of the incident, Reid's involvement in the standoff and the attitudes that existed among many whites at the time.

When the event unfolded, Reid was the immigration agent in Vancouver. Appointed to the job on April 1, 1912, he was tall, dashing and robust. He was quite imposing in his dress uniform, which included a white shirt, dark tie and a double-breasted coat with brass buttons. Topping it off was a peaked officer's cap with a crest in the shape of a crown and the words "Canada Immigration." The man was well-known and easily picked out in a crowd.

Thirty-eight years old in the spring of 1914, Reid had the countenance of a man who had seen much. His thick, black moustache, stylishly waxed at either end, covered most of his upper lip, while his steadfast eyes often looked tired with dark grey lines beneath them. Reid, whose father was from Scotland, was born in Islington, England (now a borough of London), on April 19, 1876. Two weeks after he turned sixteen, he and his eighteen-year-old brother, Roderick, boarded the *Parisian* in Liverpool and arrived in Quebec on May 14, 1892. His parents, Malcolm and Susan, and three siblings, arrived that summer.

At the turn of the century, Reid was residing in Ladner (now part of Delta, a suburb of Vancouver) when he took a teaching job at Barkerville, the main town during the Cariboo Gold Rush. By 1908, he had earned a second-class teaching certificate and was employed at the Admiral Seymour School in Vancouver, named after Sir Edward Hobart Seymour, the British naval commander-in-chief during China's bloody Boxer Rebellion.[5] That summer, Reid travelled to London to attend the Olympic Games and when he returned to Canada on August 14 on the *Empress of Ireland* he had a wife, Rose. Three years later, as a member of Canada's militia, he crossed the Atlantic again — on the same steamship — as part of a ceremonial guard participating in the coronation of King George V.

Reid was a staunch and active Conservative, and when the Conservatives under Borden defeated Sir Wilfrid Laurier and the Liberals in 1911, he was selected to replace J.H. MacGill as immigration agent in Vancouver.

The high-profile job placed Reid in the public's eye, but more importantly introduced him to many powerful and interesting individuals, including W.C. Hopkinson. A former Calcutta police inspector, Hopkinson had arrived in Canada several years earlier and was working as a Canadian immigration inspector and surveillance expert along the West Coast of Canada and the United States.

Reid admired Hopkinson and developed a strong interest in investigative work, which he pursued with great relish after he was demoted as immigration agent and made immigration inspector for British Columbia.[6]

Modern assessments of Reid's actions during the spring and summer of 1914, especially since the 2016 federal apology over the *Komagata Maru* incident, are highly critical. One online post pulls no punches, describing him as a "nasty . . . hard-boiled immigration agent" and an "implicit believer in a 'white Canada'" who "took the law into his own hands to ensure not a single immigrant made it to shore."[7] Reid is singled out for denying food and other provisions to the starving passengers while the ship remained "marooned" in Burrard Inlet — an ugly and very public tableau that lasted two months.

All of this and more happened under Reid's watch, with Vancouver City Member of Parliament H.H. Stevens working parallel to the chain of command.

Historian Hugh Johnston has described Reid as having "acted as Stevens' minion," and has suggested Reid owed his job to Stevens.[8] While Stevens certainly had an important role in Reid's appointment, Reid did have qualifications that were likely factored into the question of his suitability. Johnston notes Reid had experience as an elementary school teacher, but the immigration agent also had long service with the Vancouver militia as a member of the 6th Regiment, Duke of Connaught's Own Rifles and the 72nd Seaforth Highlanders.

Reid and Stevens were close; they communicated regularly and Reid was one of Stevens's nominators for his selection as Conservative candidate in Vancouver in the 1911 federal election. As noted earlier in regards to the establishment of quarantine facilities, the West Coast was not always the top priority of Ottawa officials and, therefore, West Coast officials were often left somewhat on their own. Stevens, a hard-working and popular member of parliament, seemed always willing to fill any vacuum and to act as bridge between the West Coast and Ottawa. He was often the physical presence of Ottawa in Vancouver and, noted Johnston, harboured fierce opposition to Indian immigration.[9]

During the *Komagata Maru* incident, Parliament had happened to go into recess. This allowed Stevens to return to Vancouver, be available to Reid and fill any communication gaps caused by the recess.

Johnston points out that the relationship between Reid and Stevens "far exceeded what ought to have been acceptable between a civil servant and a backbench member of Parliament." This may be true, but it could only occur if Stevens, who was immensely popular in Vancouver, was readily available and Ottawa was not.

One man who knew Reid well was historian and jurist Robie Reid who had the same last name, but was not related. Robie Reid was based in Vancouver at the time, working as agent for the minister of justice and therefore very involved on the Canadian side during the incident. At the time, Robie Reid was a partner in the Vancouver law firm Bowser, Reid, & Wallbridge. He described Reid as a "hard-nosed Scot, firm and inflexible in carrying out his duty as he understood it."[10]

In a 1941 article published in the *British Columbia Historical Review*, Robie Reid stated the allegations against the immigration authorities — specifically that they mishandled the affair — seemed "improper and unjust" to him. He contended he could not "see what we did that was wrong, nor where we could have done better. We had nothing to do with making the law; our duty was to enforce it. This we did. We had a difficult task before us, and I feel we did our best to perform it without fear or favour."[11]

Robie Reid exonerated Malcolm Reid from ultimate responsibility, pointing out that "Mr. Malcolm Reid took no step without consulting Mr. William Ladner or myself. If, therefore, anything was done which was improper, we were the persons responsible." Ladner was another lawyer at the same law firm where Robie Reid worked.

History has clearly shown that for the passengers on *Komagata Maru* it was a frightening, painful and ultimately tragic ordeal. The ship had been chartered by an Indian businessman named Gurdit Singh and those on board were British subjects from India. They had been led to believe they had every right to land in Canada or at least be heard by a court of law if denied. However, they were faced with a serious challenge when unwelcoming immigration authorities under Reid barred their entry and worked to block their communication with supporters on the mainland, which included a committee representing the South Asian community.

The vast majority of the local white population was not sympathetic to the plight of those on board. This nativism, along with the existing federal immigration regulations, reflected once again the common assumption that Canada was for whites. So, in their eyes, Reid was simply doing his job, while strongly determined Reid firmly believed he was acting within the best interests of the federal immigration regulations.

South Asians, mostly young men, had arrived in relatively small numbers on the West Coast of Canada and the United States during the early 1900s. They came — as most immigrants do — in search of a better life. Those who found it wrote home and shared news of higher wages, and this encouraged others. Most white Canadians and Americans pushed their elected officials to exclude any new arrivals. After all, the white North Americans were already strongly opposed to Chinese and Japanese immigration, so India was just another unwelcome source.

Meanwhile, leaders of the Punjabi communities were closely watched because of government fear over their political activity, particularly on the West Coast. Many were opposed to British rule in India and had called for independence. By 1913 Indians in San Francisco had organized the Ghadar, or Mutiny, party with Vancouver and Victoria contacts.

In 1908, the Canadian government had halted immigration from India by relying on two deceptively designed regulations. Both carefully skirted around terms associated with race or nationality. Instead, the first regulation empowered immigration authorities like Reid to prevent entry into Canada by anyone who came other than by a continuous journey from their home country. The second regulation gave immigration authorities the right to reject any Asian who arrived in Canada with less than $200 in his or her pocket. At the time, few people travelled with that much cash.

In 1913, the federal government was thrown a significant legal curve when a Canadian judge overruled an immigration department order to deport nearly forty Punjabi Sikhs. The ship carrying those men, the *Panama Maru*, had coaled in Japan. However, bunkering in Japan was not the issue. The issue was the men had not travelled by continuous voyage and on a through ticket from their country of citizenship; and, of course, did not have the $200. The judge ruled both regulations were inconsistent with the *Immigration Act*. News of this finding helped encourage people from India to view Canada as suddenly more open than the United States. Conscious of public opinion and the possibility of violent reaction, the government quickly wallpapered the opening and by January, a few months before the *Komagata Maru* sailed from Hong Kong, the two regulations were back in place. The ship sailed via Japan, called at William Head on May 21, and arrived in Vancouver two days later.

In the midst of the crisis, on June 29, a test case involving one of the passengers ordered deported was brought before the British Columbia Court of Appeal. The six judges on the bench held that the Parliament of Canada had sovereign power when it came to matters relating to immigration, and immigration authorities were justified in deporting the man. Despite this unfavourable ruling, the ship did not leave. Her discouraged passengers continued to hold onto diminishing hope.

As the crisis stretched into the hot summer, the passengers became more desperate. Their Vancouver lawyer, J. Edward Bird, pleaded with Malcolm Reid on July 9 to deliver much-needed food and water. Owing to the standoff with immigration officials, the food on board, normally considered a responsibility of the ship's charterer, had run out. Also, the *Komagata Maru* was not equipped with desalination equipment and could therefore take on fresh water only while in port. The lawyer argued that because passengers were under order of deportation and in effect "under arrest and held in detention for deportation," responsibility for their food and water lay with the immigration authorities.[12]

In his article, Robie Reid noted how the immigration officer "was moved" by the solicitor's representations and then boarded the ship along with Hopkinson, who acted as an interpreter, and a number of others. It appears Malcolm Reid wanted to assess the situation, even though he had been told by Bird how terrible it was on board. "They confronted a hostile company. The men were both hungry and thirsty and ready for anything. They threatened to hold Malcolm Reid as a hostage until their wants were supplied; they were going to take the ship's boats and make for shore, patrols or no patrols. The discussion became heated and at one time promised to end in blows or worse. After a while the atmosphere cooled down, and Malcolm Reid was allowed to leave on the understanding that a certain amount of food and water would be supplied, and this was done at once at the expense of the Department."[13]

By July 13, the passengers appealed for more food and water. Malcolm Reid refused, believing he had given the passengers enough. "He told them, however, that as soon as the ship was ready to leave for Asia he would provision her for the voyage. They were not satisfied with this and insisted the provisions should be placed on board at once."[14]

The standoff went from bad to worse and the already intense resentment from the South Asian community, due to this situation and years of unwanted government surveillance, became more explosive — as did feelings among the white population.

Five days later, a tugboat, the *Sea Lion*, with dozens of police and immigration officers, went alongside to take control of the ship. The tug's deck was much lower than the *Komagata Maru*'s and the boarding party was repulsed under a bombardment of objects thrown from the larger vessel. The police, meanwhile, were under orders not to fire back.[15]

By July 20, with the ship still at anchor, HMCS *Rainbow* entered the picture as a show of force. It was Stevens who had a pivotal role in securing the navy ship for the task.[16]

If the large crowds on shore were expecting a dramatic finish, they were disappointed. Three days later, the *Komagata Maru* left Vancouver with 355 angry passengers. When the failed immigrant ship arrived at Budge-Budge, India, some twenty of her passengers were killed in a horrific confrontation with British Indian police and troops.

There is no denying Malcolm Reid was uncompromisingly tough and unyielding in carrying out his government duties. However, his actions should be viewed within the time in which he worked, the existing anti-immigration regulations he believed he was carrying out and the prevailing attitudes among the majority of whites, including those in Ottawa who wielded greater power. The 2016 apology in the House of Commons placed the blame squarely on the Canadian government, which was responsible for the laws that prevented the "passengers from immigrating peacefully and securely."[17]

On December 31, 1914, Reid was removed as immigration agent for the busy ports of Vancouver and Victoria and then appointed Dominion immigration inspector for British Columbia. This was not a promotion, although the newspapers described it that way.[18] The man who replaced him as immigration agent, J.A. Jolliffe, was soon earning more money than Reid. However, Reid was soon doing what he relished. Well before and during the

CLC's arrival in Canada, he was conducting investigations for the Dominion Police and for Chambers up and down the west coast.

Hopkinson, meanwhile, did not live long enough to see this. His surveillance work and Reid's actions during the *Komagata Maru* incident had spawned deep hatred among members of the South Asian community. On October 21, 1914, Hopkinson was fatally shot in a very public place, the Vancouver Court House. His killer, Mewa Singh, did not attempt to flee. He pleaded guilty and was hanged in January 1915. He had been the object of a Hopkinson investigation relating to the smuggling of firearms into Canada and had recently witnessed a terrible shooting at a Sikh Temple, perpetrated by a South Asian who had worked as a Hopkinson informant. Among some South Asians today, Mewa Singh is commemorated as a martyr.[19]

Loathed as well as admired, but identified as an assassination target, Reid, despite efforts to permanently relocate him to Ontario, continued to work on the West Coast. There, the bulk of his responsibilities switched to surveillance of the Chinese with much of the work connected to the transportation of the CLC and Ottawa's desire to keep it secret.

* * *

In mid-April 1917, shortly after he forwarded the newspaper clippings regarding the smallpox cases in Vancouver, Malcolm Reid sent Chambers another secret message. The cable was copied to Colonel Percy Sherwood, commissioner of the Dominion Police. "Sir, I enclose herewith some Chinese translations of letters secured at the time of the censorship here, which I trust may prove of interest to you."[20]

The envelope of one letter was postmarked Vancouver, April 11, 1917. According to the translation it was addressed to "On Yick, Sun Cheng, Sunning, Canton," and the sender was listed as "Lee Sit Kaun of Vancouver."

It stated: "All the Allies agents are spreading throughout China to induce the people to be employed by the Allies. If they listen to these agents they will undergo all sorts of sufferings as the writer is informed that over 10,000 are working in the battlefield in Russia. They were badly treated undergoing untold sufferings. There are thousands of Chinese coming over on the Empress boats and they will be transferred to France and no doubt get served the same fate."

Another letter described as being from a "Chow Jung Shing of Vancouver" noted a ship was sunk "some time ago in the Atlantic Ocean with several Chinese on board . . . by a German submarine . . . two or three thousand Chinese from Changton Province are coming on the next boat and they are going to France to fight in the trenches . . . my brother is coming, but you (his Uncle) should persuade him not to listen to the Allies agents . . . this is a British port and I must be careful what I say."

Two other intercepted letters, obtained and forwarded to Ottawa by Reid, stated "Germany is so strong she has already won the war and . . . is pushing England out of first place as the most powerful nation." The other letter, described as being from a "Sit Sing Bok of Vancouver to Hong Fook Tung, Sun Wai, Canton," pointed the finger at China's leader for allowing the country to join the Allied war effort when "Germany has wiped out five Countries." It added the Chinese "coming by this boat by Empress Line will be transferred to the front in the trenches. On their way over several hundred had died through sea sickness, the remainder when they arrived in port had smallpox and the masters of the ships threw the bodies in the ocean to feed the sharks. Those who survived are not properly clothed nor properly fed."

Chambers promptly thanked his main West Coast contact for his excellent surveillance work, stating the intercepted letters "demonstrate the great importance of preventing the Chinese in transit from coming into connection with Chinese resident in Canada." The chief press censor, who by this time had become a lot more convinced of the need for Chinese surveillance in Canada, shared the letters with General Gwatkin. Chambers believed each one supported the decision to carefully guard the Chinese during their transcontinental train journey.

Much of the thinking here was based on perceptions of what was taking place in Canada and in China. Chambers and others believed many Chinese Canadians were pro-German, and thought Germany was going to win the war. In April 1917, when the letters noted above were intercepted, China had not yet entered the war. By August, when China finally sided with the Allies, a military government set up by Sun Yat-sen in the south accentuated China's north-south political split. News in Canada that challenged the Chinese government power in the north was, therefore, taken very seriously by officials here and in their minds had to be suppressed.

In the weeks ahead, Reid shared several more intercepted letters with Chambers, who repeated the view they revealed "a most unaccountably hostile view held by Chinamen in Canada." On May 6, he shared this opinion with Gwatkin: "I thought you would be interested in the evidence contained in these letters as to the remarkably antagonistic view held by Chinamen in Canada regarding the war." In addition to illustrating a high degree of mistrust in regards to the Chinese community, the cables raised thoughts of sabotage or other violent interference along the transportation route.

While Canadian authorities were busy reminding themselves of the importance of preventing any contact between the Chinese labourers and Chinese residents in Canada, British CLC officials in China remained concerned about the impact negative propaganda could have on recruitment.

On May 28, Reid sent Chambers a newspaper clipping from the *Morning Oregonian* published in Portland, Oregon, on May 26. Under the headline "Coolies Ship Via Canada," the article stated the "entente allies are shipping many Chinese coolies to Canada and thence to Europe, this route being chosen as the result of the sinking of ships carrying coolies in the Mediterranean, according to Harvey A. Wheeler, former student at the University of Oregon, who has been teaching in Japan."

Wheeler evidently told the press he had crossed the Pacific to Vancouver on a ship with more than 1,500 Chinese labourers.

While thanking Reid for the clipping, Chambers stated he would bring the matter up with censorship authorities in Washington, D.C. The chief press censor noted he had recently been to Washington and "secured the promise" from the chairman of the Committee of Public Relations that the U.S. would co-operate to ban anything "unfit for publication by war censorship standards." Chambers also told Reid, "Press Censorship in the United States so far is without any legal backing, depending entirely upon the voluntary co-operation of the press. On the whole the attitude of the press towards censorship has been pretty good, but there is notable objection to censorship of any kind in some quarters . . ."

Naturally, surveillance activity produced more than a few embarrassing moments. At one point, Reid thought he had intercepted an important cable between Canada and China. It turned out the cable was sent to Thomas Bourne, the man overseeing British recruitment at Weihaiwei.

In early July, in a letter stamped "Secret," Reid shared confiscated photographs taken of labourers arriving on the *Talthybius* at 7 p.m., June 30. He told Chambers they were taken by people standing at the end of the viaduct on Burrard Street. The confiscated film removed from the cameras of three individuals was not the work of spies or propagandists. They were snaps taken by a Mrs. Neth, who was travelling with an evangelist named Dr. Oliver, a CPR claims agent named E.S. Smiley, and a man whose name was not recorded.

When the CPR claims agent noticed Reid and his assistant stopping people from taking photos, he turned his film over immediately. "Of course, you can quite readily understand these people took the snaps unthinkingly and that no great political or military significance should be attached to the confiscation of them, other than the fact it does seem very lax precautions are being taking [sic] to prevent these coolies from being seen by the general public at this port," stated Reid in his cable to Ottawa.

Reid suggested a guard be placed at the viaduct to prevent the public from getting too close to the steamers arriving with the labourers.

On the same evening, the licence plate of a car was recorded after the vehicle's occupants were seen taking photographs of the Chinese. Reid told Chambers he was trying to trace the owner to confiscate his films. With no record of the car belonging to a Vancouver resident, Reid checked with law enforcement in Victoria and while he got a licence plate match, a constable reported the vehicle had never been to Vancouver and "has been in the garage for the past two weeks being overhauled." Furthermore, the car was "not in a fit condition for carrying passengers" and was used only for hauling bricks and lime. When Chambers heard this, he still insisted it all sounded just too suspicious.

Verification of the real mystery car was never established.

Meanwhile, Reid submitted invoices for the films he had processed and Ottawa reimbursed him, one in the amount of $1.61. Chambers justified the expense by stating the photos illustrated the "difficulties which occur in connection with the imposition of secrecy regarding the transfer of these Coolies from the ship . . . to the trains . . ."[21]

* * *

It took a few hours, on the afternoon of November 14, for the labourers travelling with Nettle and Livingstone to pass through the Immigration Building. From there it was a short walk to the trains, and the first men from the contingent began boarding at 3 p.m. In all, four trains (sections) were waiting for this contingent of men and their stores, and the cumbersome loading — with its various checks and balances — was completed by 6:30 p.m., noted Passenger Agent Brodie.[22] This was two and a half hours after the originally scheduled departure time.[23]

Three of the trains left that evening, while the fourth — owing to yet another delay — departed early next morning.[24] The first two trains carried six hundred labourers each. The next two departed with 550 and 535. Livingstone was on the first, so was Nettle. Also on board were forty-five members of the Railway Service Guard, including a sergeant and one officer.

The manifests for each train were made out in quadruplicate, one of which was immediately presented to the immigration agent in Vancouver. Another copy was surrendered to the senior military officer on the train, who was responsible for handing the document on to the CPR district passenger agent at Saint John, New Brunswick. The two remaining copies were forwarded to Maughan, who in turn sent one to John H. Clark, United States commissioner of immigration, based in Montreal. Clark got one because the trains had to pass through the state of Maine.

The three other trains each had roughly the same number of guards and imperial officers, and one doctor. In his journal, Livingstone notes each train "was composed of twelve coaches with a baggage car" and roughly fifty men per Colonist car.[25] He noted how the guards were stationed at each doorway throughout the train and relieved every six hours. "The car immediately behind the engine and tender was our baggage car and following it was our coach where Nettle and I, and Captain H.E. Barnes, the officer in charge of the guards, had our quarters. Some of the staff of the Commissariat car also slept there. This car was a second-class coach, warm and comfortable beds with a good-natured porter in charge. Our meals were served on two small card tables set between the seats and the meals were first-class and well cooked."

Further back was another second-class car reserved for the RSG men. Behind that, noted Livingstone, was the cook car where the meals for the guards and officers were prepared.[26]

It was dark by the time Livingstone's train rolled out of the station. From inside the coach it was difficult to enjoy the scenery, although the doctor's field diary describes mountain peaks seen through the mist and above the clouds. The diary also contains a reference to how the labourers in the Colonist cars expressed astonishment at the size of the mountains, clearly indicating they had an unobstructed view of the outside world.

As the train sped east into the night, the seating arrangements were converted into sleeping berths. At first, two labourers "slept in the lower berth and two in upper berth . . ." When it got cold, men huddled together for warmth and "occasionally there would be four in one lower berth. Sometimes during the daytime when the upper berths were supposed to be closed, we would discover a coolie sound asleep inside the almost closed berth where he thought he was safe from being caught . . . The cars were on the whole cold and the part of the coolies' anatomy that seemed to suffer the most was their noses which they would stick well down in their sleeves. Often, too, you would see them with each hand shoved away in to the opposite sleeve in the absence of mitts."[27]

*   *   *

Between mid-April 1917, when the first CLC specials rolled out of Vancouver, and mid-November, when Livingstone's contingent entrained for Halifax, some eighty-four different CLC trains had left Vancouver. From then until the end of March 1918, at least forty-seven other trains followed.

Not every labourer who arrived on the West Coast made the trip across Canada. Forty ships arrived on the West Coast with 84,473 CLC. Of that number, 80,873 crossed Canada, but 3,600 sailed on the *Empress of Asia* to Britain via the Panama Canal.

CHAPTER 16

A Journey Between Oceans

"Some nights I would wander through the cars about ten o'clock and many would be sitting up talking or lying awake and I would say to them, 'Sweejow,' meaning 'Go to sleep' and they would always repeat it after you, at the same time, smiling."

Head to foot, like sardines . . .

It was one of the little games the Chinese played in the Colonist cars to relieve boredom. Ten or more labourers encircled a volunteer who sat in the aisle with his head slightly lowered and his eyes blindfolded. Then "someone would give him a loud crack with the flat of their hand over the head. It was the victim's turn . . . to guess who had struck him and if he failed, the process would be repeated until he guessed correctly," forcing the man who had struck him into the middle. It could last an hour or more and sometimes "they would want us (the officers) to Sit [sic] in the centre, but we refused because they usually struck hard blows," noted Livingstone.[1]

Of course, there were less punishing games.

Some men dug into their haversacks and retrieved chess-boards from home. Others made do with homemade versions, fashioned out of scrounged pasteboard, but containing the requisite sixty-four squares of alternating colors. Bits of paper were usually employed as pawns and other pieces. The men also engaged each other and Livingstone in the popular finger game known as Chopsticks. Livingstone was quite good at it and the men who lost to him invariably tried to fool the next player into believing the doctor was just a beginner. As Livingstone racked up more points, "uproarious laugher" filled the railway carriage, which amused the Railway Service Guards.[2]

Although under orders not to communicate with the labourers, the guards did engage in conversation and found ways to cash in through the sale of cigarettes, candy and fruit. This activity was much to the chagrin of their commanding officer. "It has been brought to my attention that Orders issued . . . that no one must be allowed to converse with or have dealings with the Coolies enroute [sic] are being violated and that Guards on trains are not only becoming familiar with them, but in some cases are carrying cigarettes and merchandise on the trains and selling same to Coolies," wrote Major Walter Haynes. "The only parties authorized to have dealings with the Coolies are the European Officers [sic] accompanying them. All ranks are warned that any future violation of the above order will be severely dealt with."[3]

Private G.E. Peebles was docked eight days pay and sentenced to several days' detention for trafficking in merchandise and being absent without leave in early August 1917.[4]

Some men brought up on the latter charge had simply missed the train or decided to walk away from the responsibility. Private W. Metcalfe appears to be one of the latter. After disappearing on May 25, 1917, a Court of Inquiry declared him illegally absent and he was struck off strength as a deserter.[5]

Private M. Hyman was docked three days' pay and got 168 hours detention for being absent without leave and "deliberately avoiding entraining parade," while Private D.H. Whitlow got seventy-two hours detention for allowing labourers to leave the train. The list of fines, forfeitures and punishments also includes men charged for being drunk and disorderly, and improperly dressed.[6]

Discipline, of course, remained an everyday matter for the Canadian military in general, but the RSG seems to have had a particularly difficult time, even though it had drawn in mature, older men. Haynes was constantly challenged to find enough prospects who were healthy, let alone obedient and trustworthy. One man was discharged because he "was unlikely to become an efficient soldier" and there were reports of lost or missing kit, including table knives and forks, belts, shirts and socks.[7]

Haynes was not young himself. He was forty-two when he became the unit's commanding officer on August 27, 1917. Born in Charlottetown, Prince Edward Island, he was the son of a Baptist clergyman who had decided to return to England with his infant son and wife, Isabella. The family was living in Stafford when Walter decided to return to Canada during the 1890s. In February 1900, at age twenty-four, he enlisted in Fort Steele, British Columbia, in the 107th East Kootenay Regiment and served in South Africa with the Lord Strathcona's Horse. By April 1901, Haynes was a CPR office clerk at Cranbrook.

It was not long before his brothers Wilfred, Herbert and Thomas joined him in British Columbia. Thomas was the first to enlist in the fall of 1914 and was wounded in France while with the 7th Battalion. However, he returned to the front and earned the Meritorious Service Medal in June 1918. At age forty, Walter, who was working at a sawmill in Fernie, British Columbia, enlisted, but did not get overseas. Two other brothers, still living in England, joined British units and were killed: Clifford, on July 1, 1916, and Henry, on June 17, 1917.[8]

Livingstone's journal hardly focuses on the RSG, but it does reflect how he enjoyed the mid-afternoon food parades, which saw the Chinese pass the guards en route to the commissary car. The corporal in each six-man entourage carried a small stick identifying the group's carriage number. After flashing it in front of the stone-faced guards, the men carried on into the next car and invariably returned in good spirits carrying the requisite amount of rice and bread, with the dead fish slung over their shoulders. The man balancing the clattering pails and dishes also carried the salt and assorted spices that had been carefully doled out in the commissary car.[9]

After the food was prepared and cooked in the Colonist cars, it was spooned into the men's rice bowls, hot-water tins and wash basins. "Often in the evenings going through the cars you would happen to arrive at their meal time," recalled Livingstone. "Coolies would be sitting in all kinds of attitudes, scooping large chunks of congealed rice into their mouths with chopsticks and following it up with sips of hot water. They rarely drank cold water, always taking it hot and the nearer it was to the boiling point, the more they liked it. You could see men taking large bites out of the loaves of bread and it would not take long for a loaf to disappear. They enjoyed the trout too and always replied in the affirmative when I would ask them how they liked the fish. After the meal the floor was literally covered with fish bones which would be swept up by them later."[10]

Livingstone's friend Lieutenant John McDonald, who entrained at Vancouver two days before Livingstone, also witnessed the food parades. Under the command of British 2nd Lieutenant Matthew Ivy, his party of labourers arrived in Halifax on November 19. Ivy's report notes "a Chinese boy was on the train for the first day to initiate the men into the mysteries of the stoves." He also stated the "quantity of the rations was reduced considerably from the original estimate," but proved ample and there were no complaints."[11]

Tired and with little to do during their first evening out of Vancouver, many men on Livingstone's train fell asleep. Those who could not doze off sat around chatting or entertaining each other in a blue haze of pungent tobacco smoke. Livingstone also noticed men taking drags off small water pipes passed over the backs of benches or down from the upper berths. "By ten o'clock, the majority would be sleeping. Some would be lying on their backs with their faces directly under the light and snoring away quite happily. Most of them slept with their clothes on but some would remove all but their underclothes which by this time were pretty dirty. Of course, they always removed their leather slippers and placed them carefully beneath the seats."[12]

Just north of Yale, British Columbia, the train, with its head-lamp showing the way, entered the Fraser Canyon. As the train continued eastward across and literally through the province's towering rugged interior, daylight introduced the Chinese to more spectacular views. "In the Rockies they were lost in amazement at the high peaks covered in snow," noted Livingstone. "At every divisional point where we stopped for twenty minutes or so the windows would all go up and as many heads as possible would be stuck out looking at the strange sights. We [Livingstone, other officers, and guards] always walked up and down the platform and the coolies would hold out money and want us to buy candies or apples for them . . . At Field, British Columbia, near the Alberta border I bought dollar after dollar worth of nut bars from the lady in the Station then handed the bars to the chinks at the windows. Often the natives of the different towns would be at a station and would laugh at the coolies as they would laugh at them, sometimes the natives would give some cigarettes to them."

Although British 2nd Lieutenant Daryl Klein travelled to Europe with the CLC contingent on the *Empress of Asia* via the Panama Canal, he commented on a fellow officer, a captain, who took the train across Canada with the CLC. "He told amusing tales about the rail journey . . . how the coolies had exchanged salutes with the police [sic] on the train, to the immense surprise of the latter, and how when arriving at a station they had stuck their heads out the window and issued ambiguous orders to the

OFFICIAL COPY

CANADIAN PACIFIC RAILWAY CO.'S TELEGRAPH

TERMS AND CONDITIONS

All messages are received by this Company for transmission, subject to the terms and conditions printed on their Blank Form No. 2, which terms and conditions have been agreed to by the sender of the following message. This is an unrepeated message, and is delivered by request of the sender under these conditions.

W. J. CAMP, Assistant Manager, Montreal, Que.   W. MARSHALL, Assistant Manager, Winnipeg, Man.
D. A. BOWEN, Supt., Sudbury, Ont.   R. N. YOUNG, Supt., Vancouver, B.C.
E. J. LILLIE, Supt., Toronto, Ont.   D. L. HOWARD, Supt., Calgary, Alta.   J. McMILLAN,
W. D. NEILL, Supt., Montreal, Que.   D. COONS, Supt., Moose Jaw, Sask.   Manager Telegraphs, Montreal.
A. C. FRASER, Supt., St. John, N.B.   E. M. PAYNE, Supt., Winnipeg, Man.

A59, RN, S, 89 Collect and 6 Ex Rush,

WhiteRiver, Ont. April 22-17

Director of Naval Service,
Ottawa, Ont.

Please supply for use on transport. Three pounds cotton wool, one tin cyanide gauze, two dozen two inch bandages, one pound tincture iodine four ounces ichthyol, eight ounces glycerine, two hundred tablets potassium chlorate, one thousand tablets acetyl salicylic acid, two pounds soap liniment, six picric acid dressings, one pound sulphur ointment, half pound boracic ointment, half pound zinc ointment, twelve six ounce bottles, six one ounce bottles, two cases disinfecting fluid, also on board arrange for hospital and isolation fifty mumps.

Bruthon,
Captain O.C. Special Overseas Contingent.

An urgent cable sent by a Captain Bruthon from White River, Ontario, to the Director of Naval Service requesting medical supplies due to an outbreak of illness on the train.

soldiers patrolling the platform, crying out shrilly and with a gleam of teeth, 'Bout-Turn' and 'Dees-Miss' and 'Standat-ees.' Overall, the captain thought the behaviour of the Chinese was 'wonderfully good.'"[13]

During station stops in large cities, Livingstone collected small posters or advertisements, mostly promotions for new motion pictures. "They would always watch for me coming out of the nearby stores to see if I had anything under my arm . . . Sometimes Nettle and I had to run and jump on the train which had started to move then the coolies would look worried and yell for us to hurry."

Although he was the only doctor on board, Livingstone had the assistance of two orderlies he had known since Weihaiwei. During their daily and nightly rounds, all three were aware of how easy it was for one man's illness to spread throughout the cars. In Calgary, the doctor scooted off the train to purchase a bottle of Listerine for an orderly suffering from a nasty sore throat. In such moments, the doctor must have envied his father and his well-stocked drugstore.

Men, of course, continued to suffer from the mumps. The first case was diagnosed soon after the contingent left Vancouver and the patient was quickly isolated in a car at the rear of the train. The viral infection, which affects the saliva-producing glands near the ears, is highly contagious for about nine days after symptoms appear. The glands become painful and their swelling causes the cheeks to puff out, so it is easily identified by doctors. For the patient, it is very hard to chew or swallow, and the illness, which is spread through spit, is usually accompanied by a head-ache, fever, muscle aches and a loss of appetite. Among the more serious complications is hearing loss and encephalitis or inflam-mation of the brain. In such a confined space, the illness had to be treated and isolated immediately.

Earlier that year, some fifty labourers on a CLC special near White River, Ontario, contracted the mumps, prompting the contingent's commanding officer, a Captain Bruthon, to send an urgent cable to Ottawa. The April 22 telegram requested a large volume of medical supplies be delivered immediately to Saint John, New Brunswick, where the men could be treated.

For members of the CLC, mumps, while not one of the more serious diseases, was one of the worst illnesses to get because, like trachoma, it pretty well guaranteed a ticket home. Livingstone kept a close eye on those who had it on his train, although all he could do was prescribe rest while handing out cold compresses to relieve the pain. He also distributed apples, oranges and sticks of celery he had quietly slipped into his pocket during his own meal.

Every day, all six hundred labourers on the train received eye drops and, noted Livingstone, "they were all glad to get it" because they knew they could be rejected in Halifax if they had trachoma. They "would all rush to their places" and while they tilted their heads "we would flip up the lids and give them the eye water. Many of them would say their 'Ding Howla' which means good, everything good. Some would be holding their eyelids apart with their fingers to save us the trouble and a great many would come up to you again to have more drops just to make doubly sure they would not be rejected."[14]

On average it took just over three days or seventy-eight hours and fifteen minutes to travel from Vancouver to Fort William, Ontario. With the three other specials carrying men from the same contingent not far behind, Livingstone's train steamed through southern Alberta to Medicine Hat where twelve crates of apples — one for each Colonist car — were purchased for two dollars a crate. From there the train continued east through Swift Current, Moose Jaw, Regina, Brandon and Winnipeg before reaching Fort William on November 17. Coal and water were taken on at regular intervals, and on two or three occasions train equipment had to be repaired or rolled away and replaced.

When a broken wheel was discovered on one of the cars, the labourers in that carriage were escorted off the train by the RSG. While they waited along the tracks with their kit, the damaged car was removed and replaced. On another occasion, much to the delight of the labourers, a first-class coach was substituted for a broken Colonist car, "evidently on account of it being the only spare coach" at the divisional point. "The seats were all velvet lined and the floors carpeted. The coolies could be seen jumping up and down on the seats to test the springs and feeling the plush upholstered seats in great admiration," noted Livingstone. "One coolie dropped some cigarette ashes on the Carpet [sic] and at once got down on his knees and carefully swept the ashes up with his hands."[15]

As the hours slowly passed, the Chinese periodically asked Livingstone when they might expect to arrive at their destination. If there were no unexpected delays, the journey from Fort William to Montreal took roughly forty-three hours, and from there it was easily another twenty-two hours to Saint John, New Brunswick, and further yet to Halifax. "This makes a liberal allowance at divisional points for watering, and also takes care of the hour lost at Fort William" on account of the time-zone difference, noted a CPR memo.[16]

Livingstone also noticed men who were less curious, keeping mostly to themselves and sitting "cross-legged in some dark corner beneath the upper berth, playing some love song on a small Chinese fiddle." Most just sat around, "listening and dreaming of home . . . or singing to the strains of the fiddle."[17] The quieter ones often had the glassy-eyed look of exhausted or bored travellers. "Some nights I would wander through the cars about ten and many would be sitting up talking or lying awake and I would say to them, 'Sweejow,' meaning 'Go to sleep' and they would always repeat it after you, at the same time, smiling."[18]

One of the younger ones, who looked more like a boy than a man, had purchased a vivid green skullcap from a crewman on the *Russia*. He wore it proudly, but perhaps not as proudly as the conversational English he had acquired. Day or night, the young man practised saying "Good morning" to Livingstone through a smile that revealed "an elegant set of clean, even teeth."

From Fort William the train sped northeast to Nipigon, then more easterly with short stops at places familiar to the doctor, including Schreiber, Jack Fish, Heron Bay, White River and Chapleau. On November 18, he administered more eye drops and isolated another man with mumps and another one with scabies. The outside temperature had dropped significantly since entering Ontario, and, while the cars were heated, it was still cold. "Coolies all stand cold so far," noted Livingstone.

The train reached North Bay on the nineteenth and then skirted along the northern edge of Algonquin Park to Mattawa. After a quick refuelling stop at Chalk River, the special continued down through the Ottawa Valley, passing Petawawa and Pembroke. Then, instead of steaming to Ottawa, it headed south to Carleton Place, then Smiths Falls on the Rideau River.[19] An hour later, after taking on more coal and water, the train crossed rural eastern Ontario into Quebec. On the outskirts of Montreal, where another Colonist car was replaced, Livingstone enjoyed a few precious moments with his dearly missed "Ma and Pa," who had travelled to meet him after a year's absence.

On November 20, the train pulled into Lac-Mégantic, Quebec, for a thirty-minute stop before heading south into northern Maine. "In U. States right now and making good time," Livingstone jotted in his diary: "Cold weather and Coolies all enjoying themselves."[20]

The delay in Vancouver, coupled with the various equipment malfunctions, had put the train several hours behind schedule. Livingstone's field diary notes it pulled into Halifax at 2:30 p.m. on November 21. On the same day, the contingent's three other trains arrived an hour apart. Before disappearing into the darkness of a covered shed near the waterfront, passengers had a good view of Bedford Basin, the Narrows and Halifax Harbour. Livingstone noted the traffic in the busy harbour and "the many battleships and strange foreign vessels all camouflaged."

Waiting at Pier 2 was the *Olympic*, launched in 1910 and completed in 1911 as the lead ship in the White Star Line's trio of massive passenger liners that included the nearly identical *Titanic*. Built by Harland and Wolff of Belfast, *Olympic* was nearly 270 metres long while her gross tonnage after a 1913 refit was 46,358. With her "dazzle" camouflage scheme of brown, dark blue, light blue and white, she was a familiar sight in the city, having been chartered by the Canadian government as a troopship. By then she had been stripped of her peacetime fittings and had the capacity to transport six thousand troops. Although her colourful camouflage was added in 1917 to make her more difficult to identify and target, Livingstone's description of her paint was limited to "black and white in futurist design" to guard "against subs."[21]

Inside the massive shed, authorities boarded the train and handed Nettle his instructions. Soon the labourers were lined up with their kit on the platform and while it became another case of hurry up and wait, the men were glad to be off the train. They stretched and inhaled deeply while taking in the unfamiliar

Library of Congress, LC-B2-2218-5

The massive passenger liner Olympic; *shown arriving at New York after her maiden transatlantic voyage in 1911.*

surroundings. It was damp and once again the men tasted the salty air and stared up at massive ships. At the gangways to the *Olympic*, the officers gave each man the once-over and checked his registration number against the manifest.[22] "Halfway up the gangway the coolies looked up and could see hundreds of heads and shoulders of their countrymen who had crossed the Pacific on other boats but who were waiting for our contingent. There was plenty of shouting from one to the other. On board the embark officer directed them to their quarters. Some away down in the dark regions in the bowels of the ship and others to certain decks where they were obliged to sleep in the open owing to lack of accommodation elsewhere."[23]

The ship would spend the next nine days in Halifax, and during that time at least twenty-two labourers were sent by ambulance to the isolation hospital suffering from minor but contagious illnesses that could end their trip to France. Ten of the sick had been on Livingstone's train. Suffering from the mumps were Li Te Pin (Li Debin, No. 47110), Hsu Chin Sheng (Xu Jinsheng, No.

46130), Tung Hsi Wen (Dong Xiwen, No. 46221), Chang Huai Jen (Zhang Huairen, No. 46136), Li Lu Liang (Li Luliang, No. 46126) and Liu P'an Hsien (Li Panxian, No. 45828). The other four were Hsu Tien Chun (Xu Tianjun, No. 46093), Liu Chao Jung (Lui Zhaorong, No. 45675), Han Shao T'ing (Han Shaoting, No. 45957) and Wang Chin K'uei (Wang Jinkui, No. 46085).[24]

All of the men on the second and fourth trains received clean bills of health. The third train saw eight men, Chiang Chien (Jiang Jian, No. 46906), Chang Chun Lin (Jiang Junlin, No. 45171), Li Ch'ang Hsu (Li Changxu, No. 46816), Shang Wei Hua (Shang Weihua, No. 45134), Ho Ch'uan Hsu (He Chuanxu, No. 45059), Kung Tien Kang (Gong Tiangang, No. 47061), Yao Ch'ing Chih (Yao Chingzhi, No. 46985) and Ma Fu Chen (Ma Fuzhen, No. 47089), also sent to hospital with mumps. During the next two days Chao Ping Chen (Zhao Bingzhen, No. 46686), Chao Fu Kuan (Zhao Fuguan, No. 46709) and Shang Ch'I Ch'un (Shang Chichun, No. 48163) were also rejected on account of mumps while Wang Chou An (Wang Zhouan, No. 46330) was sent to the isolation hospital with tuberculosis.[25] "These poor sick boys felt very badly at leaving their Comrades [sic] and one or two commenced to cry at being left behind in the big strange city," noted Livingstone.[26]

The *Olympic* held other large CLC contingents, including many from Tsingtao, and there, among the doctors, was Livingstone's friend Lieutenant John McDonald. Finally, the schedules worked in their favour and the two had an opportunity to "get caught up."

"In the Evening [sic] after their meal was over if you passed through the watertight door leading to 'B' deck a strange sight met Your Eyes [sic]. The whole deck . . . was covered with coolies most of them lying down on their beds and many sitting in groups talking or playing chess or other games and listening to the strains of fiddles or fifes or Singing Songs [sic]. They would stretch out their oil cloth sheet then on it would place a padded blanket then after removing slippers would lie down and pile all the clothes they possessed on top of them with usually the large brown raincoat on the very top. Then, if you walked along you would often see only the top of a coolie's head projecting from under the clothes and with the black short hair standing erect, it gave them the appearance of black bears fast asleep."[27]

Livingstone noticed pairs of labourers sleeping with their arms around each other's neck for warmth. Often there were rows of a dozen men or more "packed like sardines" with one fellow's feet up near the next fellow's head. "All around . . . hanging from hooks were tins, dishes, and kit bags . . . and when the Electric [sic] lights were lit, all the windows leading to the outside would be closed to prevent any stray rays of light falling on the water and gradually the din would quiet down and except for an occasional group of gossipers nothing could be seen but prostrate sleeping forms along the long, quiet deck."[28]

On the evening of November 22, Livingstone and a few other officers went ashore and after dining at a high-end hotel headed to the Strand Theatre. "All Halifax darkened. Car lights all darkened in upper half. Blinds half down and no bright lights in street and next week they are going to be even stricter to avoid enemy minelayers finding harbour," Livingstone noted. The doctor was told the *Olympic* would be travelling with her lights out and at a good clip. "We have several six-inch guns and mine catchers, collapsible life boats, and life rafts. We must wear life belts all the time. Coolies, if they smoke on deck at night will be fired on . . . We have no idea when we are going to sail and it is hard to obtain more shore leave."

On December 1, five days before the Halifax Explosion, the *Olympic* raised her anchor and began to sail out of the harbour. For one man, however, life's journey came to a sudden end. Livingstone's diary notes that a labourer identified as Liu Chih (Liu Zhi, No. 46511) died of heart failure on the night of November 29–30. The young man had been "a strong, robust coolie" who had "never appeared on sick parade or complained to any of his companions of ill health and had retired as usual in good spirits. His mate in a near-by bunk heard him groaning and on investigating found him dead." Livingstone noted in his journal that the man's body was handed over to military authorities at Halifax. There seems, however, to be no burial record. It is believed his body was placed in a mortuary and simply disappeared in the December 6 explosion.[29]

* * *

While the preacher Napier Smith was still months away from commencing his journey from China to France, Gordon Jones, as well as other Canadian missionaries, was already overseas with the CLC by the time Livingstone left Halifax.

Jones, the Methodist from Brantford via the West China mission, and Presbyterian missionary James Blake Hattie, a thirty-five year old from Caledonia, Nova Scotia, had, on May 29, boarded one of four trains in Vancouver.[30] Like Jones, Hattie was an engineer, a husband and a father. He had married a blacksmith's daughter, but there had been no rural Nova Scotia wedding. He and his bride, Janet MacDonald, had exchanged vows in the Cathedral of the Holy Trinity in Shanghai in 1913.[31]

Altogether, the contingent of CPR specials these men had taken across Canada that spring carried 2,116 Chinese labourers, 198 guards, three doctors and eight imperial officers. Jones and Hattie were on the third train, which carried five hundred labourers plus its guard detail.

Jones wrote to his wife many times while crossing Canada. He told Clara how much he missed her and little Eleanor and how the tonsillitis he contracted at Vancouver was not as bad, but it had zapped his energy. We ". . . are on that abominable stretch between Lake Superior and North Bay," he noted in June. Meanwhile, he had formed good impressions of the labourers, who seemed to take the journey in stride. "Coolies still seem to be happy and enjoying themselves."

At the same time, Clara and Eleanor were completing their travels from China to Canada via Chicago. Jones even managed to telephone his wife from North Bay. "I have been actually talking to the dearest girl in the whole world," he wrote soon after the call ended. "When the operator told me the connection was ready and to please put three quarters in the slot, I was so excited I fumbled like an old man in getting out the money . . . It will certainly be sublime if you can come to Montreal, but if you don't I have had this talk . . . Even if there were words to say how much I love you it wouldn't do because I love you more all the time . . . And God bless our little Eleanor and let her grow up to be a fine, brave woman like her mother."[32]

By June 3, all four trains in that particular contingent had reached Montreal, where the men boarded the Halifax-bound *Ionian*, one of several steamship transferred to the Canadian Pacific from the Allan Line in 1917. "I used to be afraid you wouldn't have as much place for me when Eleanor came, but in some marvelous way you seem to make me love you more than ever," Jones wrote from Halifax on June 16.

During what turned out to be a long delay in Halifax, Jones had time to fire off several letters describing the hurry-up-and-wait nature of military movements, the busy harbour and Bedford Basin — and, of course, the great love he had for his family. On Sunday, June 24, he wrote Clara to tell her his ship was part of a small convoy en route to Liverpool. Led by the British cruiser *Devonshire*, the *Ionian* sailed with the *Montreal* and the *Scotian*. "We steamed out in single file till we got to sea and then took up our positions. It is a diamond shape with the cruiser leading and we have kept this position ever since. The *Montreal* is the slowest boat and we all go at her speed."[33]

Jones also told his wife how he hoped the "eagle eye" of the censor would skip past the heartfelt sentiments he expressed.[34]

In a postwar essay on his time with the CLC, the missionary commented on his perception of the secrecy surrounding the

Shortly after sailing out of Halifax on the Ionian, *the Reverend Gordon Jones wrote to his wife Clara. The letter included a sketch of the small convoy formation.*

CLC. "I am told that the public in Canada were never informed that the Chinese were crossing Canada, but no particular secrecy was made with us. I communicated with friends in Canada and was met at several points."[35]

Canadian Presbyterian missionary Arthur Lochead was in Halifax at the same time as Jones and Hattie. In charge of a contingent, he had crossed the Pacific on the *Monteagle* and entrained in Vancouver on May 21. There were only three trains in that group, but when they departed for Montreal they carried 1,633 labourers. When the men arrived on the twenty-eighth their time was limited to the few hours it took to embark for Halifax. "Am getting on beautifully," he wrote on the back of a June 2 postcard addressed to the Reverend Robert MacKay.

Lochead informed the secretary of the Foreign Missions Board in Toronto that he had met or heard from other North Honan missionaries while travelling across Canada. Overall, he and the other officers were "pleased with the men's behaviour. Good health. Good spirits. No disaffection." He also stated he was glad to hear from Dr. Leslie that the F.M.B. had taken "such a sympathetic view of our action in Honan." This was a reference to the decision he and other Presbyterian missionaries had made to volunteer for overseas military service.[36]

In late 1916, when MacKay learned of Lochead's wish to interrupt his missionary work by serving as a temporary officer with the CLC, MacKay's reaction had not been favourable. MacKay had thought Lochead was not healthy enough to go, but the secretary did not object to men wanting to serve.[37] "I am glad to say I have had excellent health since leaving China," Lochead told MacKay on June 16. "We do not know what may be in store for us when we reach England, whether we shall still remain as a unit or divide off into smaller companies. I am glad to hear Dr. Leslie and his men had got across to France and were at work . . . It is hard on all our patience to be tied up so long, but the labourers seem to stand it very well."[38]

MacKay wrote to Lochead on June 20, stating he was delighted to hear Lochead's health was better. He provided Lochead with a brief update on the travels of other missionaries bound for France with the CLC, noting he met in Montreal with Dr. Ernest Struthers and saw James Menzies and Thomas Arthurs when they visited Toronto on their way overseas. [39]

* * *

Being confined to a railway car or the overcrowded bowels of a ship for days on end did caused tempers to flare.

While on board the *Olympic* in Halifax, Livingstone recognized how the sheer number of labourers could easily gain the upper hand in a fight. Additional guards were usually sent for if trouble broke out in a port, but sometimes more immediate measures were required to separate or root out combatants. Serious troublemakers and agitators were quickly identified, locked up and returned to the West Coast under guard. Once there, these men were escorted onto a ship and passenger manifests were carefully checked to make sure they were actually on their way back to China.

In early October, the night before British 2nd Lieutenant Reginald Rowlatt's party of CLC arrived at Halifax, a nasty rumble occurred on the *Justicia*. Rowlatt noted the conflict was ostensibly over food, but seemed to have been mainly between rival groups recruited at Weihaiwei and Tsingtao. The commanding officer noted it had been "found necessary to call for military assistance from the barracks to restore order . . ."[40]

Up to then, the transcontinental journey for Rowlatt's party had gone well. He noted how the specials were always referred to as "silk trains" and no reference "was made to the coolies in writing or in cables." Rowlatt also mentioned a telegram received on October 5 from the officer in charge of the second train as it was crossing the Prairies. Medical assistance was needed for a labourer suffering from apoplexy. The officer in charge was instructed to drop the man off in Regina.[41] Presumably, the unidentified man was taken to a hospital. By the sixth, it was snowing hard and there were cases of mumps on board. When the train reached Fort William, Rowlatt and his medical officer went into town and purchased much-needed medical supplies, including castor oil and boracic powder, which was used as an antiseptic for cuts and burns.[42]

On the morning of the eighth, Rowlatt's train with five hundred labourers steamed into the eastern Ontario town of Smiths Falls, where the CPR passenger agent, a Mr. Lester, came on board and completed his check of the manifest in seventeen minutes flat. Every man, noted Rowlatt, was in his place and there was no one missing when United States Immigration agents checked the manifest before the train crossed into Maine.[43]

The 797 Chinese who left Vancouver on December 3 under Lieutenant A.C. Cooper had a much longer and more difficult stay in Canada, because of the Halifax Explosion. The party, which included Lieutenant W.I. Henderson of the CAMC, had left some 130 sick men behind, most of them at William Head. On the Prairies, the temperature dropped well below freezing. The locomotive on the first train broke down on December 5, near the Saskatchewan-Manitoba border. By the time it reached Fort William at 7:10 p.m. on December 6, news of the explosion had reverberated around the world. On the eighth, the two-train consignment was ordered to proceed to Saint John, New Brunswick, "owing to Halifax being in ruins."

For two days the trains pushed through blizzards. The first reached Saint John at 8 p.m. on December 10. The second train arrived exactly twelve hours later. At 9:30 a.m., the Chinese from both trains were de-trained and marched to the Exhibition Buildings.[44]

A young American, Gunner Clifton Cate, had come to Canada to enlist and was on guard duty when the first train arrived. Expecting prisoners of war, the twenty year old from Belmont, Massachusetts, was surprised when Chinese men "poured out of the railway cars." He recalled there were "hundreds of them. Herded between our lines, they trotted along to their quarters, toting heavy bags and boxes atop their heads, laughing, gesticulating, all good natured. My post was near a patch of smooth ice. Onto it ran the Volunteers of the Chinese Labour Corps. One after another went down, got to his feet, and trotted on. There was plenty of safer surface nearby, but they seemed to prefer to slide and fall . . ."[45]

The Chinese were still in Saint John when Cate sailed overseas from Halifax on December 21 on the *Grampian*.[46]

Nine men from Cooper's group were admitted to hospital with mumps while sixteen healthy men were detailed as cooks. There were not enough stoves and the rice was badly cooked, but the men ate. Another kitchen was found, although the food it produced had to be delivered by sleigh.[47]

Henderson visited the men every day, sending those with

mumps to hospital, where doctors and nurses were surprised by both the influx of patients and their nationality. Altogether, twenty-six men contracted the illness. "It was not possible to isolate contacts, and all that could be done was to enforce the regulations against spitting, and wash the floors with disinfectant daily," noted Cooper.

The Chinese remained in Saint John until December 27. This was a full month after they had arrived in Vancouver and seventeen days after they were originally expected in Halifax.[48] Rising in the cold, the men ate breakfast, lined up for one final medical inspection and then marched in two groups onto the *Ulua*. Thirteen of the sick, including one British officer, boarded the ship. Sixteen others — with mumps — remained in Saint John, bringing the total number of men left behind in Canada from that one contingent to 147.[49]

Soon, the *Ulua* was crossing the Bay of Fundy en route to Halifax, where she joined other ships anchored in Bedford Basin. The *Ulua* was a new ship, but her "latrines were continually freezing; the only place . . . where fresh water could be got was from one tap in the kitchen. There was a shortage of coal in the port" and so the ship could not sail with the next available convoy. Meanwhile, mumps continued to spread with as many as fifty cases at one time.[50]

That same month, six CLC specials were redirected to Weehauken, just northwest of New York City. The first train arrived on the morning of December 19 and hundreds of labourers were transferred to a ferry that afternoon. The sixth special arrived at 9 a.m. on the twentieth and boarding commenced around 2 p.m. From Pier 56, the ferry conveyed the men to the *Saxonia*. Although the United States had entered the war, the regulations restricting the importation of Chinese into the U.S. was very strict according to the British Ministry of Shipping. However, when the circumstances of the Halifax disaster were taken into account by authorities in Washington, special permission was granted to embark the labourers at New York. However, various conditions applied. First, an armed guard of twenty men had to be on duty at the pier prior to the arrival of the labourers and they were to remain there until the ship sailed. In addition, the vessel could not remain alongside for any length of time after the labourers were on board. This afforded very little time to transfer thousands of men from train to ship. One of the labourers, however, did not board the *Saxonia*. The man, who is not identified in the reports, was found unconscious on the train and taken to a local hospital for an unspecified operation.

Although much of Halifax was in ruins, it appears the *Saxonia* still sailed to the eastern Canadian port before crossing the Atlantic. When she left New York on December 21 there were 3,537 labourers on board.[51]

CHAPTER 17

Back Behind Wire

"Not only should no possibility of escape be permitted, but you should also see they are not allowed to come in contact with the outside public . . ."

Off the rails . . .

It was a tall order and a bit strange.

The Department of Militia and Defence was asking for fifteen thousand tins of sardines, six hundred pints of peanut oil and "Chinese" sauce, plus six hundred pounds each of garlic and brown sugar. Issued with great haste on August 2, 1917, the government tenders went to several commercial establishments at Ottawa's Byward Market Square.[1]

Each competing firm was invited by the government's director of contracts to submit its bid in a sealed envelope by August 13 to Room 95 of the Woods Building on Slater Street. On the receiving end were the Diamond Limited; E.M. Lerner and Sons, Wholesale Grocers; H.N. Bate and Sons Limited, Importers; S.J. Major Limited, Wholesale Grocers and Wine Merchants; the F.J. Castle Company Limited, Wholesale Grocers and a shop that went by "Mrs. G. Brock, Purveyor To His Excellency The Governor General Dealer in Butter, Eggs, Poultry, Game, Fruit and Vegetables."

The company with the longest name, and presumably the lowest bid, was chosen to supply two hundred pounds of garlic at twenty cents per pound. Meanwhile, E.M. Lerner and Sons won the contract to supply four hundred pounds of "Louisiana" garlic at sixteen cents per pound and a cask of soy sauce. With large local stocks of peanut oil, brown sugar and sardines unavailable at such short notice, the government looked further afield and found Mrs. Hunter and Company, conveniently located up the Ottawa Valley in Pembroke. It won the contract to supply peanut oil at twenty-seven cents per pound (delivered in one week); 600 pounds of brown sugar No. 2 at eight dollars per 100 pounds (delivered immediately); 140 pounds or roughly fifteen gallons of soy sauce at twenty and a half cents per pound (delivered within a week) and two thousand tins of sardines (delivered immediately). Elsewhere, the Leas Company of Simcoe, Ontario, won a contract to supply forty gallons of peanut oil at $1.50 per gallon, while Connors Brothers of St. George, New Brunswick, was chosen to deliver 5,500 tins of sardines packed in cottonseed oil.

This was the first and the smaller of two government orders that by early September also included "evaporated apples."

Where was it all going?

Petawawa, Ontario.

From late 1914, a facility at Petawawa served as a prisoner of war internment camp. Some 750 German, Austrian and Italian prisoners had been held there until May 1916 when it closed, notes the Petawawa Heritage Society.[2] By the summer of 1917 — three months into the transcontinental train movements of the CLC — Canadian immigration, military and railway authorities were under a lot of pressure. The war, which now involved the Americans, continued to make a very high demand on shipping and the seas were more dangerous. Despite best efforts, ships and trains earmarked for the CLC occasionally broke down and did not always arrive on time, leading to a steady buildup of men on both coasts awaiting transportation. Compounding these difficulties were the usual frustrations on account of the weather as well as the ongoing breakdowns in communication regarding the arrival of steamers and the departure of trains, particularly on the West Coast.[3]

By situating a temporary CLC transit camp at Petawawa, authorities relieved pressure at a very critical time.

Located along the west bank of the Ottawa River, Camp Petawawa was, as the crow flies, 3,422 kilometres from Vancouver and 1,082 kilometres from Halifax. It was remote, but conveniently located along the CPR's main line roughly 140 kilometres northwest of Ottawa.

On July 21, John Douglas Hazen, the former premier of New Brunswick who had joined Borden's Cabinet as minister of marine and fisheries and minister of naval affairs, wrote to the Department of Militia and Defence suggesting the camp be used for the CLC.[4] On the same day, Commander Richard Markham Stephens, the chief of the naval staff, stated that "if practicable, Petawawa would be the ideal place for a CLC transit camp being close to Montreal with good railway facilities."

Stephens was reasonably confident of the men's health, noting they had been "medically inspected before leaving China, are under medical supervision on voyage to Vancouver, and pass quarantine at William Head so there should be slight danger of infectious disease." He believed Petawawa could accommodate four thousand men, but noted such a number would be "seldom reached."[5]

On July 23, Hazen's office wrote to William Roche, minister of the interior, proposing the Chinese could be used to Canada's advantage by assisting with the fall harvest or other labour-intensive work. "It is evident there are many difficulties in the way of carrying out such a scheme," noted the letter from George J. Desbarats, deputy minister of the naval service. ". . . Mr. Hazen asked me to submit the matter to you, to ascertain if the difficulties, from the Emigration point of view, could be met. If this were possible, it would . . . be necessary to take up the question with the Imperial authorities to ascertain if they would be willing to have the coolies do work in Canada . . ."[6]

Meanwhile, immigration authorities were also looking for a solution to the buildup of men. In a July 24 cable to military authorities in Ottawa, E. Blake Robertson, assistant superintendent of immigration, emphasized the need for a holding camp in eastern Canada. He estimated between six thousand and twenty thousand Chinese labourers were expected to cross the country every month. Robertson gave, as an example, how a serious situation had recently developed on the West Coast because a troopship on the East Coast, the *Olympic*, was delayed by twelve days.

The *Bessie Dollar* had arrived in Vancouver two weeks earlier with 1,700 labourers on board and the plan had been to entrain them immediately for the East Coast. But the *Olympic* was delayed, and it became necessary to keep the CLC men on board the *Bessie Dollar*. However, Robertson explained, the "*Bessie Dollar* was wanted by the Department of Marine and Fisheries to carry a load of munitions to Vladivostok for the Russian government."[7] He noted that after "holding the boat for several days, I ordered her unloaded of the Chinese labourers, partly at Vancouver and partly at Victoria." Robertson further explained, "we have a building at Vancouver which, at a pinch, will accommodate about 1,000 coolies, but in warm whether [sic] these should not be held in the building for any length of time."[8]

Robertson did not identify the Vancouver building, but it was most likely the Dominion Immigration Building near Pier A. Meanwhile, the department also owned property in Victoria that could hold 350. "We unloaded about 1,000 at Vancouver and transferred the rest to Victoria. General McDonald of your Department was most considerate in loaning us sufficient tents and blankets to provide for about 400 men in the lot which surrounds our Victoria building and which is enclosed by an iron fence. We had to hold these men and feed them for a week, and, of course, the Admiralty will bear the expense. These coolies were loaded into trains on Sunday and are now en route to Halifax."[9]

McNabs Island at the entrance to Halifax Harbour could also be used, he suggested, so long as the CLC transports continued to leave from that eastern port. On the West Coast, he suggested William Head could be used. However, he was under the impression the director general of public health, Dr. Frederick Montizambert, was not in favour of this because of the risk of exposing the Chinese to contagious diseases and then transporting them across the country. William Head was, of course, already being used to hold thousands of CLC men.

Robertson clearly favoured Petawawa because it "would mean a break on an otherwise almost intolerable journey in warm weather . . . In any case, the men should be camped somewhere outside the city so as to guard against escapes."[10]

In the final days of July, the Department of Militia and Defence quietly selected Petawawa's West Camp for the CLC. The area had not been used since 1914. Weeds and brush had taken root and the latrines, kitchen shelters and ground drainage were rundown or in disrepair.

While the barracks were prepared, the area was made secure with barbed wire around a compound that resembled a prisoner of war camp. The fencing alone cost $775 and included four gates, each 3.6 metres high, and two smaller ones, each 1.2 metres in height.[11]

From the start, the government insisted the compound's perimeter be patrolled day and night to prevent escapes and discourage any contact with the public. The cost of making it habitable was roughly $2,800, although the final bill sent to Britain was probably higher. "The road to West Camp has already been graded but it is only a sand road and this can be macadamized for $4,000. Total: $6,800," noted a July 25 department memo.[12]

On August 1, the adjutant general, Colonel C.S. MacInnes, cabled Petawawa Camp's commandant, Lieutenant J.N.S. Leslie, telling him a thousand Chinese labourers were expected "about August 13."

The adjutant general's expectations for security were high. "As you are aware it is of vital importance these Coolies should be very carefully guarded . . . Not only should no possibility of escape be permitted, but you should also see they are not allowed to come in contact with the outside public, and all written and verbal communication with any of them should be carefully watched."[13]

On August 2 it was pointed out that although the compound was fenced, the ground was soft and therefore not too difficult to dig under the wire.

The first Chinese arrived on schedule. All 939 disembarked from two trains, which had left Vancouver on August 8. The men had crossed the Pacific on the *Empress of Japan* and passed through William Head. These were the same two special trains that went by Livingstone's regular passenger train on the night of August 11 while he was westbound to Vancouver to board the *Empress of Japan.*

When the men got off the train at Petawawa, they were still wearing socks and slippers. However, many of them were soon put to work on various camp improvement projects. According to one government file, it appears some two thousand labourers were each paid at the rate of ten cents a day. The memorandum, which was written well after the war, does not specifically name the Petawawa camp. Instead, it only refers to "the Coolie Camp in Canada."[14]

A CPR memorandum from Walter Maughan, which was written at the time, does not refer to any work scheme. This is not surprising because the CPR's priority was to move the men as quickly and as securely as possible across Canada. The intention was simply to hold the men, under guard of the RSG, in Petawawa

Library and Archives Canada, C-068863

After detraining from a CLC special, hundreds of Chinese labourers make their way to the holding camp at Petawawa, Ontario.

until the twentieth or twenty-first, when they would entrain for Halifax. The "equipment" (trains) were to be held there too "or some convenient place."[15]

Meanwhile, Canada's chief press censor, the Immigration Department, the militia and the CPR were hoping to keep this new development secret. However, on August 7, one week before the Chinese arrived at the camp, W.D. Scott sent Chambers a cable: "I notice in the 'Morning Citizen' of this date a despatch from Kingston dated yesterday, reading: 'Arrangements are being made at Petawawa Camp for the care of 2,000 Chinamen who are to rest there on their way to France where they will be engaged back of the lines. The celestials are being brought out from China.'"

Scott ended his cable with: "This is about the first break I have seen on the part of the Canadian newspapers with regard to the movement of Chinese coolies. I wonder how this got out."

Chambers promised Scott he would speak with the newspaper's editor and engage the help of Lieutenant-Colonel A.W. Richardson, district intelligence officer in Kingston, Ontario, in an effort to find the leak. "From the appearance of the paragraph I rather fancy that this news comes from the Military Authorities, but of course I may be mistaken," stated Chambers to Richardson. He asked the colonel to investigate by contacting district military officers and, while he was at it, to emphasize the need for secrecy.

The cable shows what Chambers was thinking in terms of how many Chinese were expected to cross the country. ". . . I might add for your private information that . . . half a million of these men will be passed through Canada to France before the end of the year. The enemy doubtless have an inkling of what is going on, but they are kept in the dark as to the extent of this movement."[16]

Richardson identified the leak, described as a railroad postal clerk "running out of Toronto north who had observed trains containing parties mentioned passing east." He told Chambers he found no trace of a leak at the military district's headquarters. Richardson then surprised Chambers by stating he was no longer employed as the district intelligence officer, but would be pleased to work confidentially on Chambers's behalf.

By then, keeping the news out of the press was less like keeping all of one's fingers in a dike and more like a game of whack-a-mole. Editors and reporters followed the rules, but coverage still popped up, sometimes where Chambers least expected it. On August 13, the day the CLC arrived at Petawawa, he received another embarrassing cable from Scott. "I am now informed the *Pembroke Observer*, which is a weekly paper, had a news item a week or two ago covering about three or four inches of single column space, all devoted to the movement of Chinese, where they were coming from, where they were going, and why they were being held over at Petawawa Camp."

Remaining serious, but not wanting to miss an opportunity to play with words, Scott finished his cable with: "It appears the *Pembroke Observer* has not very well observed your warning."[17]

With the word CONFIDENTIAL typed in capital letters, Chambers wrote to the Ottawa Valley newspaper on August 14. "Some time ago instructions were issued to the press of Canada to suppress any references to this very important movement of men which has been in progress for the last six or seven months without any leakage of news . . . It is very regrettable . . . the first leakage should have occurred through a paper so close to the headquarters of the Press Censorship Service, for an inquiry to this office would have elicited the information that the rules originally enforced, regarding this matter, are strictly in force."

Chambers instructed the editor to supply a copy of the newspaper article.

David Jones of the *Pembroke Observer* replied on August 17 with a copy of the newspaper. "I regret that we gave publication to this matter without consulting you, but we did so in view of the fact that within the past few months, references had been made on several occasions, in Ottawa Valley newspapers, to the effect of Chinese having passed in train-loads over the Canadian Pacific Railway en route to the coast, while in this case, the matter had added local interest through the fact they were to be quartered for a time at Petawawa Camp. We will in future refrain from giving publication to movements of the Chinese."

The newspaper article, which appeared August 2, carried the headline: "Rumours of Big Things at Petawawa Camp." It stated "in the absence of an official announcement . . . everything is conjecture and no one knows definitely what is in the air." The piece described "feverish activity" at the camp and there "appears to be a well-founded report that about 4,000 Chinese coolies en route to France are to be taken care of at the Thistle's Siding camp . . . until transports can be secured to take them across the Atlantic."

It was understood, the article stated, the "artillery camp at Petawawa will break up the latter part of this month and the forces now training there will be away by Sept. 1."

One of Chambers's right-hand men, Ernest Boag, sent the

newspaper another copy of the circular instructing Canadian editors in March to refrain from publishing news on the CLC movements. He stated the chief press censor's office was surprised to learn other Ottawa Valley newspapers published stories on the subject. Boag then asked the editor to let him know the names of the publications and the dates the articles appeared.[18]

There is no indication in the file of what became of this request.

The 939 CLC who arrived in Petawawa on August 13 also decamped on the morning of August 18. They entrained with slightly fewer guards on two trains composed of sixteen and seventeen cars, not including the locomotives. The specials headed south to Smiths Falls before completing their journey through southeastern Ontario to Quebec, where they followed the usual route across Maine to Halifax, reached on August 20.

The next three contingents of CLC did not disembark labourers at Petawawa. These trains were longer, between seventeen and twenty cars each, including eleven or twelve Colonist cars. The first party left Vancouver on four trains August 14 with 2,340 Chinese and 177 guards, including all ranks, officers and non-commissioned officers. There were also two doctors and nine imperial officers. The contingent arrived in Halifax a day after the Petawawa group arrived.[19] The two other contingents left Vancouver on August 21 and August 23. The first one utilized four specials on which there were 2,249 Chinese. The second movement featured three trains with 1,768.[20]

Camp Petawawa saw its next and final influx of Chinese labourers on September 23 when four specials rolled in with 2,289 labourers, including one man who died on the train near Chapleau, Ontario. Twenty-five-year-old Chou Ming Shan (Zhou Mingshan, No. 39038) had been in a coma for twenty-four hours prior to his death on September 22. The cause was listed as "chronic malaria," usually transmitted through the bite of a mosquito infected with the *Plasmodium* parasite. The young man had crossed the Pacific on the *Empress of Russia*, which landed

This headstone for Chou Ming Shan was scheduled for installation at CFB Petawawa in 2019.

BURIED ELSEWHERE
IN THIS CEMETERY

生 猶 死 雖

THOUGH DEAD
HE STILL LIVETH

No. 59038
CHOU MING SHAN
CHINESE LABOUR CORPS
DIED SEP 22ND 1917

Courtesy Lawrence Neville, Campbell Monument, Pembroke, Ontario

her passengers at Vancouver at 5:30 p.m., September 17. The ship's bill of health was listed as "Good."[21] But the young man more than likely fell ill on the ship, not long before he arrived in Canada.

The doctor on the train stated his patient had been suffering for eight days. At Petawawa, Chou Ming Shan's body was carried from the train by fellow labourers and quietly buried in a grave his compatriots had dug. In the summer of 2019, in conjunction with research for this book, the Canadian Agency of the Commonwealth War Graves Commission made arrangements to erect a headstone for Chou Ming Shan at Canadian Forces Base Petawawa.

These specials also brought three doctors, four Canadian officers, 172 train guards and eight imperial officers.[22] Immediately, twelve Chinese were admitted to hospital with contagious diseases. That evening the train guards and their officers commenced their journey back to Vancouver for assignment to more trains heading east. The labourers did not resume their journey to Halifax, under guard, until the evening of October 4, one day before the transit camp closed.[23] Altogether, the CPR memos indicate at minimum 3,228 Chinese labourers en route to France spent time behind wire at Petawawa.

And, of course, one of them never left.

On September 27, the commanding officer of the CLC party wrote to Lieutenant-Colonel W.C. Bryan, the Canadian officer in charge of the transit camp within the main camp. Lieutenant Angus Cannan stated there were twenty CLC in the camp's hospital as well as six Chinese orderlies. "In regard to detailing further working parties, I regret I must ask you to inform H.Q. that, owing to the state of the men's shoes, which are flimsy things at best and only intended to last the voyage, it is necessary to withdraw as soon as possible all the men at present on work outside the compound."[24]

A September 26 memorandum from the camp's engineer lists hammers and axes among tools purchased for the Chinese work details at Petawawa. "The Chinese men are distributed approximately as follows: Over 500 lowering water-mains in Central Camp below frost, Over 200 clearing up bush around Camp for prevention of fire, The balance are employed renewing beds of septic tank and filtering system, gathering and breaking stone for roads, grading roads, spreading manure, and generally improving the Camp. At the same time they are being used to help close up a portion of the Camp for winter."[25]

Though the labourers got plenty of exercise at Petawawa, allowing time for physical training (PT) during transcontinental journeys was a contentious subject between the CPR and military authorities. Officers travelling with contingents from China wrote about this in their reports, believing a little PT and fresh air would benefit the men, especially while the trains coaled or took on water. On July 18, the secretary of state for the colonies sent the governor general a telegram recommending daily exercise. But by late September it seems to have fallen on deaf ears. Scott cabled MacInnes. "I understand from Mr. Walter Maughan of the Canadian Pacific Railway that nothing ever came of the request of the British Authorities . . . I had a visit the other day from one of the transportation officials who said he thought the Government was somewhat negligent in not providing . . . daily exercise."[26]

Library and Archives Canada, C-068867

Several CLC members take a break from work detail at Camp Petawawa in
the summer of 1917. The man in the middle enjoys a smoke while resting a
sledgehammer or an axe on his shoulder.

Maughan had written to Scott on September 20, explaining
the company received no official request from the Imperial government to stop the trains for PT. His letter also stated ". . . the
Coolies are not suffering any detrimental effect by the non-
stopping of trains."[27]

After hearing from MacInnes, Maughan wrote: "I do not
favour the suggestion of giving the Coolies exercise en route
. . . We cannot stop our trains between divisional points for the
purpose without seriously interfering with other passenger and
freight train movements. The freight train movements today are
of the utmost importance, and their prompt operation is vital as
they are now practically all loaded with food stuffs, munitions,
etc. If the Coolies are allowed to exercise at divisional points
where there are usually a number of tracks, congested yards, etc. I
feel the Guards will have some difficulty in preventing the escape
of some of their numbers . . . I think the Immigration Department would object to this."

Maughan added there had been no reports of labourers demanding exercise along the way. He then suggested it was the guards themselves who wanted the exercise.[28] On the other hand, there was no mention in the memo of any Chinese having escaped or tried to escape from the trains.

Given Maughan's concerns, the adjutant general recommended to his superiors that the CPR should not be asked to make time for exercise. "Perhaps a more effective remedy would be to curtail the diet of the travellers."

From the highest levels it was soon decided if "suitable opportunities for exercising" existed, advantage should be taken of them. This included the idea of exercising the men in the Colonist cars while the trains were stopped.[29]

Meanwhile, at Petawawa Camp, the manual labour ensured such "suitable opportunities" existed every day.

Chambers remained on alert for more CLC news leaks. In September, after receiving a tip from Malcolm Reid, Chambers responded to a story in the *Ledge*, a weekly from Greenwood in south-central British Columbia. The piece referenced Chinese en route to France and asked its readers why Chinese labour could not be employed closer to home. When the editor told Chambers the piece had been scalped from another newspaper, the chief press censor handled it with his usual tact: "A very large proportion of the correspondence of this office consists in drwring [sic] the attention of Editors in a friendly way to little slips which occur from time to time."[30]

Matters became more serious on January 8, 1918, when Chambers caught wind of a report stating "twenty-five Chinese labourers en route from Vancouver to Halifax for transportation to England and France were found frozen to death in their car when it reached the Maine Border." The piece referenced unnamed railroad men who implied the "Chinese were frozen while passing through Maine in the recent cold wave when the temperature reached 42 below zero."[31]

Chambers cabled Gwatkin on January 9 stating the local superintendent of the Canadian Pacific Railway Company's telegraph office had provided him with a copy of a message sent to him by wire from the manager of CPR Telegraphs, Montreal. Chambers shared the message with Gwatkin, telling him it had been filed by the Dominion News Bureau, "operated in connection with the *Montreal Daily Star*." While checking on its accuracy, Chambers contacted Maughan, who was in Ottawa on business. Maughan telephoned his office in Montreal and concluded "there was no truth in the statement" and that "as a matter of fact such a thing was impossible." Chambers attributed it to nefarious attempts to disrupt the CLC recruitment process.

The story was published in a few newspapers so Chambers had to act quickly to suppress it. Under the headline "Wild Rumor Denied By Press Censor," the *Ottawa Citizen* included a small, but carefully-worded report on page four stating the press censor "has requested all Canadian editors to deny a rumor circulated from Bangor, Maine, that twenty-five Chinese labourers from Vancouver going overseas by way of Halifax were found frozen to death in their car when it reached the Maine border."

In addition to reminding readers of how censorship was applied to everyday news coverage, the *Citizen* article, by clearly attributing the denial to the chief press censor, gave itself an out if the report proved accurate. The article stated "military authorities declare there is not the least basis of truth in the yarn, and that it is one of many such stories circulated with a view to preventing the securing of laborers in China."[32] Chambers also arranged to issue the same caution "over the leased wires of the United States Associated Press." Despite this, Bourne, the man in charge of recruitment in China, still wanted to know weeks later if there was any truth to the story. There is nothing in the file to suggest he was told anything different.

Today, if proof of these reported deaths exists, it is elusive.

On the contrary, the CLC Medal Roll, which often notes in

the "Remarks" column the deaths of CLC travelling from China to France, does not include a list of any twenty-five men dying close together in early January 1918. Names are missing from the roll, but no evidence has surfaced to prove such a catastrophe occurred either in Maine or in Canada along the CPR route. It is also hard to accept the idea that after all these years there would be no final resting place identified for such a large group of men who died so suddenly. Also, if it was incumbent on Chambers to keep it hush-hush, why would his confidential files not include anything to encourage the impression that this was done? Instead, there is no hint in the file to suggest anything close to such a tragedy ever happened. Both Chambers and Maughan emphatically denied the story, but it is possible material could have been redacted or not included in the file. This, however, remains pure speculation until primary documentation surfaces, if it ever does. As historian Greg James points out, it is likely the labourers suffered from extreme cold, prompting someone to remark they were "frozen to death," a term still used to describe bone-chilling temperatures. If overheard, the comment may have been taken literally and caused the ensuing furor.

Meanwhile, across the Pacific, British authorities were becoming more incensed about a recurring article in the Chinese press about how abominably CLC men had been treated on their voyage to Canada in June 1917. The article, over-spilling with emotion, also claimed wounded soldiers at the Vancouver hospital spoke about how Chinese labourers — once they got to France — were armed and sent to the front to fight.

It was precisely the sort of publicity the British did not want. In addition to potentially undermining the recruitment effort in China, the article encouraged more anti-British sentiment. This was not welcomed, because even though the French and British labour schemes were well underway and China by August had declared war on Germany, there still lingered, as noted earlier, a lot of support in China for Germany.

Reacting to the article, Bourne fired off a cable from China to the British War Office. It reached Ottawa on January 10, stating a "Chinese interpreter stationed in hospital at Vancouver has written most damaging and untrue statements to native newspapers here which may seriously affect recruiting. He states . . . white soldiers in hospital report . . . Chinese in France are used as soldiers. Please see that no letters are allowed to be sent by post but that all are collected and addressed to me here for censoring."

In support of Britain and in line with the Canadian government's extensive wartime surveillance of Chinese in Canada, including the interception of their domestic mail and telegraphic correspondence, Gwatkin issued instructions for Chambers to investigate.

Chambers and Reid communicated in top-secret code which, at first, left Reid scratching his head. Chambers, meanwhile, told Gwatkin he would endeavor to further identify the source. Once confirmed, Chambers would issue specific instructions for interception and censorship of the individual's telegraphic correspondence. Chambers also assured Gwatkin he would contact R.M. Coulter, the deputy postmaster general, with the view of having the individual's mail intercepted and examined before it was forwarded to Bourne at Weihaiwei.

The chief press censor certainly knew his place in relation to the responsibilities of the deputy postmaster general, who acted as the country's chief postal censor. This was obvious in his January 19 request to Coulter and later in a cable to Reid reminding him of how the two systems worked. "If you would have the mail correspondence of the individual named and any letters addressed from Vancouver to Weihaiwei newspapers intercepted and forwarded to this office I will have them examined by interpreters and returned to you," Chambers told Coulter. "But perhaps you will prefer to attend to the matter in your own Department; at any rate I hold myself at your disposal in the matter."[33]

The coded message Reid found confusing was dated January 15. This is how it read:

> *Following in our code stop Machinate reports mucus Grotto in-terpreter stationed military Porridge grouse received by concept at Grantz contains damaging and untrue statements that white Maraud in PORRIDGE report GROTTO in GRATER being used as fighting MARAUD stop please try and have GROTTO in question located quietly without arousing suspicion and WALTZ.*

Reid replied, stating he did not understand it, and could they adopt a different code. Pressed by the urgency of the situation, Chambers shot back with a clearer copy of his message, adding: "I hope you will be able to put your hands on the little Press Censorship Code which was sent to you some months ago and that the several telegrams of this date will be intelligible. If not, we shall doubtless hear from you."

Working undercover, Reid was relying on a small team of investigators who focused on Leung Shou Yat (Liang Shouyi), who is also named in the files as Julian Leon and Julian Liang. Leung had arrived in Vancouver as a CLC interpreter, but owing to his ability to speak the languages of northern China he became a valuable asset at the Vancouver hospital that treated sick or injured CLC. While Cantonese was common in Vancouver, few people there understood the languages of Shantung.

Leung had wanted to go to France, and the longer he remained in Vancouver the more frustrated he became.

A special operative working for Reid visited the Vancouver hospital and was introduced to the man. The agent, who reported to Reid on January 18, used the cover story of "trying to locate a coolie friend who was supposed to be on his way from China to France" but had died at the hospital. When the undercover agent supplied the name, the interpreter stated he had not heard of the man. Using another approach to win Leung's confidence, the agent explained he was going to visit the Chinese Consulate and enquire there about his deceased friend. His first preference, however, was to have Leung furnish the information.

Leung told the undercover agent he too was going to visit the Chinese Consulate to speak about the conditions faced by the Chinese labourers. Feigning innocence, the agent asked Leung for his impressions on how the men were treated. The interpreter replied, the agent reported, by stating the British had "originally wanted to bring 180,000 coolies to Europe, there is about 60,000 already there. Of these 60,000 . . . approximately 6,000 have been placed in the front line trenches as fighting troops, while the balance has been distributed in France and Belgium."

This, of course, was the type of evidence the surveillance team was looking for because it was similar to what had appeared in the Chinese newspapers.

When asked by the agent if the use of the labourers as soldiers was contrary to the agreement the labourers had signed, Leung replied: ". . . well those coolies are ignorant people and what is the agreement to them, it is simply waste paper."

Leung also told the agent how the British were not honouring the contracts because the families of labourers in China were not receiving the allotments promised to them when their sons or husbands joined. Accurate or not, this assertion, of course, had deeply angered British recruiters in China. The agent also told Reid that Leung proudly admitted to being a member of the Kuomintang (KMT) "or as we call it The Chinese Nationalist League, and that he was desirous of returning home to China . . ."

Reid continued to watch Leung into the early spring. In February, authorities believed he was getting nervous, because he had sent a letter to a woman in Shanghai asking for $500 so he could return home. "He . . . cautioned the woman not to let anyone know of this, but for her to advise him as soon as she could send the money asked for," Reid told Chambers on February 25. More correspondence followed, but by early March the War Office was advising Chambers not to take action other than maintaining strict censorship. It noted "enquiries had been made and it has been found there is not sufficient evidence readily available on which action can be taken."

On March 21, Leung wrote to a friend in China, acknowledging receipt of a January 31 letter containing a clipping from the *Eastern Times* in which British consulate officials vehemently denied the previously published reports. "When I first learned the *Eastern Times* had published the original complaint about the treatment of these Coolies I felt well satisfied with myself . . . but after reading the published denial my satisfaction at once left me," wrote Leung. "The language and phrases used in the denial are absurd. For instance, the statement is made that I was influenced by the Germans to make this original complaint, but that is an untruth."[34]

By Leung's own words, captured in an intercepted letter, it was determined he was the author of the articles.

If Canadian authorities intended to swoop down and apprehend Leung or put him on the next ship to China, they were too late. On March 31, 1918, the same day the very last CLC special left Vancouver for the East Coast, Leung disappeared from the city. According to the CPR schedule, two trains carrying half of the contingent from the *Tyndareus* had already left and two more set off on the thirty-first, one carrying 600 labourers, the other 550. It is assumed that Leung made it on board one of the trains, crossed Canada, and reached France, where authorities continued to track him and where he continued to secretly criticize the British scheme.[35]

* * *

On January 15, in the midst of the Leung surveillance, dozens of CLC men were nearly killed in a train wreck in northeastern

Ontario. It occurred at 6:13 a.m., four kilometres west of Eau Claire Station north of Algonquin Park.

British 2nd Lieutenant Ashley McCallum was in command of a 3,549-man contingent. Most of the men had journeyed across the Pacific with him from Tsingtao on the *Antilochus,* which arrived at William Head on Christmas Eve. It was a very crowded ship; nine of her holds were filled with labourers and deck space was very limited. During the voyage, one labourer died of pneumonia. Twenty-nine of McCallum's men were hospitalized on the West Coast. However, several other labourers were added to his contingent before the specials pulled out of Vancouver.[36]

In addition to the locomotive, the train McCallum was on was composed of thirteen Colonist cars, two Tourist coaches, a commissary and a baggage car. There were 750 labourers on board when it left Vancouver for Halifax. Among the officers assigned to McCallum's contingent was a thirty-two-year-old Canadian, Captain John McCammon of the CAMC. Enlisted in May 1916 and commissioned as an officer on January 22, 1917, the five-foot-eleven, 162-pound doctor was loaned to the British Army on August 31, 1917, for special "escort" duty. The certificate of service in his military file states he was seconded to "Imperials as Army Medical Corps Officer in charge of Chinese Coolies proceeding to China and France, from September the 10th, 1917, to March 1918."[37]

Born south of Ottawa in the eastern Ontario village of Spencerville, the red-haired, blue-eyed McCammon was, by early 1901, living with his parents in Gananoque, east of Kingston, Ontario. In early 1911, he graduated from medicine at Queen's University. The doctor's own health, however, was not always good. Three bouts of pneumonia and a case of pleurisy had hit him before 1916. McCammon also suffered from chronic arthritis and myalgia, causing considerable pain in his joints, especially his shoulders and knees.[38]

The sun was below the horizon when the big locomotive

entered a series of curves some twenty kilometres west of Mattawa. The CPR's great steel ribbon cut east through rolling landscape where plateaus and ridges of tree-covered granite dropped into narrow gorges or descended more gradually onto frozen, wind-swept lakes. The few open fields were blanketed with deep, fresh snow and the temperature was unusually hospitable for mid-January.[39] Curled up in their upper and lower berths or sitting upright on the wooden benches, the labourers were just waking up; many had not gotten dressed, let alone put on their slippers.

Entering that stretch of track, the train was moving along at roughly forty kilometres per hour when four of its Colonist cars left the rails and careered into a field of snow. After rolling over and sliding to a stop in a cloud of white powder, the wrecked cars, each weighing more than 45,800 kilograms, were lying more than nine metres from the track. Three other cars fell off the rails and were partially damaged.

Tossed upside down and sideways by the powerful and unexpected forces inside the carriage, eighty-eight Chinese men were injured. "The depth of the snow was responsible for the marvelous escape of the coolies," wrote McCallum in his report several days later. "Immediately after the accident . . . the train guard turned out and inside of one hour the coolies from all the damaged cars had been removed. The conduct and the discipline of the coolies was wonderful. Many of them had to leave the coaches practically naked, then wade through deep snow to the track and run about 50 yards (forty-six metres) to the nearest coach standing intact. Many coolies covered this space without socks or shoes. Fortunately the cold was not extreme, the thermometer registering only zero."[40]

Anyone who has walked on snow in bare or socked feet, even for a few seconds in mild temperature, knows how it feels. The snow the men waded through while practically naked was likely waist high, so it took strength and perseverance to get out of the field once they emerged from the cars. Looking around at the wilderness, many had to wonder where they were, but it appears, at least from McCallum's report, they did it all without complaint.

McCallum noted three of the overturned cars were badly filled with gas. "This, however, did not seem to affect the coolies although the guards suffered severely from the same." The gas the lieutenant referred to was called "Pintsch" gas, named after Julius Pintsch, who had developed gas lamps for ships and trains. Tanks, loaded with the fuel, were located underneath each car with lines running up and then along the outside of the roof of each carriage to feed the overhead lamps used for lighting the carriages.[41]

McCallum and the other officers were more than likely in a tourist car, near the rear of the train. If McCammon was on this particular train, he is not mentioned in McCallum's report.

The Tourist carriage did not derail and there is no mention in the report of the RSG car derailing, but at least eight guards — two per car — were in the most severely damaged Colonist carriages. "I immediately opened what canteen stores I could reach, giving them to the coolies. These stores consisted mostly of cigarettes which kept the coolies happy and troubles were soon forgotten."

Incredibly, the train's locomotive, with its ten remaining cars jammed with shaken and injured men, reached Mattawa by 4 p.m., roughly an hour before sunset. Three labourers were admitted to hospital there, while the remaining 747 men were transferred to coaches probably assembled at North Bay and then run out to Mattawa.[42] One of those cars, a Colonist, had been quickly converted into a hospital car, and the standard practice would have been to supply it with a team of doctors and nurses, bedding and medical supplies.[43]

While no one died in the wreck, two labourers who had been on the train succumbed within days, and it appears neither man had been hospitalized after the crash. Li Chin Hsiang (Li

Jinxiang, No. 102509) died from heart failure in Montreal at 5 p.m. on January 16. Feng Chai Li (Feng Jiali, No.95167) died of pneumonia in Halifax at 4:45 p.m. on January 22 or 23. McCallum's report notes "an official investigation was at once held and it decided . . . the . . . accident was not responsible for either death."[44]

Li Chin Hsiang was buried at Montreal's Mount Royal Cemetery but his remains were repatriated to China after the war. Feng Chia Li's remains lie in St. John's Cemetery, Halifax, where a headstone was placed in 2017.

The CPR was notified by McCallum that "claims covering the injured coolies would be filed by the British Government." In addition, "claims covering lost kits and canteen supplies were completed before arrival at Halifax and placed in the hands of the CPR claims department."[45]

In Halifax, McCallum's party boarded the *Kursk*, which sailed on January 27 and arrived in Liverpool on February 6.

Five days after the wreck near Eau Claire, another Chinese labourer died on an eastbound train further to the west near Schreiber, Ontario. His name was Wang Yung Sheng (Wang Yongsheng, No. 102111) and the cause of death was internal hemorrhage due to a ruptured liver. His body was taken to Port Arthur (Thunder Bay) and buried at Riverside Cemetery.[46]

CHAPTER 18

The Western Front

"I suppose none of us are very much taken with army discipline."

Haircuts, hospitals and mental illness . . .

The razor was a broad-bladed affair, very sharp and much heavier than the standard North American razor.

While the *Olympic* was "skimming" and "pitching" across the North Atlantic en route to Liverpool in early December 1917, the barbers went to work, usually in the early evening. With a white sheet thrown around the shoulders of their "victims" or "patients," as Livingstone described the customers, the barber sharpened his blade while the men prepared themselves for "the operation" by sitting or squatting on deck. "No soap is used, simply water," noted the doctor. "The barber would commence his work . . . on the forehead and by quick movements . . . soon have the whole head devoid of hair. Then he would go over it again and when finished the man would be as bald as a billiard ball."[1]

Next, the barber would run the razor over the man's face, just as quickly. He would shave the cheeks, chin, nose and ears, "leaving only the eyebrows and eyelashes. We expected a deep gash made in the nose or cheek or even an ear . . . but no accidents of this kind happened." Many of the men only wanted the forepart of their scalp shaved, a strict custom practised in China. The "victim's" head was then washed and dabbed with "a liberal dose of some strong smelling perfume, then powdered." Between five and ten cents was handed the barber, and then each customer, noted Livingstone, went away feeling his head and repeating "Ding howla, ding howla," meaning "very good" or "feels fine."[2]

Down below, the labourers assigned to hammocks were not very anxious to climb into them. The Chinese preferred hard beds, not something resembling a swinging cocoon. Those who were not assigned a hammock curled up on the floor, atop tables or on chairs. Others slept on the steam coils running through the ship. Often, before retiring to wherever they slept, the men gathered for small theatrical shows, usually featuring a few musicians with drums and cymbals. Stories and plays usually featured "some green-faced robber or pirate who ran away with the King's wife" or some other treasure, noted Livingstone, who was admired as a special guest during the performances in the hold's damp, heavy air.[3]

While making his rounds through the crowded lower decks the doctor distributed cheap candy he had purchased in bulk in Halifax, earning him the nickname "Jang difu" or the "Candy doctor." One twenty-year-old labourer was so impressed with Livingstone's demeanour he asked the "Jang difu" to be his special guest in China after the war. There he could ride his horse and eat "peanuts, candy, crabs, sweet potatoes, and plenty of rice."[4]

Lifebelt and lifeboat drills were frequent. One man on B Deck had lost his socks and was left with only slippers for drill, but did not complain. Anticipating such shortages, the doctor had purchased extra woolen socks and handed a pair to the man who "almost cracked his skull on the deck, bowing in thanks."[5]

Since the waiving of lifebelt regulations on the Pacific, it was a struggle when lifebelts were issued on the Olympic. On the day they were handed out the men marched in single file into one of the ship's storerooms and then out the other side holding the apparatus with no idea how to put it on. Several were donned upside down and Livingstone observed "one fellow trying to get his legs through the hole for his head."[6]

Six blasts from a whistle or six rings from a bell down below signaled a boat drill. "After a few trials we managed to have every coolie in his place on deck and the interior of the ship cleared in six minutes. As soon as the first men came running . . . onto the deck with their lifebelts we would hustle them along and make them crowd well back next to the bulkheads." Within a few minutes the deck was packed with labourers standing at attention with only a yard or so between the rows. The lifeboats, meanwhile, were made ready with food and fresh water. "All of us officers had certain sections to look after and we told them in case of a real submarine attack, we would make sure they would all be saved provided they did as they were ordered. It worked fine in practice, but in reality I guess it would have been different."[7]

In addition to boat drills, deck space was used for exercise and competitive entertainment. "One day a Canadian who was handy with boxing gloves was boxing in the centre of a group of coolies which numbered several hundred. He would allow the Chink to hammer him severely much to the amusement of the Chinese audience who cheered as they thought their side was winning out, then just at the right moment the Canadian would land a terrific blow and knock the Chinaman out usually with cut lips but always with a bleeding nose. The coolie would get up slowly and then another would don the gloves and receive the same punishment."[8]

What mostly impressed the labourers was the massive, four-funnel ship and how she had been prepared for her wartime transport duty. The men learned the *Olympic* was the biggest ship in the world when she made her maiden voyage to New York in June 1911. Throughout the crossing the labourers remained curious about the mine-catchers, six-inch guns and rangefinders. On a few occasions, men got into trouble while trying to peek under the tarpaulins used to keep the North Atlantic's salty spray and ice off the searchlights.[9]

The ships leaving eastern Canadian ports often carried men who had arrived on the West Coast on different vessels around the same time, either from Weihaiwei or Tsingtao. On several occasions, this mixture — once the men were on board a single ship crossing to Liverpool — proved volatile, as it did on the *Olympic*. "One day a *Coconada* CLC labourer assigned as a policeman struck one of the *Russia*'s coolies" and men from the latter ship sought revenge. They "hammered him around but the policeman expected them and his friends piled in and our men got the worst of it . . . I had several casualties . . . in the hospital where they were brought in on stretchers, mostly cuts and bruises of the head and face. Another night we had a wild mob of our men crowding the alleyway in a very threatening mood. One of the *Coconada* officers was trying to subdue them but they . . . kept shaking their fists at him and shoving and looking very wicked. It would only have taken one Chinaman to attack this officer and the rest would have followed as he was unpopular even amongst his own men."[10]

Alerted to the commotion, Livingstone rushed in and told the ringleaders he would deal with the officer. The threat of violence ended when the doctor shepherded the labourers down the corridor.[11]

Sick parade was also conducted daily. Livingstone and McDonald, aside from the ongoing U-boat threat, did not face any life-threatening conditions, but both were kept busy. Eye drops were administered daily and there were also the usual minor complaints, including rashes and sore muscles. "Every loose or aching tooth we extracted and they (the Chinese) were certainly pleased to carry away the rotten molar in a piece of paper to show their Comrades . . . and most of them kept this as a Souvenir of the trip," noted Livingstone.[12] Four extractions were particularly challenging "but we kept at it until they were out." When the opportunity arose, Livingstone and McDonald met and filled each other in on what they had treated thus far, from abscesses and anxiety to rheumatic joints.

By December 4, the *Olympic*, noted Livingstone, had crossed into the "danger zone and everyone was pretty anxious." By 1 p.m. the next day "a great feeling of relief came over us all as 4 U.S. Destroyers . . . came up quite close as our escort . . ." There are "two boats on either side, about 3/4 mile off. They are small and very fast and painted usual colors. They dip in the sea more than we do . . . The one nearest front on portside keeps zigzagging across our bow . . . All coolies on deck and delighted to be safe now. They point to the ships and say, 'Howla.'"[13]

Livingstone learned of an SOS call received the previous night from a merchant ship that disappeared after being torpedoed.[14]

* * *

Most of the fear dissipated when the *Olympic* dropped anchor in Liverpool on the morning of December 7. Greatly relieved by the ship's arrival, Livingstone cabled his father while Nettle went ashore for a quick visit. The *Coconada* party, as it was known on board the *Olympic*, transferred to lighters while Livingstone, Nettle and the rest of the passengers known as the *Russia* party waited three more days to disembark and entrain for the south coast of Britain. During the week-long Atlantic crossing, the doctor had been noticing how well Chaug, his beloved Chinese assistant, was learning English. The lad carried a small satchel that contained candy, cigarettes, needles and thread and a bit of yarn. If the doctor needed him, the eager batman was ready to sew up a worn sock or stitch on a button. Chaug enjoyed working for Livingstone, often reminding the doctor how he hoped to remain at his side in France.[15]

The young man's loyalty was not uncommon among those who served British or Canadian officers. Most were handpicked and known previously by the officers. Missionary James Menzies, for example, had insisted his "Lucky Boy" accompany him on the voyage to Canada in March 1917. He remained at Menzies's side throughout the journey and while in France continued to polish Menzies's shoes and the buttons on his tunic, wash the bedding and even wake him in the morning.[16]

The admiration between Livingstone and Chaug was mutual, and the doctor agreed it best if they could stay together. But the war took much and gave no guarantees.

While waiting to disembark, the doctor read "the bad war news" stemming from what he described as the "retreat from Cambrai," noting how it "makes us all feel depressed . . ." The battle to establish a bridgehead across the Saint-Quentin Canal had begun well, but ended in stalemate on the day *Olympic* made Liverpool.[17]

Livingstone had no way of knowing it at the time, but CLC labourers had contributed greatly to that battle by building large bundles of tightly rolled brushwood called "fascines," which, when dropped from the front of a tank's cab, enabled the armoured fighting vehicle to cross the wide trenches of the Hindenburg Line. Some four hundred fascines and more than a hundred sledges were built by CLC men at Tank Central Workshops. The fascines were rolled in mud and then loaded onto trains to be eventually attached to tanks. In France, the sledges, carrying ammunition and equipment, would be towed across the soupy, cratered landscape.

Much closer to home, Livingstone was shocked by news of the Halifax Explosion, which "occurred near the spot where our boat was anchored and no doubt would have seriously injured us."[18]

He was deeply troubled by the civilian losses and by not knowing the fate of the Chinese who had been left behind in hospital. There was nothing anybody could do for Liu Chih, the labourer found dead on the *Olympic* just as the ship was about to sail, but what about the man's remains? Did they disappear, along with much of the city?

On December 10, Livingstone's party began its railway journey to the south coast. Compared to the CPR's Colonist coaches, the carriages reserved for the Chinese on the British trains were small and cold. Noticeable too were the rations, which consisted of bully beef and hardtack. Although the officers, Livingstone included, were treated to first-class coaches, they could easily see their breath as the countryside whipped by. It was still cold and wet by the time the train reached Shorncliffe, Kent, at 10:30 p.m. From the station the men marched to the "Coolie Tents" loosely pegged into several inches of mud. After sipping something bitter, which may have passed as coffee, Livingstone pulled two coarse blankets over his body and settled in to a long night of shivering.[19]

Rising at 4:30 a.m., the labourers ate and then marched some three kilometres east to the wharf at Folkestone, where they embarked on small boats, escorted across the choppy Strait of Dover to northern France.[20]

The last leg of the journey did not always unfold so quickly.

Before crossing the Channel, tens of thousands of other Chinese spent several days in a designated camp near Shorncliffe between iconic Sugar Loaf Hill and Caesar's Camp. Officially, it went by the pleasant-sounding name of Cherry Garden Camp, but most people just called it the Labour Concentration Camp. From the top of Sugar Loaf Hill there was a bird's eye view of hundreds of white bell tents arranged in precise rows across an open field not far from the camp's namesake, Cherry Garden Avenue. First opened in April 1917, it was built to accommodate more than just the Chinese. The caption beneath eight old photographs at the Folkestone Library notes it was reserved for "Chinese, Kaffirs, West Indians, and Fijians, and Canadians."[21] Today, the Channel Tunnel line crosses where the camp used to be.[22]

The Chinese were not confined to the camp, but most stayed put. Those who did venture into town were usually in pursuit of souvenirs, particularly hats or watches. Others were intent on having their portrait taken. The men certainly stood out among the locals, whose reactions ranged from open curiosity to suspicion and fear. For the most part the encounters went well, but there was at least one serious incident. Hsuch Liang Kung, twenty-eight; Hao Wang, twenty-five; Liu Pao Chin, twenty-three and Chang Chin Chai, twenty-eight, all with the CLC, were "indicted for criminally assaulting" Florence Stickley on January 27, 1918. A fifth man, Yuan Chang Kivei, twenty, was acquitted. According to the *Kentish Gazette and Canterbury Press* of February 23, 1918, all four were "sentenced to seven years penal servitude" for raping the woman.[23]

Stickley, who worked as a cook at the camp, was walking with her boyfriend, a private in the British Army. The attackers seized the boyfriend, held a knife to his throat, and put a second blade into his mouth. Stickley was then attacked and assaulted by three of the men until they were frightened away by another private who happened on the scene.[24]

It is interesting that these men were not amenable to military law in this case. They were tried in civil court. Perhaps the army, given the circumstances of the case, did not want to interfere with the local court system.

*   *   *

The two-hour crossing to Boulogne on an old side-wheeler covered roughly forty-five kilometres of grey, rough water. It was cold, wet and windy for Livingstone and the Chinese on his boat; several men lost their breakfasts over the side before the vessel finally reached the place where the nations of the Western World were at war.

At 3 p.m., Livingstone's group boarded yet another train, only this one had no windows and no heat, and felt like a cattle car. By 6:30 p.m., "after a cold, uncomfortable and hungry ride across the fields of northern France and through villages," the men arrived at the main CLC base at Noyelles-sur-Mer.[25]

In darkness, the labourers stepped off the old freight cars and trudged through mud to a large compound, which Livingstone estimated to be fifty kilometres from the front. At the time, prior

Members of the CLC are escorted from a ship after arriving in France, 1918.

WJ Hawkings Collection, courtesy John De Lucy

to the big German offensives that began in March and lasted into July 1918, the Allied front east of Vimy Ridge and Arras was still some eighty kilometres away. When the German offensives ended, part of the front southeast of Amiens was roughly sixty-five kilometres distant. But while the base depot was a considerable distance from the front, CLC companies were deployed to areas further forward that, although still well behind the lines, were exposed to shelling and aerial bombing, not to mention accidents and disease. Indeed, it was the latter that killed the vast majority of CLC in France and Belgium.

Exhausted, dirty and suffering from a cold, Livingstone, and McDonald, along with other officers, were introduced to Lieutenant-Colonel Douglas Gray, the depot's popular commanding officer who had worked with the British legation in Peking.[26] After an exchange of pleasantries, Livingstone and Chaug were shown to the officers' quarters, "a small, cold room, but this is war now," he wrote before falling asleep.

* * *

Situated along the River Somme only seven kilometres from the English Channel, the Chinese Labour Corps base depot in Noyelles-sur-Mer was conveniently located on the Boulogne-Amiens railway. It had been selected months earlier by Lieutenant-Colonel Bryan Fairfax, the officer in command of the CLC, and Lieutenant-Colonel Richard Purdon. The base grew to include No. 1 Chinese (No. 3 Native Labour) General Hospital, a reception centre, a holding camp and a prison.

Nearby was the ancient Crécy Forest, which in the minds of military men stood ready for wartime exploitation. Fairfax had visions of a Chinese forestry corps cutting and hauling out the timber needed for building or repairing everything from trenches and tunnels to roads, bridges, railways and wharfs. By 1917, the Chinese were busy cutting brushwood to make the fascines for the Battle of Cambrai.

By April, the base hospital had three hundred beds in half a dozen tents, which were replaced by stronger structures as the hospital grew to accommodate 1,500 Chinese patients, and the buildings at times still proved inadequate. In addition to its various wards, the hospital had X-ray facilities, a bacteriological lab and an ophthalmic department with top eye specialists. The wards were usually overflowing with patients suffering from a variety of illnesses — from bronchitis and pneumonia to tuberculosis — as well as serious injuries, including broken and crushed bones, lacerations, burns and missing limbs. The only constant was the variety of injuries. One labourer, employed in a factory, was thrown across a room after he became entangled in a revolving lathe. Another man, struck by a lorry, suffered a fractured pelvis and a compound fracture to his right femur. Some injuries were self-inflicted, including those of a suicidal labourer who drove a knife into his stomach, cutting sixteen holes in his intestinal wall.[27]

When they could be moved, men with amputations were sent

A labourer gets a close shave from a fellow labourer working as a camp barber at Noyelles-sur-Mer, France.

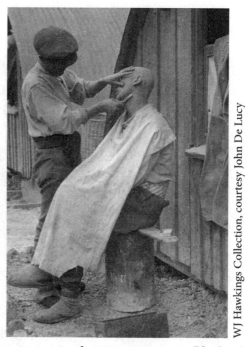

WJ Hawkings Collection, courtesy John De Lucy

to Rouen, where they were fitted with artificial limbs.

Added to these casualties were men suffering from less visible wounds. During its first two years in France, the CLC had 335 cases of mental illness.[28] The majority of cases fell into two categories, "melancholia" and "feeble-mindedness."[29] The latter included men who, when questioned, responded with strange or irrelevant answers, or "foolish jocularity and various little eccentricities." Generally, most had "no care for the future."[30]

At least six Canadian doctors, all of whom came from missionary postings in China, worked at the base hospital and earned praise from patients and staff. Frederick Auld was there, as were Percy Leslie, William Reeds, brothers Ernest and Robert Gordon Struthers and Edward Wilford. With the exception of Wilford, all came from the Canadian Presbyterian Mission in North Honan. "These ex-med-missionaries who have come have, without exception, done splendidly," noted Gray, who had seventeen such missionaries on staff helping to care for 1,800 to 2,000 patients.[31] The one drawback to some missionaries, he noted, "is they are more apt to be 'taken in' and are not keen enough to suppress gambling in a company which has a sprinkling of Tientsin Stiffs who think nothing of taking the whole of a coolie's savings off him in one night's play."[32]

A team of labourers manage a cart loaded with supplies at Noyelles-sur-Mer.

Auld, the McGill University graduate who joined the North Honan Mission in November 1910, appreciated the opportunity to serve in France and was quick to thank the Foreign Mission Board for endorsing his actions and those of other Presbyterian missionaries who were "doing their bit."[33] In a December 28, 1917, letter to Foreign Missions Board (FMB) Secretary Robert MacKay, Auld stated ". . . in view of the larger knowledge of conditions which we now have I think we are all agreed we reached the proper decision." The conscientious missionary also expressed the view "there are indications this war is a purifying fire burning up dross from the nations of the world. It is true of course a world of vice is inseparable from warfare but apart from that much that is good must inevitably arise from so great an evil as this war truly is."[34]

Throughout their wartime experience, the Chinese were often the butt of insults, racist jokes and other abuse, including physical beatings. Gray noted how officers who had never seen a Chinese man before usually "have the most absurd notions . . . and often succeed in causing discontent."

Auld had witnessed this as well and, like Gray, held a completely opposite view. "The Chinese are winning golden opinions for themselves . . . for their capacity to do work and for their unfailing cheerfulness under all circumstances."

Meanwhile, winter had started early, but the "snowfall would not be considered very heavy in Canada," noted Auld in his letter to MacKay. However, "the local French people say it is very unusual . . . They maintain the seasons have all changed greatly since the war began . . . becoming cooler . . . winter and summer . . . and more precipitation."[35]

Although he too could appreciate how much missionary work had been left behind in China, Doctor William Reeds was absolutely convinced France was where he had to be. For him it was about being in the right place at the right time, where the work offered more opportunity. The thirty-six year old had been appointed to the Honan mission shortly after graduating from the University of Toronto in 1914. He and his wife, Gladys, arrived in China in February 1915 and were posted to the Changte Station. A year later, their first child, George, was born.

In a January 15, 1918, letter to MacKay, Reeds emphasized the important role of the missionaries by stating more men from China would be needed in the months ahead.

MacKay, who always had his ear to the ground and communicated regularly with the Honan missionaries in France, was shocked to learn how close Reeds and Robert Gordon Struthers had got to the action at the front. In his letter to the FMB secretary, Reeds stated: "Yes, Gordon [as Struthers was called] and I were sent up to the front lines last July, but were recalled after three weeks. Gordon was in a hot spot, but it was very quiet where I was sent and I didn't see much. We are very glad to be back where we can keep in touch with the Chinese and continue to pick up new words and phrases in the language. Unfortunately, I was taken ill with Trench fever and Bronchitis early in October and was off duty for two months . . ." He also picked up a few French phrases which he shared with the Chinese.

Unfortunately, Reeds's letter does not describe — even generally — what he saw or experienced at the front.

Reeds, meanwhile, had a very high opinion of Gray, describing him as a "first-rate commanding officer." However, the Canadian doctor was not enamoured with military life. "I suppose none of us are very much taken with army discipline. We take it as a sort of necessary 'evil' and shall be not unwilling to say good-bye to it . . . when we doff our uniforms. Our experience here in many ways should help us in the work we hope to return to when this page is written."

Reeds, however, was confident the missionaries' work in France would establish much credibility in China. Through letters and word of mouth, news would reach home of how men such as him helped labourers through difficult situations with British officers and NCOs who could not speak their language. This good news, he added, will be especially felt in northern and eastern China. "It will doubtless have a very beneficial effect on missionary work in the years to come. I am finding the Chinese very pleasant to deal with as patients, also as servants. I am quite sure one could never expect the same amount of appreciation from a white patient as these chaps show. They respond in a wonderful way to a little kindness."

Robert Gordon Struthers and his brother, Ernest, had graduated from the same medical school. Gordon was two years younger than Ernest, who was born on May 28, 1886. Born in Galt in southwestern Ontario, the boys had grown up in a religious family, which was quite typical, in the same part of the province that produced other China-bound missionaries and doctors, including Menzies and Livingstone.

Ernest was in his second year of college when he decided to "become a Christian and try to live my life in accordance with the principles of our Master." After graduating in 1912, he earned enough money working for his father to pay for post-graduate study in England. He applied to the London Missionary Society and soon accepted a posting in Hong Kong, arriving there in 1913. At the time, tuberculosis and tropical diseases were claiming many lives in China and the few teaching hospitals were urgently requesting help from Western-trained doctors.

While still in China in 1916, the medical missionary, who by now could write and speak Chinese, decided his time would be better served in uniform in war-torn Europe. Commissioned as a captain in the CAMC, he sailed overseas with a contingent of the CLC, first to Vancouver, then across Canada by train for the Atlantic crossing. In Noyelles-sur-Mer, the sheer size of the hospital impressed him. "A huge painted pagoda had been erected at the entrance and in those final years of the war the hospital's reputation for efficiency and its unique role in the war made it one of the show pieces for every distinguished visitor to France," noted a *Toronto Star* article written on Struthers after the war.[36]

While writing his autobiography years later, Ernest noted there "is great satisfaction in being able to meet the needs of people who would otherwise receive no medical care."[37]

Disabled labourers or men too sick to return to their companies were sent to the hospital's convalescent camp in the Crécy Forest, where Ernest supervised their care. Depending on their physical or mental state, the Crécy convalescents worked in sawmills, chopped firewood, cleared brush and leveled charcoal pits. Ernest understood "the circumstances of each one and proved himself a splendid organiser and cheerful friend to them," noted Gray. "He made the Company a great success in every way, and the work accomplished proved most useful to the Army in the shape of many thousands of pickets, hurdles, fascines and other field material which were continually being sent to the Front from Crecy Forest. This Company was inspected by H.M. King George who was highly pleased with his visit."

Doctor Edward Wilford was thirty-three when he arrived in France. He, too, was born in southwestern Ontario, in the little town of Blyth. After graduating from the University of Toronto in 1908,

WJ Hawkings Collection, courtesy John De Lucy

The heavy work assigned to labourers involved in railway construction and repair included the hauling of timbers. A head ganger (right) looks on as the men walk away with another railway tie.

Wilford completed postgraduate work in Edinburgh. Accompanied by his wife Claudia, an accomplished musician, the young doctor arrived at the Central Stations of the Canadian Methodist West China Mission in the fall of 1909. As was typical of all new arrivals, the couple commenced language studies and worked out of the Tzeliutsing mission station, which had only opened in 1907.

Strongly advised to evacuate Szechuan province during the 1911 revolution, the Wilfords, along with other missionaries, heeded the warning. When they returned they helped build a dispensary, and contributed to the establishment of the largest hospital in West China. In addition to building churches, clinics, schools and orphanages the Canadian West China Mission, which served an area of more than ten million people, dealt with a variety of social issues, including child marriage, opium addiction and foot binding.

For Wilford, as for fellow Methodist missionary Gordon Jones, it was steady and engaging work right up to the time he headed overseas with the CLC.[38] Any patient passing through the X-ray department in Noyelles-sur-Mer had Wilford to thank. The images it produced identified everything from broken fingers and toes to crushed vertebrae, smashed pelvises and compound leg fractures. Most of the injuries, many of them fatal, were not caused by bombs or bullets, but sustained in accidents due to the hazardous work environment. Accidents at the docks saw men burned or crushed to death.

This dangerous work continued past the end of the war and through 1919, well after the last ordinary soldier had gone home.

While delivering a postwar speech in China, Gray told the Chinese Medical Missionary Association how the hospital in Noyelles-sur-Mer benefited from expert medical-missionary assistance. He recognized the diligent work of his staff, including the Canadians who had come from China. "In the course of time we acquired a complete X-ray plant which was installed by Captain Wilford, a Canadian medical missionary from Szechuan, who was lent to us for a time," stated Gray. "Captain F.M. Auld . . . had been studying the subject and very ably stepped into the break when Captain Wilford was recalled to his unit. Whether on the surgical or the medical side, Captain Auld proved himself the typical medical missionary, who invariably put his shoulder to every wheel with an eye to enlarging his experience for the good of his subsequent return to China. The X-ray apparatus was always kept busy."

Gray's summary of what he experienced in Noyelles-sur-Mer provides one of the best accounts of the hospital's purpose, what went on in terms of its staffing and how he perceived the Chinese.

The hospital, he noted, had three main functions: 1) ". . . the thorough examination of every incoming coolie; 2) the treatment of all those sent to it from out-companies and subsidiary hospitals; 3) the selection of cases for repatriation comprising those who were unfit for further work in France."

He explained how the first few CLC drafts, particularly those that travelled via the Cape of Good Hope, yielded a large number of men suffering from beriberi because of long voyages and poor

nutrition. This was followed by a "high percentage of coolies
. . . found to be suffering from trachoma." Most of the trachoma
cases surely arose and spread during journeys to and across
Canada or shortly after. As noted earlier, this was a very serious
situation that lead to the establishment of a separate eye department under Captain E.J. Stuckey, the former principal of a Peking
teaching hospital.[39] Stuckey was the Australian-born physician
who had arrived at William Head on board the *Russia* in April
1917 and witnessed the caning of two labourers.[40]

Gray believed all the labourers were entitled to the same type
of medical facilities offered to Allied soldiers, and he deeply
appreciated what the Chinese-speaking missionaries brought to
Noyelles-sur-Mer. "The chief success of the hospital in addition to
the treatment it gave, lay in the comfort it afforded the labourers in
being able to speak directly to the doctors, to tell all their troubles
in their own tongue, and not only to feel they were understood but
to receive a sympathetic reply which gained their confidence."[41]

He described "a perpetual stress and strain" on the men owing
to their new surroundings, and mental worries due to gambling
losses, personal quarrels, and disputes or misunderstandings with
officers and soldiers because of the language barrier. Meanwhile,
the threat of air raids and shell fire did not seem to bother those
who realized how far the camp was from the main action and that
"reasonable precautions" had been taken to protect them. Still, it
was a significant worry, especially when aircraft appeared.

In one of his letters written in late 1917 or early 1918, Gray
notes how there "is a great clamour among the army Labour
Directorate for the C.L.C. and more so now that the Egyptians
and South Africans have been sent home." The letter noted the
skilled Chinese labour being utilized at tank corps headquarters
where the armoured giants were not only repaired, but test driven
by Chinese crews. Gray also noted he had "seen the coolies in an
important Ammunition Centre reconstituting old shells, sorting
and touching up the grenades and bombs . . ."

Gray was less enamoured by the Chinese dressers or orderlies, characterizing them as "a disappointing lot." He noted "one chap not long ago who was annoyed by the clamour of a tubercular patient, a dying man asking for a drink of water; He went up to the bed and hit the patient several times over the head and made his nose bleed."[42]

* * *

After breakfast on December 12, the labourers who arrived with Harry Livingstone were fingerprinted again and checked against their identity booklets. The men "were all physically re-examined" and issued new clothes, socks, khaki overcoats, and underwear . . . and so it will not be long until they are sent out in drafts to different parts of France as labour battalions," noted Livingstone. The men were also issued boots, puttees, a towel, soap, groundsheet, blankets and an enamelled mug to replace the light, tin one issued in China.[43]

Most of the men were unskilled labourers and therefore were assigned to tough, hard and dangerous manual labour. Around the time Livingstone arrived, the British were starting to pay more attention to the various skill sets among the new arrivals. In the repair shops a welder or a riveter was in high demand, but carpenters, painters (for camouflage work) and other tradesmen were needed and there were many among the various drafts. As the British slowly fine-tuned their system for allocating labour, the Chinese assigned to a company demanding skilled labour were paid better and generally experienced better working conditions and food than those men sent to regular companies.

A full company had five hundred men, including 476 labourers and several officers and non-commissioned officers, plus an orderly. And, like members of the Canadian Expeditionary Force who travelled overseas with hometown units only to be broken up and attached to another unit in England or France, members of the CLC continued to be siphoned off depending on what labour was required and where.

The individual companies, as historian Nicholas Griffin notes, were the "heart of the Chinese Labour Corps." These men, however, did not receive orders directly from British officers, even though some of the officers spoke Chinese. As mentioned in Chapter Eight, the companies were subdivided into smaller units of men with the familiar hierarchy of first-, second- and third-class gangers acting as sergeants, corporals and lance corporals. And, just as many of them had done on the journey to France, these men relayed the orders to the labourers in the work camps. But though the gangers had greater responsibility and better pay, the job of passing down instructions was not, at times, an enviable one. Griffin notes how a ganger could easily lose the confidence of his men if he were publicly humiliated by a British officer.[44]

Within the overall British Army command structure, the CLC came under the Directorate of Labour, which by late 1917 oversaw some 387,000 unskilled workers, including Chinese. The directorate's commanding officer was Brigadier General E.G. Wace, and at first he found it rather difficult to know exactly where all his unskilled labour was working. This problem was compounded when the Chinese began to arrive and were quickly assigned to different branches of the army. "There is no doubt this special earmarking warped the potential effectiveness of the Chinese as a labour force and prevented their rational use . . . Had they been employed more sensibly, the Chinese might have achieved a great deal more than they did to further the success of the Allied war effort," Griffin observed.[45]

After examining various war diaries, he concluded the situation had been made worse by Fairfax's "persistent desire to use his Chinese as only he thought fit."[46] However, Livingstone's diary seems to indicate a better system was in place by the time he arrived and was facing the uncertainty of where he would go next — and whether it would be with or without batman Chaug.

CHAPTER 19

Death Behind
the Lines

"The little girl's mother was cuddling her very close because she was afraid a naughty bomb might hurt the little girl."

Hats and hell from above . . .

There were dozens of dirty, sweaty men squatting or standing in the hot sun around the bath house; all waiting their turn. One or two smoked cigarettes while another bit into hardtack. Everyone proudly wore some kind of hat — from straw boaters and felt bowlers to tweed caps and wool chinchillas.

When it came to headgear, fashion itself had no start or finish among the Chinese in Noyelles-sur-Mer. At the baths, clothing was optional because less time was wasted if all you had to do was remove a hat and greatcoat. Modesty and the expectation of privacy were gone, abandoned by most at Weihaiwei, Tsingtao or along the way at William Head.

Livingstone spent December 12 touring the depot, visiting the hospital wards and the crowded compound where the "coolies" lived while waiting to be sent to their work camps throughout northern France. Most of the men who had accompanied him from China had made it to France, although some had been singled out as "medical rejects" during inspections there.

The dozens of labour companies, all of them numbered, demanded strong, healthy men who could handle seven- to twelve-hour work days in all kinds of weather. While the Chinese were used to hard work and harsh weather, worse things than snow or rain could fall from the sky above the Western Front. That morning Livingstone heard the whine of aircraft engines above the dull rumble of trucks transporting artillery men along the main road. The aircraft came in low, but the machines were British and French.[1]

A few months later, during the big German offensive of March 1918, Noyelles-sur-Mer was targeted by enemy aircraft. "On different 'raids' bombs were dropped all round the hospital, some of them in close proximity, but fortunately no direct hits were registered," noted Lieutenant-Colonel Douglas Gray. "At times we were spattered with bits of burst shells which had been fired by our defensive anti-aircraft guns, and on one occasion the ground shook with the explosions of a neighbouring ammunition dump when several million shells exploded."[2]

While making his rounds, Livingstone noticed how the Chinese had been put to work at the hospital, mainly in its wards and kitchens, where they were assigned as orderlies, interpreters and cooks. Others joined sanitary gangs, responsible for the laundry, but also cleaning and emptying latrines, collecting refuse and mopping floors. Among the more skilled were carpenters, tinsmiths and painters whose handiwork included a colourful, six-meter-high wooden pagoda built out of discarded packing crates.[3]

When Livingstone heard his friend Captain Lou Sebert was on a temporary assignment back to Britain, a brief reunion was arranged at the station where trains, including Red Cross specials, passed through Noyelles-sur-Mer "every seven minutes."[4] The third part of the trio from London, Ontario, John McDonald,

Wearing an assortment of hats and clothing, some of it apparently optional, dozens of labourers wait outside a bath house at Noyelles-sur-Mer.

WJ Hawkings Collection, courtesy John De Lucy

was at that time en route to the busy hospital at Abbeville, some twelve kilometres to the southeast.

On December 14, Livingstone found out he would remain in northern France for the next while, but not necessarily in Noyelles.

While visiting Abbeville, he hopped on an ambulance that passed a road crew of German prisoners working beneath leafless, spindly trees full of crows and magpies.[5] The next day, back in Noyelles, he performed several surgeries and while getting some fresh air on the sixteenth he bought a hat for his batman Chaug.[6] On the seventeenth he received the disappointing news he was being re-assigned to No. 2 Stationary Hospital at Abbeville. This came after he had spent fourteen months caring for the Chinese. "When I awoke this morning I found Chaug in the room. He had come up to see if I was leaving for sure. I gave him a pair of socks and an old belt, then said goodbye."[7]

The doctor did not leave without an argument, but his pleas were steadfastly denied. Towards the end of the month, after dropping off a pair of gloves for Chaug, Livingstone headed

Medical officers pose in front of the pagoda built at Noyelles-sur-Mer by CLC
artisans and tradesmen.

north to yet another temporary assignment. His destination this time was No. 3 Canadian General Hospital at Boulogne. He had barely settled in when German bombers attacked on the night of December 22. "The searchlights were trying to find them and many anti-aircraft guns were firing up shells, some of the guns quite close," he wrote in his field diary. "Heard bombs fall downtown. One man with wounds and broken arm brought into hospital . . . Twenty-one British soldiers killed and about 100 civilians injured . . ."[8]

Livingstone was soon ordered back to Folkestone, but in the days leading up to his departure on January 23 he had travelled by ambulance into the countryside where he witnessed Chinese labourers at work. At a CLC railway construction camp on January 8 he watched twenty men pick up a steel rail and carry it across a soggy field. Eight days later, while strolling along the waterfront, he saw Chinese stevedores unload large, bulky shipments of ammunition and coal.[9]

The war's appetite was insatiable.

In Britain, the doctor asked again if he could be returned to France and to the Chinese in Noyelles and the CLC, and while the answer disappointed him, his time in France was not over.

* * *

The CLC companies were assigned to various labour camps throughout northern France and Belgium. Each location depended on the ebb and flow of war, and while most were within the sound of the guns the camps were still a long way behind the front lines. Along the Channel coast, the Boulogne, Calais and Dunkirk areas were particularly well served. Further inland, camps were established near villages and towns, including Fontinettes and Armentières in France, and Poperinghe and Reninghelst in Belgium, to name a few.

Sometimes bell tents just appeared overnight, much to the surprise of civilians and soldiers.

"At a bend we came across a Chinese Labour Battalion, shuffling up to work on the trenches," observed Canadian Lieutenant Coningsby Dawson. "Across their shoulders they balanced poles, with the load tied on either end. Their clothing was non-descript — the refuse of every rag-shop of Europe and the Orient. The proudest Chinaman of the lot swaggered and sweltered in the remains of a great-coat, which had belonged to an officer in the Prussian Guard . . . Beside them, rigid and regimental, marched their British non-commissioned officers, hard, uncheerful men of Indian service, who carried rods with which to force obedience."[10]

In Reninghelst, in war-torn Flanders, a village priest, Achiel Van Walleghem, kept a diary that includes descriptions of the horrific fighting around Ypres in 1917. There, as elsewhere, idyllic moments and pastoral scenes vanished beneath the whistling and thundering of exploding artillery shells. An entry for Monday, August 6, notes how the large CLC camps, including two in Reninghelst, were located on misty farmland and surrounded by barbed wire. The priest described how the labourers looked and behaved both on and off the job. "Where these men come from, and how they got here, I don't know. Many of them look very young, childlike, no better than our children of 10 or 11 years."

The diary describes their linen uniforms, rain capes and overcoats, and comments on their extreme fondness for "civilian clothes," including civilian caps or hats, which they wore constantly. He describes how their "gait is rather ungainly and you can see that they're not used to wearing such heavy shoes."[11]

Whether digging ditches or mending cratered roads, the men, he notes, were "not lazy" and performed "at least as well as our civilians and English soldiers." However, Van Walleghem expresses the view held by many British officers and non-commissioned officers, that the labourers were "like big children and they have to be handled like children." He notes how Chinese sergeants or gangers beat some men with thin iron rods or treated others like beasts of burden. Among the latter were two men who, as part of some punishment, were forced to dig ditches, one with a yoke and the other with block and chain around his collar.[12]

The priest also shares his views on how mesmerized some of the Chinese were by the sound of incoming shells, often not moving until after the shells exploded. ". . . in Poperinghe some of them were killed and then the rest were doubly shocked."[13]

For Canadian missionaries assigned to supervisory roles at the CLC camps, the war, of course, writ large the classic struggle of good versus evil.

As Gray observed, some missionaries could be "taken in" or fooled by some of the men they supervised. However, it is clear from letters written by missionaries that their strong faith did not blind them. The grim realities of war certainly challenged what they felt was crucial to the cause, even if such high levels of faith seemed out place.

And so, while they were "Somewhere in France," their faith, through the uncertainties of war, remained with Canadian missionaries, including Ted Arthurs, Herbert Boyd, Harry Forbes, James Hattie, Gordon Jones, Arthur Lochead, James Menzies, Joseph Mowatt and George Ross. "What the boy desires, the man shall have,'" wrote Lochead to MacKay after he arrived in France in the summer of 1917. "I have longed many years for an outdoor life and to sleep under canvas, and here I have my desire."[14]

Lochead, assigned to the CLC's 42nd Company, 21st Labour Group, dealt directly with the men while two British officers, both engineers, focused mostly on administration. The company's location could not be divulged in correspondence but it is clear the Chinese were kept busy transporting and stacking munitions at a dump situated near a railhead and an aerodrome. "Things were in a rather difficult state when I came here," noted Lochead. ". . . there was only one weak-kneed interpreter to depend on and the men were quite out of hand."

The missionary's ability to speak and understand the languages of northeastern China, particularly Shantung, helped resolve a bad situation. "The NCOs have got control over the men again and things are running smoothly."[15]

Western impressions of the Chinese remained mostly negative and the Chinese frequently encountered racist attitudes among soldiers, officers and civilians. For many, it did not matter that the Chinese men were there to help feed the vital supply lines or clean up after bombardments. Ongoing disrespect, coupled with fear, led to myriad problems, which often found the Chinese on the receiving end of insults and violence. There were beatings, fatal shootings, mutinies and riots. Negative stories belittling the Chinese as dirty and immature, useless and deceitful, of course, continued through the war and well after it ended, often told to get a laugh, reinforce a negative view or "white" superiority. Much of it was based on fear and ignorance.

While some of the griping or criticism about the quality of work and moments of foolhardiness was warranted, much of it was not and usually stemmed from an officer's ignorance or

WJ Hawkings Collection, courtesy John De Lucy

Under the supervision of officers, dozens of CLC men shovel brick and other debris into what appears to be a line of railway cars.

inability to communicate clearly. The labourers were not trained soldiers and therefore were not familiar with British military hierarchy, tradition and discipline.

Lochead, who was used to hearing the criticism, had great respect for the 42nd Company. "Our men are working wonderfully well; everyone is well pleased with them. One of the men trotted off the other day with a shell which weighs over 200 pounds." Lochead, while standing with a few other officers, witnessed a labourer "dancing along with a log of about 150 pounds on his shoulder." The man "gave it a toss and sent it ten feet." He then looked at the officers and suggested it would take three of them to do the same.

While the 42nd Company's other officers were clearly not churchgoers, they did not object to Christian services officiated or attended by Lochead when time and circumstance allowed. Such flexibility was not standard. Many British officers insisted the missionaries focus on their supervisory roles instead of preaching the gospel or trying to convert the men who were there to work.[16]

This presented a serious challenge for some missionaries, who saw an opportunity to save souls among the CLC as the killing spree continued on the Western Front. In a Christmas Day letter to St. John's Presbyterian Church in Toronto, the Reverend George Ross, stationed with the 84th Company, described himself as "first, last, and always a missionary" who "felt very keenly the need of missionary work among the Chinese in France." Ross included the text of a letter sent to British authorities, stating not nearly enough was being done for the Chinese from a Christian standpoint, and making the case that "a man of faith and vision" be appointed Chinese padre.[17]

Feeling strongly, Ross put his own name forward while noting someone "more gifted" could do the work by visiting every labour camp on the Western Front. "In due time, these coolies will be returning to China. The question naturally arises as to their influence on their native Province when they return. Will they learn much that is good and useful while in Europe, and bring these things back to China . . . or will they largely learn what is evil, and go back to their own land worse than when they came."[18]

The answer, at least according to Ross, depended on what could be done for the men while they were in France. "I fear . . . many . . . are learning very much more of what is harmful than what is helpful . . . all because very little is being done for them in a moral way."

Of the "1,700 coolies in the ship on which I came to France, there were about 100 Christians; yet on board the ship, and since coming to France, I have been forbidden to hold any services with them, although I have been 14 years a missionary in China; and our Canadian Presbyterian Mission in Honan has sent 13 men — all college graduates — to this work in France. We are told the work among the coolies is forbidden; that we are brought to France to superintend labour; that other men were appointed to do religious work . . . I have been here three months . . . and nothing is being done . . ."[19]

The Young Men's Christian Association was, of course, also very active in France with its canteens and recreational huts. Arthur K. Yapp, who managed the British YMCA effort there, noted in his autobiography that by 1917 there were more than a hundred YMCA huts in France and Belgium for the use of the Chinese. The smooth operation of these establishments depended greatly on "Christian men of sympathetic outlook who understood the Chinese and could speak their language." With this in mind, a request was made to the YMCA office in Shanghai, which dispatched a number of Chinese secretaries. Through these efforts, English and Chinese classes were offered as well as bible study, but as Summerskill points out, "it was understood, between the British government and the Y.M.C.A., that the granting of facilities in the camps did not include the right to try to convert the Chinese workers to Christianity."[20]

For those whose Christian work was not hindered, the opportunity to enter into prayer with the Chinese was memorable. "I was at Holy Communion this morning and the service was very warlike with the rumble of motor trucks past the door and the booming of cannon not far off," noted Lochead. "The service was in the loft of a ruined house. There are several aerodromes nearby and the air is seldom silent from the whir of the propellers. Today I saw two of our best machines climb up a couple of miles and then one started tumbling head over heels for a mile down and then restart his machine, and start climbing up again. The other came down in corkscrews and then glided off in the distance with his power cut off entirely."

Lochead finished his letter by telling the secretary he was glad to receive news from Honan. "Dear knows when we shall all get back to our work again."[21]

The hope of returning to China ended for several Chinese on the night of September 3–4, 1917. At Calais, fourteen labourers died and at least fourteen others were wounded in one of the many aerial bombing attacks that resulted in CLC casualties throughout

1917 and 1918. The same attack also killed three officers and nearly ended the life of Canadian missionary Joseph Mowatt.

The dead and wounded labourers mostly belonged to three companies and were buried at Les Baraques Military Cemetery in Sangatte, situated on the western side of Calais, France, on the Strait of Dover. The 50th suffered twelve fatalities while the 35th, Mowatt's company, and 65th suffered one each. Another labourer was wounded at an adjoining camp. The CWGC lists the deceased labourers from the 50th as Chang Chung Tai (Zhang Zhongtai, No. 7641), Wu Chin Sheng (Wu Jinsheng, No. 14724), Hsu Feng Chen (Xu Fengzhen, No. 14825), Kuo Ch'ing Shou (Guo Qingshou, No. 15555), Hsing Chao Ch'uan (Xing Zhaoquan, No. 15683), Sung Huan T'ing (Song Huanting, No. 17745), T'ien Te Sheng (Tian Desheng, No. 17784), Chang Yu Mi (Zhang Yumi, No. 18116), Ch'ao Hsi T'ung (Chao Xitung, No. 27047), Chang Hung K'uei (Zhang Honggui, No. 15537), Ts'ui Wei Ming (Cui Weiming, No. 16020) and T'ang Shih Yuan (Tang Shiyuan, No. 15447). The fatalities from the 35th and 65th were Yang K'ou Chen (Yang Kouzhen, No. 15593) and Liu Chin To (Liu Jinduo, No. 58074).

None of the mortally wounded Allied officers was Canadian. They were Major John Adams, forty-seven, of 6th Battalion, Royal Scots, attached to the 65th; Colonel Arthur Blewitt, fifty-six, of 5th Labour Group; and an Australian, 2nd Lieutenant Herbert Stubbs, forty, attached to 35th Company. Adams was buried at Calais Southern Cemetery while Blewitt and Stubbs were interred at Longuenesse Souvenir Cemetery in Saint-Omer, southeast of Calais.

Mowatt described the attack in a September 11 letter to MacKay. "A week or so ago Monday night, we had an aeroplane raid in which over 20 German aeroplanes took part. The raid lasted from 9 p.m. to 3 a.m. or six hours . . . At first we stood outside our mess quarters until shrapnel from our anti-aircraft guns began to fall about us."

Sitting in his office in Toronto, MacKay read how Mowatt and a few other officers ran to the Chinese compound, arriving just as the bombs hit. Fiery explosions ripped into the ground, sending dirt, lethal shrapnel and other debris in all directions. While many ran for cover, Mowatt was among those who remained behind amid the explosions to give directions to dazed stragglers. "I went on some distance and then lay in a ditch while bombs dropped nearby," he noted. "Soon a soldier came rushing up and said some Chinese were wounded. We hurried back to where they were and after helping fix up two coolies went on and looked for more. Soon I stumbled upon a party of men with only a few coolies amongst them who had been hit and killed or badly wounded. Out in the field . . . men were crying for help."

Stubbs, a married man from Brisbane, was hit in the head by shrapnel, but was not killed outright. He ". . . was quite conscious and gave me some messages," Mowatt wrote. "His skull was fractured and he was . . . paralyzed. I hurried for an ambulance . . . It was a sad sight for us all . . . and several times . . . I had to jump into nearby ditches . . ."

The mortally wounded Australian had also been a missionary in China prior to 1917. "Stubbs was well liked by all the officers in our mess because of his sterling Christian character and his friendly, manly bearing among his fellows," noted Mowatt who told MacKay he had written to express his condolences to the officer's widow. [22]

Enemy aerial bombings caused dozens of Chinese casualties, and, as in the incident in Calais, the men usually died in groups while working in or around the ports cities, including Boulogne, Dunkirk, Saigneville and Saint-Omer, but also further east in Belgium. "The Chinese had never experienced anything like it — death raining from the skies or fired at them from beyond the horizon — and they were at their wits' end," observes historian Greg James. "Many, on the other hand, refused to enter underground shelters, and some were killed because they stayed in the open air."[23]

Roadways or fields stacked high with munitions were particularly vulnerable to night-time attacks. The fiery explosions blew men to pieces or burned them beyond recognition. The noise and light from these enormous conflagrations were heard and seen all the way across the English Channel.

At ground zero there was no way to escape the carnage: you were either lucky or dead.

For the Chinese, it was not always easy to check up on the health or status of a fellow labourer. The same was true of regular soldiers who had been separated from friends they had signed up with or gotten to know in the early days.

After arriving in France on July 2, 1917, the labourers in Gordon Jones's party encountered the same bureaucratic fate men from other contingents had faced: they were re-organized into entirely new companies. The 52nd Company, where Jones ended up, worked around aerodromes and hospitals, built parking lots for trucks, installed water pipes and unloaded trains. "We were sent out to a little place near Doullens which was later Marshall Foch's headquarters," he wrote after the war. "From there we were moved twice to other camps in the same area. We were 20 miles behind the line and could barely see the flashes of the guns in the distance. We used to think it very peaceful but if we had been there in the spring of 1918 we would have found it different when . . . the German push came."

It was much different for Jones and the rest of the company at Poperinghe, roughly ten kilometres west of Ypres, Belgium. "Our camp was on the Ypres side of Poperinghe and if it was quiet in our last camp it was anything but quiet in this camp. The big shells used to whistle over our heads as they passed on their way to Poperinghe. Practically every fine night German aeroplanes would be overhead bombing trying to locate camps. Our first casualty was from one of these night visitors. The tents had the floors sunk below the ground level to make them safe from flying splinters but this night a Chinese policeman happened to be out when a bomb dropped beside him. He was at once taken to hospital but died within a few hours and was buried in the military cemetery at Brandhoek already filled with men who had paid the Great Price . . ."

The Brandhoek New Military Cemetery No. 3 near West-Vlaanderen, Belgium, contains 975 casualties, but only one of them is from the Chinese Labour Corps, and this same man was in fact serving with Jones's company. He was Yen Feng Shan (Yan Fengshan, No. 18060) and he died on September 28, 1917.[24]

It appears Yen Feng Shan was conducting one of his security patrols around the camp when he was hit by shrapnel. He was the only company casualty that night. Jones recalled how the enemy's artillery also claimed lives. One shell landed on a tent "and every man in the tent was killed, thirteen in all. For these coolies we made a little private cemetery beside a stream which ran past the bottom of our camp."

The 52nd Company remained in the area for three months before it was relocated toward Noyelles, where "the coolies all worked on an ammunition dump said to be the largest in France. While it was more exciting as a general rule in the Ypres salient, it was on this ammunition dump that the coolies did their best work and it was here where they had the distinction of leading the Chinese Labour Corps in the actual tonnage handled."

Jones recalled one night, following the German spring offensive, when aircraft targeted a hangar near the dump. The enemy, noted Jones, used light from the burning hangar to spot the ammunition dump, which they bombed "continuously for five hours" and "set no less than seven hangars afire, all filled with cordite."

Fellow missionary George Ross also understood the risk. "'Peace on earth, good will amongst men' has not been heard — by me at least — to-day," he noted in his Christmas 1917 letter to his hometown church. "The booming and the bombing of destructive weapons are never far away. While I write this . . . my little hut is shaking, and the windows are rattling in response to the guns on the other side of the hill. Day and night the same noise; sometimes throbbing, sometimes groaning . . . there is no let-up in the cannonading. The 'Hymn of Hate,' rather than the hymn of 'Peace and Good Will to Men,' seems to be heard now-a-days . . ."[25]

After ducking out of the cold rain and wind, missionary Ted Arthurs wrote to FMB Secretary MacKay on October 6. He was with the 28th Company and like Lochead could not divulge his location: ". . . suffice it to say . . . we are not many miles from the sea coast and only slightly further from the line of combat. So near are we to the latter that when a big strafe is on we can hear the sound of the guns, similar to the noise of not far off distant thunder, a never-ending roll, for hours and even days at time."[26]

Arthurs composed his letter while seated at a small table in the officers' hut, which had five rooms — four for the officers, one for the mess, all beneath a "galvanized iron" or tin roof. Supporting it was an arrangement of boards with cracks large enough to admit wind, rain and snow. Arthurs's room included a folding chair, cot and a small stove without any coal. Still, it was luxury compared to what the soldiers in the front lines endured, hunkered down in trenches slick with mud and polluted water, and wearing clothes infested with lice — not to mention the bombs and bullets flying overhead.

Arthurs was a modest man and he recognized how well he and others had it behind the lines. Deeply religious, he was somewhat of a philosopher when it came to viewing the grand scheme of things. He perceived his work and that of other men as infinitesimal. "I have never . . . been so much impressed with the little place any individual occupies as I have been since enlisting," he told MacKay. "The army is so vast, so colossal an organization that there seems to be very little consideration for the individual and yet . . . the reverse is equally true, that the individual is all important," he wrote while raindrops tapped on the roof.[27]

Looking up from the page crowded with his busy handwriting, Arthurs spotted the wet and muddy Chinese returning from their work on a nearby railroad. The men appeared tired and hungry, looking forward to getting into dry clothes and feeling a little warm. In addition to shoring up the railway bed and replacing the heavy rails and ties, the Chinese frequently hauled and stacked gas shells. Arthurs respected the men's work ethic and it showed. He also sensed they appreciated his ability to speak with them in their language, especially when trouble arose.

Arthurs told MacKay he considered the enlistment and utilization of missionaries in France "a wise move" and he was proud the FMB had supported the work. Time in France had made him a lot more language-proficient and knowledgeable about the Chinese way of life. "I have made greater progress in six months since leaving China than in the previous four years," he wrote. "I have not the slightest thought of not returning to China when the war is over."

This was good news for MacKay and other board members, who were anxious to get on with the important work in China.

Less than a month after Arthurs wrote his letter, James Menzies sat down to write to his four-year-old daughter, Marion. By then the missionary had crossed the Atlantic twice; first in 1910 on the *Dominion* on his long-distance way to his first posting in China, and again in the summer of 1917 at age thirty-two, aboard the *Corinthian* with a contingent of CLC. After arriving in Britain the party was quarantined for several days due to of an outbreak of mumps, a situation noted by Gordon Jones in a July 2 letter to his wife, Clara. "Saw Jimmy Menzies in the camp in England where his battalion is detained because of sickness."

Menzies's "Somewhere in France" letter was written on October 27, presumably after he had been assigned to the 53rd Company. In it, for Marion's sake, he had included small sketches of the inside of his tent, showing a table supported by sawhorses and the locations of his bed, coat rack, trunk, wash basin and books. The letter also mentioned how his trusty batman, Hsiang (Xiang Er) or "Lucky Boy" was still with him.

Dear Marion,

*Daddy writes a little letter to Marion. Daddy lives
in a cloth house like this. It is round and Daddy
has a bed made of a piece of canvas and a wood
frame. Then Daddy has a table made of an old
door and two benches like this. Then Daddy has
a wash basin of tin and a box to wash on. Hsiang
Lucky Boy has made Daddy a stool like this . . .
When the wind blows it nearly blows the tent over.
Then daddy gets out in his pajamas and hammers
in the tent pegs to keep the tent from blowing over.*

*It rains very often. All the time it rains. Outside
it is very muddy. Daddy wears long boots. Sometimes Daddy gets very wet and there is no fire to
dry his clothes.*

*Once Daddy was on a tram car and saw a mother
with a little girl asleep in her arms. The little girl
was just like Frances. Daddy watched her a long
time and wanted to see Marion and Frances and
little Arthur and mother very much.*

*The little girl's mother was cuddling her very close
because she was afraid a naughty bomb might
hurt the little girl.*

Goodbye. Kiss Frances [who was two years old]
and little Arthur [who was not quite a year
old] *and mother for Daddy and Grandpa and
grandma, too. Daddy loves you all a whole lot.
Hugs and Kisses from Dear Daddy.*

A few days earlier, Menzies had included much of the same information in a letter written to his wife, Annie. "Our floor is sand or dirty sand and mud . . . We have two little stoves and practically no coal, but our walls keep out the wind. You see we fill the cracks with loose hay that came out of hay barges."

The natural insulation was not in short supply because the party of labourers Menzies had been assigned to was hauling and stacking bundles of hay for the horses.[28]

A December 23 letter from Menzies, written on YMCA letterhead and also addressed to Marion, is one of the more poignant messages sent by a father from France. In it he included a small sketch of a sparrow resting on a pickle bottle. Menzies had been sick, but the recently promoted captain now had better accommodations, although ones not ideally situated for a man who suffered migraines.

> Daddy is living now in a big house beside a big church all made of stone. It has a big tower and away up there is a big bell. When it rings it makes a big noise right over daddy's head . . .
>
> Daddy's window looks out on a big chestnut tree so that when daddy wakes up . . . he can watch the wind blowing the leaves . . . Sometimes daddy has his dinner with some other officers in a hut where we have Chinese servants and one day a little sparrow sat on the pickle bottle all dinner time. It would eat out of your hand and come when you called it. It was just a tiny bird and had not yet grown big enough to fly away . . .
>
> You will be five years old before this reaches you . . . daddy sends you kisses for you and Frances and Arthur.

He ended the letter with three capital Xs for each child and a fourth one, with a circle around it, for Annie.

On February 21, 1918, Menzies wrote to his father to wish him happy birthday.

> *Today you are 81 years old. It is a great blessing to have had health and vigour as you have had. You have always been young and always been very strenuous in all your work. Most men are not so. Just two days ago I sent my Sergeant-Major back to base depot because he was fifty-eight and found the work and the strain too much . . .*
>
> *Twenty-three years ago we were just moving to Staples and you were beginning the work with a great milling company to organize and manage.*
>
> *The day is bright here but damp after an all-mighty rain. Clouds still cover the sky and a few birds of war (flying machines) are hovering overhead. The roar of the barrage swelled like the sea shore roars before a coming storm. The grass land is green all winter. It has never been brown. White and brown hens are hopping about pick-ing up the early worms. Fishes in the canal are in evidence again and Tommys* [a reference to British soldiers] *line and cork is once more over the banks patiently waiting for a bite. In this war it is the patient waiting that tells as much as the strenuous push.*
>
> *It is a strange land France today with the patient farmers waiting, waiting for peace — trying their best to hold body and soul together with a watch-*

*ful eye on their belonging. Waiting patiently for
the time when they can repair the damage, clear
away the sheet iron and tarpaper shelters and
restore this ancient landscape once again to red-
tiled roofs and well-tilled fields. A strange land
France with its constant pageant of war-clad figures from all quarters of the globe. The red-capped
French guard, turbaned Hindu. The Cape Hope
driver, the grey-clothed, red-numbered bullet
headed German prisoner, the swinging Canadian
railway man, the Australian with the side of his
big felt hat turned up, the Stetson-hatted New
Zealander, the heathen Chinese and now an occasional short-coated American . . .*

*A strange land with its refugees, its constant
masses and prayers with its long line of black
veiled figures leading the little ones to church to
the sound of the mournful bells. A strange land
this with its mangled crucifixes at the cross roads
and the symbols of a new world crucifixion stud-
ding the landscape like a forest. A strange land
this with its thunderous noises. The 'crump' of the
German heavies, the patter of the machine guns
. . . the steady hum of our planes and the deep
base throb of the German Gothas . . . and then the
weird eastern wail of a Chinese chant . . .*

*One wonders when the war will be over and . . .
what kind of world it will be.* [29]

Anglican missionary George Napier Smith arrived in France
around mid-1918 after spending two happy weeks in Canada
with his wife, Ruth. In Montreal, "I picked up my Chinese boys

A casket covered with the Union Jack and containing the remains of a CLC labourer is carried by fellow labourers who make up a modest funeral detail.

and we entrained for New York and the *SS Rochambeau* of the French Line. There were twenty-two passenger ships in our convoy, and we kept together to the halfway line. One morning we looked out, as we did, every morning, to see just what our position was in the convoy, only to find out that we were all alone. Our ship had left the convoy and was heading for Bordeaux, in France, while the rest of the convoy went on to England."

After reaching Bordeaux, Smith's group entrained for Paris, then continued north to Noyelles. "I handed over my charge and was ordered to England, where I received a commission as a first lieutenant, sporting one 'pip'. I felt like a general! That feeling wore off very speedily, and by the time I was ready to be repatriated I felt more like a worm, due to the superiority complex of old army sergeant-majors."

And so that was it for Smith, the dedicated preacher from Lunenburg, Nova Scotia; his history with the CLC limited to

Weihaiwei and the long voyage from China, through Japan and Canada to France. But while his service was comparatively short, it was, nonetheless, valuable. The Canadian's time with the Chinese English-speaking students who remained behind in France to work as interpreters had, in a small, appreciative way, helped narrow the language and cultural gap between East and West.

The war was still far from over, but for the Chinese, and for men like Menzies and Jones, the Western Front experience would continue well beyond the Armistice.

For one Canadian missionary, however, his time in France after the Armistice was tragically brief.

The Reverend Ted Arthurs died of pneumonia on December 6, 1918, in Le Havre, France. He was the only Canadian missionary to die while serving with the CLC and he left behind his work in China and a young family in Canada. The Reverend's grave, which lists him as a captain, is situated in Saint-Marie Cemetery in the commune of Granville-Ste Honorine, overlooking Le Havre. At the time of his death, the busy port was home to three general hospitals, two stationary hospitals and four convalescent depots. The Commonwealth War Graves cemetery, which includes dead from both world wars, has 1,690 burials from the first.[30]

CHAPTER 20

Far From Home,
Far From Over

"They say we may be here another year but we will hope for something better than that."

Good and bad . . .

Dinner looked promising in the small French restaurant in downtown London. On leave, Livingstone and a friend had journeyed by train up from Shorncliffe and were just about to take their first bite when the piercing sound of a policeman's whistle filled the air. Through the window, Livingstone saw frightened women, some cradling infants and others with small children in tow. All of them were running in the same direction past the restaurant while firemen rushed in other directions with more policemen blowing their whistles.

"Heard many anti-aircraft guns and also could hear the machine guns of our fighters in the air and could see the flashes . . . and the louder noise of the falling bombs," noted the doctor on January 29, 1918. "The firing died down around 11, but commenced again at 12 when another raid came over. They seemed to come in waves."

The two men quickly left the restaurant and joined others in the street, heading for the cover of a YMCA shelter. "The next day we saw where the bombs had dropped. One lit inside an office where people were taking shelter and it killed many. Another took the end of a house and some more lit in the gasworks. 60 were killed, mostly women and children, and 167 injured. Ambulances were tearing up the streets. In the last raid that night a bomb dropped three blocks from our hotel . . ."[1]

* * *

The first half of 1918 was not a good time for the Allies. Their armies had emerged from a disastrous year that included staggering losses, mutinies among French army units and widespread revolt in Russia that had serious ramifications for both the Eastern and Western fronts.

The Treaty of Brest-Litovsk, signed on March 3, 1918, between Germany and the new Bolshevik government in Russia, removed Russia from the war. This made it possible for the Germans to begin transferring forty-four divisions, some half a million troops, to the Western Front. While the Allies hunkered down and waited for new reinforcements and a substantial deployment of American troops, the Germans grabbed the opportunity before them. The enemy's spring offensive began on March 21. Though the initial drive toward Amiens ended some nine days later, the attacks continued into spring and early summer. The enemy gained more than a thousand square miles of territory, but while advancing developed significant logistical and supply problems. Tens of thousands were killed or wounded while thousands of others were captured.

Meanwhile, the high demand on Allied shipping had not abated, and this pressure had grown even more after America entered the war. The United States was in a position to build more ships, but it was going to take months. To make the best of a bad situation, the British War Cabinet secretly placed a much higher priority on securing transportation requirements from North American ports. This meant reducing transportation commitments at other ports, including northeastern China.

On March 3, 1918, Thomas Bourne, the top British CLC agent in China, read a cable stating enrolment of the "coolies" was to cease immediately, owing to the difficulty of supplying transport. Anyone waiting to embark was to be released. All of this was announced after hundreds of labourers had already been medically inspected, kitted out and signed to contracts.[2]

Roughly two weeks earlier, while in Shorncliffe, Livingstone had exchanged a few words with a labourer who was fresh off a troopship from Canada. The man was certainly not the last member of the CLC to reach Britain, but he had obviously left before the edict came down. In his diary, the doctor noted how the man had told him he arrived with thousands of labourers from Weihaiwei and while crossing the North Atlantic a torpedo "missed the ship by only a few feet." The ship, which is not identified in the diary, was not the only CLC transport that narrowly escaped disaster on the Atlantic.

The *Empress of Asia*, which had sailed from William Head in late May 1918, was, according to British officer George Cormack, forced to turn back after commencing her voyage across the North Atlantic to Liverpool. "After leaving the Panama Canal, and heading for New York, a Blue Funnel boat was torpedoed ahead of us. The *Empress of Asia* turned round almost on its heel. We headed for the safety of Jamaica, with smoke belching from the funnels and the Chief Officer muttering quizzically, 'Flowers for us.' When crossing the Atlantic, we heard firing from our escorting vessel the *Teutonic*. The first shot effected a 'kill,' but instead of a German submarine the victim was an unfortunate whale, which had come to the surface to blow."[3]

The *Asia* resumed her journey, but after leaving New York two of her labourers got sick and died. An embolism killed twenty-eight-year-old Wei Teng Wen (Wei Dengwen, No. 134062) on June 28. The second man, thirty-six-year-old Wang Feng Chii (Wang Fengqi, No. 133389), died on June 30 of pyaemia, blood poisoning caused by the spread of bacteria from an untreated abscess.

Livingstone, after being sent to England in January of 1918, remained in Britain until the end of the war when, instead of returning home, he was sent back to France with Lou Sebert.

Although Livingstone had wanted to remain with the CLC in France during 1918, he had made good use of his time in Britain before going back across the Channel again after the Armistice. While in Britain he had become very familiar with Ashford, Kent, roughly twenty kilometres northwest of Folkestone, where he worked in a small hospital reserved for patients of the Canadian Ordnance Corps. The work at Ashford was steady, but life was easier. There was time for morning or afternoon strolls, socializing and a bit of tennis. Evenings were often spent in a comfortable chair with his cloth-bound copy of Edith Wherry's *The Red Lantern*, which helped transport his thoughts back to China.

The small Canadian Ordnance Corps hospital there had kept him busy with examinations, inoculations and minor surgeries. On mornings or afternoons that had afforded time for a stroll, he ventured along country lanes and up into forested hills where he listened to songbirds against the distant, man-made thunder of war.

He had spied robins, thrushes, warblers and even a cuckoo that reminded him of a Longfellow poem. Livingstone had also enjoyed fairly good health, at least up until late June 1918 when he was hit with the Spanish flu which, he noted, "has been epidemic in England and Europe." Although he recovered quickly, he had also noted in his diary on July 7 how more men were falling victim during what became a worldwide pandemic with a death toll more staggering than the war. "Flu has been raging here all week. Our Brigade Hospital is full to the roof and two big huts had to be put up . . . Rapid onset with temperature of 102 or 103 and loss of appetite . . ."

Looking back, the grand-nephew of the famous Scottish missionary and explorer could see how he, too, had crossed continents and oceans. And whether it was from a railway car or from the deck of a ship, he had definitely noticed and felt the physical world around him. His travels had also exposed him to cultural and religious differences. He had also experienced racial intolerance, and the seemingly insurmountable separations between classes even among those who were, supposedly, on the same side in the great conflict. However, if Livingstone noticed or was convinced society was about to change, he did not commit the thought to paper.

By late September 1918, he had crossed out an item on his "bucket list" by travelling north to visit the birthplace of the person he simply called "Uncle David." In the town of Blantyre, Scotland, roughly twelve kilometres southeast of Glasgow, Livingstone had climbed "a winding stair to the third floor and after walking down a narrow, dirty hallway came to a small room with a brass plate on the door which read 'Livingstone Birthplace.'" A Mrs. Cook, who lived in the old tenement, showed him into the room and stood quietly in one place while pointing to where David was born. "From the window we could see the Clyde and . . . by the river bank the ruins of the old cotton spinning mill where he used to work the loom," he noted in his diary. "In the town an old woman still lives who worked beside him and said he always stood on a stool to reach the machine."[4]

Even in Britain, though, the sights and sounds of war did not disappear.

Bombing raids across the Channel and up into London occurred on moonlit nights, and during the enemy's spring offensive the guns could be heard across the Channel. "The Germans have driven a wedge eight miles into our lines south of St. Quentin," Livingstone noted on March 24. "The war bulletins are put up in the windows in town and people come up and with anxious faces read the news then walk away . . . The papers all urge the churches to have special prayers for victory . . ."

* * *

In France, the Reverend Gordon Jones continued to be impressed by what his company of labourers achieved for the Allied effort. In an essay written after the war, the former captain states the "Chinese were at the same time the best and the worst labor in France. Properly handled the Chinese could not be beaten. But sometimes a Chinese company would supply labor to some employer who didn't know how to use the labor. He might ask for fifty coolies when ten would have done."

Jones points out how time and effort was wasted when scheduled work fell through and was replaced by odd jobs that did not require as many men or was assigned just to keep the men busy. The Chinese, he adds, had to know the work was important, and if it was not deemed necessary the project could look ridiculous. "I have actually seen four men marching slowly along carrying one sheet of corrugated iron and marching at a pace that would make a snail die of envy . . ."

Although their contracts stipulated a ten-hour work day throughout the week, the labourers were given time off for special celebrations. A month before the Germans launched their spring offensive, Jones told Clara about the wonderful Chinese New Year's Day celebration he had just witnessed. "It ran from 9 a.m. to 4:30 p.m. with an hour or so off for lunch," he noted in a February 17 letter. "The hut where the celebration was held was packed all the time. Officers from all over the place were in for portions of the show and all were greatly pleased. The outside of the hut was decorated with streamers with a big Chinese flag at the top. The chaps got up [dressed up] as girls were especially good. The Chinese make good actors and some of their grimaces and gestures . . . brought roars of laughter."

The celebration included a variety of acts. There were jugglers, tumblers and magicians whose tricks — even at close range — were hard to detect, Jones noted. [5] By then, the duties of another

Canadian missionary had expanded. Instead of being attached to a single CLC company, Captain James Menzies was roving around the muddy countryside trying to settle disputes among men assigned to various companies. In a letter to MacKay, Menzies described the Chinese as "the best labourers in France, by far," but cautioned how the war was affecting their view of the Western World. "The Chinese, much less than we, understand the war. The bloodshed is horrible to them. The wholesale waste is insane to them. All their thoughts of us are turned upside down by this war."[6]

In the work camps, conflicts amongst the labourers, also between labourers and officers, occasionally boiled over into violence with deadly consequence. Most of it had to do with working conditions or overzealous applications of authority. Insults from fellow labourers and racial slurs from white officers also sparked confrontations. "I have to quell riots at times," noted Menzies, rather wearily, in a letter to his parents. ". . . I have to advise engineers on how to employ Chinese to advantage. I have to investigate cases of all kinds from stealing to murder . . . I have to examine officers on their knowledge of Chinese and to lecture to officers on Chinese characteristics and how to handle Chinese . . ."[7]

Language, of course, remained a significant barrier. The inability to communicate properly spawned fear, which led to more ignorance, racism and abuse. English words and their sounds were easily misinterpreted, resulting in angry exchanges between British soldiers and labourers. The English phrase "let's go," for example, sounds like "gou," meaning "dog" to the Chinese. Likewise, improper emphasis placed on certain Chinese words or characters conveyed inappropriate messages or responses.

Yán Yangch, better known as James Yen, worked with a YMCA colleague in France to combat this problem by improving the literacy skills among the CLC. Since the vast majority of the labourers were illiterate, teaching reading and writing was a huge challenge, given the tens of thousands of characters making up the Chinese language. Yen focused on the most commonly used characters and then developed a one-thousand character inventory or teaching aid which, when shared or used in makeshift classrooms, improved the labourers' vocabulary.

As Yen's initiative grew, a newsletter and a newspaper, the *Chinese Labourers Weekly*, were published, using the new common character scheme. It was a major breakthrough because suddenly labourers could read news stories and gain insight from opinion pieces. The issue of the labourers' behaviour on the Western Front and how it affected Western attitudes was the subject of a column by Yen, who had been educated in China and the United States. "In France you are the representative of the entire country of China and the whole nation of Chinese. Foreigners judge the right or wrong of our nation on whether your deeds are good or bad. If you have done something indecent in your own land, you lose the face of your family of Li or Wang. But if you commit something improper, the foreigners will not know your surname of Zhang, Wang, Li or Zhoa. All he knows is that 'Chinese' has done this and that. Therefore, my fellow men, if a Chinese receives a medal from his camp, then all of us Chinese are heroes. If a Chinese steals a can of beef, then all 'chinois' are bandits. Put this way, the glory and humiliation of the nation of China is all dependent on your deeds."[8]

Such messaging worked, not because it was new, but because it reinforced well-established beliefs among the Chinese. Still, it was tough to calmly ignore situations that seemed grossly unfair, disrespectful or physically threatening.

Several Chinese and Egyptian labourers were among the dead and wounded following a mutiny in September 1917. It began among British personnel stationed at Étaples. The disturbance quickly expanded to include the labourers. When the dust settled, twenty-seven strikers were dead and nearly forty others wounded.[9]

Another horrific and tragic moment unfolded at Fontinettes where, on Sunday, December 16, 1917, bullying from non-commissioned officers sparked a revolt among the Chinese. The exchange was bad for the labourers and for a Canadian private who was in the wrong place at the wrong time. Responding to the uprising, an armed guard opened fire, killing four and wounding nine other labourers. Lying dead were Yang Sheng T'ien (Yang Shengtian, No. 8278), K'Ung Chao Te (Kong Zhaode, No. 7953), Chang Ta Ch'Uan (Zhang Dachuan, No. 6698) and Chu Chien T'Ang (Zhu Qiantang, No. 8625). It is believed a fifth labourer died later.[10]

The unlucky Canadian was Private Frederick Maynard, a twenty-seven-year-old married man from Toronto, serving with the Canadian Army Service Corps. A bullet, fired by one of the guards, passed through the side of the hut he was in and struck him in the stomach. At the time, Maynard was "looking out the window at a party of Chinese rioting about twenty yards away," notes the circumstances of casualty notice attached to his name.[11] "His comrades came to his assistance and he was placed on a stretcher and taken to the medical hut where first aid was rendered. He was evacuated to No. 35 General Hospital, Calais, where he died the following day."[12]

Maynard, who was born in Croydon in Surrey, England, had worked as a butcher. He was five-feet-eight-inches tall, weighed 128 pounds, and was missing the first finger and part of the second finger on his right hand. His wife's name was Ruth, and the missing digits on his hand were more than likely lost during a work-related accident prior to his enlistment in Canada on February 5, 1916. The fatal bullet "entered in the left flank, and the wound of exit was in the left lumbar region. A considerable quantity of small intestine was hanging out through the wound of exit," noted the medical report. "The patient was extremely cold and collapsed . . . The patient did not improve and died at 5 a.m. the following day."

The wounded Chinese were evacuated as soon as possible, with the more serious going first. The four dead men were the last to be removed, and only after their fingerprints were taken. All of the deceased, including Maynard, were interred at Les Baraques Military Cemetery at Sangatte. The inscription on the Canadian's headstone reads: *"That in Calais' fatal walls God's finger touched him and he slept."*

Gordon Jones, meanwhile, had moved around quite a bit between Christmas 1917 and mid-1918. On July 1, 1918, he reminded his wife how a full year had passed since he arrived in France with the CLC. "A year from today, where will we be?" he asked. "Probably in the same spot."

By then his 52nd Company was considered one of the longest-serving British Chinese labour companies in France. However, the missionary with an engineering degree was quick to down-play his role in the war. "If there is any heroism in this business it is certainly all yours and there is a great deal," he told Clara on July 22. "I am glad to have my chance to do my bit, but there is nothing heroic about sitting in a comfortable camp miles behind the line with lots to eat, work to keep one interested, batmen to look after us, outdoor cinemas to go to, strafing superior officers to add a spice of life once in a while . . . and the chance to bluff ourselves that we are doing our bit."[13]

In a subsequent letter he told Clara there "are nearly two hundred CLC companies altogether," adding that no more "coolies are coming just now because of transport difficulties: American troops are needed more than Chinese coolies."[14]

Jones mentioned how Presbyterian missionary Arthur Loc-head was sent back to China to collect more labourers for France, but when he arrived the recruitment of labourers had stopped and there were no men to escort to France. While overseas, the Canadian missionaries often thought about the work they hoped to carry on with after the war. Most never lost sight of their original calling, and often expressed their hopes and feelings, realizing what their wartime experience had given them. "When such vast sums can be spent on instruments of destruction it is surely not too much to expect a much larger proportion of the world's wealth to be devoted to the harmonizing work that missions are doing," wrote Dr. Frederick Auld in a September 21, 1918, letter to MacKay. ". . . It is my constant desire to see each of our three main stations in China provided with a well-equipped hospital; modern and up to date."

Auld suggested the Honan Mission support the training of more Chinese doctors, establish more dispensaries in outlying areas, and hire "non-medical men" to work as administrators. He concluded by stating his work in France, including his language study, was "going along beautifully" and "all our Honan folks are well." He did, however, note that Dr. Percy Leslie had been somewhat run down, but had been on leave in England and Scotland.[15]

The urge to write home never left Gordon Jones. In the middle of the night on November 3–4, he got up from his cot and lit a small lamp. He then shook off the cold and began to write a few lines for Clara. The lamp kept going out, but he managed to finish his letter, which expressed how the "end is in sight now . . . and a great and glorious end too. Out of all this conflict a greater advance is taking place in the world situation than I would have believed possible four years ago. That is it will come if President Woodrow Wilson's ideas of the League of Nations is carried out . . ."

Jones said the war has clearly demonstrated the need for all nations — not just Germany — to put their "own house in order," including Canada. "If we are to insist on Germany being just to Belgium, we must logically insist on Canada being just to China." He noted that the $500 head tax must either be abolished, or if not, extended to all foreigners. If this is not done, he wrote, Canada must "allow China to impose such a tax on all Canadians entering China."[16]

Menzies also saw the war coming to an end and, similar to Jones, his thoughts were of home and being with family. While writing to his mother on November 5, he recalled a time when life was much easier. "How I look back on the old times when as a little boy we had Blackie the cat in Clinton and the lilacs around the pump; when I learned my letters and knelt at your knee; how I used to lie on my stomach reading the Boys Own Paper while Maggie played the piano upstairs over the store; how I remember the tick-tock of the old Grandfather clock . . ."[17]

The Armistice brought great joy and new hope to nations around the world, but it did not spell the immediate repatriation of soldiers and labourers. Thousands waited weeks and months to return home on crowded transports, and the Chinese and their supervisors were the last to leave. On November 12, Menzies was clearly exasperated while trying to convince several Chinese labourers, who had gone on strike, to return to work. "They were unloading hay and should have finished at 8:30. They did not finish till 11:30. I had no supper for I would not leave them. It was raining, a fine rain. This was the way I celebrated peace, standing over Chinks who were just moving sufficiently to make it impossible to say that they were not moving."[18]

Jones wrote home that same day, describing how he was not overcome by joy. "Fighting ceased yesterday at 11 a.m. The papers are full of the rejoicing in London, Paris, and other places, but I don't feel like rejoicing. Rather I feel like uttering a heartfelt Thank God . . . Four months ago today we were waiting with bated breath almost for the next German attack. Already our line had bulged terribly toward Amiens, again a large bend had taken place towards Hazebrouck and our hard-won Passchendaele and Messines Ridge gone as well. A further drive had brought Paris within gun range . . . I predicted another year of struggle at least."[19]

Jones noted how there was "much speculation, but no reliable information" on whether the labourers would be sent home immediately or remain behind to help clean up.[20]

The contract the Chinese signed with the British was certainly clear; it stipulated a three-year period of engagement, "counting from the day of their arrival at place of employment." It also stated that after a period of one year, the Emigration Bureau at Weihaiwei "may cancel this agreement by giving six months' notice or six months' pay in lieu of notice."

Most of the CLC labourers did not arrive in France until 1917. No one knew then how long the war would last, but keeping the men employed on the Western Front until at least early 1920 remained a viable option for the British. In their eyes it made sense to keep the men employed for at least six months after the war rather than cancel their contracts and spend large amounts on severance pay.

Another factor was the sudden pressure placed on available shipping. There was no way everyone could go home at once and so it made economic sense to keep the men working while they were being fed and housed.

The first Chinese labourers sent home after the war were neither healthy nor happy people.

Approximately 470 invalided men arrived on the *Egypt* at Tsingtao on July 19, 1919, and their health and appearance was shocking. Used as a hospital ship, the *Egypt* had sailed from Marseille with both sick and injured. Distributed among the wards or occupying portions of the poop deck were sixty-two men with some form of mental illness. This contingent did not pass through Canada, but sailed via the Mediterranean and Indian Ocean.

On board, helping to look after the men, was Canadian medical-missionary Captain Robert Gordon Struthers.

Like his brother Ernest, Robert Struthers had worked in Noyelles. On board the *Egypt* he was assisted by other medical staff, including the contingent's commanding officer, Major D.G. Bremmer. Unfortunately, many of the orderlies proved incompetent and some were even caught stealing. The terrible journey, through high seas, lasted five weeks. Twenty-two labourers died en route, including fifteen from tuberculosis. Two others committed suicide — one man by hanging himself with a strip he had torn off his blanket and the other by jumping overboard. Still, noted Bremmer, it could have been worse. "Considering the

Captain Harry Livingstone surveys a bombed out village on the Western Front in the winter of 1918-1919.

state of so many patients on admission, and the condition of the weather and the sea . . . the number of deaths was by no means excessive, and to the Medical Staff, it is a matter of satisfaction that it is not higher."

Meanwhile, the Western Front remained an incredibly hazardous place with unexploded shells, discarded hand grenades, crumbling buildings and sinkholes that could swallow a man or a truck. Trees, those left standing, were mostly stripped of foliage or ripped to shreds. Black or bone-like trunks protruded from muddy upturned earth that reeked with rotting human remains and dead farm animals. Shattered stone facades and broken foundations showed where people once lived while shell-pocked, flooded fields obliterated the former locations of little farms or roads. The rusting barbed wire, broken and twisted railway tracks, scorched rubble and maggot-covered bodies all had be removed and carted away while new roads, bridges and cemeteries were slowly built.

The Chinese Labour Corps did not do all the work, but it was heavily engaged in many phases and met with risk and disaster. To cite just one example, four labourers were blown to bits on

April 25, 1919, while stacking shells at an ammunition depot in Bourbourg, France.[21] These men, like thousands of others, had hoped to go home sooner.

In addition to the Chinese, some two hundred thousand prisoners of war and up to sixty thousand locally recruited French civilians participated in what the military likes to call "mopping up."[22]

* * *

When the Armistice was announced, Livingstone was in Shorncliffe, sitting next to Sebert and eating a bowl of Irish stew. He recalled how "a great cheer arose but no one could realize it was over." Outside, there were cheering "women and children wildly waving flags" and hugging soldiers in the streets. "One man tried to make a speech, but no one listened . . ."[23]

Five days later, the two doctors were ordered back to France, attached to a British hospital near Étaples. Sebert, the ophthalmic specialist, was sent to the eye ward while Livingstone was assigned to sick and wounded prisoners of war, many of whom had fallen victim to the Spanish flu during its most deadly phase. "I am now in charge of German influenza cases, 2 long huts full of bad cases."

In December he made emergency house calls, including a visit to a family stricken with the flu. While roving about the countryside he encountered the Chinese, noticing how well they conversed with locals and had adopted local fashions. The assortment of hats never ceased to amaze Livingstone. One fellow proudly donned "a large straw hat over another hat," which in all likelihood was on top of a third or fourth hat.[24]

The vast majority of Chinese got along well with locals before and after the Armistice. Many recruited under the French scheme elected to stay in France after the war, finding permanent work and lifetime relationships.

Still, the many months of post-war work wore men down. Frustrations grew, sparking more bad behaviour and riots that

Captain Harry Livingstone, seated with his legs crossed, poses with medical staff and German prisoners of war at a hospital in France in late 1918.

ended in bloodshed. Labour companies also had their share of deranged or nasty men who turned to crime.

In Western Europe, the Chinese stood out. Bad or unusual behaviour attracted attention and raised alarms. Actual violence — and even unfounded rumours — sparked outrage among locals who had grown tired of foreigners. Citizens urged severe punishment or immediate repatriation for criminal behaviour. For members of the CLC, this included the full weight of British military law, including the death penalty.

Between 1918 and 1920, ten members of the CLC were executed by the British — all of them for murderous deeds against fellow labourers or civilians. In one horrific case, children as well as adults were victims.

Wang En Jung (Wang Enrong, No. 10299) and Yang Ch'ing Shan (Yang Qingshan, No. 10272) were shot at dawn on Wednesday, June 26, 1918, after being found guilty of murdering a French wine shop owner on February 28. Maria Dourdent was discovered lying in a pool of blood on the cellar floor of the family-run estaminet at Sainte-Marie-Kerque. Her throat had been slashed and part of the knife's blade was stuck in the vertebrae.

Evidence showed three labourers entered the establishment where the owner was working alone. The men ordered bread and coffee and when Madame Dourdent visited the cellar to retrieve the food, the men followed her down. Wang En Jung held her from behind while Yang Ch'ing Shan pulled out a knife and stabbed her in the throat. Wang fled along with the third man while Yang stole 22,000 francs and various promissory notes amounting to 8,000 francs. The two accused pleaded not guilty, but the evidence proved otherwise. The third man was charged with a lesser offence and received a lighter sentence. The two executed men lie in Les Baraques Military Cemetery, Sangatte.[25]

Twenty-five-year old Zheng Shangong (Zheng Shangong, No. 53497), who was shot at dawn on July 23, 1918, was convicted of killing a fellow labourer. The victim was Ma Yulan (No. 53512), who was struck in the side of the head with an axe on June 17. In his defence, the condemned man stated: "I killed him because he would have killed me. He wanted me to lend him 120 francs and I refused . . ."

Like the Dourdent case, murderous offensives committed by Chinese against civilians certainly caught the attention of the press. Labourers Wan Fa Yu (Wan Fayu, No. 5884) and Yu Lung Hai (Yu Longhai, No. 4976) were each found guilty in the murder of sixty-five-year-old Amandine Boulanger and the attempted murder of her seventy-two-year-old husband, Hyacinthe. The grisly crime unfolded on the night of December 7, 1918, in the couple's grocery store at Rouen. On January 29, 1919, not long after he had been condemned to death, Yu hanged himself in his cell. Wan was shot at dawn on February 15. Both were interred at St. Sever Cemetery Extension, Rouen. The post-mortem showed Madame Boulanger suffered three head wounds from being struck with a hammer. The crushing blow to the top left side of her skull was so severe it opened up a hole fifty millimetres in diameter and sent bone shards into her brain.[26]

The one multiple homicide involving a Chinese labourer occurred on the night of November 28–29, 1918, when Chang Ju Chih (Zhang Ruzhi, No. 16174) murdered Berthe Mionnet and her three children: Marie, twelve, Andre, eight, and Maria, six. The crime scene was the Mionnet's tavern in Boutillerie, near Amiens, and the victims were horribly mutilated with a bayonet. Chang was tracked down and arrested, but managed to escape from prison the following spring. The killer made it back to China, where he failed to produce proper travel documents for legal entry. He returned to France and was arrested months later near Calais, while engaged in drug trafficking. Executed on February 14, 1920, he is buried at Les Baraques.[27]

The range of behaviour among the Chinese also includes examples of great courage. Several, through selfless acts of bravery, earned the Meritorious Service Medal. Wang Yushao (Wang Yushan, No. 15333) of the 59th Company was among them. His citation reads: "Near Marcoing near Cambrai on June 6th, 1919, he observed a fire on a dump of ammunition situated close to a Collecting Station. On his own initiative he rushed to the dump with two buckets of water which he threw on the fire and then seized a burning British 'P' Bomb and hurled it to a safe distance from the dump. He then continued to extinguish the burning dump which had spread to the surrounding grass in which rifle grenades and German shells were lying. By his initiative, resource and disregard of personal safety this Labourer averted what might have been a serious explosion."[28]

Another labourer, Yan Dengfeng (Yan Tengfeng, No. 91085) showed his courage after an explosion near Armentières on May 23, 1919. For four hours he helped prevent a larger catastrophe by drenching stockpiles of ammunition with water.[29]

As the work to clean up the battlefields continued, the desire to return home grew more noticeable among labourers and their

An officer and a couple of CLC men examine a large aerial torpedo at an enemy ammunition dump. The job of stacking or removing shells was highly dangerous with much of the work performed by the CLC.

WJ Hawkings Collection, courtesy John De Lucy

officers. Most figured they had seen quite enough of war-torn France. For some, at least, the news was good.

Doctor Frederick Auld wrote to MacKay on April 18, 1919, stating he was to be released on May 7 and expected to be on board the *Corsican*, out of Liverpool, by the twenty-second. He also updated the board secretary on other Canadian medical-missionaries, including Robert Gordon Struthers, who was still waiting to sail to China on the *Egypt*. Auld noted that Leslie was to sail from Le Havre in a day or two, while Reeds was expecting to be released from duty on June 7. He was also convinced it was going to take longer for "our non-medical brethren" to be repatriated, because of the lack of Chinese-speaking officers among the companies. Forbes, he wrote, was with a CLC company near Cambrai, while Ross and Menzies were at Rouen and Dieppe, respectively.

Writing to Clara on April 28, Gordon Jones asked if she remembered what happened two years ago that day. "It was the day I left you in Shanghai . . . I know you are about fed up waiting and want to get back to China and get settled."

He shared the good news that he was about to submit his application for repatriation. By then Jones had written to the Reverend James Endicott, the Methodist Church of Canada's General Secretary of Foreign Missions. Endicott replied on May 2, stating efforts had been made to secure the release of "all our men" from their duty in France. However, the reply from Britain's Ministry of Labour was not encouraging, noting the men "cannot be spared at the present juncture. They are of great value to the Chinese Labour Corps owing to their knowledge of Chinese and Eastern line of thought."

Endicott stated he would support Jones on any action he could take to hasten his release, including the possibility of accompanying a labour contingent back to China where he could "secure his release there." Endicott added: "We do not wish you to be kept in France or in the Imperial service a day longer than the situation really demands." Endicott ended his letter by stating two other Methodist missionaries "have been liberated from military service." These were the Reverend Homer Brown and the Reverend Edward Wilford.

By July 6, 1919, Jones was finally out of France, stationed at the Repatriation Camp at Pirbright, Surrey, England. He told Clara he hoped to be en route to Canada by month's end. Both wished to return to China. "I thoroughly enjoyed my time with the Chinese Labour Corps and was really sorry when the time of parting came," Jones noted in his postwar essay. "The British army was an immense machine with every part necessary for the proper working of the whole machine. The Chinese coolies were no small part of the machine and can well be said to have 'done their bit' and to have done it well."

James Menzies was also among the last to leave. In May, the North Honan mission made a formal request to Sir John Jordan in Peking, aimed at seeking the release of its missionaries. In Canada, MacKay, on behalf of the FMB, wrote to the Office of Chaplain Services and the Department of External Affairs to accomplish the same goal. Both departments agreed the missionaries were outside the jurisdiction of Canadian authorities because the men were, after all, officers under British Army jurisdiction.

Menzies, despite his appeals to leave the CLC, was regarded as indispensable. "I came only to assist in the war and to make it possible for the release of men for the trenches by having Chinese do their work . . . They say we may be here another year but we will hope for something better than that," he wrote to his father on February 21, 1919.

With her husband's request for repatriation going nowhere, Annie Menzies packed up her bags and sailed overseas to Britain, where she moved in with her aunts. The children were left in the good hands of the family's trusted nursemaid. James did get across to see Annie, but leaving France was not easy. "This is Monday afternoon and there seems no hope of my getting away," he wrote on September 29. "It is a wonderfully beautiful day and I wish very much that we could have a long walk together, but the Channel rolls between us. I cannot bring myself to really believe you are so near . . ."[30]

Menzies stated he had "no hankering" for an ongoing military career. He had his missionary work to look forward to as well as the astounding archeological endeavour he had begun before leaving China. Indeed, the ongoing discoveries and research associated with the Oracle Bones would keep him busy and earn him worldwide recognition throughout his life. In his short letter to Annie, James described a forest, only a short distance from his location, the site of an old Roman camp. "It is a beautiful place," he told her. "It would be a great joy just to walk alongside you. My heart would sing with joy and all the old tired brain would get rested."[31]

More than once, Menzies crossed the Channel to see the beautiful woman he had pursued all the way to China several years earlier. The couple spent his leave touring Britain, Scotland and into war-torn Belgium. In February 1920, three years after he became a commissioned officer in the CLC, Menzies was honourably discharged.

Finally, he and Lucky Boy were free to leave France and return to the people and quieter places they so dearly loved.

* * *

Livingstone and Sebert got home sooner. Their time in France ended on May 31, 1919, when they boarded a side-wheeler at Boulogne bound for old, familiar Folkestone.

CHAPTER 21

Homeward

"A few cigarettes along the way would put a silver lining in their cloud of disappointment."

An octopus's garden . . .

On June 1, 1919, after an early breakfast at a Folkestone hotel, Captains Harry Livingstone and Lou Sebert entrained for London Waterloo Station. Arriving there at 10 a.m., the officers had three and a half hours before boarding another train to the large Canadian Army demobilization camp at Witley in Surrey.

After storing their luggage at the station, the two officers took the "Tube" to Piccadilly Circus where they walked around a bit before enjoying a "dandy meal" at the Strand Palace restaurant. Unlike one of Livingstone's earlier visits to a London restaurant, this peacetime experience did not include an air raid or a mad dash to a bomb shelter. The men, however, did notice missing roofs and substantial gaps between buildings.

Elsewhere in Great Britain, there were also visible changes in some of the old parish cemeteries, which had grown to include civilian casualties as well as soldiers who had returned from the front only to succumb to wounds or disease. It was the latter that accounted for nineteen members of the Chinese Labour Corps in Britain between June 6, 1917, and August 9, 1917. These men were interred in Commonwealth War Graves Commission plots at Liverpool, Shorncliffe and Plymouth.[1]

The summer of 1917 alone claimed twelve of these Chinese lives.

While heading south toward the demobilization camp, Livingstone stared through the railway carriage's soot-smudged window. Sliding past and giving way to the English countryside were old towns with narrow streets, and gardens bursting with rhododendrons.

In Witley, the two officers observed the severe damage recently caused by bored and frustrated Canadian troops anxious to get home. Most of the violence had been directed at "Tin Town," a collection of shops along the Portsmouth Road. "Rioters had broken up all the stores, banks, canteens, etc., released all Canadian prisoners from the jails and then set fire to the theatre," noted Livingstone on June 16. His diary entry for the seventeenth states, "one man was shot in the neck scuffling for a revolver."[2]

By the end of June 1919, Livingstone and Sebert received the excellent news they were finally going home, and on July 1 they boarded a crowded troop train for Southampton.

Arriving there that same day, Livingstone and Sebert boarded the "old familiar" *Olympic* with hundreds of Canadian soldiers. The local mayor arrived the next day with his council dressed in ceremonial garb. More impressive were the thousands of people crowding the docks; men, women and children who had come to cheer the Canadians nearly seven months after the Armistice. The mayor began with a prayer, followed by a rousing "O Canada," and a heartfelt "Auld Lang Syne."

Everyone was waving flags or handkerchiefs.

The third officer in the original CAMC trio from London, Ontario, John McDonald, was not far behind. He had achieved the rank of captain and spent the last year and a half in Britain attached to various Canadian convalescent hospitals. A few days after Livingstone and Sebert boarded the *Olympic*, he sailed for Halifax on the *Minnekahda*.[3]

For Livingstone and Sebert it was smooth sailing until the *Olympic* ran into a typical Atlantic storm on July 6. As the ship creaked and pounded through the waves, an old, but familiar nauseous feeling swept over the two officers, who solemnly agreed to never "go on the ocean again."

On July 8, the *Olympic* reached Halifax, where the two doctors entrained for Ontario. McDonald's ship arrived four days later.

This time, their destination was Toronto.

*   *   *

Back on the European continent that summer there was no public flag-waving or cheery send-offs for the labourers.

Indeed, many French and Belgian citizens were glad to see the Chinese leave town and vacate the camps. By then the Peace Conference at Versailles, which had begun in January 1919 with delegates from nearly thirty countries, had produced a horrendous outcome for China. Japan continued to demand its rights in Shantung, which had already been conceded to Japan through a secret deal worked out with the Allies and then quietly agreed to by the Chinese government in September 1918. China's delegation at the conference, blindsided and angered by this, tried to argue that such secret agreements were not valid. They were unsuccessful, and left the conference without signing the Treaty of Versailles. At home, the humiliation from this led to the May Fourth Movement and changed the course of Chinese history by inspiring the rise of Chinese nationalism and communism.[4]

The labourers from China did not leave the Western Front all at once; among the last to board the repatriation ships were dozens of artisans who carved inscriptions onto Chinese headstones. In London, the Chinese embassy had strongly desired the delicate work be executed by the Chinese themselves. For the inscriptions, five standard proverbs were used: *A Good Reputation Endures Forever, Faithful Unto Death, True Till Death, A Noble Duty Bravely Done* and *Though Dead He Still Liveth.*[5]

While thousands sailed directly from France via the Mediterranean and Suez, the majority crossed the North Atlantic to Canada.

The first contingent of repatriated labourers reached Halifax on September 22, 1919, with some four thousand on board. The men disembarked from two steamers, the *Winnifredian* and *Haverford*, and then joined at least two thousand men who arrived on the Cunard liner *Caronia*. The massive movement, noted the press, required up to eleven trains with each train transporting "700 Chinese who travel in far closer company than did the returned Canadian soldiers."[6]

Once again, the labourers were quickly processed and moved along like cargo: each man recorded on manifests circulated with multiple copies forwarded by railway administrators to immigration, military and shipping officials. The governor general and colonial office were also kept in the loop. Meanwhile, the men were hastily loaded onto trains with tight schedules, placed in a temporary sheds or behind wire on the West Coast and then marched or jogged onto ships with specific destinations. It was all carried out with great efficiency with relatively little trouble. Only this time, everything was moving in the reverse direction. And while the "consignments" were heavily guarded, they were no longer secret.

By then the Railway Service Guard was no more and Petawawa Camp was no longer a CLC transit depot. The RSG had been disbanded shortly after the last labour corps contingent crossed Canada en route to France in early 1918. In its place was the newly-formed Special Guard of the Canadian Military Police Corps (CMPC), headquartered in Halifax with an establishment of 542 all ranks. Unlike the RSG, the Special Guard of the CMPC was composed entirely of men with overseas service, mostly war-seasoned, disciplined men who were used to carrying a rifle or revolver. Many were drawn from large eastern Canadian cit-

WJ Hawkings Collection, courtesy John De Lucy

A cross marks the grave of CLC labourer Chao Hao (No. 59860) who died on July 29, 1918. The man may have converted to Christianity. However, crosses were used before new, non-Christian markers were created.

ies, including Halifax and Toronto. Its commanding officer was forty-one-year-old Lieutenant-Colonel Robert Ross Napier, a twice-wounded combat veteran who had enlisted in Valcartier in September 1914 and sailed overseas in October with the first Canadian Contingent.

On March 18, 1916, while Napier was engaged in combat at Hill 63 in Belgium, a bullet entered the inner side of his left calf and passed out the other side without striking bone. His second wound, to the right forearm in 1917, was caused by shrapnel. The Scottish-born Napier, whose good arm was tattooed with the Masonic emblem and motto, had also earned a mention in dispatches for "gallantry and distinguished service" on November 30, 1915.[7]

In addition to assigning his military police to train duty, Napier placed two officers and a large group of all ranks at William Head. For those riding the rails, the work was considered "extremely difficult" and exhausting with a day or less off between return trips. In an article written for the Canadian Provost Corps Association newsletter *Watchdog*, retired Sergeant-Major Donald A. Tresham describes the unit's dress, deportment and attention to military duties as "second to none." He also noted how many men found the work "distasteful" and boring.

Ships from overseas arrived day and night with sometimes less than an hour's notice. Twenty to thirty thousand was the original estimate of the number of labourers expected to return to China via Canada, notes Tresham. "It appears that some 70,000 were transported across Canada. Incomplete CMPC records account for 48,726 Coolies. The Special Guard . . . was simply not large enough, so its members had to work double and sometimes triple time between September 1919 and April 1920."[8]

Tresham's article asserts most of the labourers did not want to return home, implying the guards had to be extra careful to prevent escapes. The research for this book did not uncover any evidence to support the view that "most" labourers did not want to return home, although such comments were certainly expressed by those travelling with the men. Many of the labourers were actually glad to leave and frustrated by decisions or delays affecting their departure.

On the East Coast, they boarded CPR specials for Vancouver. As before, the trains left quickly and stopped when they had to for coal and water. There were mechanical failures, fatal accidents and sometimes nature itself intervened. A crash at Milan, near Farnham, Quebec, on December 11, 1919, killed a conductor and a passenger on a freight train parked on a siding. A CLC special had rear-ended it, sending two cars off the track. Four other railwaymen were injured. The official statement from the CPR noted that excessive cold might have interfered with the switch that somehow was left open.[9] Near Kamloops, British Columbia, three trainloads of labourers were delayed on account of a rockslide.[10]

After reaching Vancouver, some men embarked on steamers with very familiar names, bound directly for the Orient. Most, however, boarded coastal boats that conveyed them to William Head, where Dr. Harry Rundle Nelson still worked as chief medical superintendent. In Nelson's annual report ending March 31, 1920, he stated the first returning Chinese commenced to arrive at the station on September 29, 1919, and once again the labour corps' camp adjoining the station was put to good use. The cantonment, which was still behind wire, was under even tighter security. The last of the labourers, notes Nelson's report, sailed from William Head to China on April 4, 1920.[11]

In addition to the "coolies in steerage" and their paying passengers, the big ships sailing to the Orient carried valuable cargo. When the *Empress of Japan* departed in late December 1919 she had roughly fifteen hundred labourers and approximately four million American silver dollars.[12] On Christmas Day, the *Empress of Asia* was cleared for Yokohama and Hong Kong with two thousand labourers and a cargo of silver weighing 240,000 pounds.[13]

Meanwhile, Lieutenant-Colonel Napier's guard unit at William Head certainly had its work cut out for it, trying to keep an eye on the thousands of labourers who came and went with the various movements.

On January 15, 1920, a Chinese labourer named Chang Pai Ho followed through on an arrangement he had made with a Victoria baker who conveniently went by the name of Fred Baker. On a previous visit to the camp, the baker named Baker met Chang while delivering goods to the canteen. Both spoke a little French and so language was not an issue. Chang had made it clear to the Victoria businessman he did not wish to return home. On the day in question he quietly slipped into a vehicle, got down on the floor and remained hidden as the vehicle stopped at the gate where the sentry, Lance Corporal H. Northcott, took a look inside and then waved the vehicle through.

Chang's disappearance was reported to police and he was arrested two days later on a farm in Gordon Head, northeast of Victoria.[14] Charges were brought against Baker for "aiding and abetting a Chinaman to enter Canada in defiance of the *Chinese Immigration Act*" and for "harbouring" Chang. Baker was arrested, pleaded not guilty and then released on $500 bail. The case was dismissed when the judge ruled Chang did not come within the restricted classes designated in the *Act*. "Chinese coolies who pass through Canada en route from France to their native land cannot be considered immigrants," ruled the magistrate, agreeing with the argument raised by Baker's lawyer, R.H. Pooley, who became attorney general of British Columbia.

The court heard that during the war decisions had been made without precedent, and the movement of the CLC across Canada was one of them. The lawyer representing the Dominion immigration department tried to argue that the charges against Baker had more to do with harbouring a prohibited person.[15]

During the trial a taxi driver testified he had been called to the camp where he met Baker and shook hands with a Chinese man who ducked into his car. Baker then followed with considerable baggage that was placed in the vehicle, which was conveniently equipped with window curtains. Pang Mock, the farmer in Gordon Head, told the court he visited Victoria's Brunswick Hotel on January 16 where Baker told him he had a Chinese friend from Vancouver who could work his farm for a few days.

Chang was there in bed when police arrived.

Meanwhile, the disappearance of two labourers who eluded "the vigilance of their guards" at the Vancouver CPR station did not generate much concern, according to the press. On February 11, the *Vancouver World* reported the men were "roaming at large" although "police do not anticipate much difficulty in finding them, as they are dressed in the coolie uniform, blue with brass buttons."[16]

One of the more serious events occurred at William Head on March 10 when several hundred labourers began protesting not only the amount of time they had spent there, but how they had been treated by a fellow labourer appointed as an officer. When the Chinese officer was seen to be "over-severe in his methods of dealing with a question of rations" he was chased down and beaten outside the compound. The armed guards responded with fixed bayonets, but everybody took a step back after officers talked to the aggressors and convinced the men to return to the compound and their tents. "The gates were open at the time, as rations were being brought in." At the time there were roughly 8,500 labourers in the compound at William Head."

It was easy for the local population in Victoria to imagine something far worse had occurred because the newspaper told them the "guards were insufficient to stem the onrush and the leading forces of the mutiny succeeded in getting out into the surrounding area. The report cannot be confirmed that one of the military guards was injured as the Chinese broke for freedom." Further down in the story it notes that "order now prevails at the camp."[17]

In spite of the challenges faced by the armed military police, the work of guarding the movements from Halifax carried on day and night without interruption. Unfortunately, individual accounts from the military police seem nonexistent. While reviewing available Special Guard CMPC reports, Tresham, who died in 2001, arrived at his above total by adding the 30,480 Chinese labourers who entrained between September and December 1919 to the 18,246 who commenced their journey between January and end of March 1920. Although he suggested many more crossed the country, his 48,726 fits with news reports during the last CLC voyage from Vancouver.

With the news embargo lifted on CLC stories, Vancouver and Victoria newspapers regularly updated their readers on the movements. On January 22, 1920, they reported that 31,000 Chinese from war-torn Europe had either passed through Canada or were awaiting ships in Vancouver or William Head.[18] On April 5, the day after the last CLC sailed from William Head on the Canadian Robert Dollar Company's *Bessie Dollar*, the *Vancouver Province*, under the headline "Last of China's Land Soldiers," rounded the final total to 48,000.[19]

Tresham's number seems fairly accurate because it lists the major movements through to the end of March 1920. If anything, the number could be slightly higher, not lower. By then, newspapers were reporting how the economy, which had brought in an adverse rate of exchange for the British government, was dictating a more affordable shipping route. Labourers remaining in France would be sent home via the Suez Canal through ports of call where the British pound was accepted at par. "The British

Government had planned to send 80,000 coolies through this Canadian port," stated the *Victoria Times* on February 20, "but not more than two-thirds of that number will go."[20]

In his annual report ending March 31, 1920, Nelson stated 40,314 CLC members had "passed through" the quarantine station by that time, although his figure did not include those who sailed directly to the Orient from Vancouver. The medical superintendent's annual report for 1920–21 supports what was reported by the press, that the last of the Chinese labourers embarked from William Head on April 4, 1920. It also states the "Coolie Camp" was dismantled and closed April 17.

Overall, the Chinese who endured their second trans-Canada journey faced the same tight security with virtually no opportunity to get off the trains even for a little exercise and fresh air. Their journey back across the Pacific also included the waiving of safety regulations on ships that, in some cases, had been modified to carry more steerage. Throughout their homeward journey, the labourers endured inexcusable treatment that ranged from harsh to downright inhumane.

However, without excusing any of the abuse or neglect they received, it is important to view their homeward experience within the context of the times. The transportation networks were under tremendous pressure during the war's massive demobilization. This meant cutting corners, including safety regulations, to jam as many troops or labourers as possible onto available ships and trains which had to adhere to tight schedules. Returning servicemen were definitely given a lot more freedom and slightly more space on the transports and trains, but the conditions, at least for the all ranks, were still crowded, uncomfortable and unhealthy. By design, the train schedules for the specials transporting the CLC across Canada left no time for unscheduled stops. The waiving of the head tax was still in effect and so the government and the CPR were under pressure to transport the Chinese from east to west as quickly as possible.

It is unfortunate that Livingstone and some of the missionaries did not return to China with CLC contingents, via the Canadian route. Livingstone's field diary describing the long and monotonous outbound journey does not speak of harsh treatment, but it does note how the men were carefully guarded and not allowed off the trains, even for exercise. On the return journey, authorities, rightly or wrongly, perceived an even greater need to keep the men under guard and behind wire. The war was over and it was assumed, as Tresham's article noted, many of the labourers would want to start over in a new land but, again, this assumption shared among some of the guards appears to have been somewhat exaggerated. And Canada was still an unwelcoming place for Chinese and other non-British nationalities.

Shortly before instructions were issued for Napier's new Special Guard unit, news of the CLC's return journey reached the press. As early as August 30, 1919, the *Vancouver Province* reported many thousands of "Chinese coolies, homeward bound, are expected to pass through Vancouver and Victoria within the next six months."[21]

The *Vancouver World* reported on September 6 that a naval transport officer was en route to Vancouver from Ottawa to take charge of the transport work. It also stated 75,000 were expected "as coming through this way," and the first ship to transport the men to China would likely be the *Empress of Japan*.[22]

Despite the war, Canadian attitudes towards the Chinese and Chinese immigration did not change for the better. It is also true that in towns and cities across the country people were generally too preoccupied to notice the trains or give them much thought. The press did pay attention, but the reports usually contained the same sweeping generalizations. The men, they said, looked the same, but wore odd combinations of clothing, acted like children, but also seemed strangely happy or frightened. Also appearing were descriptions of how they were moved along like livestock. Missing, it seems, are detailed interviews with the men themselves who — even if there were interest — were kept from the press. Consequently, most were simply viewed from a distance.

While lecturing at Vancouver's First Presbyterian Church in early September 1919, H.M. Clark from the Honan Mission praised the labourers for their wartime contribution. He read from a letter received from a Canadian officer in France who preferred "75 Chinese to 100 white men" when it came to handling ammunition.[23] Clark also quoted from a lecture given by British CLC officer W.J. Hawkings, whose words had appeared in the *North China Herald*.[24] "To say the coolies are doing good work is to put it mildly. They have beaten every kind of record put up by other labor, and are now engaged in beating their own." The audience heard how groups of labourers emptied a twenty-ton truck in twenty minutes and stacked 110 tons of sugar in three hours with each bag weighing eighty pounds.

Although not spoken by the Chinese themselves, such comments undoubtedly changed a few attitudes. The Canadian government, meanwhile, pressed on with a bill to disqualify "Oriental voters" in federal by-elections. The bill, noted the *Vancouver World* on September 27, passed second reading in the House of Commons and "threatened to raise the vexed question of Chinese, Japanese, and Hindu immigration into British Columbia."

Three days later the same newspaper noted the "waterfront is being deluged with trainloads of Chinese coolies who are arriving intermittently every few hours from the east." Readers were told how the men had been employed overseas and that the *Empress of Japan* was loaded with a thousand destined for China. "The *Princess Charlotte* has been taken off her regular run and for the next two or three days will continue to transport coolies from here to Vancouver Island."

Armed guards, the newspaper added, were in attendance "and from the train to the boat the coolies are herded along like a lot of frightened sheep. They are a motley crew in all sorts and varieties of uniform in which a dirty and ragged blue predominates. Some have the infantry cap, without any badge, but the majority are supremely happy in the wearing of a shapeless woollen affair which is drawn all around the head to show as little of the face as possible . . . They move along at a kind of jog-trot to the accompaniment of their plates and cups."[25]

In early October the Vancouver press was informed by Francis White Peters, general superintendent of the CPR, that the "new arrivals will not be allowed in the city until they can be immediately transported to the quarantine station . . . Those for whom immediate transportation cannot be found will be quartered up the line at Coquitlam." Peters said the labourers would be supplied with "light and water" and will "otherwise be made as comfortable as possible."[26]

On October 24, the *Vancouver Province* stated the men held at Coquitlam "will be given freedom to stroll about — under guard of course."

In Victoria it was reported that the Blue Funnel liner *Tyndareus* was in the process of breaking a trans-Pacific record in mid-October when she left William Head with the "Largest Shipment of Human Freight." The newspaper noted more than four thousand filled the ship, including regular passengers. The story stated how recent alterations at Seattle made it possible for the vessel to accommodate 4,300.[27] Meanwhile, a labourer, identified in a newspaper story only as "Lee, a Chinaman," had boarded the *Tyndareus*, but died from tuberculosis minutes before the ship sailed with 3,523 labourers.[28]

The press also explained how there was only enough shipping capacity among Pacific liners to handle eight thousand labourers per month. Meanwhile, on the Atlantic coast of Europe, demand for regular troopships for Canadian and American servicemen had "slackened off . . . and the coolies are being packed aboard."[29]

Passing through Vancouver at the time was Dr. John Ferguson, described as a political adviser to the Chinese president. Ferguson was not impressed by how the labourers were being handled by Canadian authorities, and he said that indifference would be detrimental to commercial interests between the two countries.

"If Canada wants to increase its trade with China and participate in the benefits of one of the greatest, if not the greatest market in the world, it must change its tactics towards the Chinese people."

Ferguson's remarks were specifically directed at the treatment accorded the Chinese labourers. "Despite what these men have done for the allies, and despite the fact that both France and England gave them the freedom of the country, Canada herds them off a boat at Halifax, puts them in trains in droves, brings them across the country like wild animals in cages, herds them out at this end, into sheds, and thence in cattle-like droves, into the steamer for home. Is it not shameful?"

He stated if immigration laws forbade that these men should have their freedom while crossing the continent that did not prevent the people of Canada from showing a little appreciation for the work they did overseas. "A few cigarettes along the way would put a silver lining in their cloud of disappointment."[30]

In November, a member of the Chinese Consulate in Vancouver suggested the returning labourers be used to further develop British Columbia. Speaking at a Kiwanis luncheon, Dr. Koliang Yih outlined how a contract could be made with the Department of Militia and Defence guaranteeing the men would be returned to China following a period of work. According to the *Vancouver Province* newspaper, he suggested between ten thousand and twenty thousand could be retained this way. However, the consul official was quick to insist he did not seek "a quarrel" with organized labour in the province.[31]

Meanwhile, at William Head, it was a sparrow that caught the attention of a Victoria newsman. The story in the *Colonist* described a "dirty Chinaman, well bundled up in soiled khaki" with the little bird perched on his shoulder. "*Me no compris*," the labourer said in pidgin French to a questioning Canadian officer. The man then retrieved from his pocket a dart with a fluffy red tassel which he tossed above his own head. The sparrow immediately flew up and snatched the object out of the air and then "returned to the shoulder of his master." When the labourer fired the dart against the side of a building the bird again proved dependable.

When it came to describing labourers at play, the reporter echoed the common Western views and assumptions centred on "distinctly childish" behaviour with gambling as the "premier" form of amusement. "Dice were rolling freely. It has been impossible to stop it."[32]

On Christmas Eve the *Vancouver Province* noted on page 19 that a public display "of the Far East and a flash of the battle fields of France" was evident when 1,200 CLC members were marched in a column of four across along Hastings Street. "They were a motley and a happy crowd. No two appeared to be dressed alike." The newspaper stated how the uniforms, "once the proud boast of some British or French battalion, were now faded and torn, and in many cases were relieved with a civilian hat or coat." Meanwhile, the story noted, smiles and laughter revealed "a contented state of mind and when a light-haired Canadian maiden was espied gazing upon them with interest from the third floor of an adjoining building 1200 pairs of eyes were flashed in her direction . . ."[33]

Accompanying the returning soldiers and labourers were more reports of Spanish flu cases. A story from Halifax noted how labourers were returned to their ship after falling sick. Some three thousand had arrived on board the *Minnekahda* and by January 28 one of their Vancouver-bound trains had already left. When the train reached the small town of Stewiacke, Nova Scotia, some sixty kilometres north of Halifax, a military doctor discovered a labourer with a very high temperature. "The train was run back to Halifax and the loading of other trains discontinued, the coolies being put back on the vessel," explained the *Vancouver World* newspaper on January 29.

The next day, the *Vancouver Daily Province* reported seven patients were removed from the steamer by military medical authorities and two died overnight of "pneumonia." One of the dead was Sergeant Robert C. Rayner of Norwich, England, who had accompanied the labourers from overseas. He was thirty-four when he died on January 29 and he was laid to rest at Halifax (Fort

A labourer kisses his feathered friend, possibly a canary. Taming birds was a common pastime among the Chinese.

WJ Hawkings Collection, courtesy John De Lucy

Massey) Cemetery.[34] The report did not name the Chinese victim, but death records show Liu Ching Yen (Liu Jingyan, No. 101159) died on the same date. It is clear there was disagreement between military doctors and the port's chief health officer, Dr. N. E. MacKay, who insisted there was no influenza on board, "merely a few colds in the head," a finding corroborated by the ship's doctor. The passage through Canada was continued and eight days later the trains reached Vancouver where the men boarded the *Princess Charlotte* bound for William Head.

Although there was little fanfare for the Chinese as they were transported across Canada, there were moments of kindness. The most heart-warming story involves a group of grateful Halifax women who raised money and formed a volunteer welcoming party. Some twenty thousand labourers were greeted on the East Coast in Halifax and Saint John, New Brunswick; each man was handed an apple and a little welcome card printed in Chinese. The women, who were led by their chief organizer, Clara Dennis, had agreed something had to be done because the Chinese were our allies and had worked hard on the Western Front. "The only words of greeting and God-speed were from our committee; and had it not been for the service thus rendered, these three thousand and six Chinese labor-soldiers would have passed through Saint John in the same silence and with the same absolute lack of welcome that the first few thousand passed through Halifax."[35]

Souvenirs were also obtained on the West Coast, including saplings dug up by men who boarded the *Ixion* on March 14. It is presumed some of the tiny arbutus and pine trees survived the voyage and were transplanted in Shantung.[36]

As the flow of returning labourers turned into a trickle, stories identified the last men as the dregs of the CLC. "Incorrigible Battalion Disperse Monotony at William Head Station," read one headline. "The 'Incorrigible Battalion' has proved a source of worry and trouble to the military authorities . . . The 'Incorrigible' form the last contingent of the . . . coolies shipped through here . . . and from all accounts they comprise the most remarkable crowd of 'rough necks' that ever left the inner fastnesses [sic] of China."[37]

Peters, the CPR's general superintendent, was surely annoyed by this description because he had visited William Head ten days earlier. When he returned to Vancouver he told the press: "It speaks well for the discipline of the camp and for the extraordinary even tempers of the coolies that during all the time they have been kept in their quarters, to the number of 8,000 there together at times, they have never by word or action even approached uncivility to their officers, guards or any white man."[38]

Reports of confrontations at William Head did not involve just men. On at least one occasion there was a sea creature. In 1919, Canadian Sergeant John Thompson responded to a commotion along the rocky shore, not far from the wharf. Although the sergeant's report was submitted on April Fool's Day 1920, the event itself is said to have occurred.

Sir,

In compliance with your request I beg to submit the following description of the devilfish episode which occurred some months ago, when one of our Chinese charges was attacked by an octopus while engaged in gathering mussels, crabs, and other presumably edible material on the beach.

The incident occurred somewhere about three o'clock in the afternoon, the fatigue parties had just been disbanded for the day and I was making my final tour of inspection to ascertain if the work had been thoroughly carried out in accordance with my instructions, and I had just reached that part of the camp which abuts on the wharf when I observed a large number of coolies rushing over the rocky hill which forms the southern bastion of the compound and apparently running towards some common objective, or central point of interest, as they were all moving in one general direction. They appeared to be abnormally excited, as they were gesticulating frantically, and ejaculating vociferously, a circumstance which interested me to such an extent that I too joined the procession to ascertain the meaning of their unusual perturbation.

After pushing my way through the dense crowd who were congregated on the southern slope of the hill, and on all other points of observation adjacent to the sea, I observed a struggling crowd on the further rocky shore of the small bay which lies just back of the No. 3 latrine, who were evidently the cynosure of all eyes, and on pushing through the crowd to a better point of observation, I discovered that they had effected the capture of a very large octopus, measuring fully eight feet from tip to tip of the tentacles, and weighing approximately in the neighbourhood of one hundred and fifty pounds, which according to their statement had opened the offensive by wrapping its tentacles around the leg of an incautious chinaman [sic] whose contiguity to the water had rendered such an action possible,

Dan Black

A small section of the modern artwork along the waterfront at Weihai, China, near the former location of the recruitment depot. The photo was taken in the fall of 2018 and the artwork depicts two labourers, one displaying the bracelet on his wrist.

and attempted to pull him into the sea, an assertion which was substantiated by the fact that they were still engaged in disentangling its tentacles from his leg when I arrived, and I have very little doubt that if it had not been for the timely arrival of succor he would have been dragged under water.

I may say that Lance Corporal Wilson of the C.M.P. saw the remains of the monster a short time after on the ablution table where he could form a fair estimate of its size, although by that time the major portion of it had been expeditiously converted into 'chow-chow' by the omnivorous Chinamen.

They appear to be very numerous as four others were subsequently captured here, one of which weighed in the vicinity of one hundred pounds.[39]

In his last diary entry, dated July 12, 1919, Livingstone tells of his arrival home.

David Livingstone Collection

A few days earlier, a headline in the *Vancouver Daily Province* had drawn attention to the human species and how large it could get. "Biggest Chink On M.S. Dollar: Coolie Giant Returning to Tsingtau — Steamship Carries Chinese Laborers."

The ship sailed from William Head on Saturday, March 27, 1920, "with the largest load of coolies and the largest coolie that ever left the coast." The reporter noted 4,306 labourers on board, "including one placid Oriental working man who stood seven feet six inches in his socks, and weighed over 300 pounds of bone and brawn. The Dollar Company believes the government put one over on them in regard to this human, as he is expected to eat up his share of provisions within two or three days."

All the men were embarked quickly, added the story, with the first man up the gangway at 9 a.m., and the "last passed over the rail three hours and ten minutes later."[40]

* * *

The Chinese had not commenced their homeward journeys across Canada by the time Captain Harry Livingstone arrived home on Saturday, July 12, 1919. En route to Listowel, he had come full circle, switching trains once again in Toronto. It was hotter in the city, but not exactly a scorcher, with temperatures hovering around twenty-two degrees Celsius and light rain predicted. As the train rolled west through Guelph to Listowel, Harry was intrigued by a large group of Orangemen who occupied several seats in the carriage. His attention, however, soon switched back to the anticipation of seeing his parents and his beloved egg collection. Mixed in with those thoughts of home was his longing to finally dip a big spoon into a bowl of his mother's famous "mush," a combination of warm oatmeal, maple syrup and cream.[41]

It was around noon when the train pulled in and the doctor stepped down onto the wooden platform where his mother and father waited. Settling in that evening, Livingstone wrote the last sentence in his field diary, which by then filled nearly three volumes. "Great to get home again and many changes seen in the town and people."[42]

Of course, Harry had changed, too, as did tens of thousands of Chinese men who returned to their families and villages with stories to tell about the West, what they had witnessed, and how they had been treated.

Epilogue

In China, boycotts and demonstrations followed the news from Versailles that confirmed what many Chinese already believed: that the West disregarded China and its wartime contribution. While the mostly student-led protests inspired hope that China would modernize, there remained serious political rivalries and military upheaval between governments in the north and the south.

As the warlords fought over control, many of the illiterate or semi-illiterate labourers who had returned from France between November 1918 and as late as September 1920 had little to show for their wartime experience. Those who had saved enough applied their earnings against the daily economic pressures they and their families faced, although, as Summerskill points out, the local rate of exchange on the money they earned in France was a lot less than it was in 1917.[1] For the most part, the men remained part of China's peasantry and worked to carry on with their lives and filial obligations.

Generally, life in northeastern China was extremely hard, especially with the spread of contagious diseases, including cholera, influenza and typhus. Hundreds died of the Spanish flu, but as Summerskill adds, the actual number is impossible to establish because not every death or cause of death was recorded. Adding to the misery was drought and the failure of crops, followed by famine.

Thousands of kilometres away, the country that hired the CLC men moved on through the early postwar years and the labourers were largely forgotten. When the British government was asked in late 1919 whether members of the CLC would be entitled to any medal for their service, the response was that the men would receive the British War Medal, but it would be in bronze, not silver, unlike the one issued to British Labour battalions. In addition to the different metal type, the CLC medal was not inscribed with the labourer's name, only his registered number.[2]

While articles and books have been published in the United Kingdom and elsewhere on the CLC, there was, by 2018, no memorial in the U.K. to them. However, a national campaign, launched in 2014, is underway to raise funds for the erection of a memorial in 2019. There has been other positive movement as well during the period encompassing the First World War's hundredth anniversary commemorations. Through exhibits, documentary films, conferences and online forms, the CLC story is gaining recognition.

In Canada, the story remains unknown to most, but significant effort has been made by the Canadian Agency of the Commonwealth War Graves Commission to locate the graves of CLC men who died in Canada while en route to the Western Front or on their return journey to China. "Thousands of Chinese came from their homeland to serve the Empire in time of war, and they made a significant contribution to the war effort hence those who died are commemorated by the Commission," explains David Kettle, Secretary General of the Canadian Agency of the CWGC. "Those who died in Canada or while en route across Canada are entitled to be properly commemorated by the Commission. It took significant effort — literally months of research as well as assistance from subject matter experts to locate most, if not all of the CLC war dead in our area of operations. I knew absolutely nothing about the CLC before I joined the Commission — the story of the presence of the CLC had virtually vanished from Canadian history, but once we heard their story there was no holding us back. CLC war dead were entitled to be properly commemorated and we were determined to make that happen. It is hard to explain how gratifying it is when the lost have been found."

New headstones for CLC who died in Canada have been erected or are in the process of being installed at locations across

This collection, owned by Professor Sam Chiu, shows the bronze medal (right)
issued to the CLC after the war. Also shown are two envelopes or covers.

Canada. In 2019, three Type 24 headstones were scheduled for
installation in the cemetery within the grounds of the William
Head minimum security penitentiary on Vancouver Island.
Type 24 headstones are slightly larger than standard CWGC
headstones. In an interview in April 2019, the Canadian Agency
of the CWGC explained that the three stones are to be grouped
together and located not far from the cemetery's entrance. The
central headstone features text explaining the CLC's connection to the location, while the two flanking stones list a total of
twenty-one names of CLC who are buried there. Five other CLC
men lie in marked graves within the cemetery. A commemoration ceremony for the new headstones was also, as of early 2019,
scheduled for the fall of that year.

For several years, penitentiary staff at William Head has not
forgotten the historical significance of CLC, nor the former
quarantine station. The small cemetery is maintained and there

continues to be an exhibit of memorabilia and photographs created and voluntarily organized by former librarian Kim Rempel.

If any of the Chinese labourers had wanted to move to Canada after returning to China in 1919 or 1920, the prospects were very bleak. In 1923, Parliament passed what was known as the *Chinese Exclusion Act*. For twenty-four years, the *Act* banned Chinese immigration purely on the basis of race. The only exceptions were diplomats, certain merchants, students and Canadian-born Chinese returning home from Chinese schools. In addition, Chinese already residing in Canada had to register for an identity card. If they did not, they were subject to a fine of up to five-hundred dollars or imprisonment. The *Act* was repealed in 1947, but it took another twenty years for restrictions on the basis of nationality or race to be dropped completely.

*   *   *

Dr. Harry Livingstone returned to his family practice after the war and in 1927, the thirty-nine-year-old bachelor married twenty-four-year-old Elsie Clarke, the younger sister of some boys he used to chum with. Harry continued to make his rounds at the Listowel hospital where he remained on staff until his death on June 3, 1965.[3] The former captain in the Canadian Army Medical Corps was seventy-seven when his heart stopped and he collapsed on the living room couch. His beloved Elsie, who found him there, died in 1997.

His son David, who turned ninety in 2019, explained that shortly after the war Harry built a one-room cottage along the shores of Lake Huron near Oliphant, Ontario. He completed it in a weekend, and added partitions to create rooms. It was not very glamourous, but it brought Harry closer to nature and his avian interests. "There were these tall cedar and tamarack trees between the cottage and a garage and Dad used to travel in the trees, from branch to branch, and from cottage to garage, without touch-

Part of Captain Harry Livingstone's birds' egg collection.

Owen Livingstone

ing the ground. He used to do that even when he was in his fifties and early sixties. He even built a lookout up there that was forty or fifty feet off the ground, affording a bird's-eye view in all directions."

Dr. John McDonald remained in Canada until the spring of 1922 when he returned to the United Kingdom to pursue postgraduate study. He returned to Canada in late 1923 and was married in 1933 to Hazel Huffman at Niagara, New York. The couple immigrated to the United States and, at age fifty-two, Dr. McDonald enlisted in the United States Army. He died in 1962.[4]

When Dr. Louis "Lou" Sebert returned from overseas he saw — for the first time — his new son, Louis Jr., born in 1917. From London, Ontario, Lou, his wife, Lillian, and their son moved to Toronto where Dr. Sebert's reputation as a nationally and internationally recognized eye specialist grew. A brief family biography notes he helped perform the first cornea transplant in Canada.

Louis Sr. and Lillian raised three more children, James, Mary and John. During the Second World War, Louis Jr. served overseas as a lieutenant with the Royal Canadian Artillery while Louis Sr. served at a Toronto military hospital with the Royal Canadian Army Medical Corps reserve. In 1942, Dr. Louis Sr. was diagnosed with cancer and died in December that year. He was only fifty-six. His son, Louis Jr., never saw his father again after leaving for oversea.[5]

* * *

Ernest J. Chambers served as Canada's chief press censor until the end of 1919 when the wartime position was dissolved. He continued to fulfil the duties of Gentleman Usher of the Black Rod until his death in Vaudreuil, Quebec, on May 11, 1925. He was sixty-three.

The Reverend Gordon Jones, who served as a missionary in China for more than thirty-five years, died at Brantford on October 7, 1952. He was in his sixty-eighth year.

Medical missionary Dr. Percy Leslie died in 1965, at the age ninety-four. He returned to China after the First World War and resumed his work until ill health forced him to leave 1926. Back in Montreal, Dr. Leslie joined the medical staff at Montreal General.

James M. Menzies also returned to China where he carried on with his work as a missionary and became an international authority on the Shang dynasty through his work with the Oracle Bones. He also accepted the appointment of professor of Chinese epigraphy and archeology at Cheeloo University at Tsinan in Shantung. He was seventy-two when he suffered his second heart attack and died at home on March 16, 1957. His wife, Annie, died in 1962. Among their children, Arthur served in the land of his birth as Canada's ambassador to China from 1976 to 1980 and concurrently was ambassador to Vietnam, 1976 to 1979.[6] His extraordinary diplomatic career spanned forty years and included a variety of important postings.

The controversial Malcolm Reid, the former federal immigration agent at Vancouver who served as Ernest J. Chambers's right-hand man on the West Coast during the CLC movements, died on board Canadian Pacific Train No. 3 at Beavermouth, British Columbia (between Revelstoke and Golden), on May 12, 1936. He was sixty. The cause of death is listed as Bright's Disease (chronic inflammation of the kidneys).[7]

The Reverend Canon Napier Smith died of a cerebral hemorrhage on August 26, 1953, in hospital in Buffalo, New York. He was sixty-six.

Acknowledgements

When I wrote the last sentence for this book, the joy of arriving there sprung from the people I had the pleasure of meeting along the way.

As we say, books like this are not written in isolation; its takes people with different backgrounds and stores of knowledge to produce what is ultimately a single collaboration. The valuable assistance rendered during the last three years ranged from a small but timely email confirming the smallest detail to the sharing of large files, personal family papers and photographs.

At the top of my list is David Livingstone, the son of Dr. Harry Livingstone and great-grand-nephew to the world-famous Dr. David Livingstone. David, who celebrated his ninetieth birthday in May 2019, welcomed me into his home in Waterloo, Ontario, and loaned me every file he has on his father, including dozens of photographs and the copies of Harry's three field diaries. The two of us met several times over a three-year period and on one occasion toured his father's hometown of Listowel. His abiding interest in the Chinese Labour Corps and Canadian military history goes well beyond his father's own experience. Both of us had the pleasure to meet again in Britain, where we attended a CLC conference at the University of London, and later at the annual military history colloquium at Sir Wilfrid Laurier University. I am deeply indebted to David for his generosity and patience.

Also at the top of the list are John De Lucy of London, England, Nelson Oliver of Port Moody, British Columbia, Diana Beaupré and Adrian Watkinson of Canterbury, England, Sam Chiu of Toronto, Glenn Wright of Ottawa, Douglas R. Phillips of Calgary and David Kettle, Dominique Boulais and Catherine

Paterson of the Canadian Agency of the Commonwealth War Graves Commission in Ottawa.

John De Lucy freely shared his vast collection of photographs taken by his grandfather, William James Hawkings, who served as a British officer in the CLC.

When researcher Nelson Oliver first heard from me about this project, he quickly shared his files on the steamships that transported the Chinese to Canada, and the routes they took across the North Pacific. He then tracked down everything from death certificates to newspaper articles, pertinent historical documents, biographies, photographs and even sketches of the CPR piers and the Dominion Immigration Building in Vancouver. Nelson also bravely read the various drafts and offered constructive and timely feedback. I cannot thank him enough for his encouragement, and so this book is for him, too.

In Britain, Diana Beaupré and Adrian Watkinson searched and located crucial primary documents at the National Archives at Kew, the Imperial War Museum in London and at Folkestone and Shorncliffe on the south coast. This project would not have been possible without their commitment, encouragement and eagle eyes during the final drafts.

Sam Chiu also shared images and articles on the CLC, and together we travelled to Weihai, China, for a conference during which each of us was invited to speak. Researcher and author Glenn Wright is credited for drawing my attention to the CLC while I was editor of *Legion Magazine*. He, more than anyone, convinced me more had to be done to explain Canada's historical link to the CLC. In addition to writing the foreword to this book, Glenn uncovered important files at Library and Archives Canada, and read the initial drafts.

My knowledge of railways and rolling stock was sparse until Douglas R. Phillips volunteered his expertise. Douglas freely shared articles and photographs, and his encouraging responses to my emails filled important gaps.

David Kettle and his team at the Canadian Agency of the CWGC welcomed me into their world and together we shared research in an effort to locate the graves of CLC buried in Canada. It was a two-way street that extended over a two-and-a-half-year period. My respect for the work they do is enormous.

Significant support and encouragement came from author John Boileau of Halifax; Canadian researcher and author Kent Fedorowich, University of the West of England, Bristol; author Peter Johnson of Vancouver; Diana Lary, Professor Emerita of History at the University of British Columbia, who reviewed early drafts and provided the transliteration for Chinese names and place names; Steve Lau, Chair of the Chinese in Britain Forum and architect of the Ensuring We Remember Campaign in the United Kingdom; historical Canadian mapping expert Jeffrey S. Murray of Burritt's Rapids, Ontario; Kim Rempel of Sooke, British Columbia, curator of the CLC Museum at William Head Institution; Margaret Roper of Victoria; Adele Sebert and her late husband, John, son of Louis Sebert; Roger Smith of Ottawa, grandson of the Reverend Napier Smith; King Wan, President of the Board of Directors for the Chinese Canadian Military Museum Society in Vancouver; and Frances M. Weir of Saanichton, British Columbia.

I am also deeply indebted to the Correctional Service of Canada staff at William Head Institution, a minimum-security penitentiary located on Vancouver Island at the site of the former quarantine station. Warden Trent Mitchell, Assistant Warden Peter Forbes and Anthony M. Baldo welcomed me and provided a day-pass so I could walk the grounds with Kim Rempel, visit the graves of Chinese labourers who died there and breathe in the stunning geography and vistas.

Maps, which are essential for books like these, take much time to produce and for that work I am indebted to the Information and Communications Technology Department at Algonquin College in Ottawa. Through Mike Ballard, professor of geomatics engineering, I was connected to several graduate students, all of whom could have met the challenge. I went with Yahui Chai, who is originally from North China, and Kiersti McMillan. These talented women volunteered their time and expertise to produce maps that provide overviews of the geography involved. I am also indebted to graphic artist Janet Watson of Mejan Graphic Design of Merrickville for producing the map depicting the railway route across Canada. I cannot thank them enough.

In addition, I am exceedingly grateful for the research and books produced and written on the CLC by international scholars. Highest on this list are historian/authors Gregory James, Zhang Yan and Xu Guoqi, who, in my humble opinion, have compiled the greatest amount of modern research on the labourers and their experience. Collective knowledge of the CLC would also be sadly limited if it were not for the excellent work by Nicholas J. Griffin, Brian C. Fawcett and author Michael Summerskill. Closer to home, I am indebted to historian Alvyn J. Austin for his fine book on Canadian missionaries who served in China from 1888 to 1959 and to Professor Margo S. Gewurtz, whose valuable research in 1982 first drew attention to the Canadian missionaries who served with the CLC. I am also indebted to Professor Peter M. Mitchell whose 1982 paper explored Canada's official connection to the CLC, and to academic papers or articles by Linda M. Ambrose on the 1913 quarantine investigation at William Head, Cole Harris on the 1782 smallpox outbreak around British Columbia's Strait of Georgia, Hugh Johnston on the surveillance of Indian nationalists and the *Komagata Maru* standoff, Jeff Keshen on Ernest J. Chambers, Allen Rowe on ethnic surveillance and the Chinese during the First World War and Patricia E. Roy for her work on British Columbia's fear of Asians.

This work would not have been possible without the assistance of a number of key institutions, including Library and Archives Canada, and the Department of National Defence's Directorate of History and Heritage in Ottawa; the British Columbia Provincial Archives; Vancouver Public Archives; Vancouver Public Library; the United Church of Canada Archives in Toronto, the CLC Museum at William Head Institution, the Metchosin Museum Society at Metchosin, British Columbia; the National Archives and the Imperial War Museum in the United Kingdom.

The amount of material I waded through is enormous, and any errors that show up in this book are entirely on me.

I also want to thank Angela Xianghong Ma of the Weihai City Archives, Bob Burgis of the Metchosin Museum Society; David Laurence Jones for his knowledge of the Canadian Pacific police service; John Weir of the Smiths Falls Railway Museum; Bruce Chapman; Judy Maxwell of Vancouver's Chinatown; Mary Kate Laphen, librarian at the Merrickville Public Library; friends and fellow writers Bryan Demchinsky, Jeffrey Street, and Theresa Wallace; friends Pat Remmer, Carole and Richard Odgers, Kemp McMeekin and the Voyageurs Men's Group for guidance and encouragement.

Once again, I am very grateful to publisher James Lorimer, who quickly appreciated why this book had to be written. His overall support for Canadian book publishing has helped preserve Canadian history and brought confidence to Canadian writers. In Halifax and Toronto, Lorimer's editing and production team was first-rate. Publisher Carrie Gleason, former editor Scott Fraser and production editor Susmita Dey all worked their magic. I am also deeply indebted to copy editor Laurie Miller who in addition to cleaning up the manuscript offered some vital observations.

Last, but not least I want to thank my family, Alice, Katy and Conor, for being so patient; my father, Robert Black, for bravely reading the initial drafts and my mother, Loral Spence, for her steady encouragement.

Appendix One

CHINESE LABOUR CORPS
GRAVES IN CANADA*

Name (modern spelling in round brackets with registration number)	Date of Death
Metchosin (William Head Institution) Cemetery, Vancouver Island, British Columbia	
Hsu Yung Ch'ang (Xu Yongchang, No. 27165)	11/18/1919
Chang Tien Ho (Zhang Tianhe, No. 38014)	1/31/1920
Lin Ch'ang Sheng (Lin Changsheng, No. 478)	10/3/1919
Wang Fu Wen (Wang Fuwen, No. 75789)	2/13/1920
Wang Ching Lien (Wang Jinglian, No. 99636)	2/15/1920
Wei Chen Shan (Wei Zhenshan, No. 31996)	7/28/1917
Chu Hsueh K'ung (Zhu Xuekong, No. 32626)	12/6/1919
Ting Yen Yu (Ding Yanyu, No. 65376)	12/4/1917
Wang Hsi Ch'ing (Wang Xiqing, No. 67553)	10/29/1917
Yen Chih Hsiu (Yan Zhixiu, No. 75135)	4/16/1918
Chang Yu Ts'ang (Zhang Yucang, No. 76539)	3/25/1918
Chang Hung (Zhang Hong, No. 92560)	1/9/1918
Kuo Te Sheng (Guo Desheng, No. 94941)	12/19/1917
Fan Mao Chih (Fan Maozhi, No. 100495)	4/1/1918
Hsu He Nien (Xu Henian, No. 103985)	3/4/1920
Yang Chen Hsiang (Yang Zhenxiang, No. 104041)	2/17/1920
Chang Pao (Zhang Bao, No. 106053)	3/15/1918
Ch'in Feng Ch'I (Chin Fengqi, No. 107198)	3/1/1920
Hsieh Shou Ch'ing (Xie Shouching, No. 107410)	3/12/1920
Hou Yuan Ch'eng (Hou Yuancheng, No. 108671)	3/25/1918
Chang Kung Ch'ang (Zhang Gongchang, No. 130573)	4/27/1918
P'ang K'e He (Peng Kehe, No. 130800)	5/27/1918

Ku Ch'un Ming (Gu Chunming, No. 130881)	3/5/1920
Liang Feng Hai (Liang Fenghai, No. 131682)	3/26/1918
Chang Cheng Li (Zhang Zhengli, No. 132781)	4/3/1918
Wang Wan Fu (Wang Wanfu, No. 133228)	6/6/1918
Possibly at Metchosin (William Head Institution) Cemetery	
Chang P'ei Jung (Zhang Peirong, No. 24720)**	12/27/1919
K'ung Chao Chih (Kong Zhaozhi, No. 102980)**	3/24/1920
Chang Ping Wen (Zhang Bingwen, No. 107745)**	1/12/1920
Hsi Chi Jong Wang (No. number available)	10/28/1917
Victoria, British Columbia (Record of unmarked grave Harling Point Chinese Cemetery and to be commemorated on Chinese Noyelles-sur-Mer Memorial, France)	
Ch'en T'ing Chang (Chen Tingzhang, No. 65855)	10/23/1917
Vancouver (Mountain View) Cemetery	
Li Ju Ying (Li Ruying, No. 106855)	2/21/1920
Repatriated to China from Vancouver (Mountain View) Cemetery and to be commemorated on Chinese Noyelles-sur-Mer Memorial, France)	
Ch'u I Kung (Chu Yigong, No. 14057)	5/31/1917
Han Shu Ch'ing (Han Shuqing, No. 30896)	7/9/1917
Ch'en Wang Feng (Chen Wangfeng, No. 33258)	8/4/1917
Ts'ao I Hsiang (Cao Yixiang, No. 61935)	8/25/1917
Repatriated to China from Calgary Chinese Cemetery and to be commemorated on Chinese Noyelles-sur-Mer Memorial, France)	
Sung Ming Ch'ang (Song Mingchang, No. 7934)	9/29/1919
Regina Cemetery	
Lei Chin T'ai (Lei Jintai, No. 24898)	1/18/1920
Winnipeg (Brookside) Cemetery	
Hu Yu Yuan (Hu Yuyuan, No. 46244)	1/18/1920
Thunder Bay (Riverside) Cemetery	
Wang Yung Sheng (Wang Yongsheng, No. 102111)	1/20/1918
Petwawa, Ontario (St. Matthew's Lutheran) Cemetery	
Chou Ming Shan (Zhou Mingshan, No. 39038)	9/22/1917

Repatriated to China from Montreal (Mount Royal) Cemetery and to be commemorated on Chinese Noyelles-sur-Mer Memorial, France)	
Li Chin Hsiang (Li Jinxiang, No. 102509)	1/16/1918
Quebec City (Mount Hermon) Cemetery	
Chang Hsueh P'u (Zhang Xuepu, No. 51100)	7/7/1917
Han Hsiang T'ai (Han Xiangtai, No. 31277. He is believed to have died on board the *Tunisian* at Quebec)	06/07/1917
Halifax (Fairview Lawn) Cemetery	
Liu Ching Yen (Liu Jingyan, No. 101159)	1/30/1920
Wang Chih Fa (Wang Zhifa, No. 104667)	2/5/1920
Yao Kuang T'ao (Yao Guangtao, No. 131034)	2/15/1920
Tung Shih Ch'eng (Dong Shicheng, No. 92107)	1/27/1920
Halifax (St. John's) Cemetery	
Feng Chai Li (Feng Jiali, No. 95167)	1/23/1918
Hsu Hsi Kung (Xu Xigong, No. 15608)	6/18/1917
Halifax (Burial location unknown)	
Liu Chih (Liu Zhi, No. 46511. He is believed to have died November 29-30, 1917, on board the *Olympic* at Halifax.)***	
*This list is comprised of those who died and were known to have been buried in Canada. The list is dated to April 30, 2019.	
**Names to be added to the Chinese Noyelles-sur-Mer Memorial, France.	
***This is the man noted in Captain Harry Livingstone's diary of same date.	

Appendix Two

THEORIES OF THE 1918–19 INFLUENZA PANDEMIC

Between 1918 and 1920, the "Spanish flu" pandemic killed more people than the First World War did in all the four years that it ran. Up to a hundred million died from the disease worldwide. In Canada, the death toll was approximately 55,000.

Immediately after the war, researchers began investigating the disease and its origins. While they collected their evidence, theories developed not only on the disease's point of origin, but how it spread around the world.

The name of the disease might suggest it originated in Spain, but that is far from the truth. It was named the "Spanish flu" because Spanish newspapers were the first allowed to report on the prevalence of the virus. At the time, Spain was not in the war, so its newspapers were uncensored, unlike those published in the belligerent countries.

The pandemic moved around the world in three waves, or phases. It appears to have begun in the spring of 1918, petering out that summer before a second, more deadly strain emerged in the fall. That was followed by a third wave or variant that stretched into early 1920.

The more serious possibilities put forward for the 1918 virus's point of origin are France, Kansas in the American Midwest and China. The deadly virus is related to the modern H1N1 strain known as "bird flu," and mortality was high among young children, people between the ages of twenty and forty years and those over age sixty-five. Researchers have suggested the 1918 outbreak may have originated in northern China, but was misdiagnosed as pneumonic plague. As for the spread of the disease, one persistent, if unproven, theory is that it was carried to Europe by members of the Chinese Labour Corps.

This hypothesis was supported by researchers Christopher Langford, Dorothy A. Pettit and Janice Bailie, who have found evidence of a severe form of respiratory disease that spread in China's interior during the winter of 1917–18. They contend it was the earliest recorded occurrence of the pandemic flu.

The other two epicentres also have their supporters and detractors. Because of the dead poultry they contained, frontline trenches and farmyards in France and Belgium have been perceived as the breeding grounds for the disease. Others believe it was labourers recruited by the French in southern, not northern China who introduced the virus to the Western Front. It is believed that from France the illness was easily carried across the Channel and infected a lot more people as it mutated into its most virulent stage. But, while it is usually believed the disease arrived in Canada during the summer of 1918 on board two troopships, some historians suggest it arrived earlier, in the late winter or early spring.

The third theory suggests it originated in Haskell, Kansas, during the spring of 1918, and was carried by civilians who were recruited into the army. This is based on reports of an influenza outbreak that claimed the lives of nearly fifty American soldiers. The theory is that the disease spread when troops were sent east to board crowded steamers for Europe.

While drawing attention to the possibility of a CLC connection from northeastern China, Canadian historian Mark Osborne Humphries recounts the various theories and states the "Canadian and American experiences in 1918 best fit a Chinese or early North American origin for the flu." He points to the labourers who were "shipped across Canada by the British from China."[1] Given the number of labourers who fell sick in China and during the trans-Pacific voyage, it is entirely possible that of the roughly 82,000 who crossed Canada by rail some may have been infected with the virus.

We can certainly believe whatever we want from these theories, but as of today, at least, it is hard to confirm the origin despite best efforts. One point is clear: the war came with an unprecedented volume of human transportation on land and sea. In the age of steam, ships and trains in particular were packed tightly with soldiers and labourers who came and went, and many of them brought disease.

That at least we know.

Notes

Introduction

1   Author interview with David Livingstone, March 8, 2017. Egg collecting was falling out of favour around this time — seen more as a predatory hobby. However, before and during the 1800s it was a popular pastime for adults and children.

2   Livingstone Family Papers, "Field Diary No. 1," Captain Harry Livingstone, Canadian Army Medical Corps. Hereafter: LFP, FD No. 1.

3   The source for specific Chinese Labour Corps train movements are the Canadian Pacific Railway train movement memorandums issued in 1917 and 1918 which were circulated to the secretary of state: chief press censor. These files are available at Library and Archives Canada, RG 6, E. Microfilm reels pertaining to the secretary of state, chief press censor were also viewed at: http://heritage.canadiana.ca/search/?q0.0=t101. Hereafter, the file references for the individual train movements are listed as "CPR Company Memo," followed by file number and date.

4   Xu Guoqi, *Strangers on the Western Front: Chinese Workers in the Great War* (Cambridge, Mass.: Harvard University Press, 2011), p. 55.

5   Greg James, *The Chinese Labour Corps (1916–1920)* (Hong Kong: Bayview Educational, 2013), p. 7. James presents the most accurate figures, which have ranged over the years as high as some 100,000 recruited by the British and roughly 40,000 recruited by the French.

6   Hundreds of British, British Commonwealth and French soldiers were also executed during the same period. Among the 306 British and British Commonwealth soldiers were twenty-five Canadians.

7   Commonwealth War Graves Commission (hereafter CWGC) presentation by archivist Andrew Fetherston, for Meridian Society film launch, SOAS, University of London, April 19, 2017.

8   Tim Cook, *At The Sharp End: Canadians Fighting The Great War 1914–1916* (Toronto: Penguin Canada, 2007), p. 521. This historian also points out that the estimate of German casualties did not include men who were only slightly wounded.

9   Niall Ferguson, *The Pity of War: Explaining World War I* (London: Allen Lane, 1998), p. 285.

10 Michael Summerskill, *China on the Western Front: Britain's Chinese Work Force in the First World War* (London: Michael Summerskill, 1982), p. 17.

11 Ibid., pp. 11–12.

12 Nicholas J. Griffin, "The Response of British Labor to the Importation of Chinese Workers: 1916–1917," *The Historian*, February 1, 1978, p. 254.

13 Library and Archives Canada, RG 25, vol. 229, file M60/26. Hereafter: LAC.

14 Glenn Wright, "The Chinese Labour Corps," *Legion Magazine*, September/October 2011, pp. 26–31.

15 Arlene Chan, "Chinese Immigration Act," in *Canadian Encyclopaedia, 2016*, www.thecanadianencyclopedia.ca.

16 "The Canadian Pacific Railway," in *Canadian Encyclopaedia*.

17 Peter Mitchell, "Canada and the Chinese Labour Corps 1917–1920: the Official Connection." This paper was presented by the York University professor at the Annual Meeting of the Canadian Historical Association, Ottawa, June 10, 1982.

18 CPR steamships also moved roughly four million tons of wartime cargo. David Laurence Jones, *The Railway Beat: A Century of Canadian Pacific Police Service* (Markham, Ont.: Fifth House Ltd., 2014), p. 98.

19 Ibid.

20 Wayne E. Reilly, *Bangor Daily News*, February 1, 2015.

21 www.thecanadianencyclopedia.ca.

22 "Halifax Explosion," in *Wikipedia*, https://en.m.wikipedia.org.

23 LAC, RG 24, vol. 6359, file HQ71–26–99–13.

24 James, *Chinese Labour*, p. 160.

25 *Empress of Russia* ship's manifest and summary, April 3, 1917.

26 Yan Zhang, "Shantung Navvy: Mortals under the Political Halo," p. 15. Translated by Ernest Leung, Chinese University of Hong Kong. This is a substantially revised version of an article, edited by Qiao Yinwei, published in the June 2015 issue of *Overseas Chinese History Studies*.

27 Thomas R. Gottschang and Diana Lary, *Swallows and Settlers: The Great Migration from North China to Manchuria* (Ann Arbour: Centre For Chinese Studies, University of Michigan, 2000), p. 9.

28 Zhang, p. 13.

29 Ibid., p. 14.

30 Ibid., p. 13.

31 *Daily Province*, March 29, 1920, p. 3.

32 Robert J. Davison, "The Chinese at William Head, A Photograph Album," *British Columbia Historical News*, vol. 16, no. 4 (1983), p. 19. Also see: Peter Johnson, *Quarantined: Life and Death at William Head Station, 1872–1959* (Vancouver: Heritage House Publishing Company Ltd., 2013), p. 147.

33 LFP, FD No. 1.

34 CWGC, Fetherston.

35 Louis Joseph Sebert biographical paper, unpublished. Courtesy of Adele Sebert and David Livingstone (hereafter Sebert Family Papers); LAC RG 150, Accession 1992–93/166, box 8758–25.

36 Margo S. Gewurtz, "For God or King: Canadian Missionaries and the Chinese Labour Corps in World War I," June 10, 1982. Also part of the LAC's Special Collections.

37 United Church of Canada Archives (UCCA), Gordon Jones Family Papers, Fond 3449 Accession No. 1995.103C, box 1, file 3. Hereafter: UCCA, GJFP, followed by box and file number.

Chapter 1

1 LFP, FD No. 1.

2 www.climate.weather.gc.ca.

3 Chinese Labour Corps (CLC) identification booklet issued to Han Ting Chen (Han Dingzhen), labourer No. 47557, part of David Livingstone Collection.

4 Brian C. Fawcett, "The Chinese Labour Corps In France, 1917–1921," *Journal of the Royal Asiatic Society, Hong Kong Branch*, vol. 40 (2000), p. 35.

5 Summerskill, p. 77.

6 Province of British Columbia death certificate; Canadian Agency of the Commonwealth War Graves Commission. This labourer's name appears on the death certificate as Chang Hung, labourer No. 92560. He had been at William Head for twenty-eight days, after arriving there on December 13, 1917. He died on January 9, 1918, and was buried the next day at the William Head Cemetery, which now goes by the name Metchosin (William Head Institution) Cemetery. He had been suffering from pneumonia for nineteen days.

7 LFP, FD No. 1, August 10, 1917.

8 Sebert Family Papers, p. 4. Hereafter: SFP.

9 This was Toronto's second Union Station, which opened in 1873 and closed in 1927; Toronto Railway Historical Association, Toronto Railway Museum, www.trha.ca.

10 http://afe.easia.columbia.edu/timeline/china_timeline.htm; also see "Chinese history, Shang and Zhou dynasties," in *Encyclopaedia Britannica*, www.britannica.com; Richard T. Phillips, *China Since 1911* (London: MacMillan Press Ltd., 1996), pp. 2–8.

11 Phillips, *China Since 1911*, p. 5.
12 Canada Census, 1911.
13 Phillips, p. 6; Frances Wood and Christopher Arnander, *Betrayed Ally: China in the Great War* (Barnsley, South Yorkshire, England: Pen & Sword Books Limited, 2016), p. 72; "Taiping Rebellion, Chinese History," in *Encyclopaedia Britannica*, www.britannica.com.
14 Wood and Arnander, p. 20.
15 James, p. 54.
16 Mary Gertrude Mason, *Western Concepts of China and the Chinese, 1840–1876* (New York: Columbia University, 1939), pp. 250, 256–257; cited in James, p. 61.
17 Sir John Pratt, *War and Politics in China* (London: Jonathan Cape Limited., 1943), pp. 13–14.
18 Summerskill, p. 16.
19 Wood and Arnander, p. 8.
20 John Keegan, *The First World War* (London: Key Porter Books, 1998), p. 214.
21 Wood and Arnander, p. 8.
22 Fawcett, p. 35.
23 Summerskill, p. 42.
24 Ibid., p. 44.
25 James, p. 191.
26 Zhang Yan, p. 6. The figures show 1,785 and 2,256 leaving from Weihaiwei and Tsingtao, respectively.
27 Zhang Yan, p. 6. The Chinese scholar notes that from 1916 to 1918, at the height of the CLC movements to France, there was no significant corresponding decrease in the number of migrants bound for Manchuria.

Chapter 2

1 LFP, FD No. 1, August 10, 1917.
2 Ibid.
3 Interview with David Livingstone, March 8, 2017. Hereafter: David Livingstone interview.
4 Ibid.
5 Ibid.; two other excellent sources are "Livingstones of Lanark: Dr. David Livingstone's Society Settler Relatives" by Ron W. Shaw, 2016; and "Livingstone's Brother John," http://blantyre.biz/blantyre-folk/david-livingstone/livingstones-brother-john.
6 David Livingstone interview.
7 Ibid.
8 Ibid.
9 Ibid.
10 LAC, RG 150, Accession 1992–93/166, box 5686–51, "Captain Harry Drummond Livingstone."
11 Anthony B. Chan, "Chinese Canadians," *Canadian Encyclopaedia*, July 2013.
12 Paul Yee, "Historical Overview on Chinese in Canada," available on LAC website.
13 The coldest temperature ever recorded was minus 63 degrees Celsius (minus 81.4 degrees Fahrenheit) at Snag, Yukon, in 1947.
14 CPR Company Memo, file 5–11–15-H, August 9, 1917.
15 Douglas R. Phillips interviews, November 1917 to February 2019. Hereafter: Douglas R. Phillips.
16 CPR Company Memo, file 5–11–15-H.
17 *Shipping World*, circa 1915.
18 CPR 1915–1919 news release; Douglas R. Phillips.
19 LFP, Journal, pp. 6–7.
20 CPR memo from Walter Maughan, May 4, 1917.

21 Douglas R. Phillips.
22 LFP, FD No. 1, August 11, 1917.

Chapter 3

1 "Xiaochun Qi's Enchanting Erhu," www.shengunperformingarts.org.
2 Elizabeth A. Tancock, "Secret Trains Across Canada, 1917–1918," *Beaver*, October–November 1991, p. 40.
3 David Laurence Jones, pp. 88–89.
4 Ibid., p. 100.
5 LAC, RG 24, vol.1784, file HQ683–694–4, letter from chief inspector, Department of Soldiers' Civil Re-Establishment, to Militia Council, February 6, 1919.
6 Ibid., letter from Militia Council to chief inspector, Department of Soldiers' Civil Re-Establishment, February 15, 1919.
7 Ibid.
8 LAC, RG 150, Accession 1992–93/166, box 4194–14, "Lieutenant Walter Haynes."
9 GR 2951, vol. 149, British Columbia Division of Vital Statistics, "Death Registrations 049321 to 049997"; ship manifest for *Empress of Britain*, August 3, 1911; baptisms for County Derby, U.K., September 5, 1900; Veterans Affairs Canada, *Canadian Virtual War Memorial*, "Private George F. Roe, service no. 498," commemorated on page 318 of *First World War Book of Remembrance*.
10 LAC, RG 150, Accession 192—93/166, box 2948–9, "Private Joseph Evans."
11 Tancock, pp. 39–43.
12 Harry L. Smith, MD, *Memoirs of an Ambulance Company Officer* (Rochester, Minnesota: The Doomsday Press, 1940).
13 *Globe*, January 5, 1918, p. 1.
14 Nelson Oliver files.
15 *Globe*, January 8, 1918, p. 16.
16 *Vancouver Daily Province*, January 5, 1918, p. 1.
17 LAC, RG 150, Accession 1992–93/166, box 4194–14.
18 Ibid.

Chapter 4

1 W. Kaye Lamb, *History of the Canadian Pacific Railway* (New York: Macmillan Publishing Co., Inc.) pp. 279-280.
2 Ibid.
3 Ibid.
4 George Musk, *Canadian Pacific: The Story of the Famous Shipping Line* (London, England: Canadian Pacific Steamships Ltd., 1981), p.133.
5 Ibid, p. 18.
6 Ibid, p. 137.
7 Lamb, p. 281.
8 LFP, FD No. 1.
9 *Globe*, August 11, 1917, p. 8.
10 *Daily Nor'-Wester*, Winnipeg, January 30, 1896.
11 *Globe*, February 14, 1913, p. 2; the *Winnipeg Tribune*, February 14, 1913, p. 1.
12 LFP, FD No. 1.
13 Ibid.
14 Ibid.
15 Ibid.
16 Jones, p. 100.
17 Musk, p. 127.
18 The popular "Seven Sisters" were six Douglas Firs and one Red Cedar. Constant foot traffic over their root systems contributed to their demise, after which they were cut down.

19 Nelson Oliver files; City of Vancouver Public Archives, "Hotel Vancouver." This was the second Hotel Vancouver. The Vancouver Public Archives also has an excellent photograph taken by Philip T. Timms that shows the towering flagpole in front of the court house.

20 *Vancouver Province*, August 17, 1917, advertisement for the film *Wild and Whoolly*, p. 11.

21 LFP, FD No. 1.

22 Ibid.

23 *Victoria Daily Colonist*, August 17, 1917, p. 11.

24 LFP, FD No. 1.

25 Ibid.

26 The *Oxford Companion to Ships and the Sea*, edited by Peter Kemp, notes that sailing "vessels normally heave-to when the weather is too rough and the wind too strong to make normal sailing practicable." A steamship heaves-to in stormy weather by "heading up to the sea and using her engines just enough to hold her up in position. The whole idea in heaving-to is to bring the wind on to the weather bow and hold the ship in that position, where she rides most safely and easily."

27 LFP, FD No. 1.

28 Ibid.

29 H.D. Livingstone's "Medical Officer's Journal," p. 48. Hereafter: LFP, Journal.

30 LFP, FD No. 1.

31 LFP, Journal, p. 48.

32 Ibid.

33 Ibid.

34 Ibid.

35 Ibid. There was usually a large stockpile of Welsh and native coal at Nagasaki. Livingstone's estimation of how much coal could be loaded onto a steamship in one day matches other references, including Ellen Mary (Hayes) Peck's account in *Travels in the Far East*, 1909. Peck noted the coal was loaded at a rate of 250 tons per hour with the use of bamboo ladders instead of wood planks.

36 LFP, FD No. 1.

37 Ibid.

38 Ibid.

39 Ibid.

40 Ibid.

41 Logbook for *Empress of Japan*'s August 1917 voyage to Hong Kong; Nelson Oliver files.

42 Nelson Oliver files.

43 LFP, FD No. 1.

Chapter 5

1   Reverend Napier Smith Family Papers (hereafter, NSFP), courtesy Roger Smith, p. 1.

2   This was the second Clifton Hotel. The first was destroyed by fire in 1898.

3   "Social Gospel Movement in Canada," *Canadian Encyclopaedia*.

4   Alvyn J. Austin, *Saving China: Canadian Missionaries in the Middle Kingdom, 1888–1959* (Toronto: University of Toronto Press, 1986), p. 85.

5   NSFP, p. 2.

6   Ibid., p. 3.

7   Ibid., p. 2.

8   Ibid., pp. 5–7.

9 Griffin, "Chinese Labor and British Christian Missionaries in France, 1917–1919." *Journal of Church and State,* vol. 20, no. 2 (Spring 1978), p. 288.

10 NSFP, p. 7.

11 Ibid.

12 UCCA, GJFP, box 1, file 2.

13 Ibid.

14 LAC, Arthur Menzies Fonds, R15615. Hereafter: LAC, R15615.

15 LAC, RI5615.

16 Ibid.

17 The National Archives of the United Kingdom, FO 371/2906. Hereafter: TNA.

18 LAC, R15615.

19 UCCA, T.A. Arthurs biographical details.

20 *Empress of Japan* manifest for March–April 1917 voyage to Vancouver.

21 *Montreal Star,* May 13, 1965, obituary for Dr. Percy Campbell Leslie; UCCA biographical file on Dr. Percy Campbell Leslie.

22 Professor Margo Gewurtz, "For God or King: Canadian Missionaries and the Chinese Labour Corps in World War I." Paper presented to the annual meeting of the Canadian Historical Association, Ottawa, June 10, 1982.

23 *Supplement to the London Gazette,* July 5, 1918, p. 7885; *Supplement to the London Gazette,* November 7, 1918, 13149.

24 TNA, FO 371/2906.

25 UCCA, Harry Stewart Forbes, biographical details.

26 UCCA, Harry Stewart Forbes, Board of Foreign Missions, 1942.

27 Austin, p. 3–4, 7.

28 "James Hudson Taylor, an English missionary who made his mark in China," *South China Morning Post, Post Magazine,* July 11, 2015, www.scmp.com/magazines/post-magazine/article/1835048/james-hudson-taylor.

29 Austin, p. 4.

30 *South China Morning Post, Post Magazine,* July 11, 2015.

31 Austin, p. 5.

32 Austin, p. 152.

33 Mary Beacock Fryer, *Brockville: A Pictorial History* (Brockville, Ont.: Besancourt Publishers, 1986), p. 44. Fortunately, the 1832 cholera epidemic did not hit Brockville as hard as neighbouring communities, including Prescott and Kingston.

34 Austin, pp. 27–28.

35 The island was annexed in 1683 by the Qing dynasty. In 1895 it was ceded to Japan. Following the surrender of Japan at the end of the Second World War, the Republic of China, which overthrew the Qing in 1911–12, took control of Taiwan.

36 Austin, p. 27.

37 Ibid., p. 11.

38 Ibid.

39 Ibid.

40 Ibid., p. 73.

41 Ibid., p. 74.

42 The uprising also had its origins in Zhili (Hebei) province.

43 The name "Boxer" comes from a Chinese secret society whose members practised Chinese boxing or Kung Fu. Different names have been applied to the society, from the National Righteous Group (I-Min Hui) to the League of Harmony and Justice (I-Ho T'uan).

44 Wood and Arnander, pp. 18–19.

45 Austin, pp. 76–77.

46 *Montreal Star,* May 13, 1965.

47 Austin, p. 90.
48 UCCA, Presbyterian Board of Foreign Missions minutes, April 1929.
49 Wood and Arnander, pp. 18–19, 167.

Chapter 6

1   Summerskill, p. 54; *Whitaker's Almanac*, 1916.
2   Linfu Dong, *Cross Culture and Faith: The Life and Work of James Mellon Menzies* (Toronto: University of Toronto Press, 2005), p. 37; LAC, R15615; NSFP.
3   LAC, R15615, March 5, 1910.
4   LAC, R15615.
5   Ibid., letter, August 22, 1910.
6   Ibid., journal entry, September 15, 1910.
7   Radio Canada International, http://www.rcinet.ca/patrimoine-asiatique-en/wp-content/uploads/sites/26/2012/06/2-Wedding-picture-of-Rev_-James-M_-Menzies-to-Miss-Annie-Belle-Sedgwick-Feb_-8-1911-in-Kaifeng-Henan-China. Also, see Dong ref., p. 42 for wedding date.
8   LAC, R15615, November 25, 1897, the "Friday News."
9   Ibid., p. 28.
10 LAC, R15615, journal entries, August 1905.
11 Ibid.
12 Ibid.
13 Ibid., journal entry, September 11, 1905.
14 The population for 1910 is an estimate based on the city's 1911 population of 381,383.
15 *Victoria Daily Colonist*, August 17, 1917, p. 11.
16 Student Volunteer Movement Executive Committee Report, 1913–14 convention, p. 2.
17 Ibid., p. 8.
18 Ibid., p. 11.
19 Ibid., p. 10.
20 Ibid., p. 4.
21 LAC, R15615, letter, January 10, 1910.
22 Ibid., letter, February 2, 1910.
23 Ibid., letter, January 19, 1910.
24 UCCA, Dr. Frederick M. Auld biography, minutes of Board of Foreign Missions, April 1932.
25 Dong, pp. 48–49.
26 Canadian 1911 census; the square-kilometre figure includes only land mass, not water.
27 Austin, p. 40.
28 Dong, p. 46.
29 Geoffrey York, "The unsung Canadian some knew as 'Old Bones,'" *Globe and Mail*, January 19, 2008.
30 Dong, p. 5.
31 LAC, R15615, June 13, 1916.
32 Ibid., letter, November 29, 1916.
33 TNA, cable, November 18, 1916.
34 Gewurtz, p. 1; citing UCCA, Presbyterian Church Board of Foreign Missions minutes, May 19, 1916.
35 Ibid.
36 Ibid.
37 LAC, R15615, application to British legation in Peking, December 1916.

38 NSFP, Ruth Smith, letter, September 10, 1916.
39 Ibid., letter, September 25, 1916.
40 Ibid., letter, October 2, 1916.
41 Ibid., letter, August 24, 1917.
42 Ibid., letter, September 2, 1917.
43 NSFP, memoir, p. 8.

Chapter 7

1 LFP, Journal, pp. 24–25.
2 Ibid.
3 Ibid., p. 26; LFP, FD No. 1, September 9, 1917.
4 Ibid.
5 Summerskill, p. 42.
6 LFP, FD No. 1, September 9, 1917.
7 "Silk Train," *Canadian Encyclopaedia*, www.thecanadianencyclopedia.ca/en/article/silk-train.
8 B. Manico Gull, "The Story of the Chinese Labour Corps," *Far Eastern Review*, vol. 25, no. 4, April 1918.
9 TNA, FO 371/2657, cable from Secretary of State for the Colonies Bonar Law to Commissioner Lockhart at Weihaiwei, November 1916.
10 John Marteinson, *We Stand on Guard: An Illustrated History of the Canadian Army* (Montreal: Ovale Publications, 1992), pp. 131–132, p. 125. The British, Australian, New Zealand and French forces were engaged in bitter trench warfare while occupying a shallow beachhead at Gallipoli. Among the reinforcements to arrive in September 1915 was the Royal Newfoundland Regiment, which helped advance the division line. Severe weather, including sub-zero temperatures, disease, food shortages, not to mention the fighting itself, added to the horrific conditions. By January the Allied force was withdrawn.
11 Summerskill, p. 32.
12 Wood and Arnander, p. 70.
13 TNA, FO 371/2657.
14 Ibid.
15 Griffin, "The Response of British Labor to the Importation of Chinese Workers: 1916–1917," *Historian*, February 1, 1978, see Periodicals Archives Online, p. 257.
16 TNA, FO 371/2657.
17 Signing bonuses had previously been a key part of migration from Shantung. In effect, parents were paid to send their sons away; their wages helped, but so too did the taking away of one "mouth" to feed from the family's food supplies. Source: Diana Lary, interview.
18 TNA, FO 371/2657, October 13, 1916, cable from Jordan.
19 LFP, FD No. 1, September 10, 1917.
20 UCCA, GJFP, box 1, file 3.
21 Kautz YMCA Family Archives, University of Minnesota, "Yellow Spectacles," W.W. Peter, p.3.
22 Ibid., p. 4.
23 Ibid., pp. 4–5.
24 Chiang Ching-hai, "European Journals: Twelve Months as a Coolie"; Zhang Yan, "Shantung Navvy," p. 13.
25 Zhang, p. 13.

Chapter 8

1 Simon Harcourt-Smith, *Fire in the Pacific* (New York: Knopf, 1942), p. 60.

2   TNA, FO 371/2657.
3   Ibid.
4   Zhang Jianguo and Zhang Junyong, *Over There: The Pictorial Chronicle of Chinese Laborer Corps in the Great War* (Shandong: Shandong Pictorial Publishing House, 2009), p. 40.
5   Summerskill, p. 74.
6   TNA, WO 106/33. The reference to South Africa involves the arrangement made to send Chinese labour to work in the gold fields.
7   TNA, FO 371/2905, the article was included in an Alston memo dated December 19, 1916.
8   TNA, cable from Pratt, December 29, 1916.
9   Interview with Cheng Ling, granddaughter of Pi Ts'ui Te, May 2, 2017.
10 Zhang Yan, p. 7.
11 This observation, which is cited by Zhang Yan, first appeared in H.R. Williamson's *British Baptists in China, 1845–1952* (London, England: Carey Kingsgate Press, 1957), p. 100.
12 Zhang Yan, p. 7.
13 TNA, FO 371/2657.
14 James, p. 261.
15 E.J. Stuckey, H. Tomlin and C.A. Hughes, "Trachoma Among The Chinese In France," *British Journal of Ophthalmology*, vol. 4 no. 1 (January 1920), p. 4.
16 "Official History of the War, Medical Services," *Hygiene of the War*, vol. 2 (1923), chapter 15, pp. 422–423.
17 Stuckey, Tomlin and Hughes, p. 3.
18 Summerskill, pp. 129–131.
19 LFP, FD No. 1, September 12, 1917.
20 Ibid., September 16, 1917.
21 Ibid., September 29, 1917.
22 www.wrecksite, Allen Tony.
23 LFP, FD No. 1, October 7, 1917.
24 LAC, RG 150, Accession 1992–93/166, box 2153–10.
25 LFP, FD No. 1, October 8, 1917.
26 Ibid., October, 29, 1917.

Chapter 9

1   Chaug is also spelled Chong in Livingstone's Field Diary No. 1. For consistency, I have used Chaug.
2   LFP, Journal, p. 33.
3   Ibid., p. 34.
4   LFP, FD No. 1, October 29, 1917.
5   W. Kaye Lamb, *Empress to the Orient* (Vancouver: Maritime Museum Society of Vancouver, 1991), pp. 138, 141.
6   Ibid., p. 142.
7   Ibid., p. 44.
8   Robert D. Turner, *The Pacific Empresses* (Victoria: Sono Nis Press, 1981), p. 272.
9   Musk, p. 136.
10 Frank Heath, "A Link With The American Continent," in "The Cocoanut Tree—And After, War Memories of the 4th K.S.L.I., Contributed to the *Shrewsbury Chronicle* by Officers and Men who served 1914–1918," reprinted in the *Chronicle* by Shropshire Regimental Museum, May 2004.
11 Manifests for the *Empress of Asia*, April 30, 1917, and *Empress of Russia*, April 3, 1917.

12 Daryl Klein, *With The Chinks* (London: John Lane The Bodley Head. New York: John Lane Company, 1919), p. 116.

13 1871 Canada Census.

14 Department of National Defence, Directorate of History and Heritage, vol. 3, part 2: "Infantry Regiments," see lineage Canadian Grenadier Guards.

15 Chief Press Censor (hereafter abbreviated to CPC), file 205, Chambers's speech to Canadian Press Association, August 26, 1915; Jeffrey A. Keshen, *Propaganda and Censorship During Canada's Great War* (Edmonton: The University of Alberta Press, 1996), p. 71.

16 Diane Howard, *Encyclopaedia of the Great Plains*, 2004.

17 Jeffrey A. Keshen, "Chambers, Ernest John," in *Dictionary of Canadian Biography*, vol. 15, University of Toronto/Université Laval, 2003, accessed January 3, 2017, http://www.biographi.ca/en/bio/chambers_ernest_john_15E.html.

18 Ibid.

19 LAC, RG 24, vol. 2847, file 3281, "Final Report of Chief Press Censor of Canada on Completion of Demobilization."

20 Ibid.

21 Ibid.

22 LAC, file No. CPC 331, vol. 1, Department of Secretary of State.

23 "Memorable Manitobans: William Duncan Scott (1861–1925)," Manitoba Historical Society.

24 LAC, CPC 331, vol. 1.

25 Ibid.

26 Ibid.

27 Ibid.

28 Ibid.

29 TNA, FO 371/2905.

30 LAC, CPC 331, vol. 1.

31 Ibid.

32 Ibid.

33 Ibid.

34 Ibid.

35 LAC, RG 42, vol. 255, file 37467.

36 Klein, p. 197. "O.K. Party" was the name of the specific CLC contingent travelling with Klein. Other contingents or parties were similarly named with capital letters, included D.D., E.E., and G.G. parties, all of it meant, of course, to identify and keep track of the movements.

37 Heath.

Chapter 10

1 LFP, FD No. 1, November 4, 1917.

2 TNA, WO 106/33.

3 TNA, FO 228/2892; February 22, 1918, findings from coroner Dr. E.A. Sly.

4 TNA, FO 228/2893.

5 Ibid.

6 Ibid.

7 Ibid.

8 Ibid.

9 The Canada *Lancet,* vol. 52, no. 1, September 1918, available online through the Canadian Research Knowledge Network.

10 LAC, RG 150, Accession 1992–93/166, box 7557–53, Captain Leonard Panton.

11 Ibid., box 496–66, Captain Charles Bastin; box 967–5, Captain John box; box

2156–31, Captain George Cronk; box 2653–56, Captain Philip Doyle; box 3278–40, Captain Donald Fraser; box 6807–1, Captain James McEwen; box 8852–25, Captain William Shepherd.
12 TNA, FO 228/2892, Arthur Connolly to OC, Party AB, October 11, 1917.
13 Ibid., George Lawson medical officer report for Party FF, December 14, 1917.
14 Ibid., Commanding Officer Duncan Forbes report, December 14, 1917.
15 TNA, FO 228/2892, December 14, 1917.
16 "Smallpox," Encyclopedia Britannica.
17 TNA, FO 228/2892, Forbes report.
18 TNA, FO 228/2893.
19 LAC, RG 150, Accession 1992–93/166, box 914–39.
20 David Mittelstadt, Biographical and Social History of Mount Royal (Mount Royal Community Association, 2002.)
21 LAC, RG 150, Accession 1992–93/166, box 1516–41.
22 LAC, RG 150, Accession 1992–93/166, box 2971–26, Percival Faed; LAC, RG150, Accession 1992–93/166, box 3888–4, Gilbert Gunne.
23 TNA, FO 228/2893.
24 TNA, FO 228/2893, March 3, 1918, diary entry, Lieutenant Hugh Lowder.
25 TNA, FO 228/2892.
26 Klein, pp. 129–130.
27 TNA, FO 228/2893.
28 UCCA, Rev. Arthur William Lochead biographical data.
29 UCCA, Chinese Labour Corps in France during World War I, 1917–1919, Fonds 122, Accession 1979.201C, files 1–3, Arthur Lochead letters.
30 UCCA, GJFP, box 1, file 3.
31 Ibid.
32 Ibid.
33 Ibid.
34 LFP, Journal, p. 37.

Chapter 11

1 Encyclopaedia Britannica.
2 National Research Council, sunrise/sunset calculator for Victoria, British Columbia, November 1917, www.nrc-cnrc.gc.ca.
3 Peter Johnson, Quarantined: Life and Death at William Head Station, 1872–1959 (Vancouver: Heritage House Publishing Company Ltd., 2013), pp. 31–32.
4 Ibid., p. 35.
5 Ibid., p. 44.
6 British Colonist, June 25, 1872.
7 Don Cummings and Serge Occhietti, "Grosse Ile and the Irish Memorial National Historic Site," Canadian Encyclopaedia.
8 Cole Harris, "Voices of Disaster: Smallpox around the Strait of Georgia in 1782."Ethnohistory, vol. 41, no. 4 (Autumn, 1994), p. 601.
9 Songhees: Bill Reid Centre, Simon Fraser University, www.sfu.ca.
10 Ibid.
11 Johnson, p. 27.
12 Jamie Morton, "Noah Shakespeare," Dictionary of Canadian Biography.
13 Colonist, July 11, 1884, p. 2.
14 https://www.britishcolumbia.com, "D'Arcy Island Marine Park."
15 Johnson, p. 52.
16 William Head Institution, Correctional Services of Canada, museum collection. Hereafter: William Head Institution museum. In 1871, when British Columbia

joined Confederation, the federal government expropriated eleven acres at the tip of the peninsula to establish a coastal artillery reserve battery. Source: William Head Institution museum.

17 Johnson, p. 96.

18 *Daily Colonist*, September 1, 1893.

19 British Columbia Provincial Archives, microfilm file GR-2005, B08648, Department of Agriculture, William Head Medical Superintendent Annual Report from Dr. W. MacNaughton-Jones, October 31, 1893. Hereafter: BC Archives, WHMSR, followed by specific report.

20 Linda M. Ambrose, "Quarantine in Question: The 1913 Investigation at William Head, B.C.," *Canadian Bulletin of Medical History,* vol. 22, no. 1 (2005), p. 148. This excellent academic paper covers the controversy, including Watt's death, and how politics, race and class entered the picture.

21 Ibid., pp. 139–153.

22 *Daily Colonist*, May 31, 1913.

23 Ibid.

24 Province of British Columbia Registration of Death, 70–09–012459; *Daily Colonist*, July 13, 1909.

25 *Daily Colonist*, December 2, 1936.

26 Ibid., June 7, 1913.

27 Ambrose, pp. 148–149.

28 *Daily Colonist*, July 29, 1913.

29 Ibid, August 28, 1913.

30 Ibid.

31 Ship's manifest, the *Ruthenia*, September 24, 1914.

32 LAC, RG 150, Accession 1992–93/166, box 4633–34.

33 Province of British Columbia Registration of Death, 70–09–012459; Province of British Columbia Registration of Death, 702274.

34 Lynne Bowen, "Vancouver Island Coal Strike," *Canadian Encyclopaedia*, 2006.

Chapter 12

1 BC Archives, WHMSR, 1914–15.

2 Ibid., 1915–16.

3 Ibid., 1917–18.

4 Ibid.

5 Ibid.

6 Ibid.

7 Heath, p. 28–29.

8 J. Robert Davison, "Chinese at William Head: A Photograph Album," *British Columbia Historical News*, vol.16, no. 4 (1983), p. 19. This is a translation of Joe Hwei Chun's letter.

9 UCCA, Accession 1979.201C, files 1–3, MacKay to Lochead, September 5, 1917.

10 NSFP, 8–9.

11 Ibid.

12 UCCA, GJFP.

13 Ibid.

14 BC Archives, WHMSR, 1917–18.

15 Ibid.

16 Most of the names listed here are as they appear on the CLC nominal medal roll. A few are taken directly from the British Columbia vital statistics death registration records.

17 BC Archives, WHMSR, 1917–18.

18 W.W. Peter, "Yellow Spectacles," YMCA Kautz Family Archives.
19 Ibid.
20 TNA, FO 228/2892.
21 Ibid.

Chapter 13
1 *Empress of Russia* manifest, November 13, 1917.
2 LFP, FD No. 1, November 13, 1917; LFP, Journal, p. 37.
3 *Empress of Russia* manifest, November 13, 1917.
4 LAC, RG 150, Accession 1992–93/166, box 8758–25.
5 LFP, FD No. 1, Oct. 24, 1917.
6 *Victoria Sunday Times Magazine*, August 13, 1961. BC Provincial Archives, Documents A-5.
7 Klein, p. 167.
8 James, p. 323; Wendy Fisher "Dr. E.J. Stuckey and the Chinese Hospital at Noyelles-sur-Mer," 1984, p. 37.
9 TNA, FO 228/2894, report from Lieutenant Hugh Lowder.
10 LAC, RG 150, Accession 1992–93/166, box 6817–6.
11 TNA, FO 228/2892, report from Lieutenant Horace Finlayson, January 18, 1918.
12 TNA, FO 228/2892, medical officer report, Dr. David A. MacFarlane, CAMC, January 18, 1918.
13 TNA, FO 228/2892, Finlayson, January 18, 1918.
14 Klein, p. 173.
15 Ibid., p. 174.
16 *Vancouver World* newspaper, September 12, 1917.
17 The number of labourers cited here is from the ship's manifest when she arrived in Vancouver on March 27. It is noted on the manifest that 1,898 were held in quarantine.
18 TNA, FO 228/2894.
19 Ibid.
20 Ibid.
21 Ibid.
22 Frances Weir, correspondence with the author, August 12, 2017.
23 Department of National Defence, Directorate of History and Heritage, file 322.009 (D808) Correspondence, instructions, reports, etc., re organization of special railway company to escort Chinese Coolies across Canada on their way to UK, March 1917 to February 1918.
24 Ibid.
25 Violet E. Rainey (née Rhode), unpublished accounts of the William Head Quarantine Station, 1915–1928, p. 3. Metchosin School Museum, Metchosin, British Columbia.
26 *Victoria Sunday Times Magazine*, August 13, 1961, British Columbia Archives Documents A-5 newspaper/journal clippings.
27 TNA, FO 228/2892.
28 J. Robert Davison, *British Columbia Historical News* vol.16, no. 4 (1983), pp. 18–19.
29 Nancy de Bertrand Lugrin, "10,000 Coolies and a Lost Little Girl," *Victoria Sunday Times Magazine*, August 11, 1951, p. 3.
30 George E. Cormack "Wartimes in Russia," Imperial War Museum, London, 92/21/1, pp. 19–24.
31 TNA, FO 228/2894.
32 Nancy de Bertrand Lugrin, "10,000 Coolies," p. 3.

33 Johnson, p. 152.
34 Ibid.

Chapter 14

1   LFP, FD No. 1, November 13, 1917.
2   Ibid.
3   Robert D. Turner, *The Pacific Princesses: An Illustrated History of Canadian Pacific Railway's Princess Fleet on the Northwest Coast* (Victoria: Sono Nis Press, 1977), p. 39; Robert Turner, "James William Troup,"*Dictionary of Canadian Biography*, www.biographi.ca/en/bio/troup_james_william_16E.html.
4   TNA, FO 228/2892, report from 2nd. Lieutenant Matthew Ivy.
5   Turner, p. 235.
6   Victoria Harbour History, "Princess Charlotte 1908," https://www.victoriaharbourhistory.com/transportation/sea-transportation/early-steamships/british-columbia-coastal-steamship-service/princess-charlotte-1908-2/; Turner, p. 83.
7   LFP, FD No. 1, November 13, 1917.
8   Turner, p. vii.
9   LAC, RG 24, vol. 3768, file 1048–45–2, vol. 7.
10 Ibid.
11 Ibid.
12 Ibid.
13 Ibid.
14 Ibid.
15 Ibid.
16 Ibid.
17 Ibid.
18 Ibid.
19 Ibid.
20 Ibid.
21 Vancouver *Province*, April 4, 1917.
22 Ibid.
23 LAC, RG 6 E,CPC; http://heritage.canadiana.ca/search/?q0.0=t101, Chambers to Reid, April 12, 1917.
24 Ibid., April 7, 1917, letter from Chambers to Toronto *Globe*.
25 Ibid., April 9, 1917, letter from the Reverend John Sommerville to Chambers.
26 Seattle *Sunday Times*, April 8, 1917.
27 San Francisco *Examiner*, April 11, 1917.
28 LAC, RG 6 E; http://heritage.canadiana.ca/search/?q0.0=t101, April 24, 1917, cable to Chambers from the *News-Advertiser*, Vancouver.
29 Ibid., cable from Consulate General for Japan to Chambers, June 2, 1917.
30 Toronto *Globe*, May 4, 1917, p. 4.
31 LAC, RG 6 E, CPC; http://heritage.canadiana.ca/search/?q0.0=t101, May 7, 1917, cable from Chambers to Banks.
32 Ibid., Chambers to Yates, June 21, 1917.
33 Ibid., Yates to Chambers, July 7, 1917.
34 Ibid., Scott to Chambers, July 7, 1917.
35 Ibid., Chambers to Yates, July 12, 1917.

Chapter 15

1   LFP, FD No. 1 November 13, 1917.
2   Sessional Papers of the Dominion of Canada, 1915.

3   LFP, FD No. 1, November 13, 1917.
4   Some twenty passengers returning to Canada, along with a few others were
    allowed to land. See Hugh Johnston, "Komagata Maru," *Canadian Encyclopaedia*,
    February 7, 2006.
5   Vancouver School Board Archives and Heritage, blogs.vsb.bc.ca.
6   Hugh Johnston, "The Surveillance of Indian Nationalists in North America,
    1908–1918," *BC Studies*, no. 78 (Summer 1988), pp. 13–23.
7   "The Story of the Komagata Maru," https://mickleblog.wordpress.com.
8   Hugh Johnston, *The Voyage of the Komagata Maru: The Sikh Challenge to
    Canada's Colour Bar* (Vancouver, UBC Press, 1989), p. 19.
9   Ibid. (revised edition, 2014), p. 47.
10 Robie Reid, "The Inside Story of the Komagata Maru," *British Columbia Histor-
    ical Review*, vol. 5 (January 1941), pp. 1–23.
11 Ibid.
12 *Vancouver Province*, July 10, 1914, p. 14.
13 Robie Reid, p. 14.
14 Ibid.
15 *Vancouver World*, July 20, 1914, p. 1.
16 Robie Reid, p.17.
17 Prime Minister Justin Trudeau, House of Commons, May 18, 2016.
18 *The World*, February 9, 1915, p. 1. The story cites Reid's "splendid services and
    firm but diplomatic stand taken . . . in dealing with the situation that arouse from
    the arrival . . . of the Komagata Maru . . ."
19 Melanie Hardbattle, Radical Objects: Photo of Mewa Singh's Funeral Procession
    1915. Simon Fraser University Library, 2013.
20 LAC, RG 6 E, CPC; http://heritage.canadiana.ca/view/oocihm.lac_reel_
    t101/114?r=0&s=6, April 14, 1917, cable from Reid to Chambers.
21 Ibid.
22 Brodie to Maughan, November 15, 1917.
23 CPR Company Memo, file 5–11–26-H.
24 Ibid.
25 LFP, Journal, p.5.
26 Ibid.
27 Ibid.

Chapter 16

1   LFP, Journal, p. 9.
2   Ibid.
3   LAC, RG 9, II F9, vol.1447, Daily Orders No. 113, August 10, 1917.
4   Ibid., August 9, 1917.
5   Ibid., No. 82, July 4, 1917.
6   Ibid., No. 62.
7   Ibid., No. 82.
8   https://www.cwgc.org/find-war-dead/casualty/790596/haynes,-clifford-skemp;
    https://www.cwgc.org/find-war-dead/casualty/14502/haynes,-henry-hillas.
9   LFP, Journal, p. 7.
10 Ibid., p. 8.
11 TNA, FO 228/2892.
12 LFP, Journal, p. 10.
13 Klein, p. 29.
14 LFP, Journal, p. 11.
15 Ibid., pp. 12–13.

16 LAC, RG 24, box 3767, file 1048–45, vol. 1.
17 LFP, Journal, p. 8.
18 Ibid., pp. 9–10.
19 CPR Company Memo, file 5–11–26-H.
20 LFP, FD No. 1, November 20, 1917.
21 Ibid., November 21, 1917. Group of Seven artist Arthur Lismer captured the *Olympic* when she returned to Halifax after the war. See http://www.warmuseum.ca/collections/artifact/1013868.
22 LFP, Journal, p. 13.
23 LFP, Journal, p. 14.
24 Ibid., p. 4; CLC medal roll.
25 LFP, Journal, p. 4.
26 Ibid., p. 13.
27 Ibid, pp. 15–16.
28 Ibid., p. 16.
29 Ibid., p. 23.
30 CPR Company Memo, file 5–11–7-H; 1901 Canada Census.
31 James Hattie and Janet Sutherland MacDonald marriage certificate, December 15, 1913.
32 UCCA, GJFP, letter, June 2, 1917.
33 Ibid., letter, June 24, 1917.
34 Ibid.
35 UCCA, GJFP, "With The Chinese In France," p. 1.
36 Ibid., Accession 1979.201C, files 1–3, Lochead letter to MacKay, June 2, 1917.
37 Gewurtz, p. 8.
38 UCCA, Accession 1979.201C, files 1-3, Lochead to MacKay, June 16, 1917.
39 Ibid., MacKay to Lochead, June 20, 1917.
40 TNA, FO 228/2892.
41 Ibid.
42 Ibid.
43 Ibid.
44 Ibid.
45 Clifton J. Cate, Charles C. Cate, *Notes: A Soldier's Memoir of World War 1* (Victoria: Trafford Publishing, 2005), pp. 16–17; RG 150, Accession 1992–93/166, box 1575-54.
46 LAC, RG 150, box 1575-54, Clifton Cate.
47 TNA, FO 228/2892.
48 CPR Company Memo, file 5–11–27-H; FO 228/2892.
49 TNA, FO 228/2892.
50 Ibid.
51 LAC, RG 24 vol. 3768, File 1048-45-2, vol. 7.

Chapter 17

1 LAC RG 24, vol.719, file HQ54–21-5-286, Parts 1–2.
2 www.petawawaheritagevillage.com/history/canadian-internment-camps.
3 LAC RG 24, vol. 2553, file HQC2103. See cable from Inspector General, Western Canada, to Adjutant General, Militia Headquarters, Ottawa, September 17, 1917.
4 LAC RG 24 3767 1048–45-2, vol. 3.
5 Ibid.
6 Ibid.
7 LAC RG 24, vol. 2553, file HQC2103, July 24, 1917, correspondence from E. Blake Robertson, assistant superintendent of immigration to General Sir Eugene Fiset, Department of Militia and Defence. At the time, Russia was between two

revolutions. The first, in March, had overthrown the imperial government and the second, in October, would place the Bolsheviks in power. The Russian government named in Robertson's message was the Provisional Government appointed after Tsar Nicholas II was forced to abdicate on March 2. The Provisional Government sought to continue Russia's participation in the European war.

8   Ibid.
9   Ibid.
10 Ibid.
11 Ibid.
12 Ibid.
13 Ibid.
14 LAC, RG 24, vol. 1833, file G.A.Q. 8–36.
15 CPR Company Memo, file 5–11–15–H.
16 LAC, RG 6 E, CPC; http://heritage.canadiana.ca/search/?q0.0=t101.
17 Ibid.
18 Ibid, cable from Boag to Pembroke Observer, August 18, 1917.
19 CPR Company Memo, file 5–11–16–H.
20 Ibid., file 5–11–17–H; file 5–11–18–H.
21 Empress of Russia manifest, September 17, 1917.
22 CPR Company Memo, file 11–19–H; LAC, RG 24 vol. 2553, file HQC2103.
23 By the end of September 1917 there was talk of closing the CLC transit camp at Petawawa. LAC, RG 24 vol. 2553, file HQC2103.
24 LAC, RG 24 vol. 2553, file HQC2103.
25 Ibid.
26 Ibid.
27 Ibid.
28 Ibid.
29 Ibid.
30 LAC, RG 6 E, CPC; http://heritage.canadiana.ca/search/?q0.0=t101.
31 Ibid.
32 Ibid., Ottawa Citizen, January 9, 1918, p. 4.
33 LAC, RG 6 E, CPC; http://heritage.canadiana.ca/search/?q0.0=t101.
34 Ibid., letter to C.T. Pan, Hankow, China, from Leung Shou Yat, March 21, 1918.
35 James, p. 300; Li Jun to Waijiaobu, 30.11.1918 (Chen Sanjing et al. 1997, p. 421, file 484).
36 TNA, FO 228/2892, Ashley McCallum report, February 1918.
37 LAC, RG 150, Accession 1992–93/166, box 6612–9.
38 Ibid.
39 TNA, FO 228/2892.
40 Ibid.
41 Douglas R. Phillips; https://books.google.ca/books?id=bz0OBGxRjjcC&pg= PA414&1pg=PA414&dq=railway+passenger+lighting&source=bl&ots+ZKm XxnayXT&sig=ACfU3U1ilKzyn0mcfzmQ0DdGOPDhirtaaA&hl=en&sa=X- &ved=2ahUKEwjC_ND1wpHhAhWo24MKHQRhAHMQ6AEwE3oECAgQAQ# v=onepage&q=railway%20passenger%20lighting&f=false.
42 TNA, FO 228/2892.
43 Douglas R. Phillips.
44 TNA, FO 228/2892.
45 Ibid.
46 District Record Office file No. M.D. No. 10.44-C-688, supplied by Canadian Agency of CWGC.

Chapter 18

1　LFP, Journal, pp. 16–17.
2　Ibid., p. 17.
3　Ibid., pp. 17–18.
4　Ibid., p. 18.
5　Ibid.
6　Ibid., p. 19.
7　Ibid., p. 22.
8　Ibid., p. 19.
9　Ibid., pp. 19–20.
10　Ibid., pp. 21–22.
11　Ibid.
12　Ibid., p. 15.
13　Ibid., FD No. 1, December 4–5, 1917.
14　Ibid., December 5, 1917.
15　Ibid., December 7–8, 1917.
16　LAC, R15615, December 1, 1956, letter from James Menzies to his grandchildren, cited by Dong, p. 71.
17　LFP, FD No. 1, December 7, 1917.
18　Ibid., December 8, 1917.
19　Ibid., December 10, 1917.
20　Ibid., December 11, 1917.
21　"Cherry Garden Camp During Great War 1915–19," Folkestone Library, FWW1–96.
22　Summerskill, p. 4; with files from Diana Beaupré and Adrian Watkinson, Canterbury, UK.
23　"Kent Winter Assizes," *Kentish Gazette & Canterbury Press*, February 23, 1918, p. 7.
24　*South Eastern Gazette*, February 26, 1918.
25　LFP, Journal, p. 22–23.
26　Ibid., FD No. 1, December 11, 1917.
27　G. Douglas Gray, "The Chinese General Hospital in France," address given by Dr. Gray at the Chinese Medical Missionary Conference in Peking, February 1920, and published in the *China Medical Journal*, Hospital Supplement, pp. 145–158.
28　Ibid.
29　Ibid.
30　Ibid.
31　UCCA, Gray letter extract, undated.
32　Ibid.
33　UCCA, Minutes of Board of Foreign Missions, April 1923.
34　UCCA, Accession 1979.201C, files 1–3, Fred Auld to MacKay, December 28, 1917.
35　Ibid.
36　David Jones, *Toronto Star*, May 11, 1985.
37　Ernest Struthers, *A Doctor Remembers* (Imperial Press, 1976).
38　UCCA, Board minutes, 1950.
39　Fawcett, p. 67.
40　*Russia* manifest, April 3, 1917.
41　UCCA, Gray letter extract, undated.
42　Ibid.
43　LFP, Journal, p. 23; Fawcett, p. 40.
44　Griffin, "Britain's Chinese Labor Corps in World War I," *Military Affairs*, vol. 40, no. 3 (October 1976), p. 105.

45 Ibid.
46 Ibid.

Chapter 19

1   LFP, FD No. 1, December 12, 1917.
2   Gray, 1920 address to Chinese Medical Missionary Association, cited in James, p. 821.
3   Ibid.
4   LFP, FD No. 1, December 12, 1917.
5   Ibid., December 14, 1917.
6   Ibid., December 16, 1917.
7   Ibid., December 17, 1917.
8   Ibid., December 21–22, 1917.
9   Ibid., January 8–16, 1917.
10 Coningsby Dawson, *The Test of Scarlet: A Romance of Reality* (New York: John Lane Company, 1919), book 2, *The March to Conquest*, section 4. Dawson, who was a prolific writer, was born at Wycombe, England, but was offered a commission in the Canadian Field Artillery after graduating from Royal Military College, Kingston, Ontario. He served with the Canadian Army in France from 1916 to the end of the war.
11 Achiel Van Walleghem, *1917: The Passchendaele Year, The British Army in Flanders: The Diary of Achiel Van Wallleghem* (Brighton, UK.: Edward Everett Root, Publishers Co. Ltd., 2017), pp. 193–195.
12 Ibid.
13 Ibid.
14 UCCA, Accession 1979.201C, files 1–3, Arthur Lochead to MacKay, undated, but received by MacKay on August 21, 1917.
15 Ibid.
16 Ibid.
17 Ibid., December 25, 1917, letter from the Reverend George Ross to St. John's Presbyterian Church in Toronto.
18 Ibid.
19 Ibid.
20 Summerskill, p. 172.
21 UCCA, Accession 1979.201C, files 1-3, Lochead to MacKay, August 1917.
22 Mowatt's September 11, 1917, letter to MacKay is courtesy Margo Gewurtz, Professor Emeritus, Department of Humanities, York University, Toronto.
23 James, p. 494.
24 CWGC, Yen Feng Shan (No. 18060).
25 UCCA, December 25, 1917, Ross to St. John's Church.
26 UCCA, Accession 1979.201C, files 1–3, T.A. Arthurs to MacKay, October 6, 1917.
27 Ibid.
28 LAC, R15615, personal correspondence of James Menzies, 1915–17.
29 Ibid.
30 CWGC, Sainte-Marie Cemetery, Le Havre.

Chapter 20

1   LFP, FD No. 1, January 29, 1918.
2   Summerskill, p. 190.
3   George E. Cormack, "War Times in Russia," IWM 92/21/1, p. 20.
4   LFP, FD No. 2, September 19, 1918.
5   UCCA, GJFP, letter to Clara, February 17, 1918.

6 UCCA, Accession 1979.201C, files 1–3, letter from James Menzies to R.P. MacKay, 1918, Presbyterian Church of Canada.
7 LAC, R15615, letter from James Menzies to his parents, June 27, 1918.
8 James Yen, *Chinese Weekly*, January 21, 1919.
9 Fawcett, p. 49.
10 CWGC Les Baraques Cemetery, France.
11 LAC, Circumstances of Death Registers, First World War, vol.31829_B016754, "Private Frederick Maynard."
12 LAC, RG 150, Accession 1992—93/166, box 6076A-59, "Private Frederick Maynard."
13 UCCA, GJFP, letter to Clara, July 22, 1918.
14 Ibid., July 31, 1918.
15 UCCA, Accession 1979.201C, files 1–3, Auld to MacKay, September 21, 1918.
16 UCCA, GJFP, letter to Clara, November 4, 1918.
17 LAC, R15615, James Menzies to his mother, November 5, 1918.
18 Ibid, James Menzies to Annie, November 12, 1918. Cited in Dong, p. 76.
19 UCCA, GJFP, letter to Clara, November 12, 1918.
20 Ibid.
21 James, p. 508.
22 Ibid., 651.
23 LFP, FD No. 2, November 11, 1918.
24 Ibid.
25 TNA, WO 71/654.
26 TNA, WO 71/676.
27 TNA, WO 71/681.
28 Fawcett, p. 53. James, p. 692, notes the date as June 22, 1919.
29 Ibid.
30 LAC, R15615, Menzies to Annie, September 29, 1919.
31 Ibid.

Chapter 21

1 CWGC. Five of the CLC dead are at Liverpool (Anfield) Cemetery; eight at Plymouth (Efford) Cemetery; six at Shorncliffe Military Cemetery.
2 LFP, FD No. 3, June 16-17, 1919.
3 LAC, RG 150, Accession 1992–93/166, box 6745–53.
4 Wood and Arnander, inside dust jacket.
5 CWGC, Andrew Fetherston.
6 *Vancouver Daily Province* (hereafter: *Vancouver Province*), September 22, 1919.
7 LAC, RG 150, Accession 1992–93/166, box 7233–31.
8 Sergeant-Major (retired) Donald A. Tresham, CD. "The Origin of the Canadian Provost Corps: The Canadian Military Police Corps," *Watchdog*, March 31, 1980.
9 *Vancouver World*, December 12, 1919, p. 11.
10 Ibid., November 19, 1919.
11 BC Provincial Archives, WHMSR, 1919–1920.
12 *Victoria Daily Colonist*, December 20, 1919. (Hereafter: *Victoria Colonist*.)
13 *Victoria Times*, December 27, 1919.
14 *Vancouver World*, January 23, 1920.
15 *Victoria Times*, January 30, 1920, and February 2, 1920.
16 *Vancouver World*, February 11, 1920.
17 *Victoria Times*, March 11, 1920.
18 *Vancouver World* and *Victoria Times*, January 22, 1920.
19 *Vancouver Province*, April 5, 1920.

20 *Victoria Times*, February 20, 1920, p. 12.
21 *Vancouver Province*, August 30, 1919, p. 19.
22 *Vancouver World*, September 6, 1919, p. 23.
23 *Victoria Times*, September 11, 1919.
24 While serving with the CLC, William James Hawkings took hundreds of photographs, which now form the W.J. Hawkings Collection. Thankfully, his photographs were rediscovered by his grandson, John De Lucy, and recently went on exhibit.
25 *Vancouver World*, September 30, 1919.
26 Ibid., October 6, 1919.
27 *Victoria Colonist*, October 14, 1919.
28 *Victoria Times*, October 14, 1919.
29 Ibid., October 23, 1919.
30 *Vancouver Sun*, October 30, 1919.
31 *Vancouver Province*, November 27, 1919.
32 *Victoria Colonist*, December 2, 1919.
33 *Vancouver Province*, December 24, 1919.
34 CWGC, Sergeant Robert Christmas Rayner, 704217.
35 *Halifax Herald*, February 11, 1920, p. 2.
36 *Victoria Colonist*, March 16, 1920.
37 *Victoria Times*, March 27, 1920, p. 26.
38 *Vancouver World*, March 16, 1920, p. 13.
39 Davison, pp. 18–20. The Pacific octopus is believed to be the world's largest octopus, averaging 4.8 metres across and weighing fifty kilograms. *National Geographic* reports the size record is held by a specimen 9.1 metres across and weighing more than 272 kilograms.
40 *Vancouver Province*, March 29, 1920.
41 David Livingstone interview, April 26, 2019.
42 LFP, FD No. 3, July 12, 1919.

Epilogue

1 Summerskill, p. 199.
2 James, p. 689.
3 Stratford-Perth Archives, Corporation of the County of Perth, *Listowel Banner*, June 10, 1965.
4 Chatham-Kent Physician Tribute, www.ckphysiciantribute.ca/doctors/john-mcwilliam-mcdonald.
5 "'Lou': The Life Story of Louis Joseph Sebert, 1886–1942." Unpublished biography.
6 Michael Posner, *Globe and Mail*, March 21, 2010.
7 British Columbia Division of Vital Statistics, GR 29251, vol. 514, Death Registrations 002501 to 003000.

Appendix One

Various sources, including the author's own research in collaboration with the Canadian Agency, Commonwealth War Graves Commission.

Appendix Two

1 Mark Osborne Humphries, *The Last Plague: Spanish Influenza and the Politics of Public Health in Canada* (Toronto: University of Toronto Press, 2013), p. 78.

Selected Bibliography

Books

Austin, Alvyn J. *Saving China: Canadian Missionaries In The Middle Kingdom 1888-1959*. Toronto: University of Toronto Press, 1986.

Cate, Clifton J. and Charles C. Cate. *Notes: A Soldier's memoir of World War I*. Victoria: Trafford Publishing, 2005.

Cook, Tim. *At The Sharp End: Canadians Fighting The Great War 1914–1916*. Toronto: Penguin Canada, 2007.

———. *Shock Troops: Canadians Fighting The Great War 1917–1918*. Toronto: Penguin Canada, 2008.

Crane, David. *Empires of the Dead: How One Man's Vision Led to the Creation of WW I's War Graves*. London: William Collins, 2014.

Cruise, David and Alison Griffiths. *Lords of the Line: The Men Who Built the CPR*. Markham, Ontario: Viking, 1988.

Dawson, Coningsby. *The Test of Scarlet: A Romance of Reality*. New York: John Lane Company, 1919.

De Lucy, John. *The Chinese Labour Corps: Photographs from the WJ Hawkings Collection*. Myosotis Books, 2017.

Dong, Linfu. *Cross Culture and Faith: The Life and Work of James Mellon Menzies*. Toronto: University of Toronto Press, 2005.

Dutil, Patrice and David MacKenzie. *Embattled Nation: Canada's Wartime Election of 1917*. Toronto: Dundurn Press, 2017.

Ferguson, Niall. *The Pity of War: Explaining World War I*. London: Allen Lane, 1998.

Fraser, John. *The Chinese: Portrait of a People*. Glasgow: William Collins & Sons & Co., Ltd., 1981.

Frideres, J.S. *Canada's Indians: Contemporary Conflicts*. Scarborough: Prentice-Hall of Canada Ltd., 1974.

Fryer, Mary Beacock. *Brockville: A Pictorial History*. Brockville, Ont.: Beasancourt Publishers, 1986.

German, Commander Tony. *The Sea is at Our Gates: The History of the Canadian Navy*. Toronto: McClelland & Stewart Inc., 1990.

Gottschang, Thomas R. and Diana Lary. *Swallows and Settlers: The Great Migration from North China to Manchuria*. Ann Arbor, Michigan: Centre for Chinese Studies, University of Michigan, 2000.

Humphries, Mark Osborne. *The Last Plague: Spanish Influenza and the Politics of Public Health in Canada*. Toronto: University of Toronto Press, 2013.

James, Gregory. *The Chinese Labour Corps (1916–1920)*. Hong Kong: Bayview Educational Ltd., 2013.

Johnson, Peter. *Quarantined: Life and Death at William Head Station, 1872–1959*. Vancouver: Heritage House Publishing Company Ltd., 2013.

Johnston, Hugh. *The Voyage of the Komagata Maru: The Sikh Challenge to Canada's Colour Bar.* Vancouver: UBC Press, 1980, second revised edition 1989.

Jones, David Laurence. *The Railway Beat: A Century of Canadian Pacific Police Service.* Markham, Ont.: Fifth House Ltd., 2014.

Keegan, John. *The First World War.* Toronto: Key Porter Books Limited, 1998. Originally published in the United Kingdom by Hutchinson, an imprint of Random House UK Limited, 1998.

Keshen, Jeffrey. A. *Propaganda and Censorship during Canada's Great War.* Edmonton: University of Alberta Press 1996.

Klein, Daryl. *With The Chinks.* London: John Lane The Bodley Head, 1919. New York: John Lane Company, 1919.

Lamb, W. Kaye. *Empress to the Orient.* Vancouver: Vancouver Maritime Museum, 1991.

———. *History of the Canadian Pacific Railway.* New York: Macmillan Publishing Co., Inc., Collier Macmillan Canada Ltd., 1977.

Lotz, Jim. *Canadian Pacific.* London: Bison Books Ltd., 1985.

MacKay, Donald. *The Asian Dream: The Pacific Rim and Canada's National Railway.* Vancouver: Douglas & McIntyre Ltd., 1986.

Marteinson, John. *We Stand On Guard: An Illustrated History of the Canadian Army.* Montreal: Ovale Publications, 1992.

McDougall, John Lorne. *Canadian Pacific: A Brief History.* Montreal: McGill University Press, 1968.

Mika, Nick and Helma Mika. *Railways of Canada: A Pictorial History.* Toronto: McGraw-Hill Ryerson Ltd., 1972.

Musk, George. *Canadian Pacific: The Story of the Famous Shipping Line.* London: Canadian Pacific Steamships Ltd., 1981.

Phillips, Richard T. *China Since 1911.* London: MacMillan Press Ltd., 1996.

Summerskill, Michael. *China on the Western Front: Britain's Chinese Work Force in the First World War.* London: Michael Summerskill, 1982.

Steinhart, Allan L. *Civil Censorship in Canada during World War I.* Toronto: The Unitrade Press, 1986.

Turner, Robert D. *The Pacific Empresses.* Victoria: Sono Nis Press, 1981.

———. *The Pacific Princesses: An Illustrated History of Canadian Pacific Railway's Princess Fleet on the Northwest Coast.* Victoria: Sono Nis Press, 1977.

Vance, Jonathan F. *Maple Leaf Empire: Canada, Britain, and Two World Wars.* Don Mills, Ontario: Oxford University Press, 2012.

———. *Death So Noble: Memory, Meaning, and the First World War.* Vancouver: UBC Press, 1997.

Wherry, Edith. *The Red Lantern.* London: John Lane Company, 1911.

Walleghem, Achiel Van. *1917—The Passchendaele Year. The British Army in*

Flanders: The Diary of Achiel Van Walleghem. Edited by Dominiek Dendooven. Brighton: Edward Everett Root, Publishers, Co., Ltd., 2017.

Wood, Frances and Christopher Arnander. *Betrayed Ally: China in the Great War.* Barnsley, South Yorkshire, United Kingdom: Pen & Sword Military, 2016.

Xu Guoqi. *Strangers On The Western Front: Chinese Workers in the Great War.* Cambridge, Massachusetts, 2011.

Magazines, Newspapers, Journal Articles, Essays

Ambrose, Linda M. "Quarantine in Question: The 1913 Investigation at William Head, B.C.," *Canadian Bulletin of Medical History,* vol. 22, no. 1.

Bhatti, F.M. "East Indian Immigration into Canada, 1905–1973," *University of Surrey, Department of Sociology,* 1974.

Chandler, Cliff. "Chinese Labour Corps at William Head Quarantine Station, 1917–1920," *Victoria Historical Society Publication,* vol. 17, Autumn 2008.

Cormack, George E. "War times in Russia," Imperial War Museum, London, 92/21/1.

Davison, Robert J. "The Chinese at William Head, A Photograph Album," *British Columbia Historical News,* vol. 16, no. 4, 1983.

Fawcett, Brian C. "The Chinese Labour Corps in France, 1917–1921," *Journal of the Royal Asiatic Society Hong Kong Branch,* vol. 40, 2000.

Fetherston, Andrew. "Commonwealth War Graves Commission presentation on CLC cemeteries and graves." Meridian Society film launch, SOAS, University of London, 2017.

Gewurtz, Margo S. "For God or King: Canadian Missionaries and the Chinese Labour Corps in World War I." Canadian Historical Association Annual Meeting, 1982.

Gray, Douglas G. "The Chinese General Hospital in France." Address to Chinese Medical Missionary Society conference, February 20, 1920.

Griffin, Nicholas J. "The Response of British Labor to the Importation of Chinese Workers, 1916–1917," *The Historian,* vol. 40, no. 2, 1978.

———. "Chinese Labor and British Christian Missionaries in France, 1917–1919," *Journal of Church and State,* vol. 20, no. 2, 1978.

———. "Scientific Management in the Direction of Britain's Military Labour Establishment During World War I," *Military Affairs,* vol. 42, no. 4, 1978.

———. "Britain's Chinese Labor Corps in World War I," *Military Affairs,* vol. 40, no. 3, 1976.

Gull, Manico E. "The Story of the Chinese Labour Corps," *The Far Eastern Review,* vol. 15, no. 4, April 4, 1918.

Harris, Cole. "Voices of Disaster: Smallpox around the Strait of Georgia in 1782," *Ethnohistory,* vol. 41, no. 4, 1994. Duke University Press.

Johnson, Peter. "Quarantine Was Hell at William Head," *Times Colonist*, May 28, 2016.

Keshen, Jeff. "All the News That Was Fit to Print: Ernest J. Chambers and Information Control in Canada, 1914–19," *Canadian Historical Review*, vol. 73, no. 3, 1992.

McDermott, Jon. "William Head Is A Prison With A Past," *Edmonton Journal*, July 29, 1972.

Mitchell, Peter. "Canada and the Chinese Labour Corps 1917–1920: The Official Connection." Presented to Annual Meeting of Canadian Historical Association, Ottawa, 1982.

Peter, William W. "Yellow Spectacles," Kautz Family YMCA Archives, University of Minnesota.

Reid, Robie. "The Inside Story of the Komagata Maru," *British Columbia Historical Review*, vol. 5, January 1941.

Reilly, Wayne E. "Vanceboro Bridge Bombed by German Soldier a Century Ago," *Bangor Daily News*, February 1, 2015.

Rowe, Allan. "The Mysterious Oriental Mind: Ethnic Surveillance and the Chinese in Canada During the Great War," *Canadian Ethnic Studies*, vol. 36, no. 1, 2004.

Roy, Patricia E. "British Columbia's Fear of Asians, 1900–1950," *Social History*, vol. 13, no. 25, May 1980.

Simons, Paula. "Sun-Yat-Sen and Canada: The Historic Ties between Alberta and China's Revolution," *Edmonton Journal*, September 13, 2014.

Stuckey, E.J., H. Tomlin, and C.A. Hughes. "Trachoma Among the Chinese in France," *British Journal of Ophthalmology*, vol. 4, no. 1, January 1920.

Tancock, Elizabeth A. "Secret Trains Across Canada 1917–1918," *Beaver*, October/November 1991.

Tresham, Donald A. "The Origin of the Canadian Provost Corps: The Canadian Military Police Corps," *Watchdog*, March 31, 1980.

Wright, Glenn. "The Chinese Labour Corps," *Legion Magazine*, vol. 86, no. 5, September/October 2011.

Zhang Yan. "Shantung Navvy: Mortals under the Political Halo," Chinese University of Hong Kong, June 2015.

Unpublished Materials

Gordon R. Jones Family Papers, United Church of Canada Archives, Toronto, Fond 3449, Accession 1995.103, Box 1, File 2.

Letters of James Menzies, Arthur Menzies Fonds, LAC R15615.

Violet E. Rainey, unpublished accounts of the William Head Quarantine Station, 1915–1928, Metchosin School Museum, Metchosin, British Columbia.

Livingstone Family Papers, Captain Harry Livingstone, Field Diaries Nos. 1–3; H.D. Livingstone's Medical Officer's Journal, courtesy David Livingstone, not dated.

The Reverend George Napier Smith Papers, Captain George Napier Smith memoir, 1887–1953; letters From China, 1916–1923, Ruth Langlois Smith; "My Story," by Larry Smith, courtesy Roger Smith, Ottawa.

Websites

"Chinese in Victoria During World War I: Victoria's Chinatown and the Chinese Labour Corps," https://onlineacademiccommunity.uvic.ca/wwivictoriachinese/life-at-william-head.

"Livingstones of Lanark: Dr. David Livingstone's Society Settler Relatives" by Ron. W. Shaw, 2016, http://blantyre.biz/blantyre-folk/david-livingstone/livingstones-brother-john/.

"Xiaochun Qi's Enchanting Erhu," www.shenyunperformingarts.org/news/view/article/e/QcgYSRqfEiQ/xiaochun-qi%E2%80%99s-enchanting-erhu.html.

Index

MARQUIS

Québec, Canada